The Social Origins of Islam

Mohammed A. Bamyeh

The Social Origins of Islam

MIND, ECONOMY, DISCOURSE

University of Minnesota Press — Minneapolis – London

Published by the University of Minnesota Press
111 Third Avenue South, Suite 290
Minneapolis, MN 55401-2520
http://www.upress.umn.edu

Library of Congress Cataloging-in-Publication Data

Bamyeh, Mohammed A.
    The social origins of Islam : mind, economy, discourse / Mohammed A.
Bamyeh.
      p.   cm.
    Includes bibliographical references and index.
    ISBN 0-8166-3263-4 (hc. : alk. paper). — ISBN 0-8166-3264-2 (pbk. : alk.
paper)
    1. Islam—Origin. 2. Arabian Peninsula—Social conditions. 3. Arabian
Peninsula—Civilization. I. Title.
BP55.B36 1999
297—dc21   98-42289

Contents

Introduction

The story examined in this work has thus far been largely confined to an area of specialized scholarship that, as Edward Said has effectively demonstrated, consciously resists theoretical accounts. "Regional Studies," as they are often called, are regularly restrained to "factual" narrative.[1] This work attempts, at least in part, to proceed against such a restriction. It employs interdisciplinary approaches from cultural anthropology, historical sociology, Qur'anic exegesis, literary analysis, and economic history. These approaches are employed to suggest some connective dynamics operating between grand spheres of social life. For example, what is particularly important here are such issues as the connections between the emergence of certain economic practices (such as trade and money-based exchange), cultural thought patterns (as observed in pre-Islamic poetry and ontotheology), and the reconfiguration of transtribal patterns of solidarity. The central role of such links is indicated in the trilateral subtitle, which suggests that the story of the origin of the set of doctrines that came to be known as Islam is interwoven, in a complicated process, in the sociopolitical, social organizational, and cultural employment of a system of faith. This process is embedded in conditions of material life, charted amid a maze of existent ideational contours, and elaborated against the backdrop of available modalities of expression.

In this sense, this is primarily a book in the social theory of ideological transformation. It is an attempt to understand grand cultural shifts that give rise to new systems of faith, conducted in the context of a momentous, richly informative story. It is *not* a book of history, in the sense that it does not claim to discover any new facts or to render a more "truthful" causal sequence of events than hitherto attempted. Neither is it a total thesis on what Islam is or was, in the sense that it refrains from any claim regarding an essential meaning, an invariable ideological position, or a uniform social role of the faith. In this work, my interest is extrinsic rather than intrinsic, in the sense that I want to see what the story of Islam could tell us about ideological formations in general, rather than strictly to tell a specific historical tale. In this spirit, I emphasize a theoretically informed perspective and generally refrain from pure philological digressions customary in traditional orientalist scholarship.

Thus, this work employs a different approach to the question of historical factuality than do, for instance, the recent revisionist histories of Patricia Crone and Sulayman Bashir. In the revisionist school, discoveries are not made by marshaling in new "facts" about the origins of Islam but by recombining and contrasting a variety of tales pervading well-known classical sources.[2] But according to what logic and what order of selection are such recombinations and contrasts conducted? What validity do their criteria possess? Take, for instance, Crone's three criteria for dismantling the reliability of the classical sources: contradictions, storytelling mode, and later perfection.[3] Why did such facts of discourse pose apparently little problem for the ancient audience? In my view, studying an ancient worldview requires a readjustment of the listening faculties, an attention to configurations of the world that an ancient audience could have digested with a yet-to-be appreciated contentment, and an ability to see what it could have been possible to see in the past rather than to single-mindedly insist on "facts" as if they possess the same value and appearance across the distance of centuries.[4] With some effort at listening to the interplay of ideational and discursive configurations reverberating through the classical story of Islam, almost all "contradictions" uncovered by revisionist historians can be shown to be contradictions solely in a modern logic and modality of reading.[5]

It is possible to argue that history itself does not exist as such without an implicit or explicit theoretical perspective that allows it to be discerned as being instructive. In this sense, if one drops preexisting lenses of perspective by which historical tales are organized, history begins to appear untidy, unbalanced, vacuous, or at best irrelevant and nonindicative. With no solid paradigmatic support, categories employed would be shifting and confused, concepts and definitions unrefined and porous. With no causal chain outlined in terms of acceptable rational precepts, the received chronology would appear as one sediment loaded freely upon another. With no value-oriented delimitation of the scope of the examination, visibility would be unwieldy and the focus migratory, as though one were pursuing a nomadic journey through the pages.

Thus, apart from an interminable submergence into the rich basin of the philosophy of history, what order of coherence and relevance can one propose for the story about to be told in the many pages to follow? One of the distinctions between history and fiction is not simply that one is reality and the other is not; nor is it that one is believable and the other is not; nor is it that one is subject to scientific and methodical validation from which the other is exempt. In modern times, the distinction is precisely that history is understood to contain moments along a trajectory whose temporal links are *causally rather than morally connected*—even though the cause can be shown to have a moral basis as well. History may mean a variably articulated claim to structured connections between moments, up to and including the present.

Various hermeneutic traditions address the question of the status of the present as a vantage point determining the kinds of questions history will be asked to answer. For Hans-Georg Gadamer, the present and the past could function as partners in a process of negotiation leading to some sort of relocation of both from the paradigmatic confinements of their moments. On the other hand, for a philosopher like Martin Heidegger, the present itself can be of interest only insofar as one can use it as a tool to measure the distance that has been crossed away from the past. In this sense, the interest in history would be premised upon a profound estrangement from the spirit of modernity and would thus be moved by a drive to settle contemporary accounts rather than a fixation on an essential truth lurking in the depths of time. For Georg Lukàcs, historical interest evidences a crisis-ridden consciousness, a consciousness to which the world has ceased to appear in the form of a meaningful and self-evident totality. Thus, the mind becomes confronted with a *distinction* between the phenomenon in itself and the method for its comprehension. And it is this distinction, for instance, that manifests itself between history on the one hand and the philosophy of history—whether explicit in terms of method or implicit in the choice of prisms and issues—on the other.[6] History thus becomes a battleground of contemporary ideas, whereby its raw materials are regrouped and reorganized, so that an original story may be recast, reaffirmed, downplayed, or negated.

This volume seeks to navigate somewhat different waters from those mapped out or suggested by the figures mentioned above. It revisits the ancient story from two angles: One aims at discerning the peculiarity of a worldview and its metamorphoses in light of material conditions and historical accidents and another aims at capturing atemporal logics of connection between mind, economy, and discourse. A historical sociology of consciousness, as one may provisionally call this method, entails noting links not simply between "facts" and "ideas" but, more precisely, between *records* of causally linked facts and *appearances* of logically connected ideas. Since the historical sociology of consciousness is not "history" in the narrow sense of the word, "facts" are not interesting for their own sake but for the phenomenological imprints that they leave on the records speaking of them. Such an orientation does not strive to understand *what* the "idea" of Islam was, for instance, but *how* such an idea became thinkable at a particular point in time. For the historical sociology of consciousness, the point concerns the conditions of life that could give rise to the forms of thinking that become hospitable to such an idea *as well as* to others.

I confine the analysis of the "how" to a general level, such as in tracing the growth of abstract thinking to sedentarization and the development of a money economy. This link, as I attempt to show in that discussion, does not spell out deterministic "causality," for it is not as though one came before the other, one was uniquely dependent on the other, or a reversal of the suggested sequence of the link was not possible. The connections suggested between abstract thought, money, and sedentarization are neither strictly sequential nor necessarily exclusive in nature; a money economy requires the ability to abstract the world, and the ability to abstract could grow as well out of a noticed possibility of enlarged social boundaries of exchange. But neither money nor abstract thinking is restricted in terms of its significance to the possibility of the other. Nor is it a question of money as such or abstract thinking as such; rather, the issue is the larger styles of apprehending the world that the two engender when they appear on the historical scene together.

Another set of concerns that the orientation toward a historical sociology of consciousness raises is that of intentionality. When the mind finds it necessary to communicate an idea, as in preaching, one expects to be able to discern an intention. The question here concerns whether the records allow us to decipher intentionality in this fashion. Is there an intention or a plurality of intentions? And if there is a plurality of intentions, according to what logic could they be brought into an appearance of complementarity and homogeneity rather than incidental juxtaposition? Who was responsible for the intention? Who did the intending and who received it? How was the intention (mis)understood? The "persistent major themes," which may suggest the diachronic consistency of some intentions, themselves emerge out of a complicated process of revelation, reception, social conflict, and accommodation. They cannot be presumed to exist in an unsullied fashion at the level of the unanchored, transhistorical text alone. How were they reconstituted through variations, consolidations, or mutations driven by unsuspected encounters and logics? Were they thought of as being "major" and uncompromisable by those articulating them in the first place? Were they introduced for the sake of intentions other than their face value, for example, as but one way of experimenting with many forms of expression striving to accomplish the same objective, and did they survive as "persistent major themes" only after they proved in practice to be the ones most suitable for arriving at what was intended?

And what was intended? Did the message not lose any trace of its original intentions? Did it mean, from its first day, to develop into the forms and meanings through which it found itself to be functioning at the later stages of its journey? And who took up that journey? A homogeneous group that could be described in totalizing terms such as "class," "sect," "ideologues," "reformers," "rich," "poor," "merchants," or did the riders often change seats, composition, guides, and subsequently direction? And if so, how could the "persistent major themes" be accounted for? What is one to make of all those divergent, even antagonistic lives that have been consumed along the road? How many classes, sects, rulers, ruled, ontologies, ideologies, and systems of reference claimed the same caravan? This book seeks to outline some of the ideational foundations, socioeconomic grounds, and discursive experiments through which the procession coalesced as a text, appearing on the scene in a piecemeal fashion before eventually closing the cover and thereby pronouncing the conclusion of the journey. What is significant is not what seems to be a method of textual and ideational crystallization consisting of a sequence of accidents but the various methods of signifying, articulating, and apprehending such accidents and of eventually integrating them into larger systems of interrelated beliefs by those living through them.

As the compendium of these methods, the Qur'an figures large in this book, especially in the later chapters. I consider it to be the most authentic embodiment of the metamorphosing spirit of the age, not only because of its exceptional temporal proximity to the events under investigation but also because of the unique mixture of its own moods, fruitfully comparable to pre-Islamic patterns of poetry: linguistic textures, poetics, representations, legalisms, metaphors, pedagogy, ontological foci, and the historical marks and references upon which it justifies, locates, and interprets itself. The relevance of such a text to the spirit of the age must not be merely judged by what it says, whether explicitly or through contemporaneous interpretations, but also by *how* it says it: the form and structure of the argument, the method of reasoning, the logical chain, the immersion of logic into aesthetics, the literary coating of all forms of resolution, statements of fact, promises, and threats. The point is that effective ideological pedagogy consists not merely of statements of desirable content but also of discursive reformulation, restructuring, repackaging, and re-insertion under different headings.

This orientation led me to rely on pre-Islamic poetry as a second major point of analysis. The problem with studying that more-ancient record is not only that fewer primary sources are available but also, and perhaps more important, that we have no evidence indicating that any other form of primary sources (apart from archaeology) could have ever existed at all. The only form of communication worthy of immortalizing, the only records worthy of any effort at preservation were seen by contemporaries themselves to consist of nothing other than poetry. Poetry, at that finest moment of its history, was the ultimate sociophilosophical treatise: It expressed and contained the spirit of the times not only because of the "heterogeneity" of topics it had reassembled and reorganized in peculiar ways but also because of its wide celebration. As an oral medium, it could not have been saved if it were not ubiquitous in the land or deemed to be of special standing. It became, therefore, a witness to an altogether lost life, with its values, priorities, logics, and idealizations.

Finally, a note on the sources. Wherever they appear, the Qur'anic citations are taken from N. J. Dawood's excellent translation, occasionally altered where noted. The classical histories (al-Tabari, Ibn Hisham, Ibn Sa'd, al-Waqidi, and others) have been duly consulted, together with contemporary scholarship. As for pre-Islamic poetry, I have consulted the extant compilations, which include those of Ibn Kaisan (d. 932), Ibn al-Anbari (d. 939), al-Zauzani (d. 1093), and at-Tibrizi (d. 1109), as well as the version available in al-Qurashi's (d. 878) *Jamharat Ash'ar al-'Arab*. Also of some use was the larger body of poetry extant from that period, scattered in several ancient encyclopedic compilations, such as Ibn Qutaybah's (d. 889) *Al-Shi'r wal Shu'ara'*, al-Mufaddal al-Dabbi's (d. 786) *Mufaddaliyyat*, and the infinitely resourceful *Kitab al-Aghani* of Abi al-Faraj al-Isbahani (d. 967). The emphasis here, however, is on the long odes. For that purpose, I followed the rendition offered in the compilation generally considered to be the most reliable, namely that of at-Tibrizi, although neither blindly nor to the extent that concerns of transcription, order, or matters of otherwise pure historicist detail could derail the reflective nature of the commentary. All couplet numbers refer therefore to C. J. Lyall's edition of that compilation. Quotations from that compilation are taken from the A. J. Arberry translation, sparingly modified where noted. Any translations, as well as accompanying damage, of the three less canonical odes (those of an-Nabigha, al-A'sha, and 'Ubayd) are mine. Unless otherwise noted, all dates are A.D. Finally, since I envisioned the broader affinity of this study to belong to social theory rather than strictly to the copious tradition of orientalist scholarship, I have greatly simplified Arabic transliteration, confining diacritical remarks to the 'ayn and the hamza.

Part I: The Ground

The Ideology of the Horizons

HORIZON, VISION, SETTLEMENT

We are speaking of a terrain in which life repeats itself both endlessly and precariously. Here, the eyes of the inhabitant open daily to a topography of solemn solitude, far more imposing to the soul than the minuscule islets of social life encountered thereupon. The desert is a sphere of absolute speechlessness. What is strange in the desert is speaking, thinking in words, dialogizing, communicating. In this vast expanse, ridiculing all notions of paramount subjectivity, profuse wilderness covers all visible destinations between the here and all horizons; the human actor is but an insignificant footnote to the space; to think of presence in dogmatic terms of space—where space as a *habitat* is at best a seasonal interruption—is to practically annul oneself. Only a perennially visible enigma, the *horizon*, sets the boundaries of knowable nature. Like the sea, the horizon of the desert stands out in contrast to the landscape as the unreachable terminus of nature, its inconclusive conclusion.

The Arabian Peninsula—the cradle of Islam—is dominated by the two vast deserts that occupy the bulk of the land. The great Nufud wilderness claims much of the north, while the Empty Quarter, one of the most arid and impassable deserts on earth, stretches over half a million square kilometers in the south. Such immense horizons confound the ideas of beginning and end, depositing the concept of eternity in the heart of the concrete present. This ideology of the horizons, as will become apparent in subsequent chapters, is oblivious to human structures of presence as a purposeful progression of moments where one constructs for oneself a path in time, periodizes existence, valorizes destination. In other words, such an ideology sees in the spectacle of the horizon not so much an inviting mirage as the most fundamental picture of the emptiness of grandiose human quests.

There are notable exceptions, of course, to this story. The recurrent Semitic migrations *outside* of the peninsula during the four millennia preceding Islam were clearly intended to free population groups from such a magnitude of resourcelessness. But in this volume we are concerned with those who stayed and developed sedentary societies and sedentary ways of looking that challenged the desert's inhospitability to any other life than one of permanent wandering. The story of Islam, along with many contemporaneous theological and cosmological experiments, rotates around such tensions in the ways of seeing and assessing the outside—and by extension the inside—of human society.

But before such a permanent encampment, the concreteness of existential emptiness could be derived purely by looking. No exceptional ability to see into the nature of things was required. The eternity of the same readily revealed itself to all those who had the patience to pause long enough to appreciate the horizons, the boundaries of the magnificent desert, and long enough to allow the horizon to fully transform itself into an idea, to become a part of seeing in the most fundamental way, in other words, to become an "ideology." The ideology of horizons is a peculiar production of this form of wilderness. And it is an ideology that sustains wandering. Here, the horizon, consisting of visible sameness, visible emptiness, visible lack of any promise whatever, nullifies the quest after it. But on the other hand, such a horizon speaks of the conclusion of the desert and promises an unknown beyond, a different nature that cannot be seen without wandering toward the horizon. And in this other capacity, the horizon instigates the quest for that beyond.

This perplexing appeal of the horizon situates it exactly at the borderline between two modes of wandering. One mode is to wander as a *natural fate,* preordained by the indifference of the desolate landscape to ordinary human needs. The other mode is to invest in the wandering a teleological scheme of crossing over into a land of lush riverbanks, where the horizon would gradually disappear as an invitation, goal, or boundary of permanent wandering. In both cases, the desert itself only promises traces, ruins, and betrayals of past loves and lives; nothing more. One wanders, and one forgets through wandering—in effect eliminating from view—the desert's failure to sustain other than its own overpowering expanse, eternal and normative as it seems. Here, if there is a destination, one reaches it by simply moving. No elaborate schemes are required. No scheming subject is required. In fact, no subject at all is required. Until poetic, cosmological, and thematic discourses about that nature began to be produced, valued, and preserved, there were no forms imposed on it. For the wanderer, the desert formed itself and dissipated along the way, with no everlasting images. Such a nature formed itself in the mode of interruptions, as though to encourage existence a little longer, precisely when the wanderer was about to perish. This is how the nomadic ode itself proceeded until exhaustion (and *not* conclusion) consumed its energy. But until the regular production and preservation of discourse and sedentarism, such interruptions were no more than erasable bursts of life. There was wandering, but there were no roads, no pathways, no passages into an alternative ideology or life, no meaning for time or direction. Unless one ceased to be a nomad, nothing altered that eternal presence.

Throughout the peninsula, movement was the norm and halting the exception. Agriculture, the primary precondition for settlement, was possible as a large-scale activity only in Yemen and the Green Mountain in 'Uman.[1] Some isolated agricultural colonies also developed in some elevated regions of Hijaz and Najd, the most important of which was in and around Ta'if, which supplied Mecca with much of its food.[2] Mecca itself, the birthplace of Islam, was far from being an agricultural community. In fact, it grew like a wild thorn amid an arid environment of solid rock. It survived only because of the growing world trade that passed through it (which will be explored in more detail in Chapter 2). But in spite of its world connection, Mecca, as a particular form of settlement, was left to determine its own ideology with reference to its own preconditions and surroundings, where nomadism and wandering predominated for enormous distances in all directions. With the exception of Yemen, the great powers of the time—the Romans, the Sassanids, the Abyssinians—displayed little interest in any part of the Arabian Peninsula.

Thus, the particular story of permanent halting in Mecca contains simultaneous elements of knowledge of and independence from all the great powers of the epoch (including peninsular powers such as Yemen). Mecca's location deep in the desert insulated the city from the fate of the other nascent trading centers that were annexed to such powers. Palmyra and Petra were annexed by Rome, 'Aden was dominated by the Abyssinians and Sassanids. But it was also the relations with such powers that stabilized a form of halting, which would otherwise have been devoured by a nature that does not usually allow it. The Qur'an itself registers a profound awareness of Mecca's precarious exceptionalism, nestled as it is in a resourceless terrain that under normal circumstances would not have allowed it to survive beyond a season or two. Such an exception, in turn, could be available only to foundational projects associated with prophetic effort—Abraham's in this case: "Abraham said: 'Lord, I have settled some of my offspring in a barren valley near Your Sacred House. . . . Put in the hearts of men kindness towards them, and provide them with the earth's fruits, so they may give thanks.'"[3]

In this case, an act of halting—indeed, an expression of an intention to halt forever—was seen to depend on God's leave and bounty. This is not to say, however, that a wandering nomad had no need for deities or that the sedentary God's credentials consisted in his assistance in a mere earthly and immediate task. The story is far more complex than that. As will become apparent in subsequent chapters, the decision and capacity to halt involve major metaphysical reorientations. Much of the dilemmas of Abraham's descendants, indeed, consisted of the question of how to overcome the ideology of the horizons, with all of its underpinnings. Such underpinnings had involved an attenuation of the idea of displacement, a cyclical vision of nature, a materialist rather than spiritualist contextualization of the idea of fate, an understanding of human and logical finitude in terms of processional exhaustion rather than of summary verdict or unifying conclusion, a suspicion of subjective construction and planning, a tendency to mock abstract authority, and an almost reflexive antipathy to grand political schemes in general. In an important sense, the idea of a monotheistic God exemplified a sustained attack on the ideology of the horizons and an effort to place the experiences of halting and wandering under a different order of regulation than those the nomad was willing to tolerate. This book will examine the rich dialectic interaction between that ideology of the horizons and the emergent faith and the resulting metamorphoses in all social and discursive spheres affected by both. But first, where does the story begin? If halting had accentuated for Abraham the necessity of God, what did that same halting signify for a more resilient nomad?

HALTING AND DISCOURSE

"Halt, friends both! Let us weep, recalling a love[r] and a lodging." So begins the great ode of Imru' l-Qays.[4] In the Bedouin conditions of life, the act of halting is conspicuous. There are no permanent lodgings, merely temporary territorial claims; sometimes these claims are cyclical or seasonal; other times a place is inhabited for the duration allowed by nature and then left for good. Home, to the extent that the term refers to a physical certitude, is located more frequently, as we shall see, on the back of a wandering camel than in any clearly demarcated geography. Residence is not a first principle toward which life is projected or oriented or structured: Residence is merely a state of transition between movements. It is significant, therefore, that this ode, as well as all other great pre-Islamic odes, begins with an act of halting. The poetic speech—as opposed to all other nonpreservable discourses—begins (and is perhaps motivated) when an interruption of a natural flow of movement is in order.

Thus, we have a poeticized interruption. That an oral tradition came to life, gathered the poem, and kept it from diffusing back into the mortal sphere of everyday language was perhaps a by-product of the invention of poetry itself. Such a view assumes that the poetic rendition of the act of halting was communicating with an already existent order of values, an order that was predestined to preserve for posterity the irruption of such discourse. The fact that halting is so paramountly displayed in such odes reflects that order, since halting here interrupts the normative conduct of life's course. In this, as well as in the other pre-Islamic odes, the act of halting is conducted before a ruined site of past encampment, love, memory, adventure, longing. This interruption of movement thus can only usher in the realization that life lacks a meaningful totality, that it consists of a series of irreplaceable losses as it proceeds through time. This recognition instigates a particular form of remembrance: Time is experienced not as an unfolding of potentialities but as a closing off of tangibilities. The salute is decidedly toward the past.

The ten legendary pre-Islamic odes are remarkably consistent on this score. In this ode as well as in all the others, the moment of halting is significant even if, or perhaps because, it is abrogated shortly thereafter. From this, various discussions ensue, presenting a modern reader with a scene of monumental, or rather encyclopedic, chaos. The beginning, however, is unwavering: All odes begin with halting. That is the most obvious formal unity in the tradition. That was, to be sure, how a "tradition" was recognized in the first place: A recognizable form was invoked, a form that provided the basis for the poem's belonging among poetry. Thus, halting is a formula by which discourses and meditations *other than halting* are introduced.

The elaborations that follow halting are part and parcel of the morphology of the act, especially with respect to the imposing landscape's relation to human life. Halting is obviously a spatially biased act that in some way anticipates such specifications. But this is what the ode (*mu'allaqa*, pl.: *mu'allaqat*) itself seems to be in a hurry to provide in no ambiguous fashion:

> Halt . . .
> by the rim of the twisted sands between Ed-Dakhool and Haumal,
> [then] Toodih and El-Mikrat, whose trace is not yet effaced
> for all the spinning of the south winds and northern blasts.

These are names of localities, the dwelling places of lovers from times past. The locations could indicate either spatiality or temporality, that is, they could either indicate the exact geographic point where the halting is taking place, or they could, equally probably, refer to a succession of dwellings where the lovers had once lived. The fact that the clarification is unimportant to a poet is important in itself. For the ambiguity could indeed indicate that the primordial audience knew of only one possible relationship between such locations, thus obviating the need for further deliberations. It could also be part of an economy of speech characteristic of self-dialogues in the desert. And it could as well refer to an altogether different arrangement of the world, in which confounding temporal and spatial elements posed little problem. And there is also the possibility that such conflations flowed naturally from the logic of poetry itself, that is, poetry as that preserve that discourse sets aside to all nonnormative, non-instrumental, noncommunicable experiments entrusted with the task of bringing additional conditions of being into language. There are other interpretive possibilities as well. What is more interesting about the question of the whereabouts is that names of locations always appear whenever an invocation to halting is in order. The act of halting is always anchored upon some specifiable geography. There seemed to be a need to firmly ground the halting act, so as to reproduce in it, as it were, the primal certitude of movement. One halts and ascertains the reality of such a moment in time by profuse naming.

The splash of names populating the moment at which halting is invoked accords spaciality a high order of recognition. Here, a name carves out of the infinite expanse of nature a finite space, which as it coalesces makes geographic knowledge possible and recurrent. In the descriptions of ancient Arab geographers, who wrote after the coming of Islam, one can still discern the lack of consolidation of names of places and territories. The notion of "borders" in the peninsula, for instance, often referred only to the continually shifting territories of wandering tribes rather than to stable geographic contours. Territorial designations were subsumed within an immense but monolithic topography, with enormous distances separating the habitable quarters. The five major regions of the peninsula recognized by geographers (Najd, Hijaz, Tuhama, Yemen, and 'Urud) referred to fluid and coextensive spatial generalities. Al-Alusi, for instance, supports the claim that Mecca lay in Tuhama and not in Hijaz, contrary to popular belief, and that Hijaz contained no cities other than Yathrib.[5] On the other hand, the authoritative geographer Yaqut al-Hamawi asserts that both Yathrib and Ta'if lie within Hijaz, and reports with no comment the claim by others that Yathrib could be in either Hijaz or Tuhama.[6] Apart from 'Urud (or Yamama), Bahrain is sometimes added as a sixth region.[7] Others considered Bahrain to be part of 'Iraq. Yaqut, however, considers Yamama to be part of Najd, being completely distinct from 'Urud, its supposed geographical domain.[8] Moving south toward Yemen, we encounter the same problem of determining approximate boundaries in the ancient world; thus, al-Istakhri, one of the most precise of the ancient Arab geographers, extends Yemen nearly to Mecca, so that Tuhama becomes a mere subregion of Yemen.[9] A similar hint at the extension of

Yemen is encountered in al-Mas'udi's descriptions.[10] Others distinguish Yemen from its southern expanse of Hadramaut, which had enjoyed certain periods of semi-independent social, political, and economic evolution from the rest of the Arabian Peninsula.

Such uncertain, fluid spaces are a fundamental part of the story. The different claims regarding their scope, extension, tribes, and pathways indicate an ongoing effort to clarify their relationship to each other. Like the more precise locales in the pre-Islamic *mu'allaqat,* such spaces are no longer extensions of an anonymous, vast desert extending forever between the horizons. Unlike the geographer's space, the space in the nomadic ode is more certain, fully referenced, bounded. There is, in the first instance, a wanderer who comes back, cyclically or by random chance, to a space containing a precious memory. From the vantage point of the returning wanderer, the perishability of all things except the place itself is confirmed by the singular persistence of its traces in the face of time, a persistence outlasting the love affair that had originally defined it. Realizing the stubborn resilience of the space, its power over all other natures, its resistance to disappearance, its indifference to time, in short, its negational definition of the unsettled nature of nomadic society itself, the name of the space assumes a power of its own, and therefrom is born its entitlement to a more accurate description. The space, then, is not a mere location but an essential experience by which the lover is defined: The poem thus begins here, and *not* with the unanchored self. The space works out its magic, therefore, by reminding the wanderer that he himself had lived, lost, or metamorphosed, leaving him thereafter with ponderous memory. The memory takes over and begins compiling a record of values and events that are then deposited in a distinct form of discourse.

Thus, it is not halting per se or even the naming and specifying of spaciality but, rather, the deposition of memory into discourse that allows an audible speaking subject to crystallize. The poet maneuvers from the place into himself. The place functions in the poem as it does in nomadic life itself: as a point of transition, where discourse lingers only until memory completes its search about the past amid the traces. Thereafter, the place is unceremoniously abandoned. The memory, after all, is reserved neither for the intrinsic value of the place nor for the place's empirical cohesion, exclusiveness, or natural distinction but, rather, for the actions that had constituted the place.

Life in the amorphous expanse of the desert does not guarantee a place any suprahuman self-evidence. Life, to be sure, endures *in spite of* the inhospitable sameness of the desert. And it is from this resistance to nature that a place takes its meaning. Life continues on the basis of a hope, which is continually frustrated but without which no place could ever promise the potentiality of becoming a home. The possibility of a social home, of a human togetherness persisting in the face of nature, not only stabilizes the idea of a "place" but sets the task of finding an empirical proof of such a possibility. Once found, the place is claimed with the meticulous division of labor that is seen to be incumbent upon residence and a requirement for its continuation. Such a relationship to a place allows competing discourses over land, nature, and their values to flourish, which is how a place is given a name and which is, ultimately, how the idea of place is completed with an accompanying history. Such a place, then, forms to house and collect the scattered passions of the wanderer. The pre-Qur'anic poetry here invests itself not in nature as such but in *namable* nature.

THE CAMEL, THE PATH, AND THE MARKETPLACE

The emergence of sedentary societies did not necessarily entail the oblivion of the horizons of wandering. This was especially true in nonagricultural communities, most notably Mecca. Having originally emerged as a caravan station within world-scale commerce, the city's subsequent livelihood depended on its active promotion of and participation in an annual cycle of marketplaces (*suqs*). Here, the city with the barren surroundings functioned as a locus of migratory trade that completed its cycle in it. Such moving seasonal *suqs*, in turn, functioned as a framework for commercial, cultural, and political intercommunication between the various regions. The picture that can be gleaned from various authorities provides for an annual cycle consisting of about fifteen seasonal *suqs*, which rotated clockwise around the peninsula throughout the months of the year, commencing with the *suqs* of Bahrain[11] and 'Uman, moving then southwest to the region of Hadramaut, then northward to Yemen, ending with five successive *suqs* in and around Mecca. The cycle culminated in the festive *suq* of 'Ukaz, which was held immediately before the pre-Islamic pagan pilgrimage to Mecca's sanctuary, the *haram*.[12]

To fully appreciate the nature and organizational imperatives of such an economic cycle, one must bear in mind the great distances involved, distances magnified by the dearth of settlements along the way. Historical travelers report that a caravan circling the peninsula could complete the journey in about seven months, with an average travel time of about a month between each of the major inhabited regions. By contrast, once the caravans began to venture northward into the Syrian frontiers, the distances between inhabited communities became markedly shorter.[13] Thus, although urban and agricultural sanctuaries were independent enclaves separated from each other by vast seas of sand and nomadism—especially in the central and western regions—regular communication links did form between such sedentaries. Politically and spiritually, however, such regions remained distinct from each other. Other than the marketplace routes, the *masalik* (pathways) linking them were limited in number and reach.

All these defining macrophenomena—communicative links, trade-based sedentarism, even nomadism itself—were scarcely possible in such a landscape without the camel. Some commentators argue that Bedouin lifestyle itself was a later development, since it was impossible before the domestication of the camel toward the middle of the second millennium B.C.[14] However, it was not only nomadism but commerce itself that was impossible without the camel.[15] This extraordinary animal is uniquely adapted to the harshness of the desert, with the capacity to forego water for up to five days in the summer and twenty-five days in the winter and to reuse food stored in its stomach, and its milk was an important source of nutrition. Furthermore, not only was it the only means of transportation in the desert, but it also required little upkeep. Thus, it became—as will be detailed in Chapter 2—a standard of value, with many calculations such as dowry, wealth, blood money (*diyyah*), and gambling debts being made in terms of number of camels. Nothing explains the value of the camel in such a landscape more than the number of its names in ancient Arabic; there are said to be a thousand.

For our purposes here, the significance of the camel emanates from its grand ideational status not simply as an enabler of a certain style of life but as the enabler of a certain attitude toward the world, an attitude conditioned by migration and movement. In the odes, the animal's extended attributes combine movement, escape, decrepitude, and triumph, for which the camel alone stands as the metaphor. Thus, whereas the moment of halting could only bring about the realization of time and loss, movement—as clearly symbolized in the nomadic odes by the camel—occupies multiple significations and outlines metamorphoses. The camel is no longer simply a beast of burden; rather, it is a prime signifier of the complexity of life and its events. For instance, the ostracized poet Tarafa Ibn l-'Abd, who expresses no more than a short and obligatory infatuation with the ruins before which his ode opens, wanders away from the eyesore on the back of his camel as early as the third couplet. The naming that follows is reserved to outlining the course of the journey (c. 3–4). Naming here carves out not a stability but a path. The beauty of one lovely woman who leaves with her wandering people—a scene described until the tenth couplet—is appreciated only from a distance. The poet here loves only from afar, rarely halting to actually enjoy or experience any appreciable sight. Yet when movement starts again in full (starting in c. 11), passions fly out of control over nothing other than the animal that enables movement. The unsurpassable fondness with which she is described runs remarkably consistently for thirty uninterrupted couplets, and the theme recurs frequently afterward. What is still more interesting in this masterful sequence is the presence of a rare organizing formula for this theme, with an "introductory" as well as a "concluding" couplet:

Ah, but when grief assails me, straightway I ride it off
mounted on my swift, lean-flanked camel, night and day racing. (c. 11)

Such is the beast I ride, when my companion cries
"Would I might ransom you, and be ransomed, from yonder waste!" (c. 39)

Such bounding of the discourse from both ends is a rare structure in the pre-Islamic ode. In this case, the structure is clearly reserved to elements of value, a value that is not subordinate to any other imagery. Such a thematic consistency is not restricted to the animal per se but applies more to the act of continuous movement as the discourse is being produced: We enter this discourse to find the poet riding, and we depart with him still riding. The length of the speech had not altered the act of moving. For it is in this continuity of movement that the poet finds his freedom from the dangerous human vice of melancholy (hamm).

A similar and somewhat more complicated structure is encountered in the ode of Labid Ibn Rabi'ah—to be discussed in more detail in a later chapter. When Labid abandons the ruinous site, he needs to outline the escape vehicle as well (c. 22). In the same mode, the more sedentary an-Nabigha adh Dhubyani advises a retreat along with a specification of its means: "So get away from this eyesore, there is no return for it / And gather the rafters on [the back of] a stiff-boned mare" (c. 7). In all such situations, the beast of burden, depleted by so much movement, comes to carry the distressed character away, often to no particular destination and often to a destination that only gradually reveals itself. In the meantime, the poetic discourse consumes itself with the love for the animal. It is, after all, the vehicle that empowers the subject over that moment of halting, which served only to confirm that it must not be repeated too often.

The journey away from the ruins does not consist, however, in the complete abandonment of an experience of their essence. To the contrary, the wanderer leaves the ruins on an equally ruined escape vehicle: "Break . . . with a lean camel to ride on, that many journeyings / have fined to a bare thinness of spine and shrunken hump" (Labid, c. 22). In other words, the wanderer takes the ruins along, renaming them in the process as a "camel." The paramount image of dilapidation thus engulfs the spheres of both movement and halting. But the interesting point is that such an admittedly collapsing vehicle itself contains the possibility of joyful triumph over desolate destiny:

> Break . . . with a lean camel to ride on, that many journeyings
> have fined to a bare thinness of spine and shrunken hump,
> one that, when her flesh is fallen away and her strength is spent
> and her ankle-thongs are worn to ribbons of long fatigue,
> yet rejoices in her bridle, and runs still as if she were
> a roseate cloud, rain-emptied, that flies with the south wind. (c. 22–24)

The joyous flight of this frail creature in the harsh desert is followed by similar metaphors for survival of the destitute. A she-ass and her companion roam a tortuous, drought-stricken wilderness (c. 25–35), ultimately reaching a lush oasis after an onerous journey. A wild cow searches, agonizingly, for her devoured young and is devastated by losses, but she is ultimately triumphant (c. 36–52). At a moment of absolute hopelessness, she is detected by hunters. She defends herself heroically against the hunting hounds, and the episode terminates with a festive account of her survival. We know that both the asses and the wild cow are metaphors for the she-camel because of this structure, which bounds the discourse about them with an introduction and a conclusion, both of which explicitly celebrate the camel. Thus, in this, as well as in most other poetics of that antiquity, the she-camel—the enabler of life *and* movement in the desert—is as much at the center of the speech as is the speaking subject himself. In fact, the camel seems to occur and recur with much more stability. The camel is not just an animal or even a word but, rather, a code name for order and reliability in nature. At the end of both metaphoric cycles, the camel surfaces again as the obvious *conclusion* from such experiences ("Upon such a camel . . .") (c. 53).

Thus, in the otherwise confident ode of the warrior 'Antara, it is the she-camel that reemerges at one point to rescue the poem from a sequence perilous because of its expressed uncertainty and directionlessness (c. 23–27). Without much of an introduction, the ode begins to delineate a destination, giving way to this feeling that we are already in the middle of a journey. It even seems that we have been moving all along: As far as one can tell, the she-camel comes back with a little detail from a journey already in progress (c. 28). Thus, here we have not so much an animal as an organizing principle for both life and discourse. And we find subsequent metaphors of order in general expressed with reference to the animal. As such, the camel became one of the few objects of life that, once introduced into a discourse, could not be dismissed without a ceremonious conclusion.

The beginning of the end of such an ideology is most evident in such poetics as the ode of an-Nabigha, one of the least nomadic of the pre-Islamic poets. In his ode, the camel's adventures in the wilderness and its obvious decrepitude are not metaphors for struggle, triumph, or normative or conclusive existence as much as they are a fountain of fears that cannot be dispensed with in the way of a conclusion. In an-Nabigha's ode, little space is dedicated to describing the she-camel herself; instead, her space is occupied by its metaphor, whose fate is uncertain (c. 10–19).[16] The she-camel herself, the essence of all metaphors of wandering, disappears into oblivion and never resurfaces again, save to announce a desire to end the journey in couplet 20. At such a point in the history of the tradition, wandering is not so much a glorification of freedom as a threat to existence itself; wandering is no longer normative, expected, periodic.

The wandering comes to a halt, the uncertainty of the path surrenders to the regularity of the caravan, the norm of travel becomes the continual outline of a destination. The sedentary path, conditioned as it is by a fear of this norm of recurrent loss, aimlessness, and effacement of traces, begins to lead to delineations beyond the realm of this dangerous world.

two

Socioeconomy and the Horizon of Thought

Nomadic (*badawah*) and sedentary (*hadarah*) lifestyles—along with some important subdivisions—constituted the two recognizable forms of social organization before and after the coming of Islam. Ibn Khaldun situated the *badawah* lifestyle historically before the *hadarah*, arguing that the formation of a sedentary society comes about only after an accumulation of nomadic wealth motivates a settlement.[1] Other historians, such as al-Mas'udi, also affirmed the chronological precedence of *badawah*.[2] A more dynamic picture, however, emerges when one examines geographic encyclopedias, such as Yaqut's or al-Bekri's, that outline the seasonal or temporal nature of many localities associated with a sedentary lifestyle. There are hints of an *effort* at sedentarization, an effort continuously frustrated by the scarcity of water and fertile land and the frequency of droughts. Under such circumstances, one can recognize an immutable society whose austerity regularly reproduces life just as is, without accumulation.

In itself, the barren land of northern Arabia could sustain little more than the lifestyle of the nomad, who was constantly wandering in search of water and grazing land for cattle and who was regularly forced to resort to raiding and marauding. Together, pastoralism, plunder (*ghazw*), and to a limited extent hunting provided a closed world of nomadic economy that could be broken out of only through participation in the trade of the external world, and then only as an intermediary between two or more rich civilizations, since northern Arabia had little of its own to export. But even such an intermediary role could scarcely materialize without at least one of two developments: (1) The volume of commerce passing through the desert may grow rapidly. The participation of the local population is enlisted by this enterprise in various capacities (as providers of petty services, as guides, or as protectors and agents for the caravans). Such activities may culminate in the investment of local capital in all facets of import and export activities. Or (2) the intermediary role of other agents may collapse, as was the case during the two centuries preceding Islam, with the decline of Yemen, on the one hand, and of the land route that had connected the warring Sassanid Empire and Byzantium, on the other.

There is little else to account for the birth and survival of sedentary life in Hijaz and the northern peninsula. A city like Mecca, for instance, throve originally as little more than a station for the northbound caravans originating from the port of 'Aden and elsewhere in southern Arabia, which ended their journey in such frontier markets as Petra, Bostra, Taima', or Daumat al-Jandal. Such caravans carried goods to meet Byzantium's needs. In the process, they created other markets, as will be outlined later. As the quantity of trade grew and as the states and tribes that had initially supported that trade declined in power, the inhabitants of such cities, especially Mecca, gradually abandoned their auxiliary role as dependents on caravans initiated and led by exogenous forces and began to engage directly in long-distance commerce.[3]

SEDENTARIZATION

Beyond the few fortified agricultural colonies, in such an inhospitable landscape the dynamics of sedentarization centered around trade and its infrastructure, such as caravan stations, and eventually provided territorial bases for organizing, financing, and lending to facilitate trade expeditions. Mecca offers the best illustration of such a transformation; it developed from a simple caravan station with an uncertain future into a complex center of long-distance trade, while retaining its service function and developing it into more intricate and spiritual forms. These forms were, in turn, determined in part by the nature of the diverse communities, Arab as well as non-Arab, with whom Mecca had to deal. The possibility of integrating most Bedouins into trade-based sedentarism was limited by a number of factors: the volume of the trade, the ability of powerful sedentary tribes (in this case, the Quraysh) to retain a monopoly on trade, and most nomads' lack of the necessary surplus capital. The last point is of crucial importance, particularly because the formation of the original commercial capital in Mecca had already raised the minimum surplus needed for participation in the caravans. This dynamic is alluded to in a Qur'anic passage commenting on the exclusionary behavior of the traders of Sheba, who are denounced for having asked God to make their caravan rest stops farther apart, ostensibly in order to prevent those who could not carry enough sustenance from taking part.[4]

Such conditions, coupled with the fact that there is little evidence that trade routes through western Arabia were stabilized before the sixth century, indicate that sedentarization itself was a reversible experience. Without further developments, founding a permanent settlement does not necessarily offer greater safety than nomadic existence proper. But it does have some motivating factors:

1. As Ibn Khaldun observes, one route to sedentarization is established with an increase in the wealth of the nomad. The idea of an "increase" should perhaps refer more precisely, in this context, to consistent above-subsistence-level acquisition, which could result from a prolonged period of conditions favorable to pastoralism. Within the Bedouin socioeconomy, such a surplus could neither be profitably invested nor adequately protected. Anatoli Khazanov notes that property differences among nomads are often temporary and are limited not only by the ecology but also by the "demands of cooperation and mutual aid." Such property inequalities are possible only when nomads become more strongly connected to sedentary communities or when a nomadic state comes into existence.[5] It is worth noting that the latter dynamic can be clearly discerned here, in the case of the tribes that were connected to the seminomadic dynasties at the frontiers of northern Arabia (which collapsed, as will be discussed later, shortly before the rise of Islam). Sedentarization here offered a method for protecting such wealth from the uncertainties of the *badawah* life, while it offered possible venues for its further accumulation.

2. Prolonged below-subsistence-level acquisition could also motivate sedentarization. A few years of misfortune in *ghazw* and unfavorable conditions for pastoralism could lead either to the extinction of the nomadic community or to its sedentarization in the meager hope of finding viable alternative conditions for existence. This was also a dynamic operating in the pre-Islamic epoch, when there was an increase in nomadic warfare, as will be outlined later, coupled with a prolonged series of droughts.[6] With few possessions of their own, these sedentarized nomadic communities were placed in the lowest socioeconomic echelons of the city society and thus contributed to its emerging stratification. It is likely that in Mecca communities such as al-Ahabish, al-Ahlaf, and to an extent the Zawaher of Quraysh itself, along with other lower-caste communities, had such origins.

3. Large nomadic social units could opt for sedentarization instead of the inevitable break up into smaller units that would occur if their *badawah* life was to be continued. Naturally, the area chosen for such sedentarization had to be capable of providing the newcomers with conditions able to sustain longtime residence. Yathrib is a case in point: From the very beginning it offered a proximity to agricultural colonies and caravan stations, thus allowing its inhabitants to practice both trade and agriculture. In comparison, a city like Mecca was compelled because of the barrenness of its surroundings to engage in nothing but trade and services, which furnished the ground for a complete ideological displacement of the *badawah* world outlook by the time of Muhammad. In Yathrib, on the other hand, the Aus and Khazraj newcomers joined the earlier Jewish inhabitants without losing much of their Bedouin outlook, as the city provided less of an incentive for them to concentrate all of their productive and creative energies in a single-minded obsession with trade and its concomitant forms of rationality.[7]

MONEY, TRADE, AND ABSTRACT THOUGHT

In the particular case of trade-based sedentarization (and more specifically, that concerned with long-distance, nonbarter forms of exchange), one can detect a transition away from an antecedent order of value when the sedentarizing nomads abandoned the use of direct assets—camels and herds—as media of exchange, replacing them with Roman and Persian coins so that more-complex transactions could take place. Before the introduction of abstract money value, direct assets, made up solely of herds, constituted the only meaningful acquisition for the Bedouin. Nomadic subsistence economy proper knew no abstract medium of exchange such as money. Nomadic exchange was based on consumable possessions and therefore took the form of barter, with the camel, in whose terms the significant transactions were usually calculated, having the most value in this system (while in neighboring sedentary communities, Persian and Byzantine gold and silver coins were being used more and more frequently). The development of a money economy in the trading cities was obviously a direct outcome of their incorporation into a long-distance trading system involving India, East Africa, Egypt, Persia, and Byzantium.

The growth of the abstract system of money must be seen in the context of the fact that little of the traded commodities were locally consumed, and when they were, they often were not part of a subsistence economy. In this respect, the value assigned to a commodity involved an external system of reference. This external system—empire's money—is reimported and assigned a local value that, because of local lack of experience of its genesis and meaning, becomes abstracted.

The transmutation of the camel itself from a means of exchange into a commodity occasioned the commodification of other products. The annual caravans to the northern frontiers carried gold, precious stones, ivory, wood, spices, cotton, and silk from India; incense, ebony, ostrich feathers, gold, ivory, and perhaps grains from east Africa; incense, myrrh, and other spices from Yemen; gum from Zufar; cereals from Yamama; and pearls from the coast of Bahrain, as well as cattle, leather, and a wide variety of clothes, fats, and medicines.[8] The camel, as the means of transportation of all such commodities, became itself a commodity-transporting commodity. The camel's status as a commodity was enhanced to the extent that it enabled the creation of other commodities. The main difference between the camel and the other commodities was located at the edges of the desert itself: The means of transportation remained, because of its biological limitations, a strictly internal item of value. On the other hand, transported commodities' values were determined at the borders with the empire, where the external world began. Whereas the value of the means of transportation outside the world of the peninsula was limited by its inability to adapt to the outside ecology, the value of the transported goods inside the peninsula was limited by their meager diffusion into the world of the inside, especially among the nomads. This last transition, it must be noted, has cultural as well as strictly economic foundations, as it includes generalizing the acceptance of money, as opposed or in addition to barter exchange. What was in order then was a reorientation of the mind to a notion of abstract valuation of objects in the form uniquely provided by money. In what follows, I will suggest some theoretical grounds for the possibility of such a transformation, particularly in terms of the trade economy in question.

Partially following Marx, Georg Simmel argued that money was uniquely capable of bringing the chaotic flux of objects in the world into the realm of a standardized law of value. That is, the value of an object would be ascertained not in the context of its unique occurrence but, rather, on the basis of its *form*. This form can be discerned only when the object is considered as but an incident of a more general type to which it is seen to belong.[9] As an adventure in abstraction, money establishes both a distance from the object and a link to it at one and the same time. That is, since value is an addition to the objective being of the object ("like shade and light") and since the object itself is indifferent to the value added upon its objective existence, such value cannot be determined with respect to the *essence* of the object. Therefore, the mind seeks a ground for value that could nevertheless possess the same certitude as objective existence. In other words, the source of value must be sought outside of the mind that is pondering the question of value. The mind then objectifies the addition of value by establishing a universal way of calculating it whereby the value is seen as being shared by other persons considering the same object. And since this monetary form of valuation refers not to the essence of the object but to the *method* of valuation that trading partners have in common, the question of monetary value becomes intrinsically a question of social life and social communication.

What is of concern to us is the assertion that one of the most successful efforts at sedentarization in the barren terrain under consideration required a transition into a trade-based economy that, because of the vast multiplicity of communities that engaged in it, had to be founded upon a generalized abstraction toward commodities as entailed in the experience of money. Such a transition cannot be located at an exact moment in time, which is often the obsession of historians, but must be sought along a trajectory of consciousness. This trajectory can be conceived of in terms of a diachronic continuum whereby the value-laden objects begin to have varying impacts on society's way of conceiving of the world. A preliminary cognitive trajectory can be roughly suggested by the following general steps:[10]

1. Once the value is added to an object, the object begins to be seen more and more in the context of this value and not as a pure, self-enclosed object. Value determines what and how objects will be seen.[11] The particular system of economic values prevalent in the trading community of Mecca is clearly recognized in the Qur'an, but in a way that identifies the hitherto unrecognized *source* of such values: Objects in the world are valuable not because of any intrinsic quality but primarily because of the illusory appeal imposed upon them by Allah: "Men are [made to be] tempted [*zuyyina lin-nas*] by the lure of women and offspring, of hoarded treasures of gold and silver, of splendid horses, cattle, and [crops]. These are the comforts of this life, but far better is the return to God."[12]

What stands out most clearly here is that God includes women and offspring among the known means of survival or, so to speak, with elements of use and exchange in the economy. Thus, such discourse integrates items of value in the world not so much into a system of exchange as into the essentials of the production and reproduction of life in the first place, and then within the system of value of a sedentary, commerce-based community. The preoccupation with self-preservation did not consist solely of crude economy: It was in the parallel product of human intimacy, the offspring, that an existent network for wealth accumulation recognized its eternal renewability.

The items of value enumerated in the verse cited above are not meant to be strictly equivalent to each other, however. The exposition deals with both solid and ephemeral items of wealth and prestige, beginning with monetized treasures and ending with crops. The order in which such items are listed is significant. The recognized importance of hoarded treasure speaks to a society whose economy is based on monetary rather than barter exchange, especially because hoarding indicates that the value of such treasure is trusted not to disappear in a future that is expected to continue to be sedentary. Next listed are the splendid horses, which were used neither for travel in the desert nor as pastoral assets but, most importantly, in tribal warfare. Third came the pastoral assets, and at the end of the list, the fruits of sedentary agriculture. Those different forms of wealth referred to different societies. In a way, their comprehensive listing in one condensed passage spelled out an attempt to identify a transcendental and more than simply local origin of economic value. In an age when abstract methods of assessing and recognizing economic value were being introduced, the divine effort consisted of precisely confirming such values. This was done—at least in this instance—by taking the effort to impose values on things away from both instinctive human proclivities and objective existence of commodities, providing the faithful mind with the ability to recognize a divine source for both spheres.[13]

The fundamentally sedentary nature of such a mode of thinking can best be appreciated by visiting comparable images of value in the nomadic ode. In the odes, items of values are passing and perishable rather than "hoarded," stabilized, or listed in a universal order. In the ode, the item of value in the world is that which is lost repeatedly: a ruined abode, a departed lover, or a depleted, haunted animal or human actor. Those who spend their life accumulating treasures are observed to die just as do those who live in destitution, as Tarafa most eloquently observes. The camel, the highest and most stable item of value in the ode, is conceived of not as a means of exchange but, rather, as an enabler of life, itself often being on the verge of perishing. It is the means by which the wanderer moves perpetually away from the possibilities of discerning values in abstract themes.[14]

2. Economic values in a trading community are those that define the community as one of traders. The significant aspect of the emergence of such a self-definition consists of how it supersedes other, apparently normative definitions of community—for example, those based on blood lineage, alliance, joint ownership of land, or adherence to a specific deity. Supraindividual self-definition requires a basis of commonality that would allow such a "social fact" (in the Durkheimian sense) to appear to be an unchosen norm, while at the same time basing the collective self-definition on the practice upon which the community regards itself to be founded.

One of the bases of such a value system, money, stands for a *communal* and shared comprehension of exchange values. Therefore, and *pace* Max Weber, money is not an example of means becoming ends but, rather, a communal agreement on a shared meaning for the essence of an object that could only appear as value. It is the guarantee that all would think about the object's value in the same terms and according to the same rules and that there are no other devious or hidden means (that is, means unknown to others) by which any one person could know the object better than did others. Money means that the potentially commodifiable objects that are strewn upon the earth appear to a communal mind only when endowed with value.

Here, rules by which values are measured become the object of negotiation involving external as well as internal dynamics. Several rudimentary standards for commodity exchange developed as a consequence of the introduction of long-distance trade in western Arabia.[15] The Arabs continued to use Persian and Roman coins until the advent of the Islamic state. However, the infusion of such coins eventually called for the creation of *local* standards for the adjudication of their values.[16] Such a dynamic of valuation shows that the development of local standards is not only a response to the plethora of value measurements of the outside world but also a recognition of the need to develop one's own abstraction as a result.

The development of such a value system, in turn, grounds the community upon a new system of relations and rights, so that prior values that were fundamental to communal definition—for example, tribal solidarity (*'asabiyyah*)—either become subordinate to such a system or are integrated into it. This is abundantly clear in Muhammad's eventual war against Mecca, which is interesting in two respects: First, it indicated that the new abstract method of appreciating the world had so significantly downplayed *'asabiyyah* that intratribal warfare (and in this case, using "outsiders" against one's own tribe) had become possible.[17] Second, Muhammad's war against Mecca was also a new kind of war, clearly distinct from the nomadic *ghazw*. Mahmood Ibrahim makes the significant point that, unlike in the *ghazw* situation, Muhammad's conquest of Mecca did not end in plundering the city (contrary to the wishes of many of the nomads in his army) but, rather, in sanctifying and Islamicizing Meccan capital and private property, which were retained by their owners. This concomitant redefinition of the nature of warfare was evident elsewhere throughout Arabia afterward, as Muhammad was willing to keep local rulers and local wealth in place—including the Christian Najran—subject to taxation, which here represents a new level of economic organization.[18]

3. The trading community does not emerge simply because of a proliferation of objects seen to be valuable but also because the value of such objects resides in their *exchangeability*. Such a stipulation involves what can be called a "second order" abstraction: The value that a community discerns in an object is in essence the value placed upon it by *another* community with which the first then conducts an exchange. That is, the trading community is capable of seeing the object as valuable not only because of the value it places on it but also—and sometimes only—because of its ability to see the value that outsiders to the community place on it.

In this sense, the ability to discern others' values also means that the exchange is an exchange of ideas and worldviews, and not just commodities. What is of further interest in this respect is that such a grand exchange takes place, as in the case under examination, in a largely noncoercive environment. As mentioned before, Mecca's trade partners were hardly in a position to coerce the city, given its location deep in the desert, which spared it the fate of similar trading communities that were closer to imperial frontiers.[19] This context of noncoercion meant that a variety of ideologies, cosmologies, and spiritualities could intermix in a pluralistic environment that formed the backbone of paganism. Moreover, such a pluralism meant that the textual and seemingly closed beliefs of "others" (such as Christians and Jews) or transcendental trends (such as Hanifism [a group of eclectic reform trends] and the idea of Allah itself) could be treated as experiments and possible components of pagan theodicy itself rather than as exclusive totalities. This was the spiritual status quo in Mecca, which did not even so much reject Muhammad's Allah (and it was on occasions even prepared to offer him a special status among its other objects of worship) as it did a claim to exclusive monotheism transmitted through a regular human messenger.

4. As the objects of trade enter into a circulation cycle, their value comes to consist of their capacity to remain in at least potential circulation. That is, in order to maintain a value, that is, in order to continue to be discernible, the object must always present itself as an object of desire—and thus potential possession—by another person, even if that "other person" has not seen or heard of the object. The desire of a hypostasized Other for

the object must be posited for the object to retain its status as a commodity. Such a hypostatization involves what might be called a "third order" abstraction, that is, presuming the knowledge by an *unknown* person of the value of the object.

Such a presumption is fundamental for understanding trade as a continually *expansive* enterprise, which spreads until it becomes what in today's parlance is often called a "world system." The fundamental idea here concerns not so much the expansion of the "economy" itself as the development of the cognitive prerequisites upon which such an expansion is based. Namely, this expansion—especially in terms of territory and participants, rather than simply volume—is grounded upon a *posited universalism* of desire for trade objects. This universalism, in turn, furnishes one of the grounds for thoughts concerned with universal values. Thus, at this juncture we have a presumption of universal desire, coupled with a pluralist ethic born out of the context of impossibility of coercion in that particular system.

5. The confoundment at one point in time of the stipulations just outlined establishes an unbridgeable mental distance from the object endowed with value. That is, the source of value is seen to reside outside of the mind and in the community, or outside of a trading community and in the Other with whom it conducts its commerce, or outside of both and in a hypostasized universal realm of the potential. As such, money provides for the possibility of a universal link, which then becomes the meaning of the value of the object over and above its individual occurrences and over and above the possibilities of individual experience of the object.

This means that in the context of trade as such, only a link to the object is maintained, not the object itself. That is, when money crosses the distance between the mind and the object, it places itself at the site of its value, thereby making it impossible for the object's value to appear in any form other than that of money. The experience of the object *itself* is always deferred and replaced by the *promise* instigated in the experience of a mere link to it. The trauma of such an indefinite deferral stems from what had begun as a value orienting one's attention to what could then be experienced only along the road to it. Simmel implies that only when the world is accepted as forms rather than a constellation of essences could such a trauma be overcome.[20]

This trajectory of form is evident in our story in the increasing mental departure in the sedentary community from the materialism of the *mu'allaqat* (odes)—even though the *mu'allaqat* themselves furnished a tradition of formalizing experiences deemed profound. The move was part of a continuum of abstraction that can be seen in the emergence of Hanifism and other mystical and meditative trends in pre-Islamic times. The trajectory is also apparent in the increasing disenchantment with the physical idols, a state of affairs that garnered for Islam its first few recruits in Mecca. The Qur'an clearly makes the point by expressing bewilderment at how man could worship objects that he himself had made,[21] that is, objects whose value was a product of direct human investment rather than inscribed in distanced "forms" (of deities) that one could approach only through links—as prefigured in the experience of monetized trade.

6. Therefore, money is one of the experiences of a community that, through the history of the community's experimentation with concepts of collective valuation, regularly posits abstract links to pertinent objects in its world. But because of the *abstract* nature of the link, the community becomes incapable of experiencing anything other than the link itself; and from then on, the essence of the object is indefinitely distanced. This distancing persists as a trace of unease, which becomes the learned way of experiencing objects in the world. Thus the experience of "traces" of value no longer follows the dynamic observed in the *mu'allaqa*, where a trace of a ruined site was accepted as evidence of a material end of desire. In the pre-Islamic ode, material traces of the past, notably residence, only certified the normatively tragic meaning of existence. The traditional shedding of tears at such a site, which commenced the ode, did not address the deferral of experiencing objects of longing, as in the emerging trade-based communities. Rather, it sealed an awareness that such an experience had already occurred and that it would not be repeated.

Oftentimes, such experiences are totalized and given a meaning or a voice or a legitimation from a source that is capable of legitimizing experiences of nonfulfillment, capable of nullifying or denying them, and capable of promising an eventual freedom from a collectively felt estrangement from objects. The search for such a source is evidenced in the pre-Islamic religious rituals that were concerned with establishing a connection with it, such as the pilgrimage chants (to be discussed in Chapter 4) that unified the community with its creator. Like the experience of value itself, this source is located outside of all domains over which it is to have jurisdiction. God coalesces at that site.

These remarks chart out a sociocognitive course for the emergence of a novel method of pondering the status of objects in the world, a method that could accompany the social experience of money. The background of the discussion is the assumption that the kind of sedentarization that is historically most associated with the rise of Islam occasioned a deep involvement in and dependence on trade for survival. This trade emerged out of a surrounding context of a resourceless nature and an originally nomadic society and world outlook, both of which seem to preclude the types of abstraction and valuation of objects described here. Such experiences of thinking should not be regarded as historical events in the narrow sense of the word; that is, no date could be given for the transition from one way of thinking into another. One could at best outline diachronic continua that would show, for instance, that various moments of the scheme described above had coexisted with beliefs that were diametrically opposed to them. These are the experiences in life that we refer to, for instance, as moments of spiritual tension.

Side by side with the emergence of long-distance trade, an intertribal trade within Arabia began to emerge around the seasonal *suqs* (marketplaces).[22] The *suqs* forged regular, organized links between the sedentary societies of the peninsula. They also furnished the material backbone for the emergence of a set of semilegal, semireligious rules that prefigured the later formation of the Islamic central state and its apparatus. Most importantly, such rules included the prohibition of fighting and raiding for four months of the year (*ashhur haram*, "the forbidden months") which happened to be the months during which all of the *suqs* of Hijaz and more than half of the *suqs* in the peninsula were held. Some religious concepts entailing a regularity of path or time, such as pilgrimage, developed parallel to the trade cycle and in a way that acknowledged the central role of Mecca in both regards. The commercial activity increased rapidly around Mecca as the pre-Islamic pilgrimage season neared, culminating in the great *suq* of 'Ukaz, whereafter the pilgrimage to the nearby *haram* (sanctuary) in Mecca took place.

Intermediary trade, thus, became the most important capital-accumulating occupation in the otherwise largely barren land of western Arabia. Some revisionist historians, most recently led by Patricia Crone, labor tirelessly to cast doubt on the size of Meccan trade. But they usually miss the main point here, which is that even if it is granted that the size of the trade was smaller than is usually thought, trade made possible capital *accumulation* and consequently social transformation. In a different but methodologically pertinent context, Fernand Braudel effectively demonstrated in *Civilization and Capitalism* that in a nascent world system, it was precisely the exclusion from trade of the great majority of the population that allowed for a concentration of profit and thus facilitated the emergence of capital surplus in society and among distinct elites.[23] Once it was formed, however, such a surplus had a pivotal role to play in grand social transformations. Furthermore, trade clearly left its imprint everywhere on the emerging sedentarism. The name of "Quraysh" can be traced, as many reports contend, from *taqarrush*, a word descriptive of accumulating and gaining.[24] Except in a few rare oases, such as Ta'if, agriculture played no significant role in the economic life of Najd and Hijaz. Al-Mas'udi reports that the organizing principle of the pre-Islamic calendar had no relationship to seasons,[25] whose change meant little to a non-agricultural society.[26]

Long-distance trade gradually transformed social and political life. The two centuries preceding Islam witnessed both the stabilization of the sedentary society and its increasing complexity, especially in Mecca. Throughout such developments, nomadic society remained excluded, defiant, and unchangeable. This was most evident in the crushing failure of the only monarchical experiment among the nomads, namely that of the Kinda tribes during the first half of the sixth century A.D. in Najd and its surroundings. Some intermediary societies, seminomadic and semi-sedentary, continued their transitional experimentation; Yathrib, which retained much of its Bedouin character, housed many fortifications that were used in the recurrent outbreaks of war between its main tribes.[27] The existence of agriculture in some colonies near Yathrib—later to be renamed Medina—apparently perpetuated aspects of Bedouin mentality and lifestyle; on the other hand, Mecca was forced, because of the barrenness of its surroundings, to rely exclusively on trade. Mecca was therefore forced to follow a policy of absolute neutrality and to unwaveringly insist on preserving peace in the city at all costs. The strength of the populous tribe of Quraysh was sufficient to guarantee peace within the boundaries of Mecca and its *haram*.[28]

Quraysh was the tribe most interested in preserving peace in general and during the sacred months in particular, the period when the most important commercial activities in the peninsula took place. Róbert Simon charts out a process through which Mecca emerged as the supreme trade center, a process entailing the successive elimination of the city's potential and actual competitors.[29] Although this is true to a certain extent, one must keep in mind—since this point is significant in terms of the ideological transformation and political self-concept of the city—that such an elimination of competitors was *never* done by Mecca itself. The disuse of the trade routes in Asia, the trials of the maritime route in the Red Sea, and the decline of Yemen, the northern frontier cities, and other trading peninsular tribes were outcomes of conflicts of which Mecca was certainly the beneficiary though neither a participant nor even an instigator.

The only possible exception is the so-called *hurub al-fijar* (sinful wars), when Quraysh was forced into a fight with the Hawazen tribal confederation during the sacred months, an episode that Simon discusses in the context of the struggle to eliminate competitors.[30] What is important here, however, is that during that episode, Mecca is reported to have been defending itself rather than actively eliminating others, as it was evidently *forced* into a fight after having opted to withdraw, ostensibly out of respect for the sacred month—a concept that Hawazen did not regard.[31] Thus in this case, as well as in the case of Abraha's campaign, the city was in fact seeking not so much to eliminate competitors as to protect itself from elimination by others. In both cases, there is an evident element of spiritual self-defense; in Mecca—significantly, in spite of its victory—*hurub al-fijar* were seen as being fundamentally *sinful rather than heroic* wars, and Abraha's failure was traced to divine protection rather than to the city's own effort.

The concept that peace should be observed during forbidden months, as a pseudospiritual accompaniment to trade, was often difficult to enforce. For many nomads, the concept meant little, especially if the specified months coincided with periods during which they needed to resort to raiding as a means of survival, or if they were excluded from the trade involved.[32] There is also some evidence to suggest that some tribes, though accepting the principle, contested the designation of specific months as being forbidden.[33] It is significant in this respect that at a later stage, Islam confirmed the Meccan version of the sacred months and prohibited the alternatives. In any case, observing the forbidden months was a sedentary, trade-oriented preoccupation, which for the nomads induced potential losses for one third of the year.[34]

As Mecca gained prominence in trade, its religious status was likewise enhanced. As far as ideological or spiritual developments are concerned, it is perhaps not so much the volume of trade in Mecca or even the centrality of Mecca to trade that is so significant. More important than *centrality* is the *circulatory* nature of the *suq* cycle. Circularity signifies periodicity of exposure of a variety of societies to an annually renewable routine. The fact that the process of trade involved a seasonal rotation around the peninsula, so that it came back to Mecca and proceeded out of it again, meant that the models of sociopolitical or spiritual organization of the trading community could involve not only models learned from relatively distant imperial centers (Byzantium, Persia, Abyssinia) but also those engendered by more dynamic and less controllable nomadic and semi-sedentary Arab experiences. The idea of circularity here is most evident in pilgrimage, which was not simply a visit to a distant and aloof center of spirituality but also a periodic culmination of a cycle of peninsular trade.

The idea of circularity—as opposed to centrality—is further enshrined in the fact that the pilgrims paid respect not so much to Mecca's *haram* itself as to their own tribal idols and in the fact that they chanted their own tribally distinct chants within the *common* site of pilgrimage. Neither Mecca nor its *haram* were in themselves the objects of veneration or worship; they simply housed the objects of worship of recognized *others*. The Arabic word for pilgrimage, *hajj*, is traced in one authoritative report not to any intrinsic spiritual idea but, rather, to a distinctly geographic idea denoting a regular, well-traversed route.[35]

Nearly all classical authorities attribute the construction of the *haram* in its pre-Islamic form to the Qurayshan chief Qusay Ibn Kilab,[36] whose appearance seems to coincide with the early periods of Meccans' direct engagement in long-distance trade. The foundation of a spiritual context for trade is well documented in the sources and is evident in many peninsular locations before or around the time of Mecca's prominence. Bedouins from Banu Ghatfan are reported to have built a *haram* in Tuhama explicitly after the Meccan model in order to protect their newly acquired possessions—garnered by raiding—from loss in further wars. As a result, Mecca dispatched an expedition that aimed at despoiling a *haram* that might have competed with its own.[37] Other reports mention that the Abyssinians, during their occupation of the economically faltering Yemen in the sixth century, sought to build a *haram* there in a desperate attempt to redirect the pilgrimage route, and subsequently the *suq* cycle, to Yemen.[38] Thus, many peninsular markets evidently took place in locales of cultic importance. R. B. Serjeant compared the *haram* of Mecca to sanctified sites in southern Arabia known as *hawta,* whose foundation was traced to venerated holy men, where bloodshed and the cutting of trees were forbidden, and where traders could meet and haggle in safety.[39] Other reports trace the decline of the economic status of some *suqs* to their loss of cultic prestige.[40]

MECCA

Such a spiritual organization of economic life, furthermore, seems to have entailed some institutionalized division of labor that actively promoted and maintained it. According to tradition, Qusay—Mecca's purported Qurayshan settler—added a whole set of costly functions related to the service of the *haram* and its pilgrims, the mere commitment to which would indicate the presence of wealth. Each of the five functions[41] presupposed that its holder was a person of political or economic power. Qusay's further establishment of *Dar an-Nadwah* as an institution for intratribal consultation and as a site of common celebrations and functions can be seen as an indication of the subsequent sociopolitical development of Meccan society.

The emerging need for all such functions and institutions is related in many ways to Mecca's increasing wealth and importance. But they also point to another parallel internal development, namely, the emergent class division within Quraysh itself. The sources trace class division to that time, along with the division of the tribe into Abateh and Zawaher, signified by residential segregation. The wealthier and more noble Abateh lived in the neighborhood of the *haram,* whereas the less fortunate Zawaher inhabited the rest of Mecca and the mountain terrain surrounding it. In that separation, the newly sedentarized nomad was being introduced to a hitherto rare phenomenon: visible and enduring symbols of class divisions.

Such divisions took root within a context of an almost-exclusive dependence on trade as the source of livelihood for all classes of inhabitants. (Evidence exists to suggest that Mecca lacked not only agriculture but even simple craftsmanship.)[42] This dependence, in turn, gave birth to new ways of approaching the connections between "labor" and entitlement to wealth. Trade itself was far from being an occupation universally held in high esteem. There are poetic references to its connection to avarice, disdain, and other negative attributes.[43] Trade as wealth legitimizing labor posed a novel ideological preoccupation, since it was not rooted in the older and more accepted ideas of labor permeating both agricultural colonies and nomadic pastoral and *ghazw* economy.

There are a couple of reports relevant to this problematic, both of which concern Ta'if. One mentions that Quraysh, inhabiting the inhospitable terrain of Mecca, offered to share the sacred *haram* with Thaqif of Ta'if, in exchange for the latter's sharing their fertile Wadi Wajj with Quraysh.[44] Such a proposal would indicate first that the status of the *haram,* sacred as it was, did not set it far apart from other directly negotiable items of exchange. Rather, the offer itself is generally consistent with the flexible attitudes of pagan pluralism that had enshrined Mecca's status in the peninsula. Incidentally, it also points to one of the sources of Hanifism and eventually Islam, as mystical and experimental discourses in search of a more solidly grounded and less negotiable source of divinity. Second, the report also indicates that Mecca was aware of its vulnerability due to its exclusive dependence on trade. This continuing feeling of vulnerability, in turn, was one of the grounds that Islam sought to address as well, as will be elaborated later.

Thaqif eventually rejected Mecca's offer on a very illuminating ground: The reason given was articulated in terms of labor entitlement; whereas Thaqif had made Wadi Wajj into what it became through their labor, Quraysh had simply inherited a *haram* that had been founded by Abraham rather than building or earning it through the tribe's labor. It is significant to note that the argument did not directly compare the timely values of the *haram* and Wadi Wajj; neither did it directly contest the spiritual significance of the *haram.* Rather, it grounded the comparison on two main sources: (1) the origins of values in terms of labor and (2) the right to negotiate such values. In this regard, the *haram* was no longer seen as Quraysh's to barter away or negotiate, since its value was embedded in the labor that had gone into establishing it and since the tribe was not party to such labor—not even in terms of (exclusive) genealogy. Such a view was consistent, furthermore, with the aforementioned tradition of ascribing the genesis of cultic/trade sites to *transtribal* holy men.

Thus, Thaqif's rejection of the offer was based not so much on the inferior value of the *haram* compared to Wadi Wajj as on their view that transformative labor and the ex post facto transtribal shrines belonged to different logical spheres and were thus incomparable, or inexchangeable. It is significant, of course, that Quraysh evidently thought otherwise. For it was clear from Quraysh's perspective that the value of the *haram* had been historically transformed by Quraysh's labor, which included not simply regular upkeep but, more importantly, the gradual establishment of a trade and pilgrimage cycle that aggrandized the stature of the shrine and made it *over time* the expansive house of many tribally specific objects of worship. As such, although the foundation of the *haram* was not claimed by Quraysh—and it could not claim it, if for no other reason than its necessarily transtribal claim—Quraysh was convinced of the *haram*'s comparability to Wadi Wajj precisely on the grounds of labor (and obviously not holiness per se).

Thus we have here two conceptions of labor that did not communicate or reinforce each other across the divide between trading and agricultural communities. The agricultural logic is further illustrated in another report, also concerning Ta'if but not Mecca this time, which connects a certain formulation of labor to the idea of "right." Ta'if was originally claimed by two matrilineally related tribes, 'Amer and Thaqif, with the latter being the latecomers and the former holding a recognized "right" to the land. The reports emphasize that 'Amer was nonetheless largely nomadic, spending only the summer in the elevated gardens of what came to be known as Ta'if and winters pasturing their flocks in the open expanses of Najd. Their relatives of Thaqif, having taken note of such a dynamic and becoming more aware of the agricultural potential of the area, offered to cultivate and improve it on a continuous, residential basis and in return split the harvest with 'Amer. The right of each tribe to half of the produce was explicitly articulated in terms of two distinct categories: Thaqif would receive one half because of their labor, 'Amer would receive the other half because of their right to the land. The system operated for many years. As the colony prospered, however, and the Thaqif grew in number and strength, they excluded the absentee 'Amer owners, along with branches from Thaqif itself in the process.[45]

In the absence of a central political feudal authority to enforce it, the notion of rightful ownership can be abstracted and assigned to an absentee landlord only for as long as mutual defense obligations' warrant it. Such a voluntary feudalism cannot, of course, be enforced indefinitely without the category of "right" being eventually contested on the grounds of "labor," as evidently happened in this case. Again, right (and the exclusion from it) was grounded in the ability to transform nature rather than on ancestral claims, which, although originally recognized, held only for as long as the territory in question remained untransformed or relatively defenseless.

It is in the context of established ideas of labor and right that the emergence of a Meccan trade economy must be ascertained, especially if one is concerned about its ideological connotations and problems. There is little in the ancient history of Mecca that does not link it to trade. Its foundation as a caravan station in an arid environment was made possible by the discovery of a large underground water source, Zamzam (eventually enshrined within the Islamic pilgrimage rituals), which is recorded to have been known and used for many centuries before Islam. As time went on, more wells were dug, and their discovery was both a result of the expansion of the city and a key factor in maintaining it.[46]

The reports mention that the site was successively controlled by Jurham, Khuza'ah, and finally Quraysh, even though the evidence for intertribal marriages indicates long periods of neighborly coexistence.[47] The construction of permanent dwellings, however, is traced to Quraysh, personified by the city-building, semimythical Qusay Ibn Kilab. As already mentioned, this sedentarization was also accompanied by a class-based residential division and the growth of functions and responsibilities pertaining to spiritual and consultative city life. Together with this development, the sanctity of the *haram* of Mecca began to be amplified, as it was to play a decisive role in regulating the neutrality and peace that were essential for trade. Bloody battles among tribes in and around the site were not unknown before Qusay's days, and the universal respect for the *haram* was apparently long in the coming, and it came single-handedly through Meccans' efforts.[48]

In addition to the Abateh-Zawaher distinction, a third caste, centering on the line of descent from Qusay, topped the Qurayshan hierarchy and offered a hereditary organizational vehicle for running the emergent politics of spirituality in Mecca. The sources clearly associate Qusay's sedentarization with the simultaneous introduction of an administrative apparatus. *Dar an-Nadwah*, said to be the first house to be built in Mecca after its sedentarization by Quraysh during Qusay's days, was also a communal headquarters. Everything of significance to the community was done in it, from marriages to declarations of war. *Dar an-Nadwah* functioned often partially according to nomadic principles, with the chiefs of the various clans participating in making decisions, which in turn were not binding unless agreed to unanimously. Like the principle of unanimity, other Bedouin concepts of governance were entertained in a somewhat modified form. The seniority rule around *Dar an-Nadwah* prescribed that with the exception of Qusay's sons, no Qurayshan under forty years of age was allowed to enter.[49] The exclusion of Qusay's sons from an ancient rule of hierarchy was indicative of the emergence of new criteria for eminence. It signified the addition to the old notion of social status, which emanated primarily from tribal service and secondarily from lineage, elements of leadership that were more personal rather than collective. Ibrahim traces such a development of personal leadership to the growth of merchant capital, which precludes the earlier collectivist and community-oriented credentials for prominence.[50]

As they became the economic and political elite in the gradually polarizing society of Mecca, Qusay's sons also inherited all of the spiritual functions that their father had monopolized. It is perhaps indicative of the emergence of a new form of spirituality, and of its ties to sociopolitical powers, that all of Qusay's sons' names begin with " *'Abd*" (worshipper of), unlike Qusay's ancestors. The contentions attendant on the struggle over the control of the *haram* functions was resolved peacefully, which accorded with the image of the city's sanctity, and in a way that led to increasing pluralism of duties until Muhammad's time. The five functions were allocated to different descendants, and eventually about ten more functions were created and allocated to various branches of the tribe, thereby appeasing them and assuring each of a certain degree of influence and prestige.

Meccan trade was buttressed by an array of spiritual and directly economic arrangements, ranging from sanctifying the city, housing tribal cults (*hums*), and forging internal as well as external agreements to regulate trade. Those controlling *haram* services were leading traders at the same time, as political and economic power went hand in hand in the most naked way.[51] The *haram* was an institution of fundamental importance for the city: It helped to preserve peace in Mecca and confirm its neutrality in the peninsula, securing thereby friendly relations with most of the peninsula's inhabitants. In the process, the city began to gradually gain a widespread acceptance for its proclaimed spiritual role. The most striking example in this respect is the role of *siqayah* and *rifadah,* the two most important of the sixteen or so service functions listed in connection to the *haram* before Islam. By providing the basic necessities of life, food and drink, the Meccans forged broad informal alliances with both Bedouins and sedentaries, thus facilitating the passage of their caravans through various territories. Thus the Bedouins' valorization of open hospitality, so crucial to the life of wandering and unpredictability, was firmly incorporated and organized in the ethic of a city that had to deal practically with its anarchic surroundings.[52] The first pre-Islamic taxation in Mecca, which helped cover the cost of the *rifadah,* was a direct outcome of such a necessity.[53] Testifying to their undeniable importance, such functions were always held by some of the wealthiest individuals in Quraysh.

In order to smooth out or even guarantee the functioning of such a system as a whole, a few morally and materially binding agreements were attempted. The first such recorded agreement resolved a conflict between the allies of the different sons of Qusay, who opted instead for a peaceful division of political authority in Mecca afterward in a way that satisfied most of the branches of Quraysh and maintained peace and order in Mecca until Muhammad's time. But more economically important was the agreement by major Qurayshan leaders known as *hilf al-fudul* (pact of the virtuous ones), of which Muhammad was said to have been an enthusiastic supporter (before his revelation). *Hilf al-fudul* was an agreement that guaranteed the proper collection of due credit and rights for all merchants who dealt in Mecca. There are indications that the agreement only formalized established traditions regarding rights and credit relations; by the time one incident forced it back into relevance, it had almost become forgotten.[54]

Traditional accounts mention that in the earlier periods, profits from external trade were divided up equally among Qurayshans.[55] This report must be seen in the context of others concerning the practice of *i'tifad*, whereby an individual failed merchant voluntarily banished himself and his family from the community and went away to starve to death.[56] This practice is clearly an extreme manifestation of an existent ethic of individualized destiny, in a context where commerce began to introduce novel ideas regarding rights and allocations in the community. The emergence of a stable trading society in Mecca itself introduced such novel concepts regarding the nature of collective bonds. Here, class structure began to form a second line of differentiation in addition to, or sometimes in opposition to, clan differentiations. In this light, wealth differentiation within the clan became possible, and thus so did such practices as *lending* to a relative.[57]

This development often superimposed class distinctions upon the lines of descent of the branches of Quraysh. Tribal affiliations could be incorporated into and adapted to the cause of commerce, which occasionally made lineage into another vehicle for expressing class and status position. As members of one branch became wealthy while the branch continued to exist as a distinct social entity, with clearly defined norms governing relations with the other branches, the new wealth became not only an additional recognizable feature of the branch as a whole but appeared to be most securely utilizable within it as well. The variety of preexisting *haram* service functions operated precisely in this manner: They were allocated to individuals on the basis of branch affiliation, eventually perpetuating and spiritualizing a status quo, as some functions were clearly more important and costly than others, and as the positions responsible for those functions were consistently occupied by members of the more prosperous branches.[58]

Thus, the relatively rapid infusion of wealth superimposed class distinctions, an idea of privileged functions, an abstraction of the world, an impersonal conception of the market, and a knowledge of an uncontrolled outside environment over a social and ethical framework that could accommodate it only precariously. The surrounding world, seen from the city, was in a state of complete chaos, with Mecca's competitors disintegrating, with the Bedouin society in a state of hopeless stagnation and infighting, and with the great powers of the time, the Roman and Persian Empires, tottering because of incessant wars between them, on the one hand, and crippling internal dissent, on the other.

Seen from the outside, however, the growth of the city's spiritual status paralleled that of its economic status, as outlined before. The imperatives of such a position meant that Mecca had to avoid involvement in the many tribal disputes in the peninsula and pursue a policy of heartless neutralism. Reports indicate that it rejected a lucrative offer of alliance with other powerful semisedentary groups.[59] The aura of the forbidden months, which offered spiritual shelter for peninsular trade, was supplemented by more earthly agreements, known as *ilaf*, which safeguarded long-distance trade as well. In an *ilaf* agreement, a trader purchased the right to move caravans into the lands of neighboring states and engage in commerce and in return gave a certain part of the profit or goods to local rulers.[60]

Thus, with the advent of long-distance trade, the Arabs of Hijaz broke out of their historical isolation, an isolation that is evident in their lack of knowledge about organized polities in the region.[61] The *ilaf* meant the end not only of the cycle of socioeconomic stagnation but also of a political nothingness of a barren land in which none of the neighboring powers was interested.[62] Thus, the Arabs of Hijaz began their exposure to the world outside without being subject to any previous control by great powers and without being influenced by the coercive potential of external forces.

Such an exposure was undertaken instead along annual caravan routes. The southbound caravans purchased commodities imported from India, eastern Africa, and Bahrain, products that partially fed peninsular *suqs*, before being taken northward, notably to Bostra, with the winter caravan.[63] All that movement led to the creation of a whole array of service activities along caravan pathways, such as security arrangements and rest facilities.[64] Such services enlisted the Bedouins and semi-Bedouins (that is, Bedouins who intermittently practiced agriculture or trade) at least partially in the service of trade, whose dividends were thereby distributed more widely upon the route.[65]

The many agreements, economic as well as spiritual, that engulfed this trade not only indicate the growth of commercial rationality, but they also betray the context of danger within which it took shape. The cultic *hums*,[66] *ilaf*, and other arrangements were apparently all forged within the sixth century. Simon shows that both *hums* and *ilaf* were still recent accomplishments by Muhammad's time and that trade with Byzantium, though significant, still had few established traditions around it—and trade in the direction of Iraq was even less developed.[67] The establishment of both can be traced to the "year of the elephant," circa A.D. 547.[68] This is significant, since that year was engraved in Meccan consciousness as a year of great threat to the very survival of the city. It instilled both a realization of the need for an earthly protective framework to ensure the city's survival and a sense of otherworldly involvement in such a scheme, especially since the city survived without having to confront the invader directly. It is significant in this regard that the Muslim lore also traced Muhammad's birth (A.D. 570) to the year of the elephant, clearly symbolizing thereby the commencement of divine safekeeping of the city.

The developments in trade, thus, were taking place in a world of increasing political dissimulation, both inside and outside of the peninsula. The Roman Empire was suffering from the growing strength and repeated incursions of other kinds of nomads in Europe, from internal sectarian frictions, from regional rebellions, and from eventual division after A.D. 395. The decay continued as war broke out between Byzantium and the Sassanid Empire of Persia, with the northern frontiers of Arabia in Syria and Mesopotamia becoming their battlefield. Persia itself was also suffering from symptoms of decrepitude, with internal struggles symbolized by the conflict between various theodicies, most importantly Mazdaism and Zoroastrianism. There is also evidence that both powers were beginning to lose their ability to protect their own frontiers against Arab nomads even before the Islamic conquests. The reports tell of Arab tribes who were shocked at their own victory over imperial Persia at Dhi Qar, a battle they engaged only hesitantly and after long trepidation.[69] At roughly the same time, the first successful major nomadic raids on Byzantium's territories in Syria and Palestine are recorded.

The increasing vulnerability of the great powers was also—as is well noted by historians—connected to the decline of the buffer states Ghassanides and Mundherites, which mediated between the nomads and Byzantium and Persia, respectively. These were northern Arabian tribal confederations that had settled in Syria and Mesopotamia around the beginning of the third century A.D. Their role consisted of collecting taxes from other Bedouins in their jurisdiction on behalf of their imperial patrons and protecting the peripheries of the two empires from the sporadic nomadic assaults coming from Najd. In exchange, they received imperial support for their semiautonomous rule. Both fizzled out later, with the Ghassanides' rule being abruptly discontinued toward the end of the sixth century, at a point when many of their fellowship had settled into agricultural lifestyles or become regular suppliers of soldiers to the imperial army.[70] Persia's fledgling control over lower Mesopotamia, likewise, could be maintained for as long as the empire successfully manipulated nomadic rivalries, a tactic that eventually left it with no reliable allies.[71] The third central power that had some influence on the affairs in the peninsula, Yemen, was also disintegrating because of a number of factors, such as its shrinking commercial significance, the decline of its agricultural economy, the resultant emigration of many tribes, and recurrent invasions and rebellions, which left it with a weak and uncertain political future.[72]

THE NOMADIC FLUX

Generally, the era preceding the rise of Islam witnessed not only the emergence of a particularly remunerative trade economy that consolidated and distinguished nascent sedentarization, but also a discernible political anarchy and lack of control in the same general area where sedentarization throve. In this context (but not necessarily because of it), traditional nomadic acquisition raiding (*ghazw*) not only increased but often metamorphosed into lengthy and legendary wars. *Ghazw* had always been an important component of the Bedouin economy of survival. As such, it was usually governed by a tableaux of common ethics, which justified the practice within the limits of absolute necessity and then in a way that left room for the exercise of customary rapprochement rituals. These included *diyyah* (blood money), a lien in the form of a number of boys given as captives until the *diyyah* was secured, or even the permission of the assaulting tribe to the victimized one to retaliate against specified members of the former, who had not necessarily been direct participants in the assault.[73] During an individual *ghazw*, great care was taken to keep bloodshed to a minimum. However, in the period immediately preceding Islam, central and northern Arabia became more and more anarchic. Fierce and long wars among tribes became a paramount feature of social relations. Major wars are recorded between the tribal confederations Bakr and Taghlib, 'Abs and Dhubyan, Aus and Khazraj, and many others. An entire bombastic poetic heritage developed in that era, a heritage that still survives today as the most impressive literary expression of heroism and related traits in the history of Arab Bedouins. As already mentioned, one factor contributing to that turmoil was the collapse of the peninsular powers that had partially mediated among the tribes, such as Yemen, Kinda, and the northern dynasties—the last themselves becoming involved in reproducing the Byzantine-Persian wars on a smaller scale.[74]

It was amid such surrounding pandemonium that Mecca's long-distance trade throve. As Syria and Mesopotamia became the battleground of the imperial wars, the Persian land route for Indian goods destined for Europe was abandoned. The entire intermediary trade was transferred to Mecca, including some of the sea-borne trade of the Persian gulf.[75] The imperatives of trade made the city into a unique oasis of peace, especially as many Arabs from Najd—notably those with some wealth to protect from the increasing unpredictability of the desert—moved to Mecca.

The exclusion of the nomads from sedentary possibilities imprinted two imperatives on nomadic ideology: justifying nomadic lifestyle as such and denigrating lifestyles that paraded their superiority as potential alternatives. In this sense, nomadic ideology accomplished two objectives. On the one hand, it shielded the nomad from the lure of unattainable *hadarah*. On the other, it provided a moral force that highlighted the virtues of the inescapable *badawah*. Central to such an ideology was the belief that continuous wandering was an essentially more honorable and healthful way of living.[76] The Bedouins' scorn for the *hadarah* life is well recorded and defended in a tradition that regarded their lifestyle to be not merely the one worthy of mankind but also morally and physically superior to any other.[77] Generosity, hospitality, honor, contentment, and loyalty are the traits often cited when the Bedouins boast of their lifestyle. But of special significance is their staunch adherence to a (real or imagined) line of descent (*nasab*), around which tribal loyalty coalesced and which was defended at all costs.

Khazanov notes that nomadic genealogies have generally two functions. First, they facilitate alliances and, conversely, "legitimize" inequality (more precisely, they make detachment possible) among already heterogeneous groups. He notes the flexibility of genealogical tales, which make assimilation between hitherto distinct clans possible through "genealogical amnesia" (or reconstruction).[78] Second, the formative role of genealogical imagination ascribed to it an essentiality that often superseded voluntarily (and still visibly) "manufactured" links, such as those forged through intertribal marriage.[79]

The law of cohesiveness of the nomadic tribe, *'asabiyyah*, developed around the idea of *nasab*. It entailed unquestioning loyalty to descendants of the same blood line. This idea, as Evans-Pritchard sums it up, offered a framework of "ordered chaos," offering a minimal regulator of relations and duties between separately operating small herding groups.[80] The ecological conditions often determined that members of the same *nasab* met each other only infrequently, but that did not have much adverse effect on their principle of solidarity. This seeming paradox—ritual reinforcement of blood ties in spite of the largely separate existence of small nomadic units—is observed elsewhere and is regarded by many commentators as an adaptive strategy to overcome frequently encountered hard times.[81] The limit imposed on the size of the nomadic social unit flowed from a number of factors. The more complex social organization that a larger size often entails—in order to ensure just allocation of collective gains and the settling of more complicated disputes involving a larger number of people—was fundamentally incompatible with the ecology of nomadism. Such formations were not feasible in the nomadic subsistence socioeconomy, as the failure of Kinda's monarchical experiment—to be discussed shortly—clearly illustrates.

Thus, in nomadic society it was common for one tribe to split into several subtribes, or even rival factions, whenever the size of the unit increased.[82] Khazanov remarks that "all known forms of nomadic families are closer to nuclear than to extended families."[83] The collectively wandering group could not grow in size to an extent that would outstrip the capacity of the widely dispersed oases to sustain it.[84] *'Asabiyyah*, thus, though often approached as a sacred principle, was not in essence an unbreakable creed. Once a nomadic social unit grew in numbers, it split into branches, with new *'asabiyyahs* replacing the old ones. The general *nasab* then provided a loose network of alliances between various units, alliances that, again, were not as compulsory as they are often reputed to be in theory.[85]

The limits on unit size, the fluid state of alliances, and the persistent preoccupation with survival clearly ruled out the political and hierarchical organization of nomadic society, especially when compared to neighboring sedentary settlements. In terms of hierarchy, the nomadic social unit exhibited a combination of egalitarianism and individual attention to tribal duties. Collective consultation was the rule before any action was taken, whether related to war, peace, transactions, or any matter that concerned the community as a whole. However, once a decision was made, it was binding on all members. Unlike in imperial and statelike polities, such collectivism and sense of belonging operated with little reference to hierarchical symbolism. Lacking in coercive control, the sheikh acted more or less as an arbitrator and coordinator, with little or no executive authority. Likewise, nomadic society had no built-in mechanism for hereditary hierarchy: Seniority was a key factor in choosing a sheikh, and service to the community was a key determinant of higher social status within the tribe.

Such social units were (as they still are today) at the same time "units of production," each having within itself a complete division of labor (corresponding to what in the Marxist tradition would be called a "mode of production"). Nearly all of the activities needed for the maintenance and reproduction of the Bedouin lifestyle could be undertaken within Bedouin society, virtually oblivious to what Khazanov calls the "outside world." In Arabia, such a largely pastoral economy was supplemented by barter in the *suqs*, by *ghazw*, and to a certain extent by hunting. The nomad lived on the edge of extinction, particularly in the frequent years of drought. It is in such a context that *ghazw* can be understood as a periodic activity to which the nomadic social unit could resort. *Ghazw* occurred primarily within the desert territory and often along the trade routes, with infrequent incursions into the towns. It was strictly economical: Raids were of very short duration and aimed primarily at direct acquisition, and bloodshed was kept to the minimum necessary level.

In an economy sustained partly by periodic wars, the reasons that were considered legitimate for initiating a raid were lodged in an area of concepts characterized by wide but flexible applicability. For example, the most insignificant incident could be seen as leading to one's "dishonor" or "disgrace," yet if war was not sought at the time of that particular incident, the *diyyah* provided a peaceful way of compensating for dishonor or disgrace. And in case *diyyah* was not available, other outlets were made available, as discussed before. In this way, foundational concepts like "honor" and "justice" became flexible discourses rather than objective categories that unilaterally determined collective behavior at every turn.[86]

As mentioned before, the epoch immediately preceding Islam witnessed the growth of *ghazw* into a more prominent element within Bedouin economy. The reasons may have to do with the periodically increasing demographic pressures in the desert ecology, conflict over control of the lucrative trade routes, and the decline of the arbitrative authority and power of the frontier and buffer statelets. As will be examined in the following section, on the Kinda, dynamics within nomadic society itself did arise in order to place such sources of conflict under some control. But in general, the epoch witnessed tribal wars of long duration replacing the older short cycles of raiding followed by rapprochement. The most legendary of the wars, the Basus war and Dahes wa l-Ghabra' war, are reported to have lasted each for forty years during the sixth century, with only a few years separating them and with the latter ending only during the lifetime of Muhammad.

The wars spread uncharacteristically to involve tribal confederations rather than small social units. One example of this expansion of the range of the conflict occurred during the early days of what came to be known as the Basus war, when Taghlibites attacked branches of Bakr that had initially refused to be involved in the skirmishes, thereby enlarging the raids into a complex war with multiple sources of claims and a wider range of participants.[87] Such conflicts, consequently, could not be ended by traditional means; they ended only when all the involved parties were completely and equally exhausted. These wars, however, did not change the basic organizational imperatives of the nomadic social unit, with its small size and (for most of the year) self-sufficiency. The "wars" themselves entailed not permanent mobilization but, rather, orientations of consciousness toward the larger collectivities. "Forty years" referred not so much to an ongoing struggle as to the duration of *unsettled* accounts, which sometimes during those forty years led to major battles. But in themselves, such "wars" reemphasized the need for the wandering nomadic unit to more consistently locate itself upon the map of larger tribal allegiances.

KINDA

The need for a more sophisticated social and political organization was felt only when *ghazw* was becoming unusually and consistently prominent during the second half of the fifth century. The experiment of the "kingdom" of Kinda was the fruit of that growing tendency, as was evident in the more or less voluntary submission of the tribes to Kinda's central authority. The inherent structural weaknesses of such a statelike sociopolitical organization, especially when it faced an immobile economy and an unfavorable popular ideology, led to its ultimate collapse. What the Bedouins wanted from that "kingdom" was impossibly simple: the extension of the bare structure of each social unit across the span of the entire Bedouin society. More contemporary observations reveal the salience of such a trope, whose ground can be found in the uncertain conditions of survival in a unique ecology that, as one commentator notes, lead to the definition of the family—and nothing else—"as a peaceful interior that is protected and concealed from a disorderly exterior."[88] It is in this light, therefore, that the paradox can be understood between, on the one hand, the unavoidable development of a statelike structure and, on the other, its abandonment by the nomads thereafter.

Unlike the northern dynasties, which were made possible in part by active imperial support, Kinda represented the first record of a properly Bedouin "monarchy." That experiment deserves to be outlined here, not only because it was a unique attempt at centralized nomadic self-regulation but also because it served as a precursor for the centralizing maneuvers of Islam that were to follow.

All accounts indicate that the desire to regulate the affairs of the increasingly warring Bedouin society was behind the Bakr tribes' initiative that resulted in the kingdom. Significantly, the traditional narratives explicitly locate the royal house *outside* of the feuding nomadic realm, in accordance with what the nomads themselves had sought. The reports mention that Bakr, fractured by feuds between its branches, sent a delegation to the Yemenite monarch asking him to be their king. He delegated the position instead to Hijr (Akel al-Murar), the chief of Kinda tribe.[89] Several explanations for such a choice are possible, including that Kinda were of Yemenite-Hadramite origin, which might have led the Himyari king to assume that, given the nomadic tribes' strong ancestral attachment, the Kinda were most capable of transmitting his influence indirectly, saving him thereby the cumbersome task of directly ruling a naturally uncontrollable and barren region.

Many economically oriented commentators place the story of Kinda in the context of Himyari commercial expansion.[90] There is little evidence, however, to indicate that the Himyari domain benefited in any economic sense from the Kinda experiment at governorship. Unlike the Meccan *ilaf* agreements, which signaled *economic* rather than political alliances,[91] Kinda's kingdom signaled exactly the opposite: a *political* alliance whose eventual deterioration, as we shall see, was partially because of the impossibility of constructing the economic foundations for it. If Himyari economic ambitions were a factor in assigning the monarchic role to Kinda, it is difficult to see how such ambitions could have materialized. To the contrary, it seems that Kinda itself was so unimportant in the Himyari scheme of things that it could subsequently scarcely rely on or expect Himyar's support to survive. Another, more likely reason for the choice of Kinda may have to do with the fact that until then (that is, around the middle of the fifth century), the tribe appears not to have been a major participant in the ongoing tribal wars. Another factor might have been the tribe's large size, which could ensure the stability of a medium-sized kingdom in Najd.[92]

The monarchical attempt did not last for more than a century. The kingdom disintegrated in the middle of the sixth century, although some small, loosely connected branches of it continued to exist until the rise of Islam. The kingdom could not secure an ideological hold for the concept of royalty. Its kings had no permanent headquarters; rather, they preserved their nomadic lifestyle, wandering with their tents and spending much of their time hunting.[93] Akel al-Murar's successor, 'Amru al-Maqsur, even relinquished the title king, scaling his address down to "*Sayyed* [chief of] Kinda." It can be argued that the rebellion of the Asad tribe, in which the last of the kings of Kinda was killed, signaled the violent explosion of contradictions between two increasingly irreconcilable trends: on the one hand, the attempt of the rulers of Kinda to build the infrastructure of a stable kingdom after sedentary models, a trend that included securing regular income through taxes (*etewah*) levied on subjugated tribes. On the other hand, such an attempt ran counter to nomadic society's rejection of authority that was centralized around one dynasty and accompanied by unfamiliar economic consequences.

Evidently, when they initially sought a king, the tribes did not intend to establish a "real" kingdom as such, or even to belong to one, as much as they intended to create a universally respected sheikh, whose function at the level of Bedouin society as a whole would resemble the function of the local sheikh within a single nomadic unit. He would serve as an arbiter in disputes, maintaining a minimal amount of order and overseeing the natural balance between war and peace, collective and individual responsibilities and tasks, and the just distribution of gains. Therefore, the very development of the hierarchical and functional aspects of a monarchical system posed an unacceptable challenge to a nomad used to the model of the nearly egalitarian tribe, a nomad who would submit to the tribe's unanimous decisions but not to the arbitrary will of its sheikh, who was periodically forced to reduce needs to bare minimum, who could not fathom taxation, and who relied to a certain degree on *ghazw* as a cyclical supplement to his resources. In other words, the desire to regulate the affairs of Bedouin society as a whole displayed no ideological reorientations that could justify a centralized system of hierarchical governance, all of whose aspects contradicted the basic structures of the Bedouin way of life. Once this contradiction came to the fore, the fate of the kingdom was sealed.

Yet the abandonment by the governors of Kinda of the modest stance adopted by 'Amru al-Maqsur[94] came about, significantly, not from nomadic dynamics proper but from increasing exposure to imperial politics. The expansion of the Kinda's territorial domain and the deepening of the extent of governance did not occur before the reign of al-Harith, its third chief. The first king, Akel al-Murar, did little more than regulate the affairs of his Bakrian constituents and recapture territories taken away from them by the Lachmides.[95] His successor, 'Amru al-Maqsur, restricted himself to the territory he had inherited, opting for peaceful relations with his neighbors, which he consolidated through marriages into the royal houses of Yemen, the Mundherites, and the Ghassanides. During the reign of al-Harith, however, the swelling tribes under his rule began to move northward; there are reports that he led raids on Palestine and also that he briefly displaced the Mundherites in al-Hira, probably at the instigation of the Persians.[96] Having overthrown the powerful Mundherites, the Kinda not only expanded territorially beyond its stronghold in Najd but also captured the prestige of indirect influence that the northern dynasties had exercised over their nomadic peripheries. After his victory over the Mundherites, delegation after delegation of nomadic tribes came voluntarily to al-Hira to congratulate al-Harith on his extended authority and to offer him further jurisdiction as their "king."[97]

That wide expansion, probably an unintended consequence of imperial manipulation and desire to take advantage of nomadic rivalries, became implicated in models of non-nomadic governance. Gunnar Olinder's observation that the kingdom did not consist of the tribe as much as of a coalition of tribes headed by a family from Kinda is significant in this respect, especially since that family had ongoing relations not only with the tribes but also with Himyar, al-Hira before the takeover, the Ghassanids, and Byzantium.[98] Here, the idea of a *family* rather than a tribe as a unit of rule clearly parallels and is perhaps borrowed from neighboring sedentary states. Thus, it may be argued that a model of governance exterior to nomadism itself had gestated at the heart of the experiment from the onset without being recognized as such by the subjugated tribes, since the model's impact was not fully known until the expansion of its authority, both transtribally and territorially.

Tribes were thus divided into the resemblance of "provinces," with authority over them being allocated among the four sons of al-Harith.[99] Other statelike transformations were introduced, such as establishing a standing armed force, imposing order by hierarchical and authoritarian means, and regulating state income through the collection of the *etewah*. However, the whole system was based on a short-lived geographic and demographic expansion. The rule of Kinda over al-Hira was based for the most part on the consent of the Persians. As soon as government changed hands in Persia, circa A.D. 531, and for reasons having to do with internal Persian policies, the Mundherites were reinstated in al-Hira, and they retaliated for their earlier loss by executing al-Harith and a number of the most important leaders of the Kinda.

Thus collapsed the basis upon which the monarchical experiment depended. The rule over al-Hira did not last long enough to conclude the building of all the functional, economic, and spiritual bases of the kingdom within nomadic society.[100] The fact that the source of this governance and its expansion was to an important extent not deeply rooted in nomadic dynamics proper is illustrated in the dearth of information regarding the dynamics by which the Kinda attained hegemony *within* nomadism, especially compared to the well-known reports regarding its assignment of kingship by rulers in Yemen or Persia.

In this light, therefore, the end of the rule in al-Hira signaled the beginning of the end of the royal experiment altogether. Despite the fact that the commonality of the Kinda followed Hijr, al-Harith's eldest son, after the death of his father, the nomadic preference for less-abstract governance was evident in the fact that the loyalty to the earlier division of tribes among the four sons prevailed over loyalty to a single central authority, which had lost much of its foundations. Hijr himself was killed shortly afterward during his unsuccessful attempt at forcing the rebellious Asadians to pay the *etewah*. Reports of that episode are particularly illustrative; they record that after his original triumph Hijr extended a pardon to the rebels, who then proceeded in a march of submission to his headquarters but had a change of heart along the way and assassinated him upon their arrival.[101] This story itself shows the precariousness of the grounds of legitimacy for such a distant, transtribal order, which is likely to be challenged at the slightest hint of weakness and even, as in this case, when it still commands significant reserve strength.

The large tribal confederations resumed their wars, dragging with them their nominal rulers from what had remained of the heritage of Kinda.[102] The great poet Imru' l-Qays, who was the youngest son of the assassinated king, failed to convince any of the tribes that had submitted to his father to help him reestablish the withering kingdom. His trials and tribulations in that regard are also very illustrative of the nomadic interpretation of the affair—an interpretation clearly distinct from that of the royal family. The reports indicate that Imru' l-Qays's appeal did initially generate some response from his father's staunch allies. The alliance led by the poet fought and defeated the Asad. However, as soon as the partial victory over branches related to Hijr's assassins was accomplished, the Imru' l-Qays's alliance disbanded because, according to his allies, he had fulfilled his basic revenge duty (*asab al-tha'r*), and the account was settled.[103]

This report indicates that the recovery of the kingdom meant little to most nomads, including the royal family's reliable allies. By contrast, the claimant's discourse was centered on the recovery of the kingship as an *obligation*,[104] rather than on simple restoration of justice through basic revenge. Within nomadic ideology, *revenge* is not understood as *recovery* of loss or *restoration* of past. It simply balances a natural order that has temporarily been violated, whereafter wandering can go on untroubled, as it had since time immemorial. The fact that a kingdom over nomadism had collapsed meant little, since such a disappearance was not fundamentally different from the manner in which all human effort in life is ultimately devoured by the horizon of death and departure, as the *mu'allaqa* ritually registers at its beginning.

In this sense, the emergence of a discursive difference regarding the idea of restoration of order—political in this case—becomes apparent. For the claimant, the consequence of his nomadic allies' refusal to support his mission as far as monarchical restoration meant that he had to seek support for his restorative obligation outside of nomadism. Imru' l-Qays died on his way to (or from) Byzantium in a fruitless attempt to enlist imperial help, after Arabs, including all of his brothers, had abandoned the task (but not the balancing obligation of *tha'r* as traditionally understood). This episode itself illustrates the rootedness of the discourse of Kinda's governance, especially after al-Harith, in sedentary and imperial models rather than nomadic ones. The nomadic model accepted the rule, as we have seen here, for as long as the two discourses did not come into apparent conflict.

Thus the monarchical experiment completely disintegrated, leaving behind a state of utter anarchy in the nomadic areas, which were not to be put under control until Islam reproduced a centralizing order less than a century thereafter. Islam itself, it must be noted, was not invulnerable to nomadic resistance to non-nomadic models of governance, even though the initial Islamic model of governance was less rooted than Kinda's in those of neighboring states and empires. But it was not rooted in nomadism either, introducing instead an original notion of a spiritually based transtribal order of rights and duties, much of whose origins came from sedentary and semisedentary dynamics and rules of exchange. Thus, immediately after the death of Muhammad, the nascent Islamic political order itself had to fight a nomadic rebellion (*hurub ar-riddah*) very comparable to the one that had eradicated Kinda's kingdom. But by then, it had not only the resources to crush the rebellion but also a venue of conquests (*futuhat*) that released the pent-up pressures away from the peninsula.

three

Social Time, Death, and the Ideal

Eternal subsistence nomadism and the similitude of past and present seemed to the Bedouin to be normative destiny. Austere as it was, Bedouin life seemed inescapable. Western and northern Arabia offered only a few alternatives, mostly around small-scale agriculture and trade, which in turn could only be practiced by a small number of sedentaries. One of the major features of nomadic ideology, therefore, entailed denigrating an unattainable *hadarah* (sedentary) lifestyle while at the same time morally exalting the timeless ethics of the *badawah* (nomadic) lifestyle. Furthermore, unlike the more integrated features of sedentary economy, where one activity (trade or agriculture) predominated and gave way to an understanding of the world in terms of totalities, the three activities of which the Bedouin economy consisted (pastoralism, hunting, *ghazw* [acquisition raiding]),[1] were structurally disjointed. Such a state of affairs gave way, as we shall see, to a strolling articulation of the world whereby little emphasis was placed on systematic totalities.[2]

The nomadic consciousness is an essential part of the story because of, on the one hand, its distinctive permanence and seeming extremity and,

53

on the other, the imprints that it had left on Meccan consciousness and, to be sure, on all sedentary frames of thinking. Such frames often explicitly regarded nomadism as a point of genesis, while entertaining a lukewarm or even hostile attitude toward its morality. This paradox left the sedentarizing nomads with the imposing task of representing the world anew, without recourse to the immortal certitudes of wandering upon land and in thought. As Mecca expanded and generated wealth, it emerged as the most pronounced contrast in the land to a Bedouin society that continued to be both economically stagnant and indifferent to the outside world. Mecca's trade economy increasingly made apparent the crucial role its relations with distant and foreign states and societies played in its survival, so much so that the neighboring Bedouin Arabs could only be discerned, through the city's peripheral vision, as a source of unease. The cosmopolitan vision of Mecca was in this sense predicated on a self-interest that required that the nomads be distanced in all respects, including genealogically. The dilemma consisted of an ensuing search for a "collective identity" on bases that deemphasized genealogical associations that would invariably lead the trading community back into nomadism. This crisis is evident enough in the very background that allowed the development of Islamic notions of universality—particularly in the notion of the *umma* (transtribal community of the faithful), in Muhammad's ability to abandon Mecca itself as his home, and in the enshrinement of the transtribal constitution of Medina (to be discussed in Chapters 7 and 8).

What is of interest to us here, however, is the differential rendition of the lived social world that can be traced back to such dislocation in economies, associations, and discernible options. Some of the most interesting figures in the literature of the period are those living in the gaps between sedentarism and nomadism, articulating experiences and traditions from the vantage point of their respective positions. An important literary figure in this context is an-Nabigha adh Dhubyani, as he stands near the edge of the desert, in perpetual preparation for departure toward greener pastures. Of the great pre-Islamic poets, an-Nabigha was certainly the most touched by sedentarism and thus obviously the least nomadic. The biographic fragments present him as a protégé of the northern Arabian dynasties (Ghassanides and Mundherites both, but especially the former) and as a regular in royal courts, enjoying a clear distance from Bedouin life. Yet he could still engage the poets of the period—both nomads and sedentaries—in his peculiar capacity as a critic of poetry.[3] The tradition records him as one of the most eminent judges of poetry in the festival of 'Ukaz.

Characteristically, an-Nabigha adheres to some of the important formulas of nomadic literary articulation. In his famous ode, he pays tribute to the tradition through a rather eloquent portrayal of the past functions of the remaining traces of habitation. The crucial difference between the way an-Nabigha opens his ode and the traditional way of opening odes observed by the other nomadic poets, however, consists in what he notices in the traces. This semisedentary poet pays the closest attention precisely to those material elements that had made it possible to live in the described location. Thus, neither abstract memories of love nor loved ones appear, save as a name in the opening couplet. This discourse opts to dispense with the traditional thematic not by extended mourning but by a swift resolve in favor of departing: "So get away from this eyesore" (c. 7). The speech preceding the departure serves to confirm the emptiness of the site, the dissolution of all life on it, a realization that then functions as a rationale for the resolution to follow.

The stage of the judge in the history of poetry seems to entail or presuppose, as evident here, a particular attention to systemic value. That is, the opening is not a mere tribute to tradition, to be then dispensed with rather abruptly; rather, it is a basis for what follows, a link, a justification ("so"), a rationale for constructing a conclusive sequence. This organic unity epitomizes discursive unification through an invocation of total and systemic values. The discursive movement between an observation, a contextual description, a unifying conclusion, and a statement of direction for the movement beyond posits each as a constitutive element of a grander and continuous elaboration. The entire sequence is itself posited as a conclusion that opens up another sequence.

The closest approximation of such a sequential and total structure in the other pre-Islamic odes can be discerned in the ode of Labid, who lived long enough to witness the trials and tribulations of Islam and who was influenced by an-Nabigha. After the traditional, agonized opening, Labid's movement away from the ruins commences not with devaluing them but with accepting their *normative* silence: "Yet how should one question rocks / so immovable, whose speech is nothing [intelligible]?" (c. 10). Here is the judgment on the ultimate unresponsiveness of that which had instigated the halting, whereby the discussion is reoriented toward that which is on the move, that which is of a known, experienced quality and that, by extension, can be interrogated. But here, one finds not so much a "conclusive" discourse as a traditional form of discontinuity, albeit introduced by a judgment negating the value of further reminiscence. Life emerges thereafter in the form of a caravan carrying loved ones and departing into the Beyond of the horizon. The poetics follow them until they disappear in the distance. Then, autonomous enclaves of reflection take the place of observing, recording, and concluding.

Such movement is symptomatic, generally speaking, of the legendary odes of pre-Islamic culture. They consist of an abundance of disjointed themes with little in the way of logical connections or transitional points. With few exceptions, which can be traced back to sedentary frames of influence—as can be seen in some moments in an-Nabigha—the odes seem to contain little sequential or causal order. The seminal poem of Imru' l-Qays, for instance, follows this route: reminiscences at the ruins (nine couplets), three lustful adventures with women (twenty-one couplets), description of the ideally beautiful woman and her effect on the self (thirteen couplets), night (five couplets), ethics (one couplet), an encounter with a wolf in a valley (three couplets), description of his horse (eighteen couplets), and description of the rain and other natural phenomena (twelve couplets). Although it may be argued that the first three of these eight topics are somehow related, the transition from one to the next is made abruptly, catching a modern reader by complete surprise. However, this poem shares with all other great odes an essential similarity: the existential theme of the opening. Standing at the ruins, seeing through them endearing images from the past, explaining their impact to either mythical companions or to the ruins themselves. The initial tone is powerful, sad, and hopeless. A sense of loneliness underlines the beginning of the story—if it is a story—that the ode tells. Such a psychological self-torture (or what seems to be self-torture by way of remembrance) persists until interrupted by images of hedonism, survival, and adventure. The first two visions in the ode seem to be set in opposition to each other.

Nine of the ten lengthy poems of antiquity have similar openings,[4] and all of them resemble that of Imru' l-Qays in dealing disjointedly with several topics and moving erratically from one to another. The odes do possess individual specific emphases and thematics, but they all share the tradition of the opening and abrupt departures. The profundity of lonely gloom is not the only ambiance permitted in the tradition of halting and discursively rendering experience in the world.[5] Such an opening is frequently followed by passages that, in their gay and confident manner, completely contradict the lugubrious spirit preceding them. The dichotomy of the exact opposites is not far removed from the way that changed life fortunes and rapid adjustments construe the essence of the *badawah* lifestyle, the source of much of that tradition. In the same fashion, the disjunction between the components of the Bedouin economy seem to parallel a mode of expression that is oblivious to sedentary systematization and to the construction of logic according to organic and necessary links.

It is in this light that an-Nabigha's simultaneous tribute to and negation of this tradition is significant. Being a prominent sycophant at the courts of the northern Arabian dynasties, he attests not only to a tradition at a high stage of refinement and meticulation but also to the genesis of sedentary political deployment of the poetic discourse. The poet here addresses no mythical companions such as those who had halted with Imru' l-Qays. Rather, he halts to initiate a dialogue with the traces (c. 2) and to eventually announce the end of halting for no reason other than the *practical* impossibility of past reclamation: "So get away from this eyesore, there is no return for it." There is, finally, a judgment on the ruins. The judgment does not merely assess the ruins or reconfirm the futility of all this halting; in addition it explicitly advises others to abandon this location and to go on their own way. The contrast between the past and the present state of the ruins is the crux upon which this knowledge unfolds.

The genesis of this remarkable discovery of the futility of the effort to reclaim the past can be found in other odes, notably Labid's. What Labid describes of the ruined abode does not transcend its present physical appearance, which is contrasted to what it might have looked like in the past. In other words, what the site invokes in memory is its visible concreteness. No abstract memory arises here. There is no remembrance other than that motivated by a discernible trace, which then reminds the poet only of a past state of completeness but not of any events, love adventures, duels, fables, or the like. At the "stage" of near sedentarism, the discursive tradition becomes barely capable of carrying along other than an absolute immediacy. In this sense, sedentarism entails a decreased distance between poetics and their physical object, between rendition and experience. Such a decreased distance entails not necessarily a diminution of "profundity" or "imagination" but, rather, the reorientation of thought away from the ethical cosmos of normative and perpetual loss and into a *task*. This task is then expressed in the transformation of expressive discourse into the depository of, and means for, an effort to render *experience as a piecemeal reclamation* of the estranged world. In highly idealistic language, Hegel describes this notion of experience as a journey from the abstract into its nonalienated containment: "Experience is the name we give to just this movement in which the immediate, the unexperienced, i.e., the abstract, whether of sensible being or of a bare, simple thought, becomes estranged and then returns to itself from estrangement, and is only then presented in its actuality and truth and becomes the property of consciousness."[6]

The abstract, for Hegel, is the unthought near, the unproblematized presence, rather than a hidden essence retrievable by thought alone. Experience here is practical questioning, which is oriented toward evaluating objects, endowing them with specific identities, and instilling in the place of their polyphonous presence a stable meaning, which alone allows one to claim to have experienced them so that one can proceed beyond.

This form of experience was not the property of the nomadic ode proper, as is most apparent in its normative lack of conclusivity at each juncture, in its fatalism and infusion with the sounds and movements within autonomous nature. But what the ode provided was a *form* in which further "experiences" could be deposited. The form worked in this fashion precisely because it was not uniquely nomadic. It was only uniquely formulaic, with signposts, such as the common opening theme, establishing it as a reservoir of *past*-oriented interrogation. It was, furthermore, uniquely preservable—as an oral tradition—and hence an appropriate vehicle for rendering that which must not be allowed to disappear from memory. And it was audience-oriented and thus a fundamentally *social* form of communicating experience. Here, the form becomes the foundation of a tradition precisely because it provides a *reproducible* sense of overcoming otherness and estrangement, whether in nature or with regard to past events.

But such a tradition also lends itself over time to purely formulaic appropriations, especially as it becomes disseminated and therefore accessible. General accessibility opened the tradition to the games of power. In the case of the poetic tradition proper, two sources of power play can be recognized: first, pure tribal politics, and second, the development of a definite status for the poet and for a social institution of poetry. It is perhaps this susceptibility to power that influenced the unique Qur'anic form, which was apparently advised by the trials and tribulations of earlier claimants to sagehood, and even prophethood, among poets.

With the advent of schemes of empowerment through poetics, the rendition of experience itself succumbed to more overarching social goals. The poetic rush from all directions to what became a formulaic site opened up by the earlier, lonely poets then carried a variety of packages along. And yet the crowding of words, statements, power, and institutionalizations crossed with the poets, unawares, over the site into the other side of the distance, into the depths of the other horizon, where nothing of the originary experience could be detected any longer and where there was nothing, not even traces of authentic ruins, to invigorate the fading spirits. At that other end of the horizon, the tradition—as a form for depositing experience—languished until it eroded or simply folded upon itself and reverted to the nothingness from whence it came.[7]

IDEALIZATION AND THE PAST

The nomadic formula for addressing experience, which continued to register it in an encyclopedic but inconclusive fashion, remained oblivious to such metamorphoses of the tradition. As mentioned before, the Bedouin socioeconomy entailed seemingly timeless truth and stability—in spite of the demographic pressures—and was largely excluded from trade-based sedentarism. The obvious untenability of any other style of life evidently led to the Bedouins' moral condemnation of that which was not likely ever to be within their grasp. In the process, they ennobled their misery beyond measure. The emphasis on the moral aspect was particularly suitable, since it freed the Bedouins from having to view the sedentaries from angles that showed the nomads clearly at a disadvantage. Here, nomadic consciousness became explicitly antimaterialist, as it expressed its disinterest in the supposed lure of sedentary life. Al-Mas'udi offers a succinct rendition of an account of the origins of the *badawah* lifestyle: "The Arabs regarded wandering in the land and selectively inhabiting the various locations over the days as bearing more [attributes of] glory, and [hence] as being more worthy of noble spirits . . . and they said: 'Let us not be confined by any territory, [let us] live wherever we wish. . . . So they *chose* the life of the Bedouins."[8]

What is significant in this passage is that the reference to freedom from territorial confinement stands as a sole and self-evident indicator of honor, in no need of further elaboration as to why it should be regarded as such. The self-evidence of what is honorable is a common motif in nomadic narratives, which are occasionally expanded in response to a sedentary insistence on "furnishing evidence." In such case, justifications are never in short supply:

> Others mentioned that the ancient Arabs began to contemplate settling and the value of [permanent] abodes as a result of the conditions to which Allah had subjected them: high dangers, nobility of resolve and fate, a superior sense of glory, and [a propensity to] avoid disgrace. They considered the situations of the cities and buildings, but they found them [to entail] shame and shortcomings. The knowledgeable and perceptive among them said: "Lands ail and suffer as bodies do. The proper course is to selectively choose locations according to their suitability: If air is strong [for instance], it may harm the bodies of the inhabitants and affect their moods." And the opinionated among them said: "Buildings and being surrounded limit [the ability] to use the land, hinder wandering, imprison the energies, and inhibit the instinctive quest after honor. There is no good in submitting to a predicament like that." They also claimed that buildings and ruins limit nutrition and prevent the [circulation] of the air, the passage of its currents, and the smoothness of its flow. Therefore they inhabited the open land in which they feared not confinement, settlement, and harm, [but where they enjoyed] the dispersion of matter, the friendliness of the air, and the absence of disease. As [living] in such quarters tames behavior and crystallizes the [instinct of] wandering between the homes, minds and feelings sharpen as the air does, air whose nature involves space. In [such conditions] one attains immunity from handicaps, diseases, illnesses, and pains. Thus the Arabs preferred to wander in the deserts and rest in the desert. So they are the most resolute of people, the most patient, the healthiest, the most protective of their neighbors, the most attentive to injuries to their honor, the most generous, and the most clear-minded.

They were endowed [with such qualities] because of the purity of the space and the cloudlessness of the atmosphere. Bodies contain in their parts the filterings of pollutants and refuse . . . and therefore motes, illness, and handicaps proliferated among the inhabitants of cities, invaded their bodies, and multiplied [visibly] in them. Therefore the Arabs were luckier than other, various people, for what we have mentioned of their choice of places and [preference for] wandering in the land.[9]

This passage contains an outstanding summary of a peculiar process of logical reasoning and justification. By deliberately selecting and emphasizing noneconomic criteria, such as health and moralism, the nomads chose an ideological terrain that was uniquely theirs. The visible prosperity of trade-based towns made it increasingly difficult for the *badawah* lifestyle to appear relatively superior on the basis of economic arguments. Yet although this passage does not refer to economy, transactions, or material wealth, it does address a more fundamental idea, namely, comparative well-being. According to the passage, the nomads possess a moral and physical well-being that is superior to that of the *hadaris,* even though the latter may seem to enjoy more material wealth. The passage combines two lines of argumentation to demonstrate the nomads' superiority: One shows the favorable consequence of *choosing* to live a nomadic life, while the other criticizes alternative lifestyles on the basis of the criteria set forth for the "ideal" life.

An idealized prescription for life would require a rearrangement of the time thought to contain such a life. Here, life "as lived" (daily and accidental) and life "as articulated" (sequential and total) appear to be the same. The idealized concept of life appears to be an irreducible totality, whence events are understood as chapters of an encompassing and meaningful story of life rather than as random occurrences upon the open surface of pure existence. In this context, events emanate from a large reservoir of known possibilities and are comprehensible precisely because it is always a *particular* life that lives an event, makes it possible, and ultimately grasps it as a document to be added, through the work of memory, to the total archive of a life that is discernible to the extent that it demonstrates an already known truth.

The stable order of social knowledge was most clearly evident in the primacy allocated to blood relationships, which fulfilled an ontological demand and gave a sense of predetermined order and meaning for individual existence in a widely dispersed society. The fact that a binding ethical foundation for social solidarity must come involuntarily and from without is evidenced in the supremacy that lineage had over conscious and subjective arrangements, like marriage, and that was especially evident when the two came into conflict. The story of the Basus war illustrates this principle very clearly: Incited by the murder of a Taghlib chief by a Bakrian, Taghlib prepared for war by first expelling from among its ranks the sister of the assassin, even though she also happened to be the widow of the murdered chief. Here, primary bonds are those objectively established by an unchosen birth and thus by an exterior nature; they supersede bonds subjectively established later in life, bonds that remain less certain, less inevitable, and therefore more easily breakable. There is a clear expression here of a belief in the relative profanity of all subjective rearrangement of the norms of nature, norms from which the idea of a possibly different future is absent. This view is based in the feeling that unchosen frames of social existence possess a claim to timeless and superior stability that surpasses the claims to stability of frames of existence chosen during an individual lifespan.

In a society prefigured by such an orientation, the idealization of life would be expected not to offer a guide for venturing toward the unknown but to arrange and interpret events in such a way as to avert the potential perils of nihilism and purposelessness, which are seen to lurk in purely subjective and unanchored programs. But under conditions of subsistence, survival itself is one of the prime purposes. Continued survival, by itself, is at the same time a story of continued success in attaining the purpose of life. In an above-subsistence economy, such as that of the *hadaris,* the purpose is no longer to aim at simple survival but to idealize an additional layer of life, a life larger than itself, that is, *a life larger than pure existence.* The question that follows, then, concerns the spheres of value from which the logics of idealization are drawn. The route toward such values can at least partially be charted by a brief look at the idealization trajectory evident in pre-Islamic poetry.[10]

As far as idealization is concerned, the openings of the pre-Islamic odes possessed a common feature: They remember, mourn, glorify, and re-create the *past.* Here, it is profoundly significant that one always begins with the past and not with the future, the present, or some other sphere outside the realm of time. A reference to the future, to be sure, does occur in a few scattered fragments in ancient poetry, but only in the form of pedagogic wisdom and then only in tones overshadowed by a sense of pessimism. In the unchanging Bedouin society, no grand social shifts are expected, and the material and spiritual frameworks created by millennia of sameness assume eternal legitimacy. The future is not in itself interesting because nothing other than what is already known is expected to occur in it. The lived life of the present consists of incessant wandering and fighting for survival. It is interesting in this context that the present—the moment of producing the poem—is hardly mentioned. With the exception of a few tentative hedonistic interjections, the legendary odes frequently express an unshrouded sense of estrangement from particular conditions of the present. The past thus becomes the undisputed temporal arena for the process of idealization.[11] The past is usually more eventful or glorious, both for the individual as well as for the tribe.[12]

Idealizing the past could therefore be understood as an expression of its loss, as well as a verdict on the inability of the present to retrieve or replace what was lost. For such a vision, no scene better combines the idealized past with an awareness of its unattainability in the present than that of ruins of a deserted place made meaningful by the idea that loved ones had inhabited them some time before. In addition, such a scene provides the overall vision with a sense of realism; after all, deserted places are themselves the direct product of the continuous wandering "chosen" as the proper meaning of life by the Bedouins, who in turn regard such wandering as the defining feature of their lifestyle.

This uniform commencement with a salute to the past (physically evidenced by its ruins), ends abruptly and is not revisited for the remainder of the poem.[13] But it does evidently furnish the poet with a better position from which to articulate a more far-fetched idealization of life. What follows the opening is invariably less gloomy, at times rather joyful, and it occupies the bulk of the poetic production. It is as though the difficult agony involved in confronting the question of life as a continuous totality idealized in a hopelessly distanced past gives rise to a defiant affirmation of exactly what the idealization process had relegated to the spatiotemporal realm of the ruins.

To idealize in this fashion is not open to everyone. To idealize is a right that must be acquired through a dutiful confrontation of the ethical question of life's totality. Such a progression enhances the poem as a credible representation of the course of learning in life, beginning with realizing one's embeddedness in the past through the inscription of genealogy and ending in the abrupt and unglamorous consumption by death. The construction of a credible opening here legitimates and accentuates receptiveness to what follows it, which is then no longer an unanchored individualistic creation.

The traditional sense of loss that permeates the opening of the poems and the hedonistic response that follows it are often assumed to represent opposing sets of images. But in this case, one can discern little of the consequential ramifications of the old logic of thesis and antithesis. Rather, the two contradictory ends are left standing without an apparent resolution, whereafter the thoughts of the poet travel irregularly from one topic to another with little apparent effort to connect such themes to the opening dichotomy or even to each other.

The hedonistic response (if it is a response) to the sad beginning has been conceived of, thus far, in a variety of ways: as an antithesis in the original dichotomy, as a negation of the present, as a way of relieving the original gloomy picture, and as a specific way of enabling a better rendition of life's present course, made possible after having dutifully confronted the ethical question of life as a totality. But the main idea concerns the *negation* (not necessarily the *rejection*) of current predicaments of lived life. Here, negation entails parceling out and highlighting one aspect of life, an aspect that is introduced as the most valuable endowment or entitlement at a time when the social organization makes it least accessible. In the case of Imru' l-Qays, for instance, unrestricted love affairs become a locus toward which all ideas of individual well-being gravitate.

Thus, both the traditional opening and the withdrawal from it represent two forms of the same logic of negation, rather than a thesis/antithesis dichotomy. Both are involved in reconstructing lived life and in relegating the ideal version of life to the only temporal dimension that could accommodate it under nomadism, namely, the past. The "antithesis" is in effect a continuation of an earlier attempt at idealizing the concept of life's totality. The "antithesis" is the thesis itself continued into the present. There are no contradictory ideas or intentions but, rather, an attention to a diachronic arrangement of a concept of life that is to be totalized. And along the continuum of the temporal dimension, each moment requires a readjustment of the mood of telling.

In sum, the necessity for a "process of idealization" comes from the need to account for the totality of life under conditions where the idea of the future holds little novelty, meaning, or relevance. The idealized vision, therefore, is ordinarily woven from the sphere of images constituting the "already known," that is, that which must be posited as a past along the temporal dimension. In this case, "past" means an empirically verifiable yet still instructive loss: The life constituting it has perished or wandered away yet left behind a testimony, a trace, a memory, or a lesson in the form of interrogable ruins.

The idealization attempt proceeds, then, toward the present, being carried along by an altered mood. The legendary nature of the original ideal expresses an ideal togetherness that, having been broken, challenges the unbreakability of nomadic genealogies and alliances. The idea of totality here is fundamental to this poetic enterprise in a uniquely nomadic fashion. Here, idealization must remain incomplete, and consciously so, as the proclamation of loss standing at the opening of the poem makes clear. This is a story motivated by a sense of loss, which has already been recovered in the possibility of telling itself. Since time exists, only the *articulation* of the diachronic totality of life is possible, not the lived life itself as such. Therefore, when a poetic rendition of life tells of life's totality, it can only tell of its loss. But in the final analysis, the existence of time allows no other recourse.

This tradition contrasts sharply with post-Islamic poetry, which was more oriented toward topical precision and was consequently shorter. In addition to the concern with the question of life's totality, the encyclopedic nature of the *mu'allaqat* (odes) signifies an early attempt at unifying all natural and social phenomena in a single body of commentaries, a task that was to be fulfilled by the Islamic cosmology and ethical laws shortly afterward. The receptiveness to a novel and comprehensive system of social order and natural explanations, such as provided by Islam, depends to a decisive extent on its ability to thematically and politically organize a discursive form for a movement that had already been articulating some concern for the idea of totality. Without advocating evolutionary determinism, one can still argue that the encyclopedic nature of the *mu'allaqat* represented an embryonic attempt at regulating the significant knowns under the edicts of a *singular* body of thought (that is, a body of thought to which the notion of *singularity of form* was essential). The distinctiveness of such a body consisted of its claim to aesthetic form, which set it apart from ordinary speech.[14] (Testifying to such an effect, the Qur'an itself had to compete on the literary plane with the *mu'allaqat* and came eventually to see in the poets both a threat and a potential for alliance.) This unification of totality through the *form* of articulation as expressed in the *mu'allaqat* does not in itself furnish socially acceptable truths or ideals. Rather, by establishing a model and an experience of totalization, it sets the tone for a certain range of experiments that are formulated with respect to the model and the experience. As we shall see at a later stage, the land was teeming with such experiments, of which Islam was but one.

MORTALITY AND THE FUTURE

Sedentary time is conceived of in terms of measurement. Sedentary discourse subordinates such conceptual frameworks in time's flow as period, teleology, causality, progression, and so on to either elaborate isochronisms or to other abstract structures, which are nonetheless anchored in a vision of time as a fearsome, exterior element of nature with which a hopeless duel must be waged (for example, the regular passage of years, age, and the temporal limits of expectations and projects). Either way, sedentary time is external to human life, directing life's course as it drags life along the temporal dimension. Both sedentaries and nomads saw time as a phenomenon outside of life's essential embodiment, yet they registered different conclusions: Whereas the nomad moved toward an impending mortality, the sedentary moved simply toward another point in time, a point infused with judgments about, conclusions from, and accountability for its prehistory.

The *mu'allaqat*, in general, reveal a fundamentally nomadic account of time. Yet the act of recording such poetics sought to save them from nomadic obliviousness to their potential perishability. Recording, therefore, overturned the nomadic conception of time, revealing a fundamental reorientation regarding its status. But such recording did not merely occasion the discovery of temporality according to sedentary frameworks of causal progression, salvage, and accountability for moments and authors of such moments. Here, moments or instances themselves revealed an efformable, isolable character. At the point of such an assemblage of a record of totality as attempted in the *mu'allaqat*, it was as though the gaseous flow of life in that endless expanse of the desert was corrupted. The first speech to come down to us from that wilderness belongs to that crucial moment of reorienting perspective regarding time.

Although the activity of recording is evidently related to an interest in preservation and an awareness of the temporal nature of value and its perishability, in pre-Islamic culture there was no universal account of the eventuality of human death itself. The more common attitude, traceable to the *badawah* lifestyle, showed a profound lack of concern for a world beyond. There are reports that mention a melange of beliefs on the subject, including belief in various forms of resurrection.[15] But it is also evident that even when a belief in some form of afterlife existed, it never occupied a central role in the spirituality of pre-Islamic culture.[16] Indeed, some of the most persuasive arguments used against Muhammad focused on his assertion of the eventuality of resurrection and judgment.[17] In an interesting episode, some Qurayshans made their belief in Islam contingent upon Muhammad's successful appeal to Allah to bring forth two (equally impossible) miracles, namely, changing the nature of the land and resurrecting their forefathers:

> Oh Muhammad! . . . you know that no people have more confined land, less water, or a harder life than we do. So ask your Allah, who sent you to preach, to move away those mountains that had bounded us, and let Him flatten our land and [create] in it rivers like those of Syria and Iraq. And [also] let him resurrect our deceased forefathers, and let among them be Qusay Ibn Kilab, who was a trustworthy man, so that we may ask them about [the truth of] what you are saying.[18]

Though this statement includes a clear tone of mockery, emanating from the conviction that it is impossible to fulfill the request, it also invokes a structure of judgment and credibility oriented toward the past, with the deceased forefathers having to vouch for any novelty such as Muhammad was proclaiming. Here, resurrection is impossible because the agency that terminates existence is a noninterrogable *dahr*—one of the more epochal names for time as a total, self-enclosed natural phenomenon (and not as a progression of discrete moments or as a process open to manipulation by any agency).

In Mecca, the worldly view surrounding the commercial lifestyle continued to foster in some way a materialist interpretation of life and to relegate life's finitude to an aspect of the vague idea of *dahr*. Such an attitude never had to contradict any earlier nomadic ontology. The low importance given to the interpretation of life and death in both Bedouin and sedentary societies is analogous to the low degree of adherence to the variety of religions that existed before Islam, which are to be discussed in Chapter 4. Communal ownership, interchangeability of socioeconomic experiences, and lack of social stratification among individuals in nomadic, agricultural, and early commercial communities motivated neither a mystical interpretation of difference nor a deferral of the issue to a world beyond lived life. The interpretation of the nature of life's course, especially as seen in the context of its horizon, death, was not to be informed by the model of stable socioeconomic differentiation, judgment, and justice *restoration* until such thematics began to consistently permeate an increasingly commerce-based, private wealth–oriented society.

This awareness of the ephemeral nature of all presences, and thus all unities built thereupon, permeates the odes in an often explicit way, such as in Tarafa, Zuhair, or al-A'sha. In al-A'sha's ode, the theme of love is dispensed with as soon as its protagonist, Hurayrah, begins to complain about life's uncertainties, using her occasional barefootedness as the metaphor. The poet then immediately contrasts that scene to his experience at a tavern, in which his drinking companions are described as being fundamentally unconcerned regarding the matter. They are aware that all shall perish, the barefooted as well as the shod. This theme is paralleled in Tarafa's ode, where death is entrusted with the power to erase all differences in life. In this case, the transition between the two comparable scenes is not totally arbitrary, as one clearly comments upon the other from a vantage point different from that of the ruins. As the lover's caravan gradually disappears into the distance, the poet finds a tavern, toward which he opts to wander *instead of* continuing to ponder his loss. The governing spirit of indulgence in the establishment is *defined* by an awareness of the absurdity of the lover's concerns for difference or even relative well-being, superfluous as they seem in the face of the consuming and comprehensive death to come.

According to this logic, therefore, there can hardly be a difference between lived, actual life and its potential goal. Such a difference, more apparent in sedentary societies down to the present, is often expressed in the broad term "alienation," which advises a programmed social action or a code of duties in life, activities directed toward a goal that is to be reached *before* death. To do otherwise, that is, to structure one's life more cautiously so as to programmatically maneuver through the cracks in the walls of difference (between life and its goal), presupposes an order of stability in the socioeconomy of life itself: a long-term settlement or a life programmed by the utopic *requirement* of eventual immobility, a teleologizable life, tormented by a drive to overcome the difference between the lived and the goal within the timespan allotted for one to live.

This absence of difference under nomadism is "proved" by parading death, which looms large in such instances (for example, al-A'sha's couplet 26, which is most pertinent here, but also Tarafa's couplets 63–65). For death, in effect, looms as the ultimate halt to the conditions of movement and is their final horizon. In contrast, the path of the sedentary society toward death is cluttered with structures, images, and plans for the stability and permanence of the settlement's structure. Sedentary halting is the long pause before death, but it is also a discontinuation of wandering by a means other than death. As such, the objective of such a pause is to complete life's goal before death takes away both life and its goal. Halting, thus, is this middle region at which the discovery of the difference between life and its goal appears clothed in the mantle of alienation from the present. Halting obstructs from view the phenomenon of roads existing for their own sake, roads by whose side all differences between life and its goal could be laid to rest and ignored as the journey continues into the beyond. Under conditions of permanent halting, such differences must be integrated into programs and mystiques of overcoming, or else they must be accounted for in a grand cosmological scene of stability.

The theme is intensely elaborated in Tarafa's famous ode, where individual wandering and the camel furnish the starkest thematic unities. The interesting dimension of Tarafa's case concerns—much like the case of Imru' l-Qays—a need to ponder the difference between lived life and "goal" *anew*, in the light of having been expelled from the tribe for failure to meet one's obligations. Tarafa's ode is full of oscillations between moments of the self and moments of apology for social detachment, as he knew no course other than a failed attempt to maintain normative belonging with a minimal sacrifice of the self. These "wild productions," as

Sir William Jones once called the *mu'allaqat,* could be seen, after all, as moments of the self in history. Above all, they are "productions," that is, renditions of life, philosophy, and ideals ascribed to a producer. This particular producer, Tarafa, finds it imperative to tell of the manner in which he was thrown out of the tribe:

> Unceasingly I tippled the wine and took my joy,
> unceasingly I sold and squandered my hoard and patrimony
> till all my family deserted me, every one of them,
> and I sat alone like a lonely camel scabby with mange. (c. 51–52)

The sequence following the above (c. 54–67) contains Tarafa's eloquent defense of decadence. Again, we see a common thread. The theme is launched by negating immortality (more precisely, by questioning the prerogatives of his detractor by disempowering the detractor over mortality). Thus, the hedonistic project is couched in an awareness of an *individual* finitude, regardless of the awareness that "society," as a concept, as Other, or as incubator of the eventual and detachable self, shall outlast the death of the speaker. This fact instigates an individual attempt to forestall death (c. 55: *ubadiruha,* "preempt it") through a specific strategy:

> But for three things, that are the joy of a young fellow,
> I assure you I wouldn't care when my deathbed visitors arrive—
> first, to forestall my charming critics with a good swig of crimson wine
> that foams when the water is mingled in;
> second, to wheel at the call of the beleaguered a curved-shanked steed
> streaking like the wolf of the thicket you've startled lapping the water;
> and third, to curtail the day of showers, such an admirable season,
> dallying with a ripe wench under the pole-propped tent. (c. 56–59)

Here, the importance of death is defined by the specific actions and possibilities that it takes away from life. Those are, after all, the meanings of an already lived—or already imagined—life. They are disentangled, looked at afresh, reclassified within an order of priorities, encoded as patterns of a system for the *same* life, and articulated in the context of material and sensual—rather than metaphysical—experience.[19] Those three areas of action deliver life's already experienced goal so completely that death ceases to be a worry. Thus, a project aiming to forestall death by structuring one's own finitude—beyond the impasse of generalities—

begins by emptying mortality of its proclaimed finitude, by throwing in its face an exhaustive list from the reality of the self's own resourcefulness (c. 55: *bima malakat yadi,* "with what I possess"). A vicious circle ensues: The initiative to replace life's finitude with a set of momentary pleasures reconfirms that the certainty of finitude is obviated only when the meaning of one's life is condensed in a moment of the present. Finitude, therefore, as opposed to a momentary life, is permanent. As such, this form of finitude not only appears as empirical and actual death but also as the most normative and general doctrine of stability in the world of movement.

Tarafa's "three things" are meant to be comprehensive. Life consists of them; little else is worthy of inclusion. Not only does this self know what life's worth is, but he is also able to announce an individual decision to live it according to this specific conception of worth. He wants that which constitutes the temporal domain of desire to become permanent. That is, he wants to "end" at this point, before death. That Tarafa needed to articulate such an outline in itself presupposes an enigmatic moment, borne out of social detachment and the need to interpret life anew in such a light. While one thus finds elements of a structured "project," it still occupies the figural sphere of strict materialism, as the conception of life was elsewhere in the *badawah* lifestyle. There was no elaborate afterlife, no hell/paradise duality, no God to judge, no possibility of reward, and no depleting power over human life other than that unceasing march of time, to which the Arabs attached other names full of epochal, almost atemporal overtones (for example, *dahr, zaman*), as though time were a subject capable of acting and of doing harm, as though it were a concept residing at a distance from the thinking mind and following its own course.

Yet poetry functioned also at a different, and somewhat contradictory, level. Though poetry frequently commented on perishing and loss as recurrent norms, unalterable by human action, the very fact that poetry alone was preserved in such a dismal landscape of void demonstrated the possibility of preservation in the realm of *language.* Language thus began to appear in and assume a particular social form, which became inseparable from the genesis of an interest in the idea of "future," here being defined as a realm of yet-to-be-known possibilities. Future no longer meant simply and necessarily death and the erasure of pointless difference. By demonstrating preservability, the world seemed to offer itself for a particular form of repackaging, which would allow it to be retrieved and reorganized for a variety of projects oriented toward the future. Such an experience of possibilities, as we will see, went through various metamorphoses and stages. Tarafa was one of the first observers of this issue, and he lived long enough only to take note of it, being aware of chaos's ability to overcome subjective planning, the theme with which his ode comes to an end:

> The days shall disclose to you things you were ignorant of,
> and he whom you never provisioned will bring you back tidings;
> one that you purchased never a scrap for will come to you with news,
> though you appointed no time for him to keep tryst. (c. 102–103)

According to this view, it is futile to structure things so as to make the world predictable, or even knowable. Time shall reveal to you what you do not know. If there were any worthwhile knowledge, Tarafa proclaims in an unusual expression of generalized pedagogy (which one most often associates with Zuhair), it would be revealed by itself, by time alone: It would unfold itself naturally and effortlessly. This, at its most fundamental level, is a restatement of the distrust of purposeful human effort in general. Tarafa is suspicious of planning, more trusting of chance, of which he knows himself to be a victim.

Time, thus, is both revelatory and destructive. It cannot yet be controlled, as both revelation and destruction come from without, with little contribution from those exposed to its unpredictable whims. But the fact that the odes always begin by interrogating traces from the past that time has allowed to remain just barely visible—as hints of time's power—is itself significant. Here, there is not just a simple surrender but a recognition that traces are an *invitation* to ponder the nature of the course of life in relation to the lesson infused in the traces. In the patiently conceived ode of Zuhair, in which he otherwise complains about time having left him to live much longer than desired, the poet's original interrogation of the traces places them within a more normative cycle of natural and cyclical movement:

> There it was I stood after twenty livelong years [*hijja*],
> hard put to it to recognize the lodging, deeply as I meditated. (c. 4)

Zuhair, it must be kept in mind, had lived long enough to *witness* (c. 57) the random prerogatives of fate and consequently to confine the realm of the knowable to the past and the present (c. 59). Thus he confines his action to a long wait for his coming finitude, and his wisdom to what could be gleaned through distant remembrance. Twenty years had passed since that experience that has now slipped out of the deep inventory of memory to stand at the entrance to an ode. The intervening time had not produced a better remembrance. One may say that such is a stagnant, uneventful life. How, then, does one describe an uneventful life? Indeed, what is an "event" in the context of such a life? How does memory transform a nonevent into an event? How does discourse represent the event as a particular sequence for pedagogic purposes?

The event in this case is the *measure* of time itself. Zuhair uses not the abstract equivalents to the term "years" but, rather, the more socially anchored term *hijja*.[20] The agricultural societies to the south in Yemen did have their own calendar, and the few sedentary communities, whose trade ventures depended on the seasons and increments thereof, are also known to have had a certain form of calendar before the coming of Islam.[21] But life in the desert recognized a periodicity of time only on the basis of an "event." Various events, of course, do not have the same status in memory, at least for the purposes of organizing the temporal dimension. Unlike such events as tribal wars, for instance, a pilgrimage recurs with respect to a stable destination. The meaning of the pilgrimage is located as much, and perhaps more, in the destination's geographic materiality as in its spiritual significance. None of the ancient poets, to be sure, elaborates much on the religious significance of the pilgrimage itself: It is simply a certain recurring activity that is useful to measure time with, in those instances when a measurement of the magnitude of times elapsed is called for. And it is the peculiarity of this measuring that brings into the poem this short-lived notion of an entity within time. Twenty cycles. Twenty recurrences of the same event. Twenty revivals of a sameness. Twenty interruptions by the predictable. Twenty nonsurprises. The actual event, that is, that which the memory ventures to bring forth by reflecting against a flow of nonevents, lies twenty pilgrimages ago. The poetic drama, the first instance of a strictly individual original innovation, occurs at this juncture of noticing time and bringing it back to the discourse with its full force. The speaker who takes note of meanings within time in this fashion halts to dispense elements of wisdom.

There is, after all, a certain magic for enumeration, a certain humbling impact that comes from all certitudes of regularity and cyclicity of nature. One loses the nervousness of the moment, the suspicion in the possibility of the different, hiding away in some unknown future dimension. The ruins reveal truth in its bare essence. Though minimal in dimension and barely present, nothing else in the surrounding nature obstructs their view. Though they invite lamentation and tears poured out to a point just one step away from self-annihilation, there is nothing in them that is not natural or normative. Rather, they are the *spatial* proof of time, with which one must come to terms. Thus, Zuhair adjusts, as all wise men do, bids the dwelling a hearty good morning (c. 6),[22] and proceeds elsewhere. There is no more weeping at that stage, simply a contentment with and a naturalization of the phenomenon of traces.

WAITING

The contentment with and eventual wandering away from the traces, though evident substantive themes in the odes, did not by themselves provide the "essence" of the poetic experience. In a more social and communicative sense, poetry here—the *mu'allaqat*, the *mufaddaliyyat* (the prestigious ones), and other less canonical productions—was implicated in a preservative activity paralleling but more successful than that by which the desert preserved physical traces of past lives and sociabilities. Poetry was being memorized, taught, and recited across long distances. A unique structure lodged in a living language, thus, seemed to offer a possibility of persisting and outlasting death.

The poet, however, survived only according to a certain model provided by the social context in which "his" production was involved. The preserved speech was indeed attributed to an individual name, but that name was followed by an extended genealogy, a story of trials and tribulations, and an account for the context of poetic production. The preservability and pedagogic value of such a speech—*and* of its context—also reintegrated the poet into the tribe. No longer automatic outcasts, poets became highly prestigious and valued members of the tribe.

Before their pedagogic, moral, and political value was discovered, poets were aware that they had to continually seek readmission to the tribe. To no avail, Imru' l-Qays tried to prove that he was more tenacious in upholding tribal obligations than his more conformist brothers. Tarafa died an outcast, driven to his death by a blind adherence to instructions not to read his own execution order, which he was carrying to the governor of Bahrain; his more conformist companion had the foresight to violate a similar order and, though failing to convince Tarafa to do the same, at least managed to save his own life. Tarafa's ode, indeed, seeks to make tentative amends, such as when he imagines his return to the tribe to prepare for his own death, armed with a new identity, and confident of a tenacious worthiness (c. 93–101). He speaks as though free of worries, but it is too late in the day to provide a pedagogy for the future. That was to become the business of the more established poets, those who found no reason to struggle with a problematic belonging or to undergo the tortured agony of transformation, that is, those who were speaking when poetry itself was a respected institution, indeed, the only institution to be preserved as is, unscathed by time. They were speaking at the moment when it was discovered that nothing survives time but language.

The survivability of language was to effect a reconsideration of the components of the conceptual family of useful deeds, which in its earlier version had led to Tarafa's predicament. A postpoetic version of this conceptual family addressed the enigma of eternal survival, hitherto an unthinkable notion. The immortality of the poem and similarly structured productions was grafted upon recordable dimensions of the social context—genealogy and story—within which it was produced. A sinking ship sends out a signal not to plead for an impossible rescue but, more importantly, to leave a record of its existence and to register its demise at a particular point in time, a time whose coordinates are the genealogy and the story with which the poem will invariably appear. In comparison to the poem, the entirety of lived life appears more like an event, an outburst on the undifferentiated surface of sameness, a forgettable aberration of the ongoing nonbeing, meager traces scattered about a vast sea of silence. It is those juxtaposed words that, precisely because of their apparent endurance, promise to salvage any context associated with them from the teeth of time, whose legacy is what the ode always acknowledges at its ceremonial commencement. In this manner, poetry became a carrier of a hitherto little-discerned notion of "hope," a category of thought inconceivable without an orientation toward the future. With the advent of poetry, one looks beyond the moment, beyond life itself. Life here is no longer an event but a persistent social chronicle, carried over from one vein into another.

The delineation of what is to be lost and what is to be preserved begins at the moment of recording, which interrupts the timeless dissipation of life and its events into less than traces. It is a curious point in time when the very flow of time is itself noticed, when the speechlessness of the land is brought into questioning, when the enormous diffusion of nature appears to warrant a rearrangement by designations, oral and otherwise.

The advent of preservation also changed the social nature of poetry. The wild individual spirit that had guided the earlier poets was tempered by the celebration of poetry within traditional society. The continuous search for wonders in the world by the outcasts was now to give way to moral themes. Under earlier conditions, although the poets were aware of time, they could be oblivious to it by being oblivious, simultaneously, to all preservative efforts insofar as such efforts restricted hedonism. All such efforts were regarded, not unreasonably, to be pointless. Equally aware of such pointlessness, established poets like Zuhair nonetheless found a virtue in codes of conduct advising all to be on guard lifelong and to continually search for conditions that would allow one to persist as long as possible, but certainly not forever.

Zuhair, of course, was keenly aware of the context of tribal wars permeating his moment in history, a moment whose aura required taking into account more than the free play of hedonism. In the emerging context of a dire need for general sobriety and abstention from excessive claims, codes of manner and conduct—such as were spelled out in Zuhair's ode (c. 47–58)—were posited as demure but necessary expectations from life, which itself became a long, disorienting agony. Thus, the poetic codification of manners of (modest and temporary) survival were couched in an aura of a necessary humility and attention to the pointlessness of any grand schemes of preservation. Thus, *neither hedonism nor survival became possible.* The weary man who had composed such a code announced likewise his reasons, his conclusions, his fatalisms: "I have seen," Zuhair says, "the Fates trample like a purblind camel; those they strike / they slay, those they miss are left to live on to dotage" (c. 57).

"I have seen": Zuhair is a witness. A very old one indeed, convinced that he himself had been missed by the Fates too many times, so much so that he became weary of waiting for death. He knows that his code of manners, pronounced in a context governed by the imposing presence of mortality, is no more than a feeble offer of compromise with the forces of destiny, a compromise intended to allow the human actor a bit of control so as not to be crushed prematurely. Here, waiting becomes a phenomenon. There is, on the one hand, the promise of overcoming a set of destructive forces in the nature of human society by adhering to the code. On the other hand, there is the march of time, which ensures that any such overcoming is only temporary. In this context, overcoming the destructive potentials of human society becomes an attempt at waiting for the more legitimate victory of time. The code, which pedagogically advises individual *action,* contemplates as well the torment of *passive* waiting.

The question, then, becomes how to valorize waiting. The search for a purpose behind waiting not only makes it more possible as a standard practice but also brings closer to consciousness the depleting operation of time that accompanies or even defines it. Purpose, here, is the ethic that accounts for waiting for an exterior and natural progression to take its proper course. As he discovers this agony, Zuhair endows his own life with a purpose, which is to dispense his accumulated wisdom to a new generation. It is that accumulation itself that proves that the elapsed time had been doing more than simply elapsing. Since it could be preserved as a reservoir of learned wisdom, it was defined by more than pointless waiting. Since wisdom is transmittable, waiting provides communicative action with a purpose as the locus of a preservationist endeavor. Since such preservationist efforts stabilize the practice of waiting itself, waiting becomes possible not on the basis of the code of behaviors provided earlier in Zuhair's *mu'allaqa* but on the basis of waiting's potential to add to social and collective knowledge. Waiting thus becomes a complicated activity, with an ontological status superseding lonely presence within a monotony of time. It is through this operation that knowledge—transmittable, preservable, earned, recordable, forthcoming—infuses the practice of waiting with a life other than that defined purely by the span of time:

> I know what is happening today, and what passed over
> before that yesterday,
> but as for knowing what tomorrow will bring, there I'm
> utterly blind. (c. 59)

In the final words of Zuhair's phenomenal speech, this verdict is delivered on the relationship of the self and the ode to knowledge. This is a speech infused with the knowledge that time has made available. That the future is not known is announced as a *fact*. In an important sense, the future does not *need* to be known. All one needs to know about the future is already in the code of manners (c. 47–58). The code, after all, is premised on the predictability of outcome of the instructed behavior. The unknowability of the future could therefore relatively easily be dispensed with, even though it is the sphere of time that is certain to arrive. So this foreknowledge, which is the stuff of waiting, is already stabilized by being lodged in the depth of a general structure of grand and comprehensive ethos.

Such a structure is oriented trilaterally. It is grounded first and foremost on a certain *fatalism,* which underpins the practice and ethic of waiting for finitude and downplays the unknowability of the future. Second, it provides a structure and promise of *predictability,* articulated as a guide in the form of code and consequence. Third, it grounds knowledge upon a certain *naturalism:* that which is worth knowing shall be revealed because of its own virtue, without advocacy or effort (see, for instance, couplet 58). One's own nature, so the discourse professes, cannot be hidden. There is an unanchored faith in the necessity of this natural unfolding of the self. After this search for an instrumentality, at the end of the speech, at the final moments of this journey, when a conclusion was to seal the series of adventures with the stamp of a totality of knowledge made available by time elapsed, there stood faith with arms outstretched to receive the inquirer and share with him a permanent abode, outfitted with nothing but an elaborate scheme for waiting. There they were to rest, poet and unanchored faith, from then on together, until a transcendental God anchored the faith in a realm beyond the vagaries of unaccountable time.

four

Pre-Islamic Ontotheology
and the Method of Knowledge

Spiritual life in the immediate pre-Islamic era consisted of paganism, book religions, and Hanifism. None of these could be confidently thought of as a "finished product" in its own right. Such movements and practices are best conceived of as trends of belief, open to diversity, amendment, and experimentation. As we shall see, trends of spiritual life were defined more on the basis of verbal pronouncements than on the basis of doctrinaire following. Traces of this oral priority can be detected in Islam, whose first pillar of faith was the *utterance* of the formula professing that there is no God but Allah, and that Muhammad is his messenger.

Before Islam, manifestations of irreverence toward existing religions were abundant. This phenomenon notwithstanding, much of narrative history concerned with the period deals with pre-Islamic "Judaism" and "Christianity," for instance, as if they were finished and well-defined bodies of belief. Little mention is made of their specific and peculiar shape in that society, the underlying assumption being that "believers" have the same interpretation or degree of attachment to their faith regardless of the various historical and social contexts within which an expression of faith takes place. In much of orientalist literature, one finds a prevalent normative assumption of bodies of faith as separable conceptual realms.

"Jewish tradition," for instance, is presented as an exclusive body of thought, from which elements could be seen to be "borrowed," even if they follow a different developmental trajectory.[1] Such a perspective ignores the essential fluidity of spiritual concepts through much of pre- and even post-Islamic Arabia. While the concept "Jew," for instance, could be treated as a marker of tribal identity—among other things—it did not necessarily designate a unique repository of particular ontotheological or cosmological principles, which, even before Islam, could float across tribal lines.

Apart from the factors that can be attributed to its relation to tribal politics (to be examined later, especially in Chapter 7), the triumph of Islam, according to the hypothesis being introduced here, was precisely due to a situation in which it seemed to offer a persuasively comprehensive, interpretive schema and guide for life, with respect to a particular sociohistorical moment. Though the existence of spiritual precursors to Islam during the *Jahiliyyah* (pre-Islamic era) is symptomatic of a crisis, their irrelevance manifested itself in their parochial or uncertain hold over society. Islam itself, thus, can be understood not as a unique doctrine but as a product of a long social learning process. While presenting itself as an alternative system, it incorporated elements that predated it in spiritual life, folk traditions, and biblical ontotheology.

PAGANISM AND THE IDEA OF THE RITUAL

Paganism was the belief against which early Islam had to wage its fiercest fight. Such a struggle consumed a great deal of Muhammad's efforts and ultimately determined the direction of much of his teaching. The argument here is not that paganism was strong but only that it was widespread. The pervasiveness or even persistence of a certain belief does not necessarily indicate its strength; it merely indicates the absence of a more historically and socially grounded alternative. Pagan deities were relatively weak, and their level of abstract eminence, as Muhammad duly noticed, was embarrassingly low for a god worthy of increasing duties assigned to the realm of deity. In addition, though the traditional narrative emphasizes pagan resistance to Islam and the persecution of the early believers, it is worth keeping in mind that the speed with which Islam consolidated itself as a formidable force, even before the death of Muhammad, is astonishing, especially when compared to histories of other world religions. Such a fact may indicate that Islam's main spiritual adversary was already in no condition to put up a genuine and sustained resistance.[2]

Paganism entailed the worship of a multitude of idols, many of which were objects of local worship and restricted to certain tribes. But although they existed among various Arabs, pagan rituals and beliefs were much more evident in Mecca than anywhere else in the peninsula. The development of the central spiritual role of Mecca before Islam, as shown, closely paralleled its ascendancy as a trade center. Other objects of worship, such as stars and fire, existed as well among the Bedouins, but the preeminence of the idols to a large extent shaped the contours of the ontotheological campaign of early Islam.[3]

On the one hand, paganism offered the pre-Islamic Arabs an explanatory framework for nature. But on the other, such a framework was devoid of guidance for practical life or warning of ethical consequences. Reports exist of consulting an idol before embarking on a journey, war, or other significant affair in life. A well-known report, which concerns Imru' l-Qays, shows that it was neither necessary to obtain nor obligatory to follow the advice of the idols. According to the legend, Imru' l-Qays consulted his idol three times before he set out to take revenge for the murder of his father. Consistently receiving discouraging advice, he cursed the idol, remarking that it would not have given such an answer had the affair concerned its own father. What is interesting in this story is the clear indication not only that the idol's verdict was by no means binding but, moreover, that, as Imru' l-Qays compares his own predicament to a possible one concerning the idol's father, he discerns little distance between the two. There are reports that indirectly confirm the idols' distance from local traditions, asserting that idol worship had no local peninsular roots, having been imported from Syria by a Meccan chief who learned that they were used to bring rain and as a moral aid against enemies, and that they were only modified within Arabia.[4]

Pagan idols do not seem to have had any division of labor among them. Unlike in other pantheist mythologies, the various idols had no specific functions and responsibilities ascribed to them, even though some were more greatly honored than others.[5] Only a few had a mythology giving the origin of their holiness, and even then, such an interpretation made little impact on their status. Usaf and Na'ila were, according to myth, two fornicators in the *haram* (sanctuary) who were punished by being transformed permanently into idols.[6] Their sinful origin clearly had little impact on their status as objects of worship. Ibn al-Kalbi's account stresses the fact that their holiness stemmed more from the fact that they resembled the stones abundant around them in the *haram* than from the moral lessons of the story of their genesis.

As weak deities, idols were incapable of doing harm or good, as Muhammad was to repeatedly remind Meccans. Such an invocation of the need for *action* on the part of a deity was in some way original, since pagan objects of worship never pretended to offer a complete system of life. The social virtues stressed by Bedouins and Meccans bore no necessary relationship to paganism, and furthermore they probably preceded it. There is a paucity of reports offering any credible hints that such deities had much to do with moral direction or guidance to everyday, practical life. Rather, most social arrangements and bonds continued to be prefigured by given genealogical traditions, in the context of a past-oriented society. This orientation continued to frame Meccan consciousness even after nomadism was far from view and outside society's regular options. The intensity of the past as the only legitimate venue of mores was most directly registered in Mecca in the innumerable pagan objections to Muhammad that he had violated the spiritual order given by the forefathers—and not simply that his logic was wrong. More systematically and eloquently, however, the heavy weight of the past was ritually affirmed in the ponderous possibility of its loss, the generalized tradition seen most clearly in the openings of the odes adjudicated in 'Ukaz, the marketplace near Mecca, at the conclusion of the annual trade cycle.[7] Standing at the ruins, as mentioned before, became the traditional image with which to begin an ode.

There are some qualifications to be made here, however. A discursive *tradition* does not always immediately indicate an experienced resonance, even though the origin of such a tradition may be traced to such an experience. Normally one speaks of a "tradition" when a *form* of expression or practice is seen to have survived beyond the original moment of birth or utterance, when such a form or practice has been reproduced according to a relatively stable order of recurrence. Whether the notion of a "tradition" could also refer to the continued survival of the original experience that had unleashed the form by which it was expressed is a more difficult question. It is always possible that widely different experiences could express themselves through a single ubiquitous form, that quite divergent orientations could inhabit, claim, or utilize a form of discourse that signals a certain "tradition." Such notions are common currency in late-twentieth-century criticism. Here we have our hands on a peculiar variant of a form of discourse, commonly referred to as a "tradition," that functioned in interesting ways. For many Arabs, this was the first tradition to become firmly, but perhaps not exclusively, lodged in language rather than in physical objects. There are other fragments from the period that do not begin with the ruins theme; nor are they of the same length, intensity, expressive vigor, or legendary status as the *mu'allaqat* (odes). There are also less elegantly preserved fragments of rhymed, ordinary language, commonly addressing issues of cosmology, ethics, and wisdom, ascribed to certain prophetic characters about whom little is known.

But, in standing at the ruins, we have the genesis of a form of speech that many aspired to revisit. There is therefore the first constitutive element of what we call tradition, namely, a recognizable point of return. How is that appeal constituted? Is it the potency of its delivery? Is there, therefore, an essential communicable nature peculiar to this point of return, or does it survive precisely because of its enigma, its open-endedness, its responsiveness to a multitude of manipulative and cumulative possibilities? Or, perhaps, is there a residue of the original experience that the form spelling out the discursive product allows later listeners to smell and thus hope to revive through an act of emulation? How was it that, of all other possible forms, this expression of a perpetual loss of the past became the foundation of a tradition? Or was a "tradition" being attempted in the way of forms, and was this one clung to not because of any reason latent in its essence but, rather, because of an unanchored but refined character of its word sequence? Or was it not "refined" character that was the determining factor but simply the accident of it having been spoken first?

What we know with the highest degree of certainty is how the tradition was expressed. By discerning the various openings of the *mu'allaqat,* certain suggestions regarding the nature of the tradition begin to emerge. Tarafa Ibn l-'Abd, generally regarded by the ancients as the heir to the legendary poet Imru' l-Qays, almost copied the latter's opening couplet in the prominently placed second couplet of his own ode: "There my companions halted their beasts awhile over me / saying, 'Don't perish of sorrow;

bear it with fortitude!'" In the original language, this and Imru' l-Qays's rendition differ only by one word, the last, which occurs at the crucial location determining the rhythm. Only this line, together with the first couplet, constitute the traditional opening of Tarafa's ode, whereafter different digressions ensue. Thus, half of Tarafa's extremely short flirtation with the traditional opening theme is a near word-for-word duplication of the master. The disseminating oral tradition, as it seems, was troubled neither by such a "plagiarism" nor by the brevity of Tarafa's salute to the tradition. And in a similar vein, Zuhair Ibn Abi Sulma imitates those poets preceding him: In his *mu'allaqai,* the second couplet pays homage to Tarafa's opening line and his third to Imru' l-Qays's third!

In this light, tradition seems to include ritual plagiarism, at least at the expressive, formulaic level. The theme of perpetual loss and ruin, as the "substance" of this tradition, resonated differently within Bedouin and sedentary societies. For the nomads, loss and dying were regular norms of nature; they needed no metaphysical camouflage, and the ode did not venture to offer any. Only the language of mourning itself mitigated the loss. The Bedouins' materialism was associated with the relative simplicity of their life. The nature of their economy was seen as a direct result of the natural surroundings. Here we have a society with no surplus production and no class distinctions, an economy of bare and uncertain survival reflecting itself directly in the culture, a social equality of chances of fortune and misfortune and thus no hidden secrets of survival. None of the stones or idols that the Bedouins worshipped ever neared the status of the ones worshipped by the sedentary tribes, and the Bedouins evidently had little trust in their own idols. Death itself had no explanation beyond time and aging.

These elements, which consolidated an unchanging tradition and attitude among nomads, were not as operative in a sedentary society that had to redefine its posture toward the notion of loss. It was in Mecca that paganism reigned supreme, to a degree almost unparalleled anywhere else in the peninsula. The efforts of the city contributed most singularly to the spread of paganism, as well as to enshrining the resulting sanctity of Mecca. Evidently still inspired by the nomadic model of permeability of culture and economy, many of the city's competitors clearly saw parallels between its economic and spiritual centrality and sought likewise to enshrine parallel sanctuaries, although without as much success.[8]

Though the connection between transtribal, supralocal exchange and holy sites or sanctuaries was evident elsewhere in Arabia, the specific expression of such holiness in idol worship cannot be as directly connected to banal interest. One of the ancient accounts mentioned earlier simply saw idols as "imports" from Syria, much like any other trade item, but another account stresses at least the local mutation of such a tradition. Ibn al-Kalbi traced the worship of stones to the ancient migrations away from Mecca after the lost times of the Amalikites, when each migrating group took with it a stone from the *haram* as a sign of reverence and a constant reminder of Mecca. Out in the wilderness, they began to "worship what they loved" (*'abadu ma s-tahabbu*).[9]

At the semiological level, the endowment of physical objects with meanings is premised upon anchoring such objects in a larger origin (the *haram* in this case) that becomes periodically distant with the need for nomadic migration. Such objects thus operate at the same level as the ruins in the pre-Islamic ode, namely as discernible, interrogable remains of a more meaningful but disappearing whole. In both cases, one sees an elaborate effort to delineate the exact distinction of the object. With paganism, the object becomes a tribally specific deity, detachable from the larger spiritual ensemble of the *haram*. In the ode, a curious effort can be seen, usually at the opening, to delineate the exact location of the ruins. This is readily evident in a variety of odes, from Imru' l-Qays to Labid Ibn Rabi'ah. The intensity of the moment of halting is not exclusively invested in facing the traces of a vanishing abode or in sensing nature's way of reclaiming what humans had once sought to claim for their own. Rather, the gradual reclamation of a place by wilderness calls for an elaborate documentation. First, the location of the ruins is strictly delineated by extensive naming. (Consider, for example, Labid's c. 1–2: "The abodes are desolate, halting-place and encampment too / at Miná; deserted lies Gaul, deserted alike Rijám, / and the torrent-beds of Er-Raiyán," or Imru' l-Qays's c. 1–2: "Halt, friends both! Let us weep, recalling a love and a lodging / by the rim of the twisted sands between Ed-Dakhool and Haumal, / Toodih and El-Mikrát, whose trace is not yet effaced.")

A name here operates as a primal identity. It is the last step in a laborious process by which an enclosed, self-referencing identity is brought out from its prior gestation within a larger domain (the *haram* for pagan objects, the previous encampment for the ode). As a discursive product, such a name is also the final stamp, the last signature of a specific creator. The Qur'an itself registers this discovery in the contentious *surah* (chapter) of an-Najm—to be discussed at length in Chapter 7—in which the prominent idols are explicitly condemned as *nothing but names* assigned by the forefathers and followed blindly by their descendants. In that Qur'anic passage, a "mere" name is contrasted to actual authority in the world, which God denies to the idols.[10]

But in the ode, and presumably under paganism as well, the name had little to do with an act of creation. It was, rather, a reservoir, that portion of an identity by which it could become easily discernible for the sake of a future discourse about it. As such, it guaranteed that a discourse could be reproduced indefinitely and economically. In this form, a name is much like the paradigm defined by Thomas Kuhn: an invocation nullifying the need to reiterate a lengthy multitude of significations, characteristics, and rules anew. Such a paradigmatic significance of the name is premised on an assumption of a unanimity regarding what the name signifies. It is also based on an assumption of synonymity—a complete and natural confoundment, an absolute elimination of distance—between the name and the essence of the object that it signifies. The name, thus, functions most ideally when it is subjected to a condition of hearing that senses in its utterance the collectivity of possible deliberations about the object. A name that met such requisites signified an identity that was seen to be timeless. Before existence across the span of time could be ordered by an abstract divinity, the most successful form of resistance to the phenomenality of time was paradigmatic naming.

On the other hand, names of places as they occur in the traditional openings signify an emergent crisis. The ode usually begins by noting that the volumes of experiences that had been wrapped up by a name are about to disappear in a remarkably unsparing way. The habitat is about to slip away from the grips of the creative human subject. The promise of permanence first certified by the name is aborted. *A project at creation is halted and then reversed.* We could see how transient the whole project was in the fact that in order for a speech about a place to begin, it required several geographic references and anchoring points. There was in that construction a lurking teleology, an invitation to wait for a stable meaning to come about. Instead of that delivery, now the poet comes back to the site to witness it at the final moments of its dispersal back into the enormous diffusion of nature from whence it came. In this recurring, ritualistic termination, the ruins reveal an element of their ontology, for here they are no longer mere remains from a past into which a lover is irretrievably deposited; rather, they are the remains of an arrested birth of permanent and total construction, for which the name was a placeholder.

Thus, whereas for the nomad the ritual of regarding ruins coincided with periodic interruption of the regular flow of time and life, Meccan idols enshrined such an interruption in the form of a total social meaning of tribal isolation and self-sufficiency. Thus, with the idols, the status of the ritual moved from interrupting the flow of nature and time to arresting the flux of continual social rearrangements. In Mecca, idols proliferated in and around the *haram* in a way that allowed most of the tribes in the peninsula, *as tribes,* to anchor a spiritual claim in and obligation to a distant but stable house.

Mecca's idols fulfilled both external and internal functions.[11] Externally, they became an integral part of the process of providing Mecca with a central sociopolitical role in the peninsula. Pilgrimage, as a periodic voyage toward sacred tribal objects housed in the *haram,* was a fundamental ritual in that process. But it was the *haram* as a *house* of sacred objects, not the *haram* itself, that was the pilgrim's destination. This reflected—at least in part—the fact that the various social units in the peninsula lacked central political authority, lived separately for most of the year, spoke different dialects, inhabited a desert terrain marked by enormous impediments to communication, and were primarily connected by a trade cycle that took form prior to any political consolidation, leaving trading partners in relative cultural isolation from each other. In his study of today's Bedouins, Meeker observed that the Bedouin image of God involved attributes that resonated strikingly with the Bedouin lifestyle, that visions of hell and paradise addressed the problems of desert landscapes, and that assignment to either was seen in terms of tribal affiliation rather than in terms of an individual's deeds.[12] This shows a lack of belief or interest in the possibility of transcending existing horizons and conditions, but it also shows a firm ground for the tribal self-reference in terms of irreducible totalities. Recent research argues that totemism was a prevalent form of accounting for a tribe's origin and legitimacy in pre-Islamic Arabia.[13] In this case, the totem must be interpreted not exclusively in terms of psychoanalysis but as a protopolitical sign of tribal independence.

The dialectic between the norm of tribal distinction and the interruption of that distinction by transtribal cycles (trade, migration, intertribal marriage) paralleled a ritualistic system typified by a place-centered combination of local and general spirituality. Distinct tribes had distinct objects of worship, though they observed the general sanctity of the *haram* that housed such diverse objects. This pattern, which is strikingly similar to a dialectic of local spiritual autonomy coupled with reference to a common holy center, can be observed elsewhere in the ancient Near East (for instance, Nippur in ancient Mesopotamia), testifying to a long tradition of confluence between year-long local isolation and cyclical patterns of supralocal communication. In this case, the combination of the tribal specificity of each idol with the general sanctity of the *haram* provided Mecca with a nonhegemonic form of spiritual centrality in the land.

This phenomenon of nonhegemonic spiritual centrality closely paralleled a trade-based economy, territorially extended far beyond the reach of the available means of coercive control. The source of Meccan wealth was based on the surplus of transactions with the outside world rather than on exploitation within the city itself. The increase and stabilization of trade required a move beyond monopolistic efforts and earlier attempts to limit the number of participants to a system characterized by an expansion of the network of participants and the extension of *common* forms of spiritual citizenship.[14] One of the marks of such a shift is the end of the practice of *i'tifad* (individual family withdrawal from the community after commercial failure and subsequent suicide by voluntary starvation) in the trading sedentary community through the introduction of the principle of shared investment and responsibility for collective well-being.

Though some holy sites and objects may have existed in more diffused states prior to the inception of long-distance trade, the significance of the contacts brought about by trade induced an added and regular spiritual investment in such spiritual guides. In itself, this added layer of ritualistic regularity does not necessarily infuse paganism with strongly binding guiding principles for practical affairs, with explanations for the nature of things, or with ethical directions that would be expected to form in a society based on exchange and borrowing. Before the coming of Islam as a comprehensive system of explanation and guidance, such voids set the stage for various reform figures and movements, as well as for ad hoc protopagan attitudes toward such problems, to be explored shortly.

The socialization of the phenomenon of poetry before Islam also points to such ethical directions. In the odes, one can detect a variety of stages in the ideas of sociability and obligation, some of which have already been discussed. But in general, one can see a move from an exiled, highly *individualistic* involvement in the objects of pristine nature, represented by ostracized poets such as Imru' l-Qays and Tarafa, to the formation of the poetic form as a *tradition,* as epitomized by the likes of Zuhair, Labid, 'Antara, and many other less well known poets. Here, poetry becomes not simply a mode of commentary upon exterior nature but a reservoir of moral ethos and logics of social attachment. In a third stage, the poets become exclusively defined by specific sociabilities, whereby the poet largely represents a collective subject, as the cases of 'Amru and al-Harith illustrate. Thus we see the metamorphosis of a distinct *form* of discourse and commentary, from ontology to ethics to sociability. With each metamorphosis, the range of poetic reflection is narrowed, precisely as the poetic form becomes more socially expansive.[15]

The socialization of this form of discourse reflects not so much something essential in language itself as an interest in taming an observed loss in the perpetual encounter with the ruins. When the poet becomes a spokesperson for the tribe, it is because the tribe sees itself as a stable and transgenerationally present audience, in spite of the ruins everywhere in sight. Thus, as a preservatory discourse, poetics became the depository of all elements of value to be shipped across time. Value, thus, began to be moved in bits and pieces under the jurisdiction of this language.[16] The historically recurrent irony, which can also be discerned in prophetic experiences, is that the very introduction of such discursive forms is attributed to individuals who are totally oblivious to social norms—in this case to a few posthumously celebrated outcasts.

REFORMERS, HANIFISM, PAGAN MONOTHEISM

According to traditional sources, pre-Islamic "prophets" or reformers do not appear to have been in short supply.[17] They are frequently reported to have made the same observation that Muhammad made regarding the idols, namely, that they were "harmless and helpless" creatures. References to a transcendental power, and even the word "Allah," are frequently encountered, albeit in vague connotations, in the pre-Islamic literature.

(Indeed, many commentators have used such recurrences as evidence that Islam fabricated an older tradition rather than as evidence that Islam itself was embedded in pre-Islamic traditions.) At least one of the figures in this story, al-Mutalammes Ibn Umayyah, is reported to have offered a "compromise" whereby Allah was to be worshipped exclusively, albeit as the "lord of the idols."[18] One of the earliest recorded references to a transcendental God is traced by the sources to a period long preceding Muhammad, namely, to the days when Mecca was inhabited by Khuza'ah, before Quraysh.

The few available records regarding pre-Islamic pilgrimage rituals hint at the roots of some monotheistic beliefs that were later highlighted in Islam. These include the famous *talbiyat* (responses to divine calling) uttered during the pilgrimage, of which no fewer than two dozen were in circulation among various tribes.[19] Compilations of *talbiyat* seem to indicate that various tribes believed in a supreme God, *in addition to* their own, more specialized ones. The tribally specific rendition of *talbiyat* accentuates separate tribal identity by emphasizing the *uniqueness* of its response to a divine call while simultaneously affirming the universal nature of the addressee and the call.

Paganism and monotheism thus should not be regarded as stark and exclusive contrasts. Kister shows that although Carl Brockelmann and Hamilton A. Gibb start from different foundations and use different sources, they arrive at a similar conclusion, namely, that Islam was grounded more in the *Jahiliyyah* than in Jewish or Christian traditions, contesting thereby some important lines of orientalist inquiry.[20] Though this argument can itself be contested on the conceptual ground of the clear distinctions it presumes between pre-Islamic textual and nontextual traditions, it does acknowledge the monotheistic aspect of paganism. It would be more to the point to say that there was also a certain degree of confluence between paganism and the book religions.

God, as evidenced in the *talbiyat*, occupied a higher realm within a pantheist hierarchy, but as a *concept* he became clearly distinct from the materialist pagan idols under his common jurisdiction. "God," in this sense, was not destined to be an abstract concept through some logical necessity. Rather, he could also be seen as a placeholder for a specially magnificent idol, who would come to place the other idols under its sway as the power of the tribe worshipping it was enhanced. As mentioned before, there is evidence that tribes vied to have their idols predominate, or even sought to house the *haram* in their territories. The aforementioned *hurub al-fijar*, the confrontation between Quraysh and the Hawazen tribal confederation, can be seen as the last episode in that struggle, when Quraysh's victory finally decided the Meccan centrality in that regard.

If the ritual regularly reveals and revels in the distance between the sensible and the abstract, then one would presume that it was the routinization of the patterns and rituals of pilgrimage that engendered the gradual removal of the concept of God from the concept underlying the idols. This means that, eventually, God could scarcely be conceptualized as the "lord of the idols," even though the offer was made to Muhammad in an avowed attempt to mend a tribal split. The elevation of God into a heavenly realm beyond representation or comprehension also means that divinity would now replace for all material and sensible deities at the same time. Gradually, they become more than unnecessary: Their very presence diluted the conception of deity as an unreachable being. Thus, though Islam fought the idols adamantly, it retained the idea underlying the sanctity of the *haram*. The latter only housed questionable deities and, like God himself, was a sign of universality that was at the same time not in itself the object of worship. Furthermore, the *haram* was a specifically and uniquely Meccan institution, unlike the idols, whose semblance proliferated everywhere in the land.

The observation that the idols were "harmless and helpless" clearly indicates an interest in guidance, which in the context of the trading community entailed to a significant extent an ethical dimension. Schemes to protect traders' rights and to define their obligations—notably the *hilf al-fudul* (pact of the virtuous ones)—were obviously part of that trend. Reports also mention that commercial agreements in Quraysh were opened with the statement "In your name, our Allah."[21] In the trading community, the question of justice posed a novel dilemma about the practicality of guaranteeing and executing justice. Under nomadism, by contrast, good and bad fortune had to be dealt with as it arose. The importance attached to settling accounts through revenge or blood money, for instance, illustrates such an investment in earthly, material justice, which could become a transgenerational obsession before it could be relegated to an otherworldly realm. In that subsistence society, such a relegation could only be the beginning of social extinction.[22] Amendable loss, after all, is a luxury open only to a society possessing expendable surplus. Barring that, any "injustice" must be dealt with on the scene and very swiftly, as unpleasant surprises in desert conditions presented the Bedouins with life or death issues with regular frequency. Such is not the image that can be discerned in the poetic tradition of the ruins, with its normativization and surrender to the eventuality of loss. But it must be kept in mind that such a tradition was established by (or, more importantly, *attributed to*) outcasts from the tribe. Though emulated by socially more established poets, other themes—pedagogy and wisdom, love, belonging, and so on—usually counterbalanced the initial image of complete surrender to the work of fate.

But it is in the poems of those poets entrusted with being tribal spokespersons that we detect an element of derision toward the ruins traditions and, subsequently, toward the notion that perpetual loss could be a norm of nature, over which the individual would have no control. Thus, the heroic ode of 'Amru Ibn Kalthum is the only one from that period to open with a theme other than that of the ruins.[23] Indeed, 'Amru's unique defiance of the traditional opening has led many commentators to speculate that the first seven to nine couplets were additions to the original *mu'allaqa*, although, so the theory goes, they would be very early additions. Yet this is what the oral tradition has delivered, by way of a long poem whose tone, from beginning to end, seems to be consistent: 'Amru's is an ode of explosions and heroisms, flavored with a bit of love and some drinking. It is a mix of sorts, all conditioned by a mood of uncontrollable, almost lawless tempest. The ode opens with the dawn. The day to follow is about to be *made* by the hero. He mourns no already-made ruins, no past, and no otherness. More precisely, he manifests no longing for a lost or sought-after authenticity. A self-confident hero seeks no roots in a primal identity. Rather, he makes his own world with his own hands, recognizing in the ruins not a loss but a world offering itself for an encyclopedic rendition. 'Amru, thus, demolishes the ruins and begins anew in the early hour. Temporality is dissociated from and made to overpower spatiality, with no names or specification of any location. Now a different logic flows. This logic seems to be articulated with respect to a spirit of indulgence, where praiseworthy wine

> . . . swings the hotly desirous from his passion
> when he has tasted them to gentle mellowness;
> you see the skinflint miser, when the cup's passed him,
> suddenly holds his prized property in derision. (c. 3–4)

The key is transformability. (And while we are at it, it might be added that we are all mortals [c. 7]). The claims of 'Amru's ode concern a reconstitution and, in a very peculiar way, a reaffirmation of the idea of the acting subject, a recasting of the idea in the context of an awareness of mortality. But such an awareness does not take place in an inert state of consciousness. Seeing that the tradition has become congested with images of ruins proving the power of time, the poet proclaims his indifference to mortality, indeed, his power over it. His indulgence is constructed so as to defeat all purpose in life. He constructs his own destiny, indeed, his own ruin, rather than awaiting the blind force of time to do the work. But his preemption of time targets not only time as an inert concept but also a tradition that had expressed its surrender to fate by proclaiming the power of time over all things, places, lives, and loves.

The initiative of the hero-poet to introduce or restore justice commences the second movement of 'Amru's ode, which many commentators regard to be the "true" opening. A scene of an impending separation is presented. The ruins are yet to appear. The poet, so to speak, is standing at the preruins stage, preempting their emergence: He is an active rather than a reactive character. He is also a hero who, unlike the other legendary heroic poet 'Antara, possesses the confidence of belonging; his folklorized biography lists him not only as the poet of Taghlib but also as its leader. So this is an ode delivered by a political authority. Thus, he is acutely aware of the role of tribal conflict in his world. As his lover's tribe prepares for departure, he reminds the audience of a previous skirmish with them, now to be seen as a "hateful day." He ponders the impact of that possible injustice (or norm) on the present; now it is time to clear up all records, so that the impending separation can be properly remembered. Tribal wars themselves were remediable instances of separation and never reached the point of total annihilation of an enemy tribe. An awareness of the normative status of war conditions the tone with which war is addressed in this sequence. However, that "hateful day" imposes an additional weight on the moment of recording memory, now that a migration is threatening to usher in a separation less rectifiable than the separation caused by war itself. It is noteworthy that this preruins moment infuses in this speaking authority the delusion of being able to transform the flow of time itself into a perfect stillness of a permanent, full record; that a memory works its magic in such a way that the prehistory of separation annuls the torture of its remembrance; and that, at this moment of standing so close to a loss that one can foresee it, an encyclopedia of the past is assembled to assess certain moments as being preservable, others as being instructive, and the rest as to be abandoned, mourned, declaimed. Justice here consists of the proper balance of such mental and discursive operations.

The oral tradition opposes to the force of this subject another poet, al-Harith Ibn Hilliza of Bakr. His ode is set in the context of a rivalry with 'Amru and, by extension, with the latter's kinfolk. Thus, the opening of this purported antithesis, unlike 'Amru's, is extremely orthodox in form. There is abundant naming of locations. The all-too-common weeping—and the equally common expression of its futility—follows. The reasons for this predictability and excessive adherence to formal orthodoxy, seen in light of al-Harith's competition with 'Amru, becomes more obvious as al-Harith's political references are spelled out later in the ode. The opening introduces several reversals that address 'Amru's mood with contempt: couplet 1 ("Asma' announced to us . . .") is comparable to 'Amru's sonorous invocation in his couplet 8 ("Pause yet . . ."). Unlike 'Amru, al-Harith is preempted by the departure resolution, even though he, like 'Amru, begins his ode just before the separation that would eventually leave the physical traces by which it will be remembered. Al-Harith accepts the inevitability of the formation of the ruins and makes no effort to halt the process. The "certainty" is lodged not in a knowledge to be constructed by the subject but in realizing the inevitability of what is to become (that is, it is as if the poet says, "I do not tell, because I have no foreknowledge to expound, no certitude to exhume from the inventory of my memory: To the contrary, I am *told* that she is leaving"). What one is being told is what will happen. The speech pronouncing the separation occupies the same moment in time as the separation itself. In pronouncing the separation, the poetic discourse acknowledges not only such contemporaneous actuality but also its powerlessness to reverse that actuality. Thus, it quickly reverts to the ancient practice of naming of locations of past encounters, which is now understood to indicate the irretrievability of a loss to be documented.

Thus, unlike in the case of emerging, trade-based sedentarism, loss under nomadism did not in itself correspond to the concept of "justice." In fact, permanent loss was impossible, since the world was either prearranged so as to make loss within it invisible ('Amru), or documented and entrusted to a preservatory tradition (al-Harith), or deposited into a perennial, earthly, and possibly transgenerational project at revenge. In Mecca, in contrast, such attitudes toward the idea of justice began to be reformulated. Class divisions and fluctuations of fortune no longer presented an immediate and necessary threat to life as such, especially since the end of the practice of *i'tifad* and the commencement of collaborative capital investment and caravan expeditions. In that context, the main issue was not daily survival but *relative* position and well-being in a stratified society. Here a high God capable of rewarding and punishing on the basis of ordained ethical relations to fellow society members was both harmful and helpful. With the concept of justice being increasingly deposited in him, one ingredient at a time, such a God was also becoming the formative subject; the reference point; the witness of documents, transactions, and agreements; and the model of empowerment invested in symbolizing collective societal resources.

In addition to the set of practical uncertainties that the growth of Meccan economy brought to the fore, there were further problems arising from the nature of trade itself. A wide range of day-to-day transactions placed a demand for market regulations that, in their abstract nature, would be adequate for the market's growing impersonality and scope. It was no longer simply the buying and selling that mattered but, rather, a range of transactions that included borrowing, insuring, and valuation. God makes an appearance after a long period in which increasingly complex transactions lead to a piecemeal development of regulations. In other words, God, among other things, epitomizes and represents the concern for regulative efficiency. The absence of an earlier experimentation with a state apparatus that could accomplish such tasks made the introduction of a high God all the more urgent.[24] In this case, he had to take on such a task from scratch, since the *badawah* lifestyle had provided no comparable models of transcendence.[25]

EXAMPLES AND COMMENTARY

Qass Ibn Sa'idah, "the sage of the Arabs," is one of the better known among pre-Islamic "believers." He was praised by Muhammad, who was reported to be among his audience in the marketplace of 'Ukaz.[26] His sayings, which revolve around the idea of resurrection, begin by pointing to the certainty of death and the ineluctable eventuality of the future.[27] This orientation toward the future makes the speech itself novel and noteworthy, since the theme is largely absent from recorded Bedouin literary heritage, especially in the *mu'allaqat*. In the odes, the future held little promise of being any different from the present. The vantage point of sedentarization processes, by contrast, led to the realizations that social metamorphosis was possible and that the general ethical contours of the future were thus less predictable. There are scattered references in the literature that suggest a connection between sedentarism and a tragic understanding of death. M. M. Bravmann has unearthed apparently seminomadic references to death as a sedentary condition (the deceased as *muqim*, "someone who settles permanently").[28] Elsewhere in poetry, one sees either an unconcerned attitude toward death, as in Tarafa and Zuhair, or, less frequently but more tellingly, an attitude toward death that considers it to be a tragedy only when it happens in settled towns.[29]

In the Qass's speech, after his initial observations (mortality and the future), he proceeds to reflect on the grounds for nature, especially those elements of it that are distant or seem to belong to a different realm than human life: heaven, stars, seas, night, and so on. Thus, the earlier observations regarding individual fate are combined with observations on nature to convey a sense of estrangement from both. The next step resolves the suspicious status of being by tracing both nature and life to a single source. Since nature itself is seen to control the arrangement of human life by allowing certain methods of survival and restricting others, then the force that is capable of controlling nature comes to be defined as the source of a *common* origin of being. A discourse that asks, in the same breath, questions about the nature of things unrelated by existing cosmology (for example, death, stars) is fundamentally interested in universal laws, in the origins of all phenomena, and, by extension, in the *origins of their difference.* In the case of Qass's discourse, the conclusion follows smoothly: There is another world in which there is to be a resurrection. Thus, the certainty of death, pronounced with a tragic tone at the beginning of the discourse, is downplayed at its conclusion.

This belief in resurrection assures not only a continuity of individual physical life but an eventual reunification of this life with the society to which it once belonged and knew before its temporary lapse into death. The emergence of a nonegalitarian, sedentary society, in which there was the possibility, and even the certainty, that there would always be some members more fortunate than others, gave new impetus to the idea of resurrection. The classical Marxist position on this issue traces it to the need to assure the less fortunate members of society that they would certainly have an opportunity to reclaim that from which they were alienated, given a learned inability to overcome alienation on earth in this life. On the other hand, resurrection was part and parcel of an enlarged conception of life: Questioning what a life was about, what a person was to be, became large and acutely present obsessions, obsessions to which the nomads had shown absolute indifference. The question of what one must accomplish in life gains an immense legitimacy as a question when, by positing in their faces differentiations they can see, a differentiated society offers its members the possibility of *comparison*. That is, the nomads realized their destitution not while they roamed the desert but, rather, when they came to a city and saw its relative fortune. Only then did they conceptualize the idea of destitution, and only then did they see themselves as the object of such a concept. The idea of resurrection postpones—practically and remorselessly—the need to recompense life for what the possibility of comparison had revealed as a deficiency in it. With the book religions, we have a material foundation for the idea of rectifying injustice: As earthly deprivation took place in a *social* context, so will the recompense after resurrection. Resurrection is not an individual privilege; the whole society is resurrected, but after resurrection each member will be assigned a completely different value than he or she held in earthly society.[30] Such a social and hierarchical notion of resurrection is one of the hallmarks of the book religions, fundamentally this-worldly and social as they were. By contrast, the pre-Islamic meditations of someone like Qass still presumed resurrection as a basically individual experience.

Other pre-Islamic "believers" possess what the tradition itself acknowledges as more prophetic qualities. Khalid Ibn Sinan, for instance, was reportedly called by Muhammad a "prophet lost by [the indifference of] his people." According to the sources, Khalid's daughter, who once encountered Muhammad as he was praying, commented that the words he used to assert that Allah is the only God were similar to those used by her late father.[31] Another such figure is Zaid Ibn ʿAmru, who is reported to have called on Qurayshans to follow him in adhering to the "faith of Abraham," which highlighted the idea of an active God. He is also said to have directly criticized the worship of the "harmless and helpless" idols, while finding both Christianity and Judaism to be inadequate alternatives.[32] Both, however, pointed him to the religion of Abraham, which in its undiluted, primordial form entailed the worship of nothing but Allah.

Muhammad, too, referred the vaguely defined religion of Abraham. This vagueness is part and parcel of the anticipation of the coming of a prophet, whose task would be to reestablish a forgotten tradition rather than to begin a new one. With such a remote background, the prophet to come could symbolize or effect a complete and irrevocable break with the present while at the same time basing such a break on the authority of an authentic past. At least one figure is reported to have refrained from believing in Muhammad out of envy, since he was hoping that he himself would be the anticipated prophet.[33] At least two other famous figures are reported to have adopted Christianity explicitly as a *transitional* belief, in anticipation of the coming of the "true" messenger.[34]

Such a state of affairs does not in itself necessarily make the task of the coming prophet any easier, since the empirical prophet, as Muhammad was to find out in both Mecca and Medina, will be evaluated against preordained and demanding, almost superhuman standards. Muhammad's early failure for Mecca, as will be discussed later, can be clearly attributed to this anticipation. But even for Medina, where his authority was considerably more established, the literature is replete with stories of dissension on both practical and ideological grounds. For example, one of the most important figures to oppose Muhammad in Medina, Abi 'Amer, did so because he believed that he was a truer follower of the faith of Abraham (*Din Ibrahim*) than Muhammad. This may indicate that for some, Hanifism may not even have needed a prophet, or at least not one who matched Muhammad's description, attitudes, and behavior.[35]

Others, however, like Waraqah Ibn Nawfal, anticipated the coming of the prophet based on their conviction that the Arabs had lost track of the religion of Abraham, which Muhammad was now thought to be in the process of rediscovering. As a Christian, Waraqah helped in part to formulate a link between Islam and the other book religions. According to him, Muhammad was indeed the prophet promised by Moses and Jesus. At a later stage, Muhammad was to vehemently capitalize on that point, for he envisioned Islam not only as a fraternal doctrine to the book religions but also as a logical conclusion to a divine plan of historically progressive revelations leading to the true faith.[36] Thus, such a conceptualization ascribed a unity to various traditions anchored upon the same divine source while sharply distinguishing it from the profane practice of paganism.

References to the omnipotence of Allah and his divine justice are likewise encountered throughout pre-Islamic literature, most notably in the legendarized odes of Zuhair Ibn Abi Sulma and 'Ubayd Ibn l-Abras,[37] often in ways connected to the idea of justice. Under the *badawah* lifestyle, rectifying injustice was an earthly matter with no metaphysical substitutes. A story depicting the increasing lack of certainty regarding this notion of justice as society underwent a transition from *badawah* to *hadarah* illustrates the point through the words of 'Abd l-Muttaleb, Muhammad's uncle. Among his memorable sayings was one affirming that no "unjust" man would pass away before being punished for his deeds. However, one day, so the story goes, an unjust man died without receiving due punishment. After contemplating the event, 'Abd l-Muttaleb concluded that there had to be another world beyond death, in which justice would finally be done.[38] The story is remarkably simple, but the fact that it had to be recorded—apart from the need to show the pious nature of the house of the prophet—illustrates a fundamental conceptual transition, here regarding the concept of justice per se rather than that of Allah. It is worth noting that 'Abd l-Muttaleb posits the otherworld as an undefined possibility, without explicitly structuring it around the idea of an abstract God.

When justice in the course of life becomes uncertain (that is, justice understood as a balance of rewards and punishments), the challenge is either to reformulate the concept of justice or to redefine the course of life within which justice is to be assured. The problem poses itself thus: One must choose either a concept of *life* as it has traditionally been understood (that is, as exclusively earthly), in which case one will have to accept the possibility of injustice, *or* a concept of *justice* as it has traditionally been understood, in which case one will have to rethink life's duration so that it includes a sphere within which justice is assured of a final triumph. When life is understood as a total record of a physical entity rather than as a set of haphazard diachronic fragments, it can scarcely be imagined without a posited value at its conclusion, without the possibility of a verdict on it as a totality, and thus without the possibility of *redemption*. Once conceived of as a totality, life cannot exist without the concept of justice.

For the concept of justice is the sum of all such conditions of existence, as a record being accumulated *for the purpose of making verdict possible.*

This idea of life as a totality divided between two worlds is fundamental to early Islam. In fact, the very word "Islam," according to one thesis, meant not only resignation or surrender (to Allah) as it is usually rendered but also "defiance of death."[39] In either case, the will to outlast death cannot be separated from life's transformed meaning under sedentarism, where it was coupled with a requisite of justice that could not be safely entrusted to the material horizons of life. In the pre-Islamic era, at least two figures exemplify best the multitude of ramifications stemming from such reconceptualizations of life, justice, and resurrection: 'Amer Ibn ad-Darb and Luqman al-Hakim, or Luqman the Wise.

'Amer Ibn ad-Darb thought of existence in terms of logical necessities of origin and destiny: "I never saw a thing which had created itself, neither an object which had not been created, nor an arrival [of someone who] did not depart. If people died of illness then they would have been resurrected by the cure." Resurrection, according to him, came about through the intervention of an exterior power, a power that must be capable of creation in the first place. The necessity of coming back to life (that is, *continuing* life) after death is deduced from the logic of creation itself: "The dead come back to life, and the Nothing comes back as a Thing, and therefore heavens and earth were created."[40] At first glance, there does not seem to be an obvious or causal relation between observing human inability to create nature and believing in resurrection. But if nature and time are posited as unattainable mysteries, and if social life is seen as only able to produce differentiations that allow self-definition via *comparison,* then one's identity will appear to be formed via an essential otherness.[41]

This account of an exterior source of self-identity revokes the possibility of thinking of creation in terms of autogenesis. One becomes an object under the control of a mysterious force that has become differently thinkable: One dies and fails to come back through human effort, such as by the administration of a cure. The power that controls such incomprehensible processes is set outside of the realm of the knowable and is gifted with capabilities unclaimable by the living. When it resurrects the dead, such a power thereby brings justice to life. Until then, one could comprehend such a power by assigning to it a range of capabilities that include hitherto present but unaccounted for accomplishments: It is capable of resurrecting the dead because it could create heaven and earth. In this assertion there already lurks the dogma of systemic totality, whereby natural appearances and moral and social life are no longer separable items of knowledge, in the manner of encyclopedic disjunction typical of the *mu'allaqat*. Rather, these items are causally connected through a grand source and purpose.

Another figure who illustrates a reconceptualization of life, justice, and resurrection is the famous sage Luqman the Wise, who was praised by Muhammad and who is legendarized in the Qur'an, to a degree that it alludes to his near prophethood. Commentators have noted that figures possessing the same attributes as Luqman are also known to have circulated in other ancient traditions—for instance, Ba'laam of the Old Testament or the Greek Aesop.[42] Like Luqman, Ba'laam is semiprophetic, with a problematic and uncertain relation to political authority. Whereas in such traditions those figures combined an aura of holiness with mischievous playfulness and earthly pleasures, thereby providing a truly resourceful and varied fountain of wisdom, the figure of Luqman as noted in the Islamic tradition is largely cleansed of any potentially sinful attributes. This reinterpretation of a folk character may indeed have been going on well before the introduction of Islam itself.

According to the lore, Luqman was "given a thousand chapters of wisdom, each of which was divided into a thousand sections, each of which was divided into a thousand branches, each of which comprised a thousand of the different types of knowledge."[43] His character encompasses a set of contradictions. First of all, he is at the same time the most holy and the most humble of men. Luqman "never slept during the day, and no one ever saw him spitting, urinating, defecating, bathing, playing, laughing ... and he was once married and children were born to him and they died, [but] he did not mourn their loss."[44] On the other hand, Luqman was at the same time a freed black slave (*mawla*), that is, he belonged to the very bottom of the social hierarchy. The tradition also states that his wisdom began to be apparent while he was still a slave, that it was divinely endowed, that he continued to live a humble life after his freedom was granted, and that he was a contemporary of David. In fact, together with David he forms an illustrative dichotomy that furnishes Luqman's credentials and illuminates his distinction.

God needed an earthly governor to adjudicate between the people (that is, a governor *and* a judge). While Luqman seemed at first to be the most likely candidate, he knew that governing *of necessity* entailed the likelihood of injustice. Such an early sign of remarkable wisdom spared Luqman the agony of error-prone governance, a task that was assumed by David instead.[45] First of all, God intervenes in the world not directly but, rather, by asking for assistance in adjudicating among the people on earth. The contrast between Luqman and David illustrates a significant point, namely, that governing and arbitrating justice are not necessarily the same thing, that in fact, they may be *contradictory* tasks.

In Bedouin society, the chief of the tribe was little more than a judge-like figure. This tradition apparently informs Luqman's stance, which in five steps expresses the inadequacy of a governing role for humans: First, a dichotomy of opposites between judging and governing is established. Second, Luqman the Wise, who is humble and close to earth, as opposed to David, who is a prophet and close to God, notices that to be a judge in the age of the activist God—and moreover to be able to do so because of God's power—means also to assume the still undesirable role of coercive governor. Third, as a consequence, Luqman declines the judgeship not because it is needless but because it has become contaminated with the necessity of governing. He takes wisdom instead of either, and continues his individual existence on the sidelines of the new state of affairs. Fourth, David, who took up the divine offer, shows human failings in the task and a propensity to sin. In the last step, when it is too late to rectify the damage, David is reduced to envying Luqman's happy freedom from the sin-borne instruments concomitant with ruling.[46]

In this way, wisdom and knowledge are not only set apart from governorship but are opposed to it in the terms of outcome. In one sense, this stance expresses a resistance to the replacement of traditional regulatory bonds through the introduction of political hierarchy. David necessarily goes astray precisely because of the contradiction between the nature of his role and the nature of the social life over which he is ruling. With his infinite, legendary wisdom, Luqman wanders like any other ancient Bedouin, free from ruling and being ruled, disdaining both situations. On the other hand, David, as a God-sent and God-aided prophet, ceases wandering and halts to dedicate at least one-third of his days to governing and adjudicating conflicts.[47] Thus only God can change immemorial norms regarding the idea of governing, especially when governing is posited as a source of justice rather than as a pure exercise of power. But as soon as God commences the project through David, an opposite, earthly character makes his presence known, a character who is legitimated precisely by having been asked to do the scornful task *before* the prophet was summoned. Eventually, the faltering prophet comes to wish to trade places with him. David's weaknesses are thus exposed by virtue of his contrast to an outcast, *not* through a direct confrontation with the society he is ruling. Society itself is not directly challenging God's decree and prophet. Rather, it is a symbol on its periphery that effortlessly discredits the new order and, without acrimony or rebellion, highlights the virtues of the time-honored abstention from the stakes involved.

The selection of an ex-slave to reveal David's shortcomings addresses an important contradiction. At one level, Luqman's actual socioeconomic position at the bottom of the social hierarchy is compensated for by his unreachable spiritual status. Such a plot restores equality to a society that had only recently begun to experience the phenomenon of stable, visible political and economic hierarchies. It also points out that a less-stratified past was still within the purview of a society, as it witnessed the construction of material and spiritual institutions for its reproduction as a differentiated entity. In this respect, David and Luqman can be regarded as merely one set of a potential sphere of symbols,[48] symbols that not only stand for a transitional phase but also express an *awareness* of this fact through the continued survival of a vantage point to the past.

In the *mu'allaqat*, the relation to political hierarchies becomes more prevalent the closer the poet is to sedentary or dynastic settings, and thus closer to the Islamic era, to which the recorded Luqman shows at least some exposure. An-Nabigha, for instance, while duly standing at the ruins as he opens his ode, clearly shows no desire to mourn too much and is in fact eager to depart shortly thereafter. After showing the perils of life in the desert, the poet calls his she-camel out of its metaphorical hiding place, whence the animal is instructed to take the poet home at once: "And through her I am told of an-Nu'man's favors, / bestrewed as they are among the near of the people, and the far" (c. 20). An-Nu'man is the source of this speaker's wealth, including perhaps this she-camel, his well-being, his distance from nomadism. From an-Nu'man's court the poet was expelled, and to that institution he endeavors to return on the strength of an extended apology, whose delivery seems to motivate the very composition of an ode here.

The following line in the ode, thus, adds an equally empty praise for the sovereign. Afterward, an-Nu'man mercifully disappears, leaving the scene for two extremely interesting metaphors, two legendary folk figures who, much like Luqman, are extracted from circulating folk mythology: Solomon and Zarqa' l-Yamama. Yet unlike in the contrast between Luqman and David, it is Solomon's virtues that are illustrated through being contrasted to Zarqa' l-Yamama, rather than his earthly shortcomings. The sovereign, through his immediate presence, could solicit no more than an obviously flat praise, and when he is addressed directly once more in the ode—starting at couplet 32—he is clearly no more than a source of a wealth to be apportioned among loyalists. By himself and without moral support from historical and traditional metaphors, the sovereign has no other virtues. His moral meaning must be found in and connected to the parables of the past in which the duties of his office can be imagined. It is interesting, therefore, that the poet constructs his metaphors at the moment when he seems to suspect a lack. The image of sovereignty is buttressed by symbolization. But the relative dearth of authenticity means that it is the *symbol* that will assume a reality of its own upon usage.

Taken together, Solomon and Zarqa' l-Yamama here illustrate the combination of governance, wisdom, and knowledge, spheres that the Luqman-David contrast had separated. In the ode of an-Nabigha, Solomon is explicitly introduced (c. 22 and after) in order to illustrate the unmatchable (yet inexplicit) feats of an-Nu'man. The transition is couched by the statement that none among the living matches (in favor or in "doing") the sovereign, "except" for Solomon (thence commences Solomon's story). This exception is, in essence, the whole story; it is the exemption of Solomon from incomparability that allows the goodness of the existing sovereign to appear to be universal. An impossibly broad virtue is demonstrated by an extension of the tale of the existing sovereign to cover what is allowed through exemption to reside outside of it. On the other hand—and this is what allows this exemption itself, disarmed as it is of the flagrancy of offense—the exception concerns an ancient figure of recognized sovereignty, whereby sovereignty is not seen (through the eyes of a Luqman, for instance) as a potentially malevolent novelty but, instead, appears as a "tradition" in the land, simply reawakened and invested in a new claimant.

This method of structuring discourse, it must be added, bears a strong resemblance to the early Qur'an, where "forgotten" traditions are awakened and claimed to be the basis of the new faith. And as in the case of Islam, since such traditions are assumed to be generally "known," they furnish a residual justification of the status quo (sovereignty and hierarchy in this case) that the present has failed to complete on its own. Thus the story of Solomon, hurriedly assembled under the pretext of telling of an "exceptionalism" (that is, complementarity), seeks at the same time to obviate the profound moral void of meaning from which a present sovereignty suffers, a void that could inadvertently be exposed by an unanchored, general praise.

In a scene reminiscent of traditional poetic openings, Solomon, a majesty from times past, enters the ode standing in the face of the open nature (*barriyyah*), commanded by God to cause it to desist from error (*fanad*). His first observation, however, is not of a ruined site of past harmony and togetherness but of an exactly opposite and *future*-oriented activity: Solomon detects the first signs of *permanent* sedentarism in the ongoing activity of the jinn who, by Allah's leave, are busy building him a *city*. Thereafter he receives rightly guided subjects (rightly guided being *both* their virtue and their reward for having that virtue: the closed circuit of virtue). Those subjects, in turn, are *not* equal. Solomon here is further instructed that he has no need to curtail invectives (*damad*) except toward those who are "equal" to him or "slightly" inferior (c. 26); thus the notion of an "elite" and special subject, to whom regular rules do not apply, and whose relation to the sovereign is to remain, therefore, more structured by favors than by abstract ethical strictures.

These highlights are all that is told of Solomon's state. A state here is viewed as a stable order of domination, with vague (a weak deity's instruction) or inexpressible ground of normativity. The need of such an order of governance for obedience confronts all subjects with the choice of either accepting or refusing. Negotiating a third way is allowed only to those "equal" or "slightly" inferior to the sovereign himself. That is all that this nomad could say about the state. Yet in the history of the nomad, that was indeed a novel proposition. Suddenly there was an external political entity standing there and demanding that the wanderer halt long enough to give an answer to the question of the nature of the wanderer's relation to it—a relationship that was now to have more meaning than being a sheer accident of inhabiting its jurisdiction. Such an answer was essential for the state's conduct of its business. The answerability was fundamental, for it was to show Solomon how to undertake the task with which he alone was entrusted. God had delivered a general commandment and then quickly vanished, as was his habit in those amorphous pre-Islamic times. He had made a simple designation, delivered an impossibly general instruction, and personified its act of interpretation, and he had said no more. All subsequent decipherments of the divine message were left for Solomon to ponder. So Solomon constructed his knowledge here according to the hints, models, and parallels he was allowed to discern. God had instructed him to ban evil in this God-forsaken country and, while withdrawing, had left a little instrumental hint: The city and its builders were all Solomon's.

So Solomon had an army, a city, a divine commandment, and a responsibility to interpret it. The interlocution of the last two items, especially, anticipates a movement beyond the city, for the city itself is introduced neither for its own sake nor as a self-contained locus of authority, but as the condition of actualizing the statement. The divine command applies not only to the city, where it first begins to be put into effect, but also to the vast nature outside—the *barriyyah,* to which it is contrasted and upon which it finds itself sprouting like a wild flower carving for itself a lonesome way of being. And it seems to itself, as it stands out, that to be a city means to uninterruptedly observe the *barriyyah* outside, that imposing silence of the noncity, congesting the distance from that point to the horizons in all directions.

Solomon's knowledge is possible because he can be trusted to interpret the founding statement of the city. The holder of such a trust is, in turn, a ruler of the city, in essence, its only possible ruler. His capacity to interpret, which the tradition elsewhere invests in Luqman, is thus indistinguishable from his capacity to demonstrate the interpreted knowledge, which elsewhere was David's domain of operation. But since life in the city, unlike the *badawah* lifestyle, cannot be based on a sequence of discrete and nonadditive moments, Solomon must *continually* demonstrate the interpretation. This, in turn, requires the validation of the statement through action. The originality of this modus operandi can best be appreciated if one compares it to similarly expansive projects at governance within nomadism proper, such as in the case of Kinda. The fundamentally fleeting, intermittent nature of such governance is evident throughout

nomadic societies down to modern times.[49] By contrast, the model offered here, half sedentary and half mythological, is based on continual re-
generation of legitimate outcome as the condition of stability of an original, founding statement or principle. Such a structure for knowledge is
the basis of authority, and conversely, authority is its basis.

We see here, then, the emergence of a protected reciprocity between a
generally expressed statement and an interpretive capacity of sovereign
authority. The reciprocity is also guarded through the simple duality of
reward and punishment, which seems to suffice for a while. A general notion of ethics to ontologize the sovereign beyond such a duality was a site
of much contention, of which our poet here seems to know little. Such an
ethic was to be a later addition, with basis and models in versions of the
idea of prophethood, legitimate succession, and exegesis of holy words. It
had to wait until that nomad could halt long enough to construct from
the certainty of the state, the irremovability of this imposing transtribal
order of abstract sovereignty, a certain notion of ethics. At its point of
origination, the city itself knows about itself little more than an association of postsubsistence abundance with residence.

The absence of an elaborate notion of ethics notwithstanding, there is
a certain virtue of right-guidedness (c. 24: *rushd*), which is equally inelabo-
rate and unclassified. It is Solomon's responsibility to assure its exercise.
Yet to be expounded in coded forms, it constitutes nonetheless an objective of a recent state. Ethical normativity in the realm of the state is here
defined by the sovereign for the benefit of the contending, obedient subject. Naturally, one should not expect the narrator, himself accustomed to
the sedentary state as more of a source of bestowals than of ethical codes,
to know more, or to provide more, or even to be willing to talk of this
strange topic. Yet there was another item of state that he must have noticed clearly: that states are always engaged in violence, that they fight
other states, that their wars—his own patrons themselves waging wars as
clients of imperial states—could be very large compared to the customary
nomadic raids, and that, occasionally, the ruler must lay more modest
claims toward a sovereign who is or who is suspected to be an equal than
toward his subjects, who by nature must obey.

The last couplet in the Solomon sequence registers this fact of state affairs, not a happy note to the mentor, a bit mischievous, but nonetheless
more known to the poet than the details of the normative code, which

were yet to be laid down, standardized, or deciphered. This poet, standing at the beginning of history, could discern a crude and naked power game. His decision to confront the problematic with cynicism comes out glaringly in couplets 32 to 36: successive, fragmentary, disconnected images of wealth, the easy life, and all the potential offerings to a loyal subject by the state. That is all that the state means to him. Yet his is the kind of decision that, unlike a puritan attitude, could take note of a discontinuity between the "original intention" behind the state (for example, God's statement) and what emerges at a later stage as consequences to the self from the state's coming into being. *A commandment to intervene in the world in order to stop the potential malevolence of untamed nature ushers in a structure of power, which could act only under the dictates of self-preservation.* There is no necessary continuity between the two sets of concerns, and it is this middle region of doubt between the two at which the cynical option offers itself as a response modality for those unprepared to endure the rigor of the wilderness outside.

The other set of images through which the image of sovereignty is consolidated in an-Nabigha's ode concerns the legendary Zarqa' l-Yamama, fabled for a miraculous power of sight. She could see, so the legend goes, for a distance of several days. There is a short interval between Solomon's story and hers, an interval that an-Nabigha uses to remind the audience that he is still addressing the existing sovereign (c. 27: ". . . and rule like the girl of the clan . . ."). Thus, what follows is to continue the instruction on the rules of ruling, adding what Solomon did not provide, perhaps another "exception." The sagaciousness of Zarqa' infuses the idea of "ruling" with a possibility of knowing the future. To see in the distance is also to see through time, to see who or what is coming toward the observer. The future is a spatial dimension, for the nomad has no purely temporal sense of time: Time is simply that which is required to cross a distance. It has no independent self-confirmation. The future is thus known simply by looking. To have a powerful, discerning eye is thus an essential ground for a claim to knowledge. And thus the myth of Zarqa' l-Yamama epitomizes the possibility of knowing that which time shall in its own course reveal. The common, ordinary kinfolk (*hayy*) are the ones who shall live to confirm the truthfulness of her prediction, and their confirmation, in turn, becomes the ground of the authenticity of her vision.

On the other hand, in the age of the visionary, secure knowledge could reside beyond simple immediacy: It could now be the property of those who are naturally more endowed with a power to discern a truth that shall become. This becomes, then, one of the forms of knowledge that the state is expected by definition to possess: to be able to see from above, to be capable of forewarning and of being forewarned as well. The inexplicable sagaciousness of the state lavishes a spiritual aura upon its hitherto naked presence as power. Its phenomenal certainty consists no longer of the menacing, detached presence of a sovereign, city, or army. Just as is God's statement, this knowledge is also entrusted to the sovereign. The state, therefore, becomes a form of certainty predicated upon the dual aspect of knowing: interpreting the already delivered statement of the hidden sovereign (God) and delivering a new statement on the otherwise hidden knowledge by the existing sovereign. In other words, the meaning of the state consists in bringing into presence that which must otherwise remain nonimmediate and that, if it so remains, would be destined to perish on account of its uncertainty, undecidability, and uselessness.

It is to this towering structure that our an-Nabigha finally comes to ask forgiveness and seek readmittance. He is fearful of the natural world outside. The poet of the city is accustomed only to an approving audience and its possible generosity. Once that home is taken away, he discovers that the loss of the fluidity of nomadic lack of concern for regularities of sedentary structures and hierarchies is irreversible. Sedentarism itself is also irreversible. Such a state of affairs heralds some major aspects of post-Islamic poetry to come: precisely topical; less encyclopedic; more attentive to conflicting, constricting, and solicitous institutions of power and counterpower. In this particular case, the dilemma is clearly spelled out in what immediately follows the image of a windswept Euphrates in which the navigator must continue to hold on to the shipwreck, despite a corrosive exhaustion, lest he collapse into the river:

> A better day, when the bestowals flow:
> may today's giving not forbid tomorrow's. (c. 46)

The giving, thus, assumes the same nature of the antecedent nomadic path: not a one-time experience but a continually renewable tradition, a new way of life paralleling the same continuity the path had once promised. This city is continually contrasted to the stormy nature of outsidedness, no longer to be desired. Nothing, in fact, outside of the city is desired any longer: At the very end of the ode, the poet throws it at the gate as a price for entrance:

> Such is my atonement; may it find a course,
> for its composer has gone astray in the country. (c. 50)

By contrast, Luqman, while rejecting the role of governing and retaining his distance from city gates, expresses his wisdom through a more morally established and universal channel of authority. The bulk of Luqman's wisdom is preserved in the form of advices and instructions given to his son (in a manner remarkably reminiscent of the Old Testament's Book of Proverbs). The communication is unidirectional, as the opinions, questions, and responses of the son are never mentioned. This style was in harmony with a tradition that deposited the most normative hierarchy in the father-son relationship rather than in the sovereign-subject channel, which was more visible to a poet like an-Nabigha. The parental line offered an enormously valuable channel for transmitting ideals, old and new, since coercion was neither required nor expected—a rather profound concern for a society lacking in a centralized means of coercion.

Luqman imparts many truths to his son, truths encompassing ethics and the nature of things. Those aspects of Luqman's transmitted wisdom preserved in the tradition are significant not because of their "authenticity" but because they tell us a great deal more about the Islamic paradigm (and its earlier roots in some aspects of pre-Islamic culture) within which they were compiled than about any actual historical figure. Thus, one might find it interesting that the father, the hitherto uncontested source of control, himself broadens the potential domain of social forces capable of directing and conditioning the behavior of the son: "Son, attend [the councils of] the wise men and strive for a place [in them]. Do not argue with them so that they would not deprive you of their sayings, ease the question on them if they allow you [to ask], and do not complicate [things] so that they would not be burdened by you."[50] Such a vague council of the wise ones was to find a concrete expression in, among other places, the sedentary hierarchy. Although the merchants who controlled pre-Islamic Mecca did not precisely conform to the esteemed ideals expressed by Luqman, his teachings did at least point the way to a nascent social hierarchy whose features might not have been predictable but which was certain to include more than just the father. The most prosperous Meccan traders, for instance, could, by assigning to themselves specific *haram* service obligations, occupy a position within a *spiritual* hierarchy as well, which was recognized by Qurayshans from *various* lines of descent.

Luqman's concept of hierarchy, however, was far from being specific on details, conditions, or instances. The only criterion for the validity of a hierarchy here consists of it being a depository of "knowledge," whose acquisition is stressed by the father without qualification; the son has to fight for a place in the councils of the more knowledgeable men, since it is a virtue in itself to be with them; and then he will only be a listener rather than a full participant in the manner of the Bedouin tribal councils. Thus Luqman signifies, among other things, a transformation of the practice of hierarchy, whereby the "son" has to make a continuous effort not to burden authority by his very presence. He has to find a way to incorporate himself into a certain type of social hierarchy, which he could expect to demand proof of grateful submission.

The addition of the wise men, as an intellectual foundation, to the legitimate chain of control is augmented by an instruction on the virtues of submission to *political* power as well: "Son, if you sat down with a man of power, let there be between you and him a man's sitting space, so that you would not be belittled and humiliated by him asking you to give up your place for a visitor who is more valued by him than you are."[51] As he surrenders in the face of *knowledge,* the son must now show a similar respect to *power.* Whereas the men of knowledge are beyond reach and could not in any case be burdened, the men of power could in principle be reached, but the son is advised to keep his distance. For the harm they can do, which defines them as men of power in the first place, stems not so much from their crude prowess as from their ability to *value.*

The ability to value is no longer seen to be rooted in an arbitrary will, which, because arbitrary, could be disregarded. Rather, it is the property of a power that is capable of detecting an *actual* value in nature and then displaying it in view of all with eyes to see. The council giving audience to this power must believe the truthfulness of this value judgment, since it is the raison d'être of power to discover value and to present it as unquestionable. The distance of this attitude from the Bedouin ethical realm can best be comprehended by contrasting it with some of the values permeating the ode of 'Amru Ibn Kalthum. Though himself a man of power,

'Amru's fiery speech seethes with indignation at the ill-advised attempt by an ostensible superior to impose a less-than-equal status on 'Amru's tribe. The legend, in fact, asserts that the poet produced his ode immediately after having slain the said adversary in his outrage.

While expanding on the sources of social control, Luqman does not forget to accentuate his own position, emphasizing the need to please and obey one's parents, which was an aspect of Luqman's wisdom that the Qur'an clearly registered and approved.[52] Right in the midst of a dense pedagogy, the father reasserts his own right to continue to deliver it, but not because of any normative expectation of obedience to the father. The source of Luqman's own authority now is God, the ostensible *source* of his wisdom, which in this case becomes the *outcome* of his wisdom as well. That is to say, since the pedagogy that the son is being exposed to is recognized to be fundamentally beyond the norms of the tradition, the traditional instructor can no longer instruct solely in his traditional capacity as a father.

After all of this intensive, mystified hierarchy places its weight upon the son, he becomes prepared to swallow the grand conceptions of life and world that will follow. The centerpiece of the new worldview is the dichotomy of life and afterlife. Luqman himself had declined the caliphate for fear that it entailed a potential loss of favor in this world or the other.[53] That is, he recognized that potential sin was associated with governing, as well as with all material yearnings. Doing harm to others through governing them, invariably becoming unjust in the process, and *having to* restrict their original freedoms, are plainly constructed as *social* sources of sin. But it is significant that the concept of sin operates in the exact opposite order when it comes to *individual* life: Here, one must place one's own individual world under strict control so as to avoid falling into sin. Mere entanglement with earthly enjoyments of life leads only to illusions and potential losses afterward: "Son, attend funerals and not weddings, for funerals remind you of the other world while weddings awaken your desire in this world."[54] The Qur'an clearly endorses such teachings, highlighting Luqman's instructions to his son to bear misfortune with fortitude, to be humble, to lower his voice, and to walk upon the earth without showing excessive, undue pride.[55]

Though loathsome, the quest to survive the mortal conditions of life is portrayed as leading people to endure the pain of authority, hierarchy, valuation by power, and the new forms of self-control for the moment. The futility of those schemes is illustrated in two simple steps: First, it is argued that all humans seek immortality. Then, a myriad of mythico-historical records are marshaled to prove the impossibility of attaining such a dear aspiration. Immortality, thus, is possible only as a gift from an exterior, invisible, and extraordinarily powerful source. The Bedouin son is presented with a problem, which he had probably never thought of as such before, only to be made aware of his own weakness and need for help in order to overcome it. This idea is sometimes emphasized by presenting Luqman himself as an example. When Allah offered him anything he wanted, with the exception of immortality, Luqman chose longevity, the closest possible alternative. Allah then gave him the age of seven eagles. Luqman attempted the impossible, trying to outlast this time limit; he chose the strongest eagles at their hatching and associated one of the seven given lives with each. Ending with the seventh, he chose the strongest eagle he could find on earth, to whom he gave the name Labad (eternity). But Labad eventually died, and so did Luqman.[56]

In this parable the deity is introduced neither as a sporadic entity nor as a strictly transcendental entity but, rather, as a source of action on daily concerns and operations in which harm and help are possible and frequently encountered. Luqman's passive philosophy avoided the *harmful* aspect of God, leaving that task to Islam at a later stage; Luqman's God could only reward, and then not with respect to one's earthly work but only in a possible, misty world beyond. Here, a divine figure of immense power makes its presence more frequent in a materialist society with little concern for the otherworld. The materialist conception of the world so abundantly encountered in Bedouin thought, wisdom, and poetry rejected the idea of resurrection or, at best, conceived of it as a pseudonym for a questionable search after immortality. To appreciate either concept in transcendental terms, they had to accept the idea that such concepts were not invalid just because human effort was inadequate to attain them. Because such concepts were valued despite their transcendence of human limitations, a provision was made for divine work. Thereby, God's work consisted not only in the production of the promise but, moreover, in furnishing further evidence of human incapacities, the increasing awareness of which had allowed for God's introduction in the first place.

Luqman's wisdom is not confined to the questions addressed here, as it also covers—through sayings and parables—issues of everyday manners and ethics. In a sense, it may be compared to the codes of ethics encountered in the odes, especially Zuhair's. It represents yet another significant source of common ethics, referenced to a transtribally relevant, distant, but familiar and earthly author. This structure partially anticipates grand organizing principles and partially retains and inflates a preexisting but vague idea of God. Thus, though Luqman was one of the more nomadic sources of inspiration for Islam, he remained much more limited in scope than what was being called for by the dictates of sedentarism, a trade economy, and the fragility of the encompassing order in Muhammad's era. For a while, at least, and in certain quarters, these scattered fragments of variably effective instructions for individual life seemed to suffice. A reported encounter between Muhammad and a prospective convert hints at the perceived nature of the relationship between the two sets of doctrines, obviously regarded by Muhammad in evolutionary terms. The man wondered whether Muhammad's doctrines resembled the doctrines to which he himself subscribed, which in the process were revealed as consisting of Luqman's sayings. Thereupon, Muhammad commented: "Those are good sayings, but what I have is better. It is a Qur'an revealed to me by God almighty."[57]

five

The Discourse and the Path

Do you not see how God compares a good word to a good tree? Its roots are firm and its branches are in the sky.

—*Qur'an 14: 26*

'Ilm al-Kalam, or scholasticism (literarily, "the science of speech") was one of the most foundational components of early Islamic philosophy, as it began to take form a little less than a century after the death of the prophet.[1] The centrality of language analysis to many Islamic systems of thought is one of the most striking historical features of the intellectual offshoots of the faith. A leading commentator has expressed bewilderment, in the context of contemporary debates in literary theory, at how little is known of the fact that many of the contours of the lines of thought regarding language and representation under discussion today can already be discerned in debates surrounding Qur'anic exegesis some ten centuries ago.[2]

There is little question that the relationship between language, representation, and truth has been a central and recurrent feature of Islamic civilization since its inception. A common argument—which for Muslims became one ground for the miraculous nature of the revelation—was that the literary plain through which the Qur'an expressed itself emanated from a temporal context prefigured by the experience of poetry, which then highlighted the idea of the *form* of speaking as a venue of truth. For Muslims, the literary superiority of the Qur'an to the odes itself proved its

115

unmatchability by human means (*i'jaz*). In other words, for the Arabs to whom Islam was first disclosed, the field of language was itself the field of the miracle, in the same way that, as some classical commentators have noted, medicine was the field of the miracle in the age of Jesus, who had to prove his credentials by miraculous healing, or magic was in the age of Moses, who likewise had to prove his credentials through that venue of truth production.[3] In one of the few contemporary studies to revisit such a notion of discursive centrality to Islamic thought, Nasr Hamed Abu Zaid seems to endorse this same ancient point of view by asserting that the Islamic civilization can be regarded primarily as a "civilization of the text."[4]

In some classical as well as much of contemporary orientalist scholarship, examining a language-oriented civilizational frame has entailed following a rather narrow path of meticulous but largely inert philological deductions, in a way that obscured the philosophical and sociohistorical complexities surrounding discourse production. With rare exceptions, the field has remained largely closed to the contemporary advances in the philosophy and cultural studies of discourse production that have benefited so many other fields of inquiry. There are a few exceptions, such as Mohammed Arkoun, who argues for a multilevel approach to the Qur'an, more richly embedded in contemporary philosophical and anthropological debates. The three approaches selected by Arkoun for illustration include a linguistic one, where emphasis is placed on detecting deep, orderly structures; an anthropological approach, which would be oriented toward a different level of structure, namely, the mythological one; and a historical approach, which would be oriented toward and advised by the philosophy of history as it pertains to this field, already referenced by the traditional genre of *asbab an-nuzul* (grounds of Revelation).[5]

The examination of the full scope of this langauge-oriented focus within Islamic culture and philosophy is well beyond the limited scope of this chapter. Rather, the emphasis here will be confined to the foundational period, and more specifically I will focus on some important transformations in representation between *jahili* (pre-Islamic) and Qur'anic forms, especially in the context of the odes. The exposition cannot, needless to say, be exhaustive, but I hope that it will illustrate some major ideological and expressive attitudes toward being, representation, and the recording of items of value, particuarly as they relate to sociological shifts in lifestyle and mentalities.

In both the Qur'an and poetic speech, the *form* of expression assumes paramount importance, since it first indicates the classification of the speech. It was after that primary classification that the "substance" of the speech could then be introduced. It is such a form that, for instance, allows an ode like that of al-Harith to be counted among the great odes. If the traditional opening (c. 1–14) were removed from the body of the poem, for instance, al-Harith's production would appear to be a rhymed political speech (*khutba musajja'ah*) rather than a poem with some level of autonomy from the immediate concerns of a mortal society. Apart from the opening, everything else in the piece has a clear political character, refers to particular events, clarifies the position of the tribe in each case, and appeals to the wise judgment of the king of al-Hira, in whose court the ode is said to have been delivered. Except for the traditional opening, all else has an instrumental communicative purpose and is delivered to an audience that is expected to *act* upon this delivered knowledge, on behalf of another audience that is to be redressed by its effects. Such is not, needless to say, necessarily a "misuse" of or a "betrayal" to an eloquent form of discourse. (After all, al-Harith's mission was to rescue his tribe from the erratic whims of a dangerous king.) Given the stakes involved, there follows the temptation to protect the story and point of view of the tribe with the relative security of a highly regarded form, and in some cases, such as this one, to adhere to such a form in an excessively orthodox fashion. Two observations follow in this regard.

1. By the time of al-Harith, poetry had already been granted a superior capacity to render truthful accounts, natural orders, and stable conditions, to an authority or an audience. In other words, a distinct discourse was elevated from being a deviant act warranting expulsion from the tribe into a result-oriented, solid fountain for sociopolitical communication, ideals, and ideas.

2. That tradition, in turn, was founded upon a formal discursive stability. The opening of the speech became the location at which the specific type

of discourse was determined. In other words, the *opening formula* directly defined the nature of the piece to follow, hinted at its reference point in terms of tribal politics, served to adjust listening faculties to a diversity of possible themes, and also established the credentials of the work as another component of an emerging "canon." The typification of speaking was determined in terms of how it began rather than in terms of how the speech unfolded, its substantive themes, or how it tied such themes together. The ending in all of the *mu'allaqat* (odes) is unimportant, inconclusive, a mere continuation of the theme that happened to be circulating at that point of poetic flight. It was usually a moment of sudden, unexpected landing. The poem itself did not attempt to tie its themes together. Thus, the only point at which a determination as to the collective nature of the speech could occur was at the beginning. What was important, however, was what followed the opening: Once the speech was classified as such, the audience gathered itself to hear that which had been designated as poetry. After the classification of the speech as poetry, the audience became absorbed in a different dimension, launched by a pronouncement for, of, or about *halting* with which the ode invariably began. Thus, what seems to us to be enormous disjunctions within each ode could seem to be perfectly smooth terrain when heard under the tutelage of a different aura of listening. The smoothness of such a terrain is determined not by a continuity of empirical experience but by a *primal* act of "standing." It was at the moment of halting that all determinations of the general nature of the path to follow were made.

The Qur'anic *surah* (chapter) also exhibits an obsession with *indicative* form. The challenge for the Qur'an was to find an appropriate form, one that would indicate divine as opposed to poetic speech. The resort to *saja'* (rhymed speech) in the Qur'an of early Mecca partially accomplished that distinction. But *saja'* itself had already been in circulation as a form long before Muhammad; it generally distinguished the *kahin* (soothsayer), who had jurisdiction over mysticism, prophesying, and sagehood, from the poet. As will be discussed in Chapter 7, many Qurayshans also thought that Muhammad could be described to the Arab pilgrims in Mecca as either a *kahin* or a magician—and less convincingly as a poet— exclusively on the grounds of the nature of his *sayings*. A leading commentator argues that since it was generally accepted that *saja'* and poetry could be inspired by the jinn or other spiritual forces, it was not so much the *form* of Muhammad's revelation that was a source of contestation as it was his claim to a *unique entitlement* to communication with a hidden source of the sayings.[6]

Thus, when Quraysh resolved to explain Muhammad's phenomenon to the outside world in terms of magic, the emphasis was not on the formal aspects of his sayings but, rather, on the socially disharmonious *consequence* of those sayings, which for them served to dissolve normatively indivisible social bonds. While the *form* proper could be mobilized within already existent norms, worldviews, and ideologies—as the case of al-Harith's ode clearly illustrates—it was the employment of the form in a process of codification that entailed social and moral consequences. Through codification, the amorphousness of available knowledge is structured so as to become efficiently retrievable. The code of ethics discussed in the ode of Zuhair, for instance, shows that it was possible for disparate, sometimes contradictory behaviors to stand together as the building blocks of a coherent corpus, since they were spelled out in a single formulaic sequence. The idea of the Qur'an as the final book into which such codes were deposited in revised and refined ways, and according to a systemic order, may not have been conceived from the outset. While the idea of "the book" can be partially traced to the circulating model of *ahl al-kitab* (Jews and Christians), it can also be shown to be rooted in the phenomenon of codifying the world through words, as the experience of poetry illustrates.

The ancient Arabs saw themselves living within a massive profusion of words, with the camel and the sword each claiming a thousand different names, the lion enjoying two hundred, and many other facets of life being expressible through dozens or hundreds of words as well. This phenomenon evidently furnishes some of poetry's arsenal. In al-A'sha's ode, for instance, we are told that he was followed by a *"shawen mishallen shalulon* [or *nashulun*] *shulshulon shawelu* [or *shamilu*]."* The exact meanings of all the words do not concern us here, but it is important to note this construction, for the words are obviously arranged in order to produce the effect of a tongue twister. Yet although this may seem to be the "authorial intent," we need only look at the classical commentaries to find that philologists could easily find enough meanings for each of those words to allow them to make sense when placed together. It was as though the poets became possible simply because of this dense air of words surrounding them, so many words competing with each other for the privilege of designating the same object.

Thus the ease of the flow of poetry was supplied from an inexhaustible reservoir of words. Between the poet and the object, there stood a congested traffic of words, each carving for itself a territory from the life of the object. The limitless supply of words could thus destructure all totalities in the world to their smallest constitutent components and isolate their most specific manners of movement, stability, or relation. It was a condition of life in which words, as products of the conditions of wandering, were so unleashed as to form layers of signs upon all externalities, and even upon each other. As such, they confirmed their power to bring externalities closer to consciousness and claim them in the words, while at the same time infusing empowerment projects with the vigor of this language. That was the lesson that was soon to be fully appreciated by textual Islamic religion, as it firmly grounded itself upon a second order of systematic assemblage beyond the ode, namely, that of the "book."

It is in this light that the book can be understood, namely, as a second order of abstraction, when linguistic *forms* are made into *codes,* when such codes are referenced with respect to an authority beyond the world itself, and when, in a tautological fashion, such an authority is premised again on the claimed uniqueness of the linguistic form by which it is expressed. In this regard, one can suggest that whereas the Meccan Qur'an was infused with formulaic structures that served largely indicative functions, the Medinian Qur'an displayed a transition into a language of codifications, which served as grounds for advising action in the world.

First, the importance of organizing words as indicative, primary signs is incorporated into the story of creation, where Adam's first task in heaven is to prove his knowledge to suspicious—and hitherto ignorant—angels by telling them the *names* of all things, as taught to him by Allah. This vast knowledge that Adam acquires and transmits anchors the entire project of book-oriented codification and encompasses the entirety of life and nature ("[And] He taught Adam the names of all things and set them before the angels, saying: 'Tell me the names of these.'").[7] Thus, the credentials of the encyclopedic project of codification and interconnected signification are premised first and foremost on the singularity of the source of their *names,* which allows them to be discerned as distinct objects. At another level, the project of the book is also premised on the impossibility of its accomplishment by existing frames of knowledge, demonstrated by the ignorance of the angels (whose existence, in a parallel fashion, *predates* Adam's).

Words, though connected to knowledge retrieval in the fashion indicated above, also serve in this context to differentiate human and divine knowledge. The mystical, uninterpretable sequence of letters commencing some *surahs*, though relatively few, were objects of a disproportionate effort at decipherment and were obviously seen as encapsulating an unimaginable amount of knowledge in single, scattered utterances. Significantly, Muhammad himself made little effort to bring forth their meaning, since they were seen to offer only a glimpse of a higher and humanly unreachable form of relations between language and signifieds. The prophet was thus strangely silent on reported numerological interpretations by some Jews of such letter sequences, which for them signified the number of years that Islam would predominate.[8]

Regardless of the specificity, historicity, and impact of floating interpretations, the most significant aspect of such words was the prophetic and divine silence surrounding their possible referent in the world, or beyond. It was a silence that confirmed the connection between the word and the knowledge presumed to hide within it, yet in exactly the opposite manner in which Adam's recitation of names disclosed the nature of the world as being made up of distinct objects and, hence, distinct missions. With the mystical sequence of letters, a code locks in a congested site an incomprehensible cosmic order or an eternal sequence of events. And in doing so, this impenetrable code conceals an unknown magnitude of knowledge in an indeterminate realm. The parceling out of knowledge, furthermore, occurs not by pure assertion of divine wisdom or prerogative—as it is explicitly justified elsewhere in the Qur'an—but by a linguistic formula: Language itself "proves" knowledge as well as its impossibility.

NATURE, TEXT, RUINS

In the poetic tradition, the aura of a textlike production was primarily oriented toward preestablished rather than revelatory knowledge and was attentive to the model of nature rather than to that of transformative human labor. In the eloquent opening of Labid's ode, the poet ponders the enigma of "text" as a metaphor for preservation, as he meditates upon the meaning of the ruins:

> ... and the torrent-beds of Er-Raiyán—naked shows their trace,
> rubbed smooth, like letterings long since scored on a stony slab. (c. 2)

> ... Then the torrents washed the dusty ruins, until they seem
> like scrolls of writing whose text their pens have revivified. (c. 8)

Labid's extended halting allows him to carefully observe and record the workings of nature. Here, nature speaks, nature acts, nature washes away a previous "text" from its pages and writes a new one in its place. Does the poet realize that his own ode is itself a text? What is the nature of this "authorship" that delivers him to us as a distinctive personality? What of preserving an otherwise amorphous presence through textual deposition? In the second couplet, a "text" is given as a trace, almost a near shadow, but as the only preservable mark nonetheless. One has to come near to be able to read it. But the contents (*mutun*) of texts themselves seem to be unimportant. They could wash away, vanish, or be reinvented (*tujaddad*) or rewritten. So there are two things that persist: the creator of the text (composer, nature, or the text's own power to self-generate: "by their pens" [*aqlamuha*]), and the *form* of textual presence. And so is the ode: It is a *form* of speech, new to the historical scene, coming together with a clearly recognizable, highly esteemed author. Once uttered, it echoes endlessly through the desert. It functions like a trace, that is, like that fragment from a past state of totality that had enabled the poet, after all those years (c. 3: "many years have passed over, months unhallowed and sacrosanct") to recognize ("like letterings") the lodging place of past lovers.

Nature erases; nature preserves. Furthermore, nature erases and preserves what it wills. Since there is no perceptible order that enables the observer to predict what will last, the observer ascribes that power of willing to nature. Why a scroll of writing on a stone is preserved while the lodging of the lover is not—even though both belong to the same semantic unity of a place's name—is an opposition that can only be understood as a blind, formidable will of nature. Now the poet, anxious to preserve (himself, his memory, a past project at identity, and so on) emulates nature: He produces a preservable discourse. What is inscribed on stone, after all, is a *record* of loss preserved through a primal act of willing the record itself.

The content of such a record—which is scarcely mentioned—is insignificant to our poet, to all poets, to anyone who happens to pass by. The willer had long disappeared, perished, wandered off, wandered away. In the desert, the passerby would not recognize the original willer but would be more likely to be struck by the power to survive of the willer's speech. Thus a continually revivifiable text came to be seen as a frame of reference for halting in general rather than as a signifier of an implied or expressed purpose, code, wisdom, or content.

This mode of preservation through textual recording, while emulating nature's observed mode of preservation, also acts in a reciprocal fashion to discern how nature's mode is reflected in human signs. Immediately following the reference to textual revivification, Labid's ode adds another twist to the metaphor, where reclamation by nature is seen to resemble the revelation of the tattooing on a woman's hand. This recalls very similar images by composers of other odes:

> There are traces yet of Khaula in the stony tract of Thahmad
> apparent like the tattoo-marks seen on the back of a hand. (Tarafa, c. 1)

> A lodging where the abode in Er-Rakmatán, that appears
> like criss-cross tattooings upon the sinews of a wrist. (Zuhair, c. 2)

Thus, what we have here is an apparently widely diffused image, an image that must have been captivating. The poets here are fully aware that the two items being brought together belong to two distinct spheres of existence, that the object to be described is so impoverished in and of itself as to require an external support, that it is barren and yet must continue to be addressed.

The various interpretive possibilities suggested by this metaphor seem to all point to nature as the model for preservative and creative activity. To liken nature's reclamation of a former abode to fading bodily decoration could be premised on the discovery that the creative subject operates upon the world "like" nature does. Rather than being posited as an anti-human externality, nature is seen to be acting in a mode that parallels human transformative efforts. A different interpretive possibility could be that the poets lament the very idea of *change* rather than the abortion of a promised teleological march, the deconstruction of a totalizable identity, the distance between memory and the present, or the triumph of disorder over order. Thus, the ordeal of a transformative project with lustrous, decorative intent is as much lamented as the transformation of a promise of perfection into rubble. The common element in both operations, again, is the success of an impenetrable, unconquerable, unstructurable, unpredictable, exterior *will* and the subsequent definition of will as an external power *over* the self.

In any case, the metaphor entails a clear recognition of symmetry. Though not directly related, both material construction (the abode) and aesthetic appendage (the appearance of the self) are equally subject to erosion over time. Both occupy the same lamentable plane for the poet, who knows that even though he must learn from the model of nature, nature itself will always be one step ahead of him. Unlike nature, he must act, create, change, defend, make decisions, and above all, will consciously. Nature, on the other hand, seems to will, and to transform by the magic of its will, effortlessly, anonymously, subjectlessly, speechlessly: The only thing it leaves intact, it seems, is a willed speech. And hence the poetic discourse itself: responding to nature in kind, with the only weapon time seems to be unwilling to erase. With this weapon, however, one does *not* confront nature. Rather, one *accepts* nature's terms of destiny. One preserves and wills and creates with the only capacity nature allows one to keep *beyond the self*, namely, the capacity to speak, to preserve, to will, and to create through speech. Only through speech, thus, could such an observor become *like* nature.

The paradigmatic shift observed in Qur'anic speech, as opposed to the ode, is first and foremost indicated by the derisive tone with which the Qur'an addresses the ruins. For the sedentaries, among whom the Qur'an appeared and to whom it spoke, the nomadic horizon and the ideational imperative of the ruins had become distant memories, even though they continued to inform a formulaic poetic tradition. Qur'anic speech, rather than being oriented toward *preservation*, following the model of a normative and overpowering nature, is oriented toward the *retrieval* of a spatio-temporally distant (transcendental and historical) truth. Nature here is no longer the model but only one of the symptoms of such a truth. When the work of nature ceases to be the reference point of knowledge, it is no longer seen to belong to the essence of nature itself; rather, it appears as just another manifestation of the spatiotemporally detached truth. This was no more apparent than in the idea of the ruins, which in the Qur'an was reoriented away from its paradigmatic hold over the nomadic ode. There were two basic reorientations in that regard:

1. For the Qur'an, as opposed to the ode, ruins are metaphorical rather than geographically specifiable reference points. They are scarcely used to open the speech itself, let alone anchor it. As such, ruins signify through this usage a further departure from the model of ideationally formative nature and of nature as an empirically verifiable container of the limits of experience.

2. Ruins in the Qur'an, furthermore, are not the result of normal cycles of human departure, as they are in the ode. Seen from a sedentary perspective, ruins are an indication of *social malfunction*. As such, they usually appear in the Qur'an as evidence of sin, and consequently they result from divine displeasure.[9] With the advent of sedentarism, ruins lose their normativity and begin to require an ethical explanation for their deviation from the model of successful settlement.

The abandonment of the ruins in this fashion was not entirely abrupt, however. Some nomadic poets—albeit following different motivations—had themselves registered an awareness of the confined figural space of the ruins but had found little to replace them with. This is evident in the ode of the legendary warrior-poet-lover 'Antara; the ode opens with otherwise traditional and dutifully presented motifs: highly praised ruins (c. 5); naming and localizing (c. 4, 9); contextualizing within an inhospitable realm (c. 6–7); direct speech to the ruins (c. 2, 5); halting for the explicit purpose of mourning the unattainable (c. 3). But then there is the strange, discontinued protest of the ode's very first verse: "Have the poets left a single spot for a patch to be sewn? [*Hal ghadara ash-shu'ara'a min mutaraddimi?*]." Is there still any image, idea, gesture, or other intensities of the experience of the ruins not yet claimed in one poem or another? Could this body of poetics still be added to? Has the archive been completed? Yet the very next half of the couplet abruptly aborts the questioning, making the swift decision to drop the enigma for the comfort of the tradition: "Or did you recognize the abode after long meditation?" Another questioning, yet of a thoroughly secure nature.

The first question of the ode itself reveals that it belongs to a form of discourse: 'Antara does not question poetry itself as a medium for higher thoughts or even as a tradition. He does, however, notice something from within the tradition: It has become too congested, having re-created life, or so it seems, in its sum total. The magnitude of its accomplishment, paradoxically, leads to its exit from history. Its representation of life is so complete now as to have become an *appropriation*. After all, representation is an activity that, by definition, must occur at a distance from the represented, allowing that which has already been represented to be represented once more. Once such an activity seems impossible—except by sheer cynicism—the poet halts, now no longer strictly facing the ruins, his view of them clouded by all that poetic clamor about them, and asks, as though to clear up the suffocating jumble of previous words standing between him and the sight: What is this speech that seems to have laid claim to all prefigurations?

A tradition allows a claimant a regulated entrance into a prefigured world with known boundaries. Questioning, or even noticing, its congestion does not entail a rejection of the world it prefigures. Thus, 'Antara's halfhearted unease must fail to produce anything new, since only a radical departure from such a tradition—in fact, from poetry itself—could allow the prefigured world to be represented again as an experience or could re-create a totally new arena of representation. But for the time being, 'Antara could only do more of the same, attempting once more to overdo the ritual of the ruins. Poetry had finally covered up, through the enormity of its presence, the representative claim of an antecedent language of everyday life. Poetry's claim to being the language that engulfs all things in its adventures of representation was not yet to be contested. The experience of poetry itself confused things, with its project of confining the world into variable images, all introduced by loss and departure. One could spend a lifetime in that figurative location, hoping now and then to perhaps expand the chambers of experience a bit. For the time being, nothing more could be done, until the ruins were finally out of sight, languishing where they could offer advice no longer.

THE WANDERING LOGIC

The ruins, however, had provided a semblance of unity in discourse, in a way that suggests other modes by which logical unities were established in representative speech. Al-A'sha's ode, for example, contains a second lengthy act of halting (beginning in couplet 26), situated in a tavern. The variety of discourses and thematics inspired by that locale—wine, conversation, love, longing, and lust—possess a peculiar unity governed by the scene in which this halting takes place, namely, the tavern. As Hurayrah—the departing lover with whom the ode begins—assures the return of all thematics and images to the scene governed by her presence, so does the scene of the tavern, which governs the unity of all that is spoken in it. The only common structure of such unities is that of a *presence* within a spatial scene, so that when the departing Hurayrah finally disappears or when the tavern closes its doors and throws the drunkards out, the presences maintaining these discursive unities are finally aborted. In the representational discourse of a society whose norm is movement, diverse themes are not brought together on the basis of transcendental or formal logic. They could only manifest their unity in relationship to a halting act confirmed by a singular scene that is, in any case, temporary.

In some cases, however, a self-contained theme—as opposed to a self-contained scene—takes over through a particular form of potent moral "introduction." 'Antara's impressively uninterrupted sequence of heroic poetry (c. 63–76), for instance, is introduced by an opposition of ideas, an opposition that is soon left behind: couplet 63 portrays a betrayal; couplet 64, an act of faithfulness. Two irreconcilable poles of the morality of attachments set the scene for the clash to follow:

> I am told that 'Amr is ungrateful for my beneficience,
> and ingratitude is a heaviness to the soul of the benefactor.
> I have minded well the counsel my uncle gave me in the forenoon
> when fearfully the lips drew back from the mouth's white teeth
> in the thick of death, of whose agonies the true hero
> utters no complaint, other than a muffled cry. (c. 63–65)

It is clear that such an "introduction" is not meant to historicize the war or to present a cause, as in the case of the poets speaking for the tribe, such as 'Amru or al-Harith; nor is it meant to introduce its direct protagonists or to shed a light on their nature. Here, introducing a persistent theme entails bounding it by the ropes of a moral milieu, which would then invite a discourse of justification (for example, 'Amru), adjudication (for example, Labid), or settlement (for example, Zuhair). The moral milieu which for 'Antara introduces heroic qualities addresses neither a network of causalities nor the protagonists themselves or their virtues. Rather, it establishes a general situation of opposition between moral ideas. This technique of introducing could be seen as characteristic to a wandering society: *As nature seems to form itself in a piecemeal fashion along the way of the wanderer, its elements forge their connectedness in the order by which they are encountered rather than through a preconceived or posterior system of interdependencies.* The latter conception is characteristic of the settled society, where fundamental themes are juxtaposed with respect to a system, an enclosure, a closed territory to which all things must come back to be judged. Such a trope is condensed in the Qur'anic reinterpretation of life as a journey *back* to Allah. But under conditions of wandering, themes and observations seem to accumulate along a chronology of forgotten openings and within an expedition oblivious to its conclusion or otherwise unaware of the sedentary status of a conclusion as a unitary "lock" upon thematic variety.

For the wanderer, the introduction does not entail the necessity of being revisited at the end of speech. The traditional opening, as we have seen, does not "introduce" as much as lay the poem's claim to be in the realm of poetics, thereby differently adjusting the listening faculties. The occasional moral milieu within the poem is not so much the *context* for what is to follow as a force moving the discourse into one of several possible directions. The ending of a theme in nomadic poetry, therefore, is always provisional. One way to "end" a heroic sequence, for instance, is with a conclusive note of healing, which by no means ends the poem. For example, at the end of the long heroic sequence in 'Antara's ode, the poet proclaims his satisfaction and indicates his readiness to cease the battle: "And oh, my soul was cured, and its faint sickness was healed" (c. 76). The healing was premised on 'Antara's identity being finally acknowledged. The mere invocation of his name is now sufficient to solicit an expected response: "By the horsemen's cry, . . . 'On with you, ['Antara has come!].'" For the sedentaries, a healing would readily offer itself as one of the most appropriate sites to conclude the adventure and the speech. Yet unlike in the edicts of the salvation religion rearing its head slowly in the land, recovery here is not in itself an objective. When the eye can still discern a bit of a yet-to-be-crossed distance, no matter how mediocre, and contrast that to the virtue of a unifying conclusion presenting itself shortly before that horizon, continued wandering wins. The virtue of unifying conclusivities had not been discovered yet. Thus the ode crosses into the last remaining distance (c. 77–80), where it ends while 'Antara is still on the move, still on the back of his camel. Only the horizon, the boundary of natural exhaustion, shall end the speech.

Such an attitude, which typifies the odes in general, emanates from an ingrained suspicion of the purpose of subjective planning in life. The most extreme manifestation of this mind-set is spelled out in Tarafa's ode, in which all the notions of differential status that could result from a purposefully conceived life were seen to be fundamentally empty. When Tarafa embarked on his fateful trip to Bahrain (where he was predictably put to death by the governor), it was as though he was following a destiny, being fully aware of the consequences, and being fully aware as well that consequences were not the essence of a life conditioned by a free flow of movement. To be, after all, is in this case to be on the move, even if the source of movement happens to lie outside of or be independent of any notion of the self. Movement was in the nature of things. The act of halting, which, as we have seen, occasioned a discursive outgrowth in the form of poetry, was a moment of interrupting nature's eternal course. The journey was to continue thereafter, carrying the poetic baggage along. The poem, after the traditional halting, continues into unforseen, unpredictable, inconsequential, inconclusive gesticulations in the mode of movement. The endings of the odes seem to be unimportant. There was no effort at "concluding," tying the themes together, deriving a final lesson, reformulating an original thesis, re-posing a question, returning to the beginning, and so on. The imagery, character, content, spirit, and discontinuous occurrence of the end are similar to those of any other point in the poetic narrative. The end, in other words, was interchangeable with any other point in the story, save for the traditional opening. There did not seem to be any conception of an "end." Where it ends, the ode could also go on.

The end of the ode is a matter of natural exhaustion, like the end of wandering itself, an activity that included rest stops, after each of which a whole new journey began, a whole new speech. This was the manner of movement, as lived by a discerning eye, recording as it moved along the road the variations of themes and the continuous displacement of views and thus topics. An eye attentive to all that could be observed and rendered through a form that would preserve it after it had been passed by. This collecting speech transforms all externalities on the road into possessions to be taken along. At the "end" of the journey, naturally, an immense weight of objects would have been acquired. This weight, in turn, was simply laid down by the side of the road. The only major observation about it was that a "production" (or a collection of images of a journey) could outlast the life of the producer (or the collector). That was an entirely new phenomenon in the desert; before, nothing had seemed to promise this survival except the faint hope that the creating patriarch's blood would be preserved in his descendants, which was one of the ingredients aggrandizing blood kinships, genealogical tables, and the collective subjectivity of the tribe. It is not as though the search for everlastingness is posited here as a primal human instinct. Rather, like other possibilities, this one became perceptible in the vigorous survival of a reproducible record.

With this fundamental observation, life begins to appear as a project, which provides the idea of conclusion with a unique status in speech, a status to which the ode was oblivious. For a society living upon the path itself and not toward its culmination, "conclusion" had only entailed the termination of life itself. The nomadic logic conflated the notions of conclusion and ending, unlike the sedentary logic, in which the conclusion was made to be the harvest of labor and the zone of preserved essence. But under nomadism, the conclusion was merely scattered like dust over the arbitrary site where halting occured. With every step along the path canceling out the one before, nomadic ending was such a perpetual occurrence that it no longer appeared distinctly. Indeed, if there was a conclusion, it was located at the beginning of the ode, where the perpetual disruption of all schemes to end wandering was ritually announced. In a life conditioned by a mode of departure, there were no conclusions: Nothing was brought "back" home. Home itself was no more than the back of the faithful camel, the journey *itself* toward the mirage, toward the horizon, toward the ruinous site, or into the memory; home was the mythical companionship of cotravelers.

Under sedentary conditions of discourse, a successful conclusion is a successful crossing *back* into familiar lands, languages, audiences, habits of thinking, and methods of presentation, in order to give a summary of an adventure, a summary that could—as a permanent record—substitute for the adventure itself, even obviate the need for its repetition. Thus, the idea of salvation, where the record is central to adjudication, becomes a prime posited purpose for the journey of life. Indeed, influential trends in Qur'anic exegesis have explicitly conceived of life as a voyage (*safar*) toward God. This journey, in turn, presupposes the necessary support institutions, such as rest stops and signposts.[10] The sedentary notion of a conclusion consists of the effort to rescue the essence from the teeth of the "excessive ground"—too many surrounding words, too many possible meanings. The sedentary conclusion is the reward and meaning for a new conception of labor, whereby labor is no longer synonymous with life but an outgrowth conspicuously added to the meaning of life. Sedentary society thus encapsulated labor within a concept of "return" to the ground of stable residence, whereby it became governed by a cyclical nature. Under nomadism, the essence was neither a brief occurrence, a condensation of a totality, nor an activity of cyclical return but, rather, a ubiquity of equally poeticizable events and nonevents along a path. Crossing the path was no more than a profound listening to the whole story, until it terminated itself in the mode of an exhaustion. This path was not an excessive ground to be discursively reconfigured and narrowed down. There was no specific reclamation of labor that a conclusion could bring back. Uttered from the outset as in the ode, the nomadic conclusion could only announce the perpetual effacement of the product of labor and the perpetual departure and hopeless disappearance of the laborer.

One of the clearest manifestations of this operation, especially as compared to its use in Qur'anic speech, is the use of symbolization. In the ode, the symbol parallels the experience of wandering in the sense that—with notable exceptions—it ceases to reinforce its original referent shortly upon invocation, calling new referents instead. In Zuhair's ode, the metaphors used to describe war include fire, millstones, a breeding she-camel, and a crop:

> When you stir it up, it's a hateful thing you've stirred up;
> ravenous it is, once you whet its appetite; it bursts aflame,
> then it grinds you as a millstone grinds on its cushion;
> yearly it conceives, birth upon birth, and with twins for issue—
> very ill-omened are the boys it bears you, every one of them
> the like of Ahmar of 'Ad; then it gives suck, and weans them.
> Yes, war yields you a harvest very different from the bushels
> and pieces of silver those fields in Iraq yield for the villagers. (c. 30–33)

One sees here two sets of images. First, there are instruments—fire, millstones—which operate in a predictable manner (fire burns and millstones grind). Then come productive processes whose outcome is more unpredictable, thus requiring further explanation. The difference between the two sets of metaphors is not that of a "rational" mind making a distinction between a form of life and a form of nature; nor is the difference that between the items associated with production and those associated with consumption. Rather, judged by the relative amount of elaboration allotted to each, the distinction seems to be between operations or objects, on the one hand, whose effects on being are known, predictable, normative, and thus economizable out of speech and, on the other hand, operations or objects whose effects on being are uncertain, problematic, disorderly, and therefore matters for discourse, elaboration, enumeration, and classification. Thus, on the one hand, the fire and the millstone, once operative, consume the victim at once and cease their animation together with the devoured body, without any further deliberation. On the other hand, what this yearly conceiving she-camel is to beget is unforeseeable. The produced, here, is an actor. The identity of such an actor is definitely announced in couplet 32: All offspring produced by such a creature (a metaphorized war) are evil, treacherous, mother killers.[11]

It is obvious that the "ill-omened" offspring will not be killing war by killing its metaphor, the fertile she-camel, but will, strictly speaking, be killing their mother. The meaning of the relationship between the producer and the product is therefore strictly internal to the meaning of their natural link. Symbolization, which portrays the producer and the product as standing for something external to their nature, leads not to a judgment on that exteriority but to a demonization of an otherwise natural link. The symbolized, once having infected the body of an otherwise natural link, takes over its life and forces it to speak to the world exclusively in terms of the symbol, forgetting in the meantime both its previous normativity and the original metaphorical intent. Even though in some cases, such as this one, the poetic discourse resumes speaking directly of war, it is the use of the symbol that here interrupts nature, in the same way that war is portrayed to do. But the symbol itself assumes, soon after invocation, an identity of its own as an object with full standing, referencing no other.

Symbolization is a process predicated on dividing the world into substance and metaphor, whereby the latter confirms the former and complements its lack of a desired identity, definition, or appearance. In the case of the odes, the symbol maintained a close proximity to the world of substance. Discourse had its own reality, a phenomenon conducive to Qur'anic and other mystical literary productions. Things, categories, operations, orders of being—all merely needed to be spoken of according to particular formats, in order for them to blossom into a self-contained reality. To speak symbolically was to add the symbol to the world. The distance between the invocation of the name of God and feeling God's presence—itself confirmed by hearing God's words—was accomplished. Since the encyclopedic understanding of the domain of the ode meant that there was no reality safe from the reach of words, there were also no new realities that could fail to be summoned by words to the infinite inventory of the archive of the times. Reality was not simply detected by the sense experience, evident in the effort invested in specific geography at the moment of halting. Rather, it also became all that could be salvaged from nonbeing by a form of discourse. Everything was added together: the symbol, the empirical, and the experiential. The entirety of disconnected experiences associated with wandering, such as in the case of Labid or 'Antara, were united only by the path upon which they occurred. Under nomadism, it was not the destination but the path upon which life was to be lived.

Elements of this priority of path over fundamental, unified referent are also available in the *sira* tradition (biographies of the prophet) as it pertains to the piecemeal revelation of the Qur'an. In fact, it was not until Muhammad was firmly entrenched as a source of unifying political authority in Medina that he began to pay specific attention to logical and practical doctrinal unity. It was at that point that believers were pronounced to be equivalent to the infidels if they believed in one revelation while disbelieving another.[12] The additive nature of the revelation now had to be refocused to a fundamental point of return, especially in light of the discovery that simply and openly following one's desired gaze—as in the ode—would destroy the whole corpus. This was never more obvious than in the experience of a lonely and overwhelmed Muhammad in Mecca finding himself praising the idols, as if they were simply another component of the idea of deity. At a somewhat less problematic level, Muhammad and the early believers saw clearly and accepted that the Qur'an, rather than anticipating events, was commenting on them as they occurred, that it had changed its mind on some matters, and that some later instructions either expanded on, ignored, rendered pointless, or even contradicted some earlier revelations. Although he blamed major blunders, like the praise of idols, on the intervention of the demon, in a very rare confession, Allah admitted that he himself was responsible for many minor alterations, since otherwise it would be too aggrandizing to the demon's authority to assign them all to him: "If We abrogate a verse or cause it to be forgotten, We will replace it by a better one or one similar."[13] Thus, here there is in the Qur'an a demonstration of the path-inspired logic of progression that one usually associates with the nomadic ode. But the Qur'anic additive logic involves an important qualification. The path is no longer simply cumulative; rather, it assumes the structure and logic of a unified—though tactically amendable—mission. This mission required, in turn, certain forms of structural discursive stabilities, many of which paralleled existing or emerging tropes of poetic speech.

SOURCES OF STRUCTURAL STABILITY

Though the themes and images prevalent in the Qur'an, odes, and other circulating discourses are difficult to compare fully in the narrow scope of this outline, two basic sources of structural stability can be found throughout, sources that emerge from logical orientations to be found outside the field of language proper. The first has to do with a discovery of "value," which then advises cyclical structures that return to value. The other has to do with scenes of confrontation, which advise structures that are defined by a continually present adversary.

In the odes, items of "concrete value" (such as the camel, which makes life in the desert possible) tend to enjoy a particular resilience in memory. In such cases, memory operates so as to prevent the metaphor from stealing the original object, as was the case otherwise with all objects not endowed with a comparable assessment of value. Memory here acts like an extended tether that would allow the metaphor to throw its weight into the depths of the distance, while ensuring that it would neither fly away and assume its independence as the logic of wandering would otherwise dictate nor dissipate in a way that left behind a bewildering void. The most remarkable instance of such a structure is provided in Labid's ode, where metaphors are presented in a structure of circles, one woven into the web of the other, folding and unfolding to face a layer outside and another inside.[14]

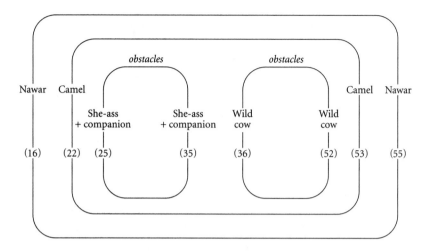

Both internal metaphoric cycles (the asses, the wild cow) pose the question of survival against immense odds. They commence with portrayals of loneliness and austerity. Destitute, disoriented, exhausted, the animals spend the bulk of their story doomed to movement, dislocation, and search. In the first case, the arduous venture leads to an oasis, a discovery celebrated in two couplets. Thereafter the poet finds nothing more to add. So a similarly structured metaphorical cycle is unleashed. The second cycle is even more laborious, and includes three successive moments of distress. A wild cow searches for her supposedly devoured infants. In the process she is exposed to floods, and after that she is detected by hunters. The first set concludes with confirming the irretrievability of loss (as at the end of the traditional opening). The second is a moment of pondering the next step (pondering, that is, while nature does its usual work: rain, night, dawn); the third comes from without, while the pondering had produced nothing other than the acknowledgment of loss and also loneliness. This movement comes to the wild cow, thus, in her state of surrender to fate, to destiny, to the laws of the wilderness, to the muddiness of the inhospitable landscape. From the depth of this existential abyss, she is forced now to fight for her life. It is her final chance to reemerge, lest she perish altogether (c. 51). She emerges victorious. The cycle ends. The she-camel reemerges, also triumphant, undoubtedly reliable. The loss has been redeemed not by bringing the dead back to life but by a show of vigor that guarantees the continuation of the already-present life. Loss is overcome through strength, *not* retrieval, a theme more appropriate for the nascent sedentary conception of justice. In this case, the one who survives is the one who is capable not only of fighting but also of forgetting, precisely as one repeats the same cycle shortly thereafter.

Furthermore, the metaphoric cycles here are ordered hierarchically in accordance with a system of values. Thus, Labid does not bring his most valued endowment, namely, the she-camel, out of her metaphoric hiding place until he guarantees that all danger has been eliminated. The first sequence was apparently not sufficient, neither in learned attributes of drama, complexity, compassion, endurance, or vigor. Couplet 36 thus witnesses an unsure reemergence and a quick retreat behind the curtains of the metaphor (*afatilka, amm . . .* , "is [she] so, or . . ."). The attributes of the animal are then buttressed by experiences of search for lost kinfolk, enduring the trials of the wasteland, and staying put in a struggle *against others* for survival. Thus, the sequence of the asses brings out substantiations of character, which then supplement the *original* item of value. Thus, such an ordered, planned speech also admits of experimentation. Yet it values experiments in a uniquely path-oriented way: Rather than being confined to the best of that which was said or attempted about its topic, it *adds* the experiment to the finalized version.

This elaborate experimentation following cyclical structures is absent from the other great portrayals of the camel in the *mu'allaqat*, especially Tarafa's. Tarafa's she-camel always stands as her own figure and metaphor. There are no great cycles of memory; there is merely a linear progression of elements, an extended look at all occurrences of the animal's anatomy, features, and ways of moving. In both cases, however, the camel's discourse is begun with a seemingly eccentric characterization of feebleness, which is properly contextualized shortly thereafter. But her essential character is not normative decrepitude but age, a sign of endurance rather than decay. Figures of speed and swift movement follow, fully counterbalancing any suspicion of uselessness. Labid, however, orders the speech in the form of cycles of memory, whereby the item of supreme value is poised to reemerge from the grips of successive metaphorical cycles at the end of the speech. With such a planned speech, the camel can run through a substantial portion of the ode without being detected by name. That is, it waits in gestation for the series of experimentations to lead to its metaphorized perfection. Only then does the camel appear in name again, only to announce its already demonstrated faultlessness.

Perfecting the image of the camel, which leads to its departure from the ode, opens in this case a yet larger cycle of memory encompassing it. Immediately thereafter (c. 55), we witness a sudden reawakening of the figure of the lover Nawar, after nearly forty verses of absence. She enters not as an uncontextualized figure but as she was before her story was interrupted, being still compounded by the thematic of breaking. That crucial thematic, as it is structured here, rapidly invites a series of problematic oppositions: break versus choice, subjectivity versus freedom, hedonism versus austerity, dream versus discipline. We have crossed a blinding figural jungle only to return, after thinking that the poet had acknowledged the overpowering distance and flown away, back home, precisely on that camel that resembles a "roseate cloud, rain-emptied, that flies with the south wind." But it was on this instrument, it turns out, that the poet had been flying *toward* Nawar's forbidden land. In a remarkable cyclical structure, Labid reminds the audience of the original—now almost forgotten—problematic, restating the original case before reentering Nawar's figural territory. He revisits the possibilities of choice and freedom over breaking, paraphrasing the couplets immediately preceding the original abandonment of Nawar's theme (c. 21–22). It appears, thus, that the discourse that is bounded by couplets 16 and 56 constitutes a closed, autonomous space within the sphere of Labid's ode. The couplets before couplet 15 are a matter of tribute to tradition; those after 56 are a new movement, which is not as readily structurable.

Examples of this structure abound throughout the Qur'an, where metaphors of nature as well as tales of earlier prophets (which are presumed to be already familiar to its readers) explicitly serve as moral lessons, *not* as self-enclosed themes. Yet unlike the structures evident in Labid's ode, for instance, images of decrepitude and weakness on earth do not necessarily establish the ground for metaphorical or symbolic survival. Nor do they instigate a semblance of the ruins-oriented meditation, where loss is acknowledged as a norm of nature and henceforth is left to stand. Rather, death and injustice, which can result from earthly predicaments, are possible and indeed recurrent historical events. But since life itself is little more than a cyclical journey back to God, tales and metaphors regarding it cannot be—in sum—other than cyclical metaphorical structures.

The major departure from this cyclical predicament occasions the earthly realities of confrontation and actual struggle, which require a different posture and structure of stability. This was to be in abundant supply during Muhammad's later career. Many Qur'anic *surahs* (for example, al-Fath, al-Anbiya') teem with thematics presumptive of stable confrontational scenes. The general *jahili* structure of a confrontational scene is expressed most obviously in the ode of 'Amru Ibn Kalthum, which is largely maintained by an extended and unilinear heroic posture. Here, the "skin rusted from the long wearing" of armory (c. 71) refers openly to a weariness with a confrontation that cannot be aborted or made to shift direction, since it had been presented as being irreconcilable. So how does it end? If the metaphorical reservoir of themes of confrontation is of a confinable and exhaustible dimension, then such an ode could be expected to collapse under the weight of its own unilinearity of motive. But in this case, 'Amru's ode is poverty-stricken on metaphorization, particularly following the setting up of the sober scene of confrontation (c. 20). Thereafter the speaker had to be continuously on guard against the imposing reality of such a scene, which disallowed journeying into the unpredictable, consumptive land of symbols.

Thus, 'Amru could use neither Zuhair's mode of symbolization, in which the symbol assumes a life of its own, nor the retrievable metaphorization with which Labid infuses his cyclical structure. In 'Amru's ode, there is no cycle assuring the return of the symbol to the place of its launching, nor does the intensity of the conflict allow a flight away via free-spirited symbolization. When the women of the tribe are brought in (c. 89), they operate as but one more step in the endless fortification of the scene. Their praise is relatively quick-paced, nervous, almost inattentive, as though the speaker is on guard for other dangers looming around this and all previous signs of tribal might and virtue. Thus, no hedonism is allowed to cause a rupture at this juncture: The discourse of the collective subject must be always attentive to duty.

Under the dictates of irreconcilable confrontation, duty entails conditions that would make triumph over others possible. The confrontational Qur'anic *surah* of al-Fath concludes by pointing out that the maturation of the believers into a credible force is intended as a divinely inspired fact to be paraded in front of their adversaries: "They are like the seed which puts forth its shoot and strengthens it, so that it rises stout and firm upon its stalk, delighting the sowers. Through them He seeks to enrage the unbelievers."[15] Here, the product of nature and labor attains significance not because of an intrinsic virtue that would allow it to appear cyclically as its own self-referent but, rather, because it registers the promise of a final victory after a protracted battle against the *same* enemy. The need to maintain a solid front is clearly behind the severe, unforgiving Qur'anic denunciations of unreliable allies, whether nomads (the *a'rab* in al-Fath) or sedentaries (the *Munafiqun,* "two-faced," who constituted Muhammad's proclaimed as well as clandestine opposition in Medina).[16]

Since these forms of confrontation are seen, both in the Qur'an and in the odes, as interruptions of norms, they usually invite a search for conclusive modalities of ending. 'Amru's remarkably consistent panegyric, thus, does indeed have the semblance of a conclusive sequence (c. 91–96), which parades the grandiose attributes of the tribe, leaving the audience with this final warning:

So let no man act foolishly [*yajhalanna*] against us,
or we shall exceed the folly of the foolhardiest [*fanajhalu fauqa jahli l-jahilina*].
(c. 92)

There is a semantic play here that establishes a total, impenetrable stiffness, which is the condition of a safe withdrawal: *Jahl* had the dual meaning of "ignorance" and "temperamental insensibility." It is introduced as a "truthful" knowledge, the arrival at which had been announced early on as the objective of the whole speech (c. 8, 20). Here, the only knowledge that could assuredly protect this collective subject, after all, is the enemy's knowledge of its ability to attain catastrophic ignorance.

In contrast, Qur'anic confrontations highlight the power of knowledge, which is *uniquely* available to the believers and is explicitly introduced— against *jahl*—as a source of tranquil and confident power, even if, or precisely because, adversaries are unaware of it.[17] 'Amru, on the other hand, is aware that only the paraded virtues of the tribe could offer at least a negotiable withdrawal from or an abrogation of a confrontational scene. Such virtues include in this case the tribe's uncultivated, rugged nature, frightening as they confirm the *universally knowable* consequences of ignorance. The power of the Muslims, by contrast, was based on knowledge whose dynamics of communal empowerment were known to them *alone*.

Scenes of confrontation usually invite a search for sources of empowerment, which in this case are found in existing social structures. For the prophet, they are found beyond this world altogether and by way of abstract and distant examples, since this world, along with the knowledge it provides, cannot produce success in this novel venture.[18] Failure to achieve consistent success is still possible but is no longer necessarily calamitous. While *jahili* disempowerment led periodically to accepting finitude as the norm—as can be observed in the case of 'Ubayd or in the practice of *i'tifad*—loss now could be accepted as an ingredient within a cyclical cosmic plan: "If you have suffered a defeat, so did the enemy. We alternate these vicissitudes among mankind so that God may know the true believers and choose martyrs from among you."[19]

Part II: The Faith

six

Prophetic Constitution

THE LAND DREAMS OF A PROPHET

The pre-Islamic epoch witnessed a profusion of prophets and sages. Reports abound of mystics and diviners preaching doctrines and even sayings not far removed from what Muhammad was to articulate with more decisive impact. In addition to the *hanifs* (Abrahamic reformers) already discussed, some claimants to prophecy disputed Muhammad's entitlement, and one in particular—Musaylimah—posed a serious threat to the nascent Islamic polity after his death. The Qur'an itself indirectly registered the anticipatory mood by assigning to Muhammad the three roles of bearing conclusive good news (*mubashsheran*), conveying warnings (*nadhir*), and serving as a *witness* (*shahidan*) for the direction of his times.[1]

Delegating responsibility for spiritual transformation to a prophet is no arbitrary matter. Entrusting an epochal project to a mere individual raises the specific question of why venues other than prophethood were not seen as suitable for the accomplishment of the task at hand. It also introduces problems with regard to the interplay between the requisites of the task and those encumbent upon a more customary communal leadership role. The emergence of such a figure cannot simply be attributed to "individual genius," although personal attributes do no doubt play a role. More importantly, the prophetic figure must demonstrate otherworldly links and proceed beyond the threshold of ordinary sagehood. The establishment of these credentials is usually judged in the context of prevalent notions of individuality and customary venues of prominence. Thus, examining the idea of prophethood as such would tell us more about an ancient social landscape than about the trials and tribulations of the prophet himself. It is in this spirit that I wish to examine the emergence, constitution, and condensation of the idea of prophethood in Muhammad's case, rather than simply narrate once more well-known biographical details.

Who Is a Prophet?

The question of prophethood, as a phenomenon predicated upon a unique and distinct individuality, is intricately linked to the question of uniquely legitimate and nonreproducible authority. Who would grant such an authority to a mere kin relative like Muhammad, whose life had been so constantly ordinary before the moment of proclamation? Within the ideational confines of ordinary, experienced, traditional society, which abhors novelty and lives according to the claimed example of the forefathers, perhaps only a few detached souls. The legitimacy of the prophet, therefore, comes from elsewhere. It emanates not only from "above" but, in a significant way, from the *past* itself. The prophet here descends from a tradition more authentic and everlasting than that of mortal society. Throughout the Qur'an, the prophets of ancient history appear as founding fathers of society, and in the context of pagan Mecca they are resurrected from the dust of moral oblivion in which they had languished for centuries in order to testify in one voice to their coming from the same divine source. In this spirit, the idea of prophethood is couched in terms of stories of social origin, now introduced as an advisory prehistory for the present.

Muhammad's prophetic genealogy is not ascertained only through abstract scriptural revelation; rather, it commences with rare direct contacts with that tradition. In a story that illuminates the significance of this trope, al-Tabari relates an episode in which Muhammad recalls being taken by the archangels Gabriel and Mikhael to see his "fathers"—Adam and Abraham—who reside in the first and seventh heavens, respectively.[2] In the intervening heavens, he saw his "brothers" Jehova, Jesus, Idris, Aaron, Moses, and Joseph.[3] Here, prophetic identity is grounded upon images of traditional tribal relations, as they operate in a spatiotemporally distant realm demanded by the abstract and universal nature of God. The final paternal nature of God consolidates the familial imprints through which prophetic entitlement is addressed. The prophets of this family embody stories of incomplete success with their constituents, but through no fault of their own. Thus, both Moses and Jesus are excused in the Qur'an from the "revisionism" of their followers, with the blame being placed squarely on the latter. The prophets resemble brothers of one family, who are infallible only to the extent that the will of Allah dictates. Allah himself is often introduced as a merciful-vengeful parental character who frequently interferes in order to shield his messengers from the mockery and brutality of their constituents—in a manner unmistakably similar to that of a father who intervenes to protect a son from the mistakes of his first independent venture outside of the home.

Such a formulation takes the image of familial relationships in Bedouin and sedentary societies as its model. As the most homogeneous and cohesive social institution, such a family was unquestionably patriarchal. In subtribal feuds, the degree of closeness to any *nasab* (line of descent) largely determined the alliances, and the immediate brothers were bound together, right or wrong. The preeminence of one member of the family translated into preeminence for all, and likewise for shame. If all prophets are viewed as brothers, then together they acquire sufficient distance from the traditional bonds imposed on them by their accident of birth, while the model for the relation among them continues to be the family. But this holy family establishes a distance from the traditional family, a distance that allows prophets to experiment with the dual role of struggling against and belonging to their communities of birth.

Brothers share a destiny, a similarity of character, and the source of their inspiration. Once the realization comes about that they had been relaying the same message of the same God from the beginning of time, then the boundaries of the family are immediately met. That is, by providing a concrete example of the concept "family," the addition of new members must be controlled rigorously, since the quality of each member will reflect on all. And if this family is discovered to have been in transhistorical existence in an unparalleled way, then additional members can only *decrease* the sanctity of its conceptual integrity.[4] And from such logics (boundedness of the concrete, revealing the plan as an act of conclusion) came Muhammad's emphatic assertion that he was the last of the prophets; the one to whom the plan is revealed is at the same time the one to be entrusted with the task of bringing it to a conclusion.

As retold in the Qur'an, the stories of the prophets anticipate the rejection of prophetic claims by society as an almost inevitable outcome of the project of prophethood itself. But more importantly, ancient prophets are consistently unrepentant for having disrupted the status quo. If anything, they do not even claim to be bringing anything new, but rather stress that they are restoring an old order that had been suppressed by contemporaneous society. In the story above, Ismael, the "father of the Arabs," and his own father Abraham clearly abhor the departure of the Arabs from a *forgotten* tradition that was explicitly antipagan.[5] This construction, with the founding fathers testifying against their distant offspring, was effective not only because it invoked portions of existing stories of social origin but also because it redirected their purview to a teleological seal, while at the same time neutralizing the ever-present alternatives of other book religions, namely, Christianity and Judaism. These were recognized as links in a chain of a divine plan, although both entailed criticizable shortcomings. Both were imprisoned within the sociocultural contexts of their moment of introduction, with Judaism being confined to exclusive tribal enclaves and Christianity leaving little impact on the collective morality of the tribes adhering to it, not to mention its sectarianism, which Islam decried. Thus, though the prophetic qualities of Moses and Jesus were confirmed, their followers were denounced on a variety of theological and behavioral points, ranging from diluting monotheism,[6] to factional infighting,[7] to betraying their prophets,[8] to lacking relevant rules of social ethics.[9]

The Audience of the Prophet

As one aspect of the process of ascertaining credentials for an audience, the interrogation of the past had some foundations in pre-Islamic pedagogies. In pre-Islamic poetry, a number of evocative symbols that establish the poetic flow address directly both the past and an audience. Standing before a ruined site, as mentioned in previous chapters, was the traditional formula by which the pre-Islamic ode opened. The ruins were conceived in no unambiguous fashion as referents to a *lost* past in which the life of the poet was implicated. The traces were moreover directly addressed and interrogated as if they were themselves an *original audience*. Eventually, the ruined site is abandoned in the ode in exchange for a more present audience of companions, who accompany the poet in halting in front of the past as a ritual of discourse initiation. In Imru' l-Qays's seminal ode, the ordeal of halting is assisted by two companions, who watch the poet's lamentation and listen to the flood of memories they provoke. Silently, this audience watches the entire transformation. But it consists of more than passive listeners. They lift the poet from the abyss of self-annihilation-by-remembrance: "There my companions halted their beasts awhile over me / saying, 'Don't perish of sorrow; restrain yourself decently!'" (c. 5).

They say no more for the rest of the ode. Yet this "saying" is sufficient to rescue the one who remembers from the impasse brought about by the ruins' fundamental infertility and unresponsiveness. At the point of recognizing the audience, the poet stands again, acknowledging them and proclaiming a recovery, and leaps into the second movement of the ode. The audience has become present. It confirmed itself first by halting when an invocation to that effect was delivered and then by speaking. This constitution of an audience rescues the narrator from the loneliness of self-reflection, for which the desert landscape can only offer the mock consolation of a ruined site—a sign of the impossibility of reclaiming the past. The companions in pre-Islamic poetry invite the narrator to depart from the silent ruins and come back to the adventures of the present. The act of "speaking" by the companions confirms more than a simple dialogic presence. It also delivers a trust in the power of ordered (poetic) words and re-proves, at the same moment, that listening has already been occurring. The moment of halting is the moment of examining not merely the meaning of residence (which, as the ruins testify, is temporary), but also the meaning of presence. Now both, poet and audience, are to linger in the halting. The flux of unregistered time stops. There emerges an ode, registering what had been lost and anticipating what is to be gained, and a world is made for the sake of listening. At the moment of halting, therefore, history begins: It becomes possible to tell a story.

The idea of prophethood, on the other hand, is premised on a drive to *regain* the past rather than simply to lament its irretrievable loss. As such, it requires a different procedure of audience constitution. Here, the past has a singular, teleological meaning precisely because it points to an *ongoing* transhistorical story that is about to be concluded. This feature means that such a story cannot be abandoned in the unceremonious manner by which the ruined site is habitually forgotten in the ode; rather, the very essence of the ancient tale is the ground for its resumption in the present. Here, the story is not only narrated, it is also brought back to life by adding another character—a prophet—who resembles its protagonists and who for that reason is the only character who can end it. The uniqueness of such a story is itself underwritten by the conception of a prophet, simultaneously an actor and a voice for synthetic and uncontested interpretation.

Pre-Islamic society, however, offered no stage from which a speaker who did not claim to be a poet could address an audience in this fashion. Bedouins recognized no strictly binding hierarchy, especially one to which they had not consented, and their material ideology and near egalitarianism rendered claims to prophecy highly suspicious. Thus, the Bedouins were the last group to join Islam in Arabia, and many of them reneged immediately after the death of Muhammad, only to be brought back into line by force during the short reign of the first caliph, Abi Bakr. On the other hand, the more differentiated society of Mecca posed a different problem for the notion of a prophet. There, social and economic hierarchy was both noticeable and recognized. Muhammad himself was partially immune from reprisals for many years, largely because he belonged to the relatively influential Hashemites of Quraysh. But in any case, he was neither close to the helm of the branch nor a distinguished Meccan in other ways. Many well-to-do Qurayshans refused to listen to what a common man had to say in his capacity as a prophet, as they equated legitimacy of discourse with personal prominence, and personal prominence, in turn, with economic well-being.[10]

In the traditional *sira* (biographies of the prophet) that impasse was overcome by suspending the prophet-audience dialectic for several years and replacing it with a dialogic God-prophet cycle, which finally established a prophetic right to an earthly audience on the basis of Allah's capacity to reverse human standards and reality. Here, the idea of the prophet did not evaporate into reclusive, otherworldly mysticism, precisely because ordinary social values were not rejected in their entirety; the prophet was possible precisely because such values could be *reallocated*. The tiny early *surah* (chapter) of al-Kauthar concluded as much in one quick stroke. There, a certain nemesis of Muhammad is addressed as an *abtar* (a derogatory term for a married man who had no male heirs), who in reality was none other than Muhammad himself.[11] The Qur'an here acknowledged the shameful substance of the word when it reallocated it to the enemy of the prophet. How a man with male heirs could become an *abtar* in Allah's world was never made clear, since the *surah* expressed a will to revenge rather than an articulation of reason.

The act of revenge must reproduce the original transgression in the name of justice, since it was revenge for a specific act rather than an articulation of a universal principle of justice. It must therefore return to the perpetrators their transgression as it was understood, that is, in its quality and language as a transgression. In one sense, that is why the will to revenge is so capable of displacing the universality of abstract reason. Such a conception of the will to revenge was uniquely adapted to a God who was under no obligation to explain the unexplainable. The insult to Muhammad was understood as an insult, not only because the intention was to insult but also and especially because every occurrence of the word *abtar* was understood to entail a *natural* diminution of status. It was not the concept of the *abtar* that was rethought but the will to revenge that threw it back, as it stood, onto the perpetrator, who was not logically exposed to it. The logical impasse expressed in the *surah* of al-Kauthar did not merely signify an original failure at acquiring a passive audience in the manner provided for the pre-Islamic poets. It also motivated a conscious and elaborate drive to ascertain a proper audience as a *precondition* of prophethood rather than as a possible outcome of it.

Thus for three years after the first revelation, Muhammad preached the early, largely cosmological segments of the new religion "secretly." A small constituency began to take shape, which not only confirmed for Muhammad the seriousness of his mission but also added to his confusion, as it demanded of him further elaborations on what Allah's intentions were beyond vaguely introducing himself and assigning an earthly carrier of his message. The recruitment of the early followers apparently followed no specific social or economic pattern. The earliest *Sahabah* (companions) included the respected affluent merchants Abi Bakr and

'Uthman Ibn 'Affan, the slave Bilal the Abyssinian, the austere Bedouin Abi Dharr al-Ghafary, Muhammad's adopted ex-*mawla* (slave) Zaid Ibn Haritha, and members of Muhammad's close family, namely, his wife Khadija and his adopted nephew 'Ali, who were reportedly recruited after a *hanifi* endorsement by Waraqah Ibn Nawfal. The diversity of the original base, though not signifying a challenge to traditional clan bonds, did nonetheless give rise to a new method of looking that detected the lack of spiritual content in traditional social bonds.

Beyond that small social enclave, open propagation later revealed the practical difficulty of constructing a prophetic audience, mostly because Arab societies that lived in or frequented Mecca during the pilgrimage and *suq* (marketplace) season had different reasons for rejecting specific claims to prophethood, even when they entertained some notion of its anticipation. The Bedouins showed the least interest in Islam, even when Muhammad used overt tribal appeals in approaching them.[12] The Bedouins, however, barely respected theological orders, especially abstract ones. Other Bedouins understood Muhammad's approach as an invitation to join an alliance to conquer other territories, and they subsequently offered their help on the condition that after "Allah gives you power over those who deny you," they would inherit sovereignty. They very explicitly told him that they would not sacrifice their lives for something as trivial as an Allah unless that Allah allowed them a privileged status among the Arabs after the victory of Islam.[13] Only then would they be ready to follow a prophet, be it Muhammad or anyone else.

The naked way in which the Bedouins spelled out their tribal conditions caused great tactical and even strategic difficulties for the emerging Islamic evangel, even though it failed to detour the development of his cosmology in a lasting way. In a characteristic gesture, the leader of the later nomadic rebellion, the aforementioned Musaylimah, reportedly used a strictly tribal tone in his correspondence with Muhammad shortly before the latter's death, demonstrating thereby that the newly consolidated religion still left almost no trace of an impact on nomadic political perceptions of the world. Musaylimah reportedly wrote a letter to Muhammad offering the following compromise: "From Musaylimah, messenger of Allah, to Muhammad, messenger of Allah: Peace be upon you; I have been designated to share the matter [prophethood] with you, and been told that half of the land is rightly ours and half is Quraysh's, even though the

Quraysh are transgressors." To which Muhammad reportedly replied: "From Muhammad, the messenger of Allah, to Musaylimah, the liar: Peace be upon he who follows the true guidance; the land belongs to Allah, Who passes it on to whomever He wills among His worshippers."[14]

Thus, from the perspective of Musaylimah and his followers, the notion of prophethood did not necessarily presuppose a deposition of a divine task in a unique individual instance. It did, however, correspond to claims to political authority in a more open manner than sedentary communities were ever willing to entertain. Thus, the unreliability of the nomadic audience was registered clearly in many passages in the Qur'an, such as this one: "The Arabs of the desert declare: 'We are true believers.' Say: 'Believers you are not.' Rather say: 'We profess Islam,' for faith has not yet found its way into your hearts."[15]

In this respect, the distinction is made between two acceptable declarations of allegiance, "Islam" being only one—and the weaker one at that—of the two. In the above *aya* (Qur'anic verse), the word "Islam" is used in the literal sense of submission (to peace, to Allah) rather than in the sense of *active* undertaking of diverse and more detailed practices encumbent upon faith. This "offer," which is made in the Qur'an only to Arab nomads and to no one else,[16] signified the agony of a tactical decision that had to be made with communities that were themselves offering practical alliances but were unwilling to submit to continuous command or central supervision.

Muhammad's dismal failure to construct a prophetic audience in Mecca and among the Bedouins contrasted sharply with his decisive success in Yathrib (later Medina), where, significantly, the audience constituted itself largely in the *absence* of the prophet. According to traditional Islamic accounts, the Islamicization of the Yathribites began during one pilgrimage season when, among the flood of visiting peninsular Arabs, the busy Muhammad finally stumbled upon a band of Khazrajites of Yathrib, from whom "Allah willed good to come." According to the sources, the half dozen men went back to their town to tell their people of the new prophet in the land. They returned to Mecca during the next pilgrimage season, twice as many in number and with a broader representation and more dedication, promising loyalty to Islam. By the time Muhammad and his followers left Mecca to go to Medina during the *hijra* (migration), most of the people of the city had already been Islamicized.

This accomplishment was as decisive as it is illustrative of the unintended course through which the prophetic audience coalesced. As such, it requires a brief pause to explore its grounds. In comparison to Mecca, Yathrib was less heavily involved in the trade economy, although it played a part in it. Its society, which consisted of periodically warring tribes (Aus, Khazraj, Jews) living behind fortifications, revealed more visible fissures than Mecca's. And as an overall sedentary unit, it was much closer than Mecca to nomadism. Those conditions offered an order of reception to Islam that was free from some of the restrictions that Mecca had to impose on new theological contributions. In Mecca, the monotheistic Allah lacked one major factor, namely, a socially sanctioned means of dissemination; Mecca's most emphatic rejection addressed not the notion of a monotheistic Allah as much as Muhammad's unsolicited prophethood. In other words, it rejected the uncustomary notion of boundless authority for a fellow citizen. In Yathrib, such an insurmountable barrier of social communication did not exist, for Muhammad was not a regular member of its society. Most of the Yathribites saw Muhammad for the first time only after they had already joined Islam. In his absence, he enjoyed an aloofness second only to Allah's. Unlike the Meccans, Yathribites never experienced the perfectly human prophet "eating and walking about the market squares"—as the Qur'an registered Meccan responses to Muhammad's prophetic claim—before they had already committed themselves to the faith. Faith, in this sense, indicates just this accomplishment: An audience is so firmly constituted in the absence of the source of its dissemination that when the human features of the prophet appear in the distance, prophethood as an empirically discernible notion will have forsaken the precondition of miraculous and credentializing presentation. An audience so constituted could be counted upon not to disperse thereafter.

The constitution of this audience, however, was pathbreaking in another respect. Traditional sources mention two successive agreements (*bay'ah*) between Muhammad and Yathribite delegations, the second of which was to instigate his migration to the town. In the first, Muhammad delegated a trusted Meccan follower, Mus'ab Ibn 'Umair, to teach the elements of Islam to the Yathribites. The main traditional sources also point out that it was the Yathribites themselves who asked Muhammad to send an outsider to regulate their affairs, as the long history of infighting among them had left them without a local arbitrator who had not been tarnished by the spillover of tribal wars.[17] This episode is greatly reminiscent of the dynamics that had preceded the commencement of the monarchical experiment among Kinda tribes almost a century before in the central peninsula. In that case, the distant king of Yemen was approached to assign an outsider to arbitrate the increasing disputes in Najd. In this case, the same experiment addressed antagonistic sedentary tribes, which could be controlled more effectively than the widely dispersed nomadic following of Kinda could be controlled by its kings. Moreover, this experiment was now buttressed by an ontotheology and underwritten by an Allah demanding to be feared.

The preaching of Islam through a representative of an absentee prophet, rather than by the prophet himself, proved to be an astonishing success. Unlike in Mecca, Muhammad was not at hand and so could not be continuously implored to produce convincing prophetic credentials. The knowledge that there was a prophet in the land, his detached remoteness, his anticipation, and his instrumental role as a needed arbitrator of conflicts encumbent upon sedentarization—all provided a dialectical scene through which the audience coalesced. Furthermore, Yathrib had little affinity with Mecca's need to populate the *haram* (sanctuary) with stones and engulf them with spirituality, which protected and enhanced its magnetic economic role in the peninsula. Yathrib was not the center of either the *suq* route or the pilgrimage. Like many non-Meccan Arabs, the Yathribites had no great dedication to the idols. And the presence of a large Jewish community in Yathrib and in neighboring towns, such as Khaibar, introduced newly sedentarized Bedouins to a different spiritual order, one centered on an abstract God.

Thus, when Islam was introduced to the semi-Bedouin, non-Jewish Yathribites, it progressed among them very smoothly, as it had to demolish nothing in its way. There were no deeply held beliefs against the thrust of its message. But even at that early stage of its introduction to Yathrib, Islam had more to offer its people than a pure ontology: It used the force of Allah to regulate a social life that could no longer afford the heritage of some aspects of the old Bedouin economy, namely, intertribal raids. In the following year, the delegation of the Muslim Yathribites in Mecca, who came to be known in Islamic history as the *Ansar* (Backers), concurred with Muhammad on the following conditions: that they worship none but Allah; that they refrain from stealing, adultery, infanticide, and propagating falsehoods; and that they obey Muhammad insofar as his teachings involved social benevolence (*ma'ruf*). In return, Muhammad promised them paradise if they followed their part of the agreement. If they did not, they could expect punishment that was not necessarily certain: Allah could either absolve them of the oath if they so wished by hardening their present life, or he could merely make them wait until the Day of Judgment, when he might forgive them just as well.[18] It was not a bad deal. It spelled out a gradual intrusion into the life of two antagonistic tribes of a set of beliefs and a system of authority that ordained that from that point on, they would submit to Allah rather than to one another.

The second agreement was a historical landmark. Its conditions betrayed a synthesis between the old worldview and the revealed pieces of the new ontotheology, between tribal identity and a new form of transtribal unity, between the existent social conditions in Yathrib and the ideals of the prophet and his Meccan followers. In addition, it set in motion the Muslims' total break with the Mecca of the past, where their movement had been stagnating for years: Shortly afterward, they left for Yathrib en masse in what became known as the *hijra*.

The traditional historical sources narrate the story of the second pact as follows: More than seventy of the *Ansar* came to Mecca to meet Muhammad during the pilgrimage season. He went to them accompanied by his non-Muslim uncle al-'Abbas Ibn 'Abd al-Muttaleb, who was the first to speak at the meeting. The uncle began his speech by announcing to the *Ansar* that Muhammad was enjoying an honorable unassailability in Mecca because his clan protected him. However, the messenger of Allah was prepared to abandon that luxury and join the *Ansar* in their dwellings. Al-'Abbas concluded by warning the *Ansar* to abandon Muhammad and his teachings at that moment if they had the slightest doubt about their dedication to his protection once he moved to their territories. The immediate readiness expressed by the *Ansar* led Muhammad to finally proclaim his unity with them in a strict tribal manner, signaling a departure from the theological aloofness through which Islam had been proclaimed up until that moment.[19]

This prophetic audience continued to enjoy a certain distance from the prophet even after the *hijra*. Muhammad refrained from ruling in Medina directly, delegating authority instead to twelve *nuqaba'* (keepers, overseers) selected by the Khazraj and the Aus to guarantee the pact. The *naqibs* were told that they were to account for *their* people (the *Ansar*) following the example of Jesus's disciples, while the prophet would account for *his own* people, meaning the Meccan Muslims who migrated to Medina (the *Muhajirun*). This division, which was to leave its imprint on later developments, answered the question of the audience for God's message by contouring such an audience along earthly social structures, which the phenomenon of prophethood was in the process of remodeling.

CONSTITUTION OF SAGEHOOD: KNOWLEDGE, FOREKNOWLEDGE

Recluse Quest

According to traditional accounts, Muhammad's first revelation came during one of his extended seclusions in the mountain terrain around Mecca. The first phrases to be revealed of the holy book emphasized little other than the modality of transmitting the forthcoming knowledge: "Recite in the name of your Lord who created—created man from clots of blood. . . . Recite, for Your Lord is the Most Bountiful One, who by the pen taught man what he did not know."[20] Sacred knowledge is an outcome of a piecemeal process of passive recitation. As such, it must be sought through ritual purification, signified in this case by Muhammad's recurrent seclusions away from the perils of ordinary society for many years. The outcome of this process is a particular kind of knowledge, available not through ordinary pedagogical channels but, rather, through a reclusive quest. The search itself, *unlike the knowledge it was to produce,* was a socially sanctioned practice. A story from the tradition tells that one day Muhammad, along with his young nephew, were discovered practicing a strange form of worship by the nephew's father, who, while declining the invitation to join their quest, did not object to it either. For the quest itself did not threaten the established order.[21]

The intensity of the seclusion is also confirmed by many other early Qur'anic statements, which instruct that meditation should be performed at night, away from the clamor of the ordinary society of the daytime.[22] Sleeping, on the other hand, was a possible route to seclusion insofar as it protected the prophet from the temptations of sin, which, according to the traditional narrative, reared its head twice during his youth.[23] This freedom from sin is not only an outcome of a determined reclusive quest for knowledge but, moreover, a symptom of a strong denigration of mortal society. The first signs of prophecy, as Muhammad was to recount many years later, involved an encounter during a lonely stroll in the wilderness with two angels, who proceeded to ascertain whether he was indeed the promised one. The verification procedure they employed involved weighing him against one man, then ten, then a hundred, then a thousand, only to find him tipping the scale consistently. They concluded that he was indeed the promised one, who would still tip the balance even against his entire nation.[24]

This procedure is itself interesting because it presupposes the social embeddedness of the seclusion itself; Muhammad is judged on the basis of a *comparison* with other ordinary mortals from his own nation rather than on the basis of self-referencing attributes. This social comparability is an outcome of the seclusion process; the spatiotemporal sanctuaries from this world—the cave and the night—allow a discourse of world denunciation to take form, but in some cases they also prepare for the reintegration of an exhausted soul back into society as a reformer who possesses knowledge gathered from the wilderness outside. In Muhammad's case, the periodic recurrence of time of reckoning with ordinary social life (for example, dawn) does not signify the end of the reclusive quest; as the time of revelation nears, Muhammad experiences visions as powerful as the sudden break of the dawn (*falaq s-subh*) itself.[25] At such a point, the reclusive quest is over. The knowledge accumulating through the time-space dimensions of seclusion begins to encroach upon the time-space of society. The dawn is reminiscent no longer of the end of the quest but, rather, of its success.

The reclusive quest is one model of knowledge transmission that operates according to particular dynamic. In the pre-Islamic ode of 'Antara—an ex-slave who exists on the margins of social belonging—we find a comparable process of reflection, which renders a different order of knowledge nonetheless. At an early point in the ode, 'Antara hears a voice that instigates a particular quest, a departure from his regular discourse of love and heroism. Whereas in the case of Muhammad the voice that commands him to "recite" comes only at the conclusion of the reclusive quest, the voice for 'Antara reverberates at the outset and induces a movement toward its point of origination. That unknown point exists in a region distinct from the anonymity of a nature in which this nomad travels.

Until the source of the voice is found, the poet refrains from describing nature, which then ceases to interfere in human life. 'Antara gathers himself at that point, places all faculties in attentive order, and proceeds to interpret the sign for himself. His aim to render the call as "smooth, comprehensible" offers a direction for his journey. He is set in motion by a promise, a task, or a goal, to be certified (thus completed) at the point of destination by an act of "interpretation," that is, ordering the barbarous nature of the primal voice. The essence of his project consists of a continuing movement toward the source of a call.

Unlike the prophetic call, the nomadic encounter with a potential source of otherworldliness is recorded as a voice within poetics that, distrustful of moral rigidities and faithful to an erratic encyclopedia, is tolerant of the continued presence of strangeness within its confines *as strangeness.* Even though the movement is invited by the possibility of making sense of a primal voice, there is nothing in the voice that stands in need of reclamation through elaborate schematization. With such an openness, the quest after the voice leads to no particular destination, after all. Under such nomadic conditions of detecting new missions, where movement is the nature of life and halting is the exception, strange callings float without a home in which they could be deposited or classified: Under conditions of wandering, everything that invites a quest will eventually slip away from sight. The nomadic quest is not otherworldly in the sense that it is *against* the world but in the sense that the otherworld is a component of the self. As an entity that is equally open to all absurdities of the strange and the familiar, *this self is a continuous act of recording* and is thus a projected encyclopedia. Here, the knowledge accumulated through any act of seclusion is not *transformative,* as it is under the prophetic experiences of sedentary life, but *cumulative.*

Similar quests can be found throughout pre-Islamic poetry, for example, in the odes of Labid and 'Amru Ibn Kalthum. 'Amru's otherwise sonorous, confrontational ode gives way at the end of couplet 14 to a monumental withdrawal by the poet, who lets externalities overwhelm him. Voices from the past and from other places appear as though uninvited and with little transition. The poet then becomes the antithesis of the tribal leader he otherwise is, receiving signs as they occur, as though dreaming, incapable of reclaiming loss or pausing to condense the clutter of signals down into a coherent voice. The joy and promise of the dawn with which the ode opens has been frustrated, the project of standing in the face of time and molding it to one's own end has been thoroughly shattered. And to complement the degeneration, the gnostic, revelatory project announces in couplet 19 its complete surrender to the unknowabilities not only of the future but of the present as well. This sequence ends on that note. Nothing more is added to the void, the region of ignorance, lying one step ahead, and from then on extending to the limits of sight. Thereafter, the invitation to respond to the invasion of signs and voices by a reclusive quest is pushed to the background, as a more clearly political and communal project, to which the ode is ultimately oriented, takes over.

Knowledge and Prophetic Credentials

Unlike the sage, the prophet is sent by God. His knowledge comes from God, without whom the prophet-to-be remains simply another illiterate member of the tribe. In fact, even his selection as a prophet flows not from any specific prior credentials or personal qualities but simply from God's right to make arbitrary selections.[26] Furthermore, Muhammad's relationship to the deity is largely passive, nondialogical, and prone to fear. The prophet does not actively seek God and his knowledge but, rather, is forced to absorb divine instructions as an unsolicited reward for his quest. The *sira* emphasizes the extreme horror and helplessness that engulfed Muhammad during the early episodes of revelation: He frequently fell to his knees, pleaded with his wife, Khadija, to cover and hide him, and even contemplated suicide. Divine knowledge, which the prophet was to propagate, gradually took the form and style of what eventually became known as the Qur'an. As "knowledge," this corpus required the employment of particular codes and insignia and also the endowment of its vehicle—the prophet—with the requisite credentials.

Self-enclosed systems of knowledge require unique codes that set them apart. The code, however, does not simply consist of linguistic forms through which the knowledge can be heard distinctly. The speaker must seek and find a location of authority from which to speak. The distinct codes recorded in pre-Islamic poetry all came with tales that also described the status, trials, and tribulations of their speakers. Zuhair's biography, for instance, introduces him as an "organic intellectual" (in the Gramscian sense), as a sage who spoke from within the tribe. One crucial background for his wisdom consisted of his awareness—akin to Muhammad's—of a lack of an instrumental authority that could enforce the code of morals and manners outlined in his ode. There were other speakers, needless to say, who could also lay a claim to a privileged speaking position from which to dispense wisdom but who were less traumatized than Zuhair by the dilemma of instrumentality. 'Amru Ibn Kalthum, who personified the position of a poet-leader, offered a modality of code transmission that contrasted sharply with Muhammad's trials, which exhibited—at least in Mecca—the agony of the unenforceability encountered in Zuhair's case. 'Amru's ode includes some intriguing viewpoints incumbent upon the particularity of his belonging, namely, to a society in which the author of a "legitimate" code of knowledge (the poet) also happens to be entrusted with instrumental authority.

'Amru's speech not only defies the tradition of standing at the ruins but actually attempts to preempt their formation. His speech preceding the traditional contemplation of the ruins, lacking in any foundation in the tradition, compensates by furnishing an encyclopedic record of things past instead of contending with the loss imprinted on the reality of already formed traces. As couplet 8 has it, the function of this encyclopedic composition is "to be certain," "to *tell* that which is sure knowledge," "to be *told* of that which is sure knowledge." The speaking leader, therefore, is himself the instrument of certitude that has eluded Zuhair so frustratingly. Rather than fruitlessly mourning a loss, 'Amru preempts its occurrence by assessing its real value. The record, thus, evaluates what had elapsed and what, on the basis of what is known from what had elapsed, could be seen to be following suit. At a certain level, the act of recording involves a desire to anticipate the future or, more pointedly, to premourn the loss that is to occur so that, when it lands with its full ferocity, one could endure it by claiming to have already experienced it.

It is this preexperience that projects into the personality of the leader an element of foreknowledge. A leader must know and must have anticipated the way things are from an earlier point of commencement. So he has to choose a point of beginning earlier than all possible others: Standing at dawn, with which his ode begins, replaces standing at the ruins. In other words, the replacement of a spatial halting by a temporal genesis prepares the leader to act to preempt the work of nature rather than waiting for nature to present its bill. Time is not to run its natural course but is to be made by the author. He shall decide the course for the rest of the day, rather than wait for the traces to be formed for him by the natural flow of time. When the inevitable happens, and the lover's tribe begins its departure, an emphatic plea registers a protest rather than a strict lamentation: "Pause, and we'll ask you whether you caused this rapture / the wrench being so near, or to betray the trusty" (c. 8). The questioning mode replaces the customary expression of sorrow at the site of the ruins: A leader wonders where others weep.

From the vantage point of conscious power, the reality of pain is transformed into a questioning of its existence. Power is the capacity to postpone loss indefinitely. If the questioning mode is to ever dissolve into an admittance of the loss, the wreckage, the break, the absurdity of further questioning, it would find itself confronted with this lack of control, which the concept of "treason" alluded to earlier brings to the fore in the most challenging way; for the leader himself is defined by the existence of an "order," whose undermining defines treason. On the other hand, a leader is himself defined by the possibility of treason: As an eternal play of opposites, power is at the same time the susceptibility to subversion.

Prophetic knowledge, on the other hand, is the foreknowledge of God. Unlike the experience of instrumental (tribal) authority, the prophetic experience is such only because the formula of knowledge/foreknowledge is distributed to different agencies rather than condensed at the one locus from which discourse emanates. The very first word of the Qur'an was the command to recite, repeat, or read (*iqra'*) an already formulated yet humanly unknown wisdom. In this fashion, the prophet's legitimacy is premised precisely on his lack of contribution to the discovery of prophethood. The question of reason becomes subordinate to the demonstration of will: Muhammad has not sought the divine; rather, the divine surprised the contemplative, ordinary wanderer along the road and told him that from then on, the relationship between his self and the divine was to be that of *repetition*. Muhammad was taught from the beginning that the being of a prophet meant neither subjective responsibility for a mission nor a speculative rendition of God's instructions but a strict verbal reiteration of God's exact words. The anticipation of prophethood, and subsequently of the revelation of the stored foreknowledge, furnishes in itself a readiness to repeat. Reportedly, the prophet's first response to the command was not "why recite?" but "recite what?" The anticipation instigates a search for signs of the divine's presence in and communication to the world. The fact that the divine's first order of business is the transmission of an already formulated body of instructions rather than self-justification indicates, among other things, the prior establishment of the idea of the divine itself as a distinct storehouse of knowledge, communicated to the world only through words whose source cannot be seen.[27] Even the prophet himself is one step removed from the ultimate source, since the Qur'an is revealed through an intermediary, the archangel Gabriel. Allah is not directly involved even in transmitting his own religion. When Allah is situated above the medium carrying his own words, he registers thereby the validity of the words on the basis of the impossibility of comprehending their source.[28]

Since the only experience of the divine that could possibly be transmitted to society is his utterances, such utterances must then stand for the idea of the divine in its entirety. But since one of the qualities of the new conception of the divine is his unapproachability, the utterances must then also stand for that which cannot be expressed. Therefore, the first experiment with a solution to such a dilemma dictated that neither the utterances nor the prophetic experience of receiving them can find a resemblance in the world. The unapproachable divine cannot appear in an approachable format. The format consisted for the most part of the quasi-poetic tradition of rhymed utterances (*saja'*), which was known long before Muhammad's time. The Qur'an expanded the range of topics expressed through *saja'*, and in many instances it registered its pride in its unmatchability on literary grounds.[29] Such an extensive use of a comparatively little used literary medium—which occurred less in sage discourse than did poetry—liberated the Qur'an from having to compete in the much more contested and regulated literary medium of poetry. It added an aesthetic dimension of authenticity that was crucial for the reception of the text without having to dilute its sanctity by reverting to more popular, thus more profane, means for the dissemination of ideas. The Qur'an openly resorted to glorifying its own literariness as a sufficient material evidence for the authenticity of prophethood in the land.[30]

In Meccan society, however, the crisis of prophethood was generated not so much around Qur'anic discourse as around Muhammad's own credentials. Muhammad had no instrumental authority until his migration to Medina, had no inherited distinct clan honors, and subsequently had no traditional entitlement to ideological or spiritual positions of leadership. Thus, for the first seven or eight years of preaching, Muhammad accomplished no significant breakthrough in Mecca. His followers continued to comprise a small minority, and major elements of his teachings, like the resurrection of the body, were openly ridiculed.[31] Many of his significant followers had to migrate to Abyssinia for a second time, and many of those who stayed behind recanted, whether because of social pressure or dwindling enthusiasm. The less powerful or wealthy believers found themselves bearing the brunt of harassment, and only those who enjoyed the protection of recognized clans, including Muhammad himself, could debate the rest of the community without fear of repercussions. Muhammad was pressed hard to produce miraculous prophetic credentials, but the aloof Allah consistently frustrated him. Ultimately, he had nothing other than the Qur'an to show, but even that hitherto unique form eventually became just another background for literary competition among the poets and storytellers, who were eager to emulate it.[32]

Thus, though for the prophet the constitution of prophethood was structured entirely around discourse, the earthly community to which he ultimately belonged privileged other credentials, namely, preordained tribal prominence. It was a question of entitlement to embody tribal destiny, a theme whose most illustrious celebrant in pre-Islamic discourse is 'Amru Ibn Kalthum. Unlike Muhammad or other poets (for example, Zuhair, Labid, Tarafa, Imru' l-Qays), 'Amru never addresses his own kinfolk; rather, he addresses their enemies on their *behalf*. After a brief submergence into the mist of history, love, dawn, wine, transformations, and sorrows, the bulk of 'Amru's poem is dedicated to addressing the major nemesis of the tribe, the king of al-Hira, all the way to the end of the ode. This registers a remarkable consistency in ancient poetry, which is maintained by virtue of the stability of the two sides of the communicative scene. This rare thematic stability, which the Qur'an itself did not begin to attain until its Medinian period, flows from a predicament similar to that of the prophet in Medina: A thematic consistency here is directly related to confrontational imperatives.

Similarly, 'Amru's addressee is less likely to leave, to slip away as easily as a lover, whose theme adorns earlier segments of the ode. The king of al-Hira, much like Mecca as seen from the perspective of the Medinian Qur'an, is a threat, an enemy, an antithesis, a traitor to the project for harmony, and thus could be counted upon to inform the entire discourse, disappearing only after the account has been settled. The enemy is a less elusive addressee, a nonmirage. It is an existing, known quality, a more stable form of concreteness than the vanished prehistory alluded to by the ruinous site or the lost prophetic traditions, which respectively instigate the nomadic ode and the sedentary gnosis. In both cases, scenes of animosity and confrontation stabilize the flow of "knowledge" and speech, where "to tell" or "to inform" (the adversary, infidels) are formulas that often begin and are interspersed through many couplets and *ayat*. In the case of 'Amru, this kind of knowledge flows from an instrumental authority and is delivered on behalf of the tribe, whereas in the case of the Qur'an it is provided *to* the tribe for the sake of saving it from itself.

Instrumental authority—at least in Muhammad's case—was only a later concern, born out of the failure of knowledge *in itself* to incite in the larger community a similitude of the recitational response, which molded Muhammad's prophetic career from its onset. The later shift in emphasis in the direction of attaining instrumental authority navigated through behavioral models that different heroic pre-Islamic poets revisited, notably 'Antara and 'Amru. To simplify the matter, 'Amru is a poet-hero-leader and, as such, a discursive prototype of the later Muhammad. 'Antara is a poet-hero-lover and, as such, a prototype of the early Muhammad. In the case of 'Antara, the substitution of the lover for the leader reorients the notion of heroism, and the poetic discourse addresses the notion of knowledge *without* the traps incumbent upon leadership. To be sure, the substitution makes the scenes of confrontation less stable. As a prototype, 'Antara's case shows that the lover shall never become a leader; as a freed slave, 'Antara is guaranteed to remain an outsider to the blood genealogy—an indispensable criterion for eminence—in a manner paralleling Muhammad's predicament of lacking tribally recognized criteria for prominence.

'Antara's is an ode of a legendarily long time of war (the same one that we have seen problematized in Zuhair's ode). Yet war here is but one more of the conditions of life. It has been going on for many years; it has become natural. And so the discourse finds little trouble in interrupting the battle scene with imageries of love, yearning, tranquillity, reflection: moments of lull, soon to be shattered by a resumption of fighting. Conflict and disharmony are not temporary conditions to be stamped out systematically, as sedentary societies thought of them, but simply other ordinary facets of life. The dialectic operating between struggle and tranquil reflection is not wholly arbitrary; rather, it is an operation through which proper credentials become evident for all to see:

> Praise me therefore for the things you know of me; for I
> am easy to get on with, provided I'm not wronged. (c. 36)

"Praise me . . . for the things you *know* of me." Not for the things I am about to tell you, nor for the sake of this tribal togetherness in which we are bonded, nor for what I do not manifestly possess. Praise me, rather, for the things you *know*: You already possess the knowledge that enables you to perform the act of praising. The praise is here an outcome of foretold knowledge. Since you already know, therefore I am known. I am not a subject tormented by the task of making myself known; no, I have myself disappeared as an actor on behalf of the self: I have been *made* known. And to be so naturally made known means that I shall not be asking the praise from a stranger. My strangeness, which itself defines the stranger in the other, had already been erased by this body of knowledge about me, which seems to have disseminated in the land.

On the other hand, you do not know me yet. I must make myself known with my own speech. My self-description shall deliver me to you. A stranger could not have possibly been so readily made known, at least not in a way that is naturally conducive of unmitigated praise. Now it is time to reappear, as though a cataclysm, to effect a disappearance once and for all. Here, I am throwing at your feet my unparalleled heroism. In its place I would like words: just that praise which alone would allow me *not* to be with you, but with the anonymity of the tribe, to wander, assured that while away, I am already deposited with you as this value, guaranteed by your words to survive as such, irrespective of my location in the vast land, where I could perish and never return.

So, who am I? On the one hand, I'm easily summarizable, "for I am easy to get on with, provided I'm not wronged." On the other hand, now as a hero, I am still easily summarizable, for "if I am wronged, then the wrong I do is harsh indeed / bitter to the palate as the tang of the colocynth" (c. 37). *I am a reactive but naturally dormant hero.* That is, in essence, all of me, or, in other words, all of me that my speech was required to deliver. The rest, as you know, is known. My contribution was to make known my performance in a scene of confrontation, and now that all unknowns are thereby rectified, I am prepared to leave, with the confidence that my own speech, when combined with the already known, shall redeem me against all danger.

Like this hero-lover, the prophet is not intended to be an empirical person spending a great deal of time and energy to make known that which must have been so, or even to defend his face, subjective being, and entitlement to spiritual leadership. The Qur'an, especially the Meccan Qur'an, explicitly allocates to Muhammad little more than the role of a bearer of good news and warnings. The crisis of prophetic entitlement in a tangible community, however, and unlike 'Antara's affair, made the trials of subjecthood all but unavoidable. In 'Antara's case, by contrast, one can recognize a remarkable ease of transition, engendered by the preentrustment of all knowledge about the hero unto the tribe and the lover. Thus he easily leaves a well-lit scene, going off to drink wine, and, after lingering there for a while (c. 38–41), he departs the inn only after reminding the audience that the loved one already "knows" unmentioned qualities, which were on the verge of being spelled out but are now left unsaid for the sake of more important business (couplet 41 ends the wine scene with ". . . my qualities and my nobility being as you have *known them*").

The need of such a hero to speak, however, stems from a condition of living in which one encounters continuous alterity, self-defense needs, and a sense of unfreedom that his distant objects of desire bring to the fore. Such forces always pose for him, therefore, the question of identity. Within a social hierarchy attentive to (real or imagined) blood genealogies, identity was an issue of unalterable naturalness and thus was not an object for plain and direct meditation. Under such circumstances, identity, to the extent that certain events reallocate the right of its thinking to the self, is an enigmatic feeling of a relation to the self and society that must be thought anew, since the past archive of the tribe offers it no reference point. At this juncture, discourses of individual identity and entitlement—'Antara's as well as Muhammad's—belabor experimentation and add layers of sameness, for they are attempting to capture a feeling for which no word was yet in existence.

In 'Antara's case, the enigma is assaulted, circumvented, discursively altered, or relegated to the domain of the "already known." His ode points this out most clearly in the sequence in which he describes his drinking habits. For wine causes a shift in identity; it causes an other side to appear, a less controllable side, a hint at a difference lurking within. It seems necessary for 'Antara, therefore, to deny the transformation: Drunk or sober, he is the same moral entity: generous, honorable, bountiful, noble, or of otherwise "known" qualities (c. 40–41). In a similar gesture, in some interesting early passages the Qur'an offered the faithful in heaven a special kind of wine, distinct in that it caused no shift in personality and no lapse in reason.[33] The fact that wine was eventually prohibited in this world points to the need for the faithful to possess psychic stability, since after the faith there would be no reason to *change* one's identity and temperament.

In the case of 'Antara, the resilience of identity, belabored in the context of wine consumption, also stabilizes in one location a number of behaviors that together inaugurate an unshakable, unique character. From the vantage point of this privileged, stable position, change could be foreseen and resisted, whereas identity endures a quest after a phenomenal unity preservable in the economy of a summarily proclaimable rendition. The search is after a *word* that could deliver the enormous entirety of a hero-poet-lover (in addition to other secondarisms), a word that would preserve the reservoir of experiences that had formed the identity, so that the subject could keep on moving, beyond them, into the yet to be "known." This word, in other words, is that verdict that is to settle the account with the prehistory of the speaker. And in the preinscriptional era conditioned by a normativity of movement, such a search, unlike the highly referenced history that was to follow, was indeed arduous. To find a verdict on experience was a matter of chasing a smell of possibilities emanating from a variety of directions rather than simply choosing from the classified givens of an ideological tableaux.

Under prophetic conditions, by contrast, the "word" became the endless project inaugurated by the divine command to recite. Rather than delivering exactly that word that the command of recitation implies, Qur'anic discourse postpones the delivery a little further: "Recite in the name of your Lord, Who . . ." Thus, as in the case of the nomadic poet, the prophetic quest inaugurates a movement that, unlike the nomad's, is fixed from the beginning on a single source of voice. In either case, the promised identity is indefinitely postponed as a dynamic *discourse* begins to unfold. The duality of prophet/community in the case of Muhammad and hero/lover in the case of 'Antara provide audiences against whose backdrop the identity of the speaker is continually adjusted and made known.

In the case of 'Antara, the story of heroism concerns the warrior's performance in war. Yet the story must in some way be already known, even before the heroic identity is confirmed by its retelling. The audience's presence is the first item to be ascertained here: "I could advise you, daughter of Malik, to ask the [horses] . . ." (c. 44). Heroism, indeed, war itself, is a performance for an audience. And it is especially so in this case, where concerns of communal defense, even the tribe itself, are hardly mentioned. Neither is the "daughter of Malik" subject to any discernible threat. She is there to listen to another alteration of moments of this duality of knowns and unknowns, a cycle that is meant to introduce the fighter in his full heroic bloom, his collected history of victories, his totalization as an active identity. Thus, she is now to be told, in a rather confounding mode of speaking, of what she is yet to know.[34] This knowledge, which in any case is to be provided by a witness (c. 47: "Those who were present at the engagement will acquaint you . . ."), ushers in the hero's acquisition of an identity (unique, unified, totalized, certain, confining, confident). Such shall be the identity through which this speaker would enter history and last in it forever.

Thus, we have a scene of telling stabilized, whereby the audience is clarified, and the warrior moves on, confident of the naturalism of a mode of telling that no longer requires him to halt and address the audience in the first person. The constructed and stabilized scene will allow him to be described by the witnesses. Thus, the very next scene finds him moving, as though he had been moving all along, rather than recommencing after a rest: "for I'm [still] on the saddle of a strong swimmer" (c. 45). He plunges into enemy territory. A great war is to ensue. Before the enormous cloud of dust and the noise of colliding armories erases all else from view, the warrior reemerges and addresses the lover for one last time, "informing" her—still by way of a witness—of one important detail, lest she misinterpret the battle:

> Those who were present at the engagement will aquaint you
> how I plunge into battle, but abstain at the booty-sharing. (c. 47)

This mode of fighting is different from the normal and regular nomadic raid (*ghazw*): A hero is to be detached from such trivialities. Once an audience is formed and for which it is performed, the battle assumes a different moral structure. The socioeconomy of the *ghazw* situation required no particular witness, order, or report. The war to be witnessed here is waged in the closed circuit of audience-identity: Identity here is a matter of acknowledgment by the audience, and the audience ensures that the performance does not deviate from the behaviors and codes required for an entitlement to an identity. Thus 'Antara is aloof to the common economies of the situation and abstains from sharing in the booty, which is made known by the witnesses. *An item of knowledge which ought to have been "already known" is that which is delivered by a witness,* not by the hero. Like the prophet, what is *not* to be given through his own voice is a general description of his own qualities and habits. That, *in general,* is assumed to be known. That is, he already possesses the requirements of the claimed identity that the audience presumably anticipates. *In their general capacities,* the hero and the prophet must be already known. Thus the discourse emanating from such identities addresses only further details: As a known commodity, the hero tells in the first person only those details, specifics, twists, and variations of a more stable and general phenomenon that, in its larger form, is already namable as 'Antara and is therefore foretold.

In a similar vein, the qualities of the anticipated prophet are already foretold in the myriad of stories of prior apostles sent to the world by the *same* God. The Qur'an thus spends a great deal of time on retelling such stories rather than on defending and explaining Muhammad's character and actions. Moreover, such tales are often told not as original stories but as parables, whereby Qur'anic discourse quickly moves on to drawing conclusions from them, assuming that their substance is already known, that prophethood as a general identity is already prefigured in the land, and that the dilemmas it faces are historically recurrent rather than specific to Muhammad's case.

The added element in Muhammad's case, which was to be of important ramifications for the ethical dimension of prophethood, consisted of a set of known general life conditions condensed in Muhammad's own identity. In an early *surah,* the prophet is made aware of the fact that his role in society consists of reproducing his relationship to Allah. In the brief *surah* of ad-Duha (Qur'an 93), the prophet is told that as Allah had sheltered the orphaned Muhammad, the latter shall oppress no orphan; that as Allah had guided the imperfect Muhammad, the latter shall respect everyone who seeks help; that as Allah had enriched the poor Muhammad, the latter shall proclaim the generosity of the former. These acts of *reproduction* of divine goodness parallel the formulation of the project of prophethood as a *recitation* of divine words. But in deeds—as opposed to the case of words—the prophet is never allowed to exactly reproduce the work of the transcendental deity, whose actions must keep a respectable distance from those of mortals, just as his nature must transcend their imagination. At that early stage of prophethood's formation, Muhammad was merely instructed to acknowledge the actions of God in the world, and to *make known* the fact that any present bounties anywhere derive from him alone. The collective knowledge that Allah was behind every fortune in social life would in itself assure the irreversibility of such fortunes.

Since the source of prophetic identity is situated outside of the self and is defined as incomprehensible via the customary methods of inquiry, the identity and the project become themselves irreversible. A prophet no longer ponders identity. The heroic identity, by contrast, requires continuous reinforcement, performance, retelling, and granting by an audience. Whereas a hero is impossible without an attentive audience, a prophet lives and dies as such in spite of the indifference of the audience. 'Antara's report on his heroic virtues succeeds only when the appeal for a heroic identity is granted by the audience. But here, the "audience" is simply a placeholder for the finitude of knowledge transmission. 'Antara's ode ends by relieving all anxiety about fate thereafter, so the burial of the speech can be undertaken with equanimity. All danger of the "unknown" in the world has been eliminated: Should 'Antara now be killed by his enemies, he says, he is not worried, for he has done them greater harm than they could ever redress.

With this certainty, he surrenders to the openness of the desert and goes on. There is no teleology awaiting him, no destination: He is fundamentally *unworried*. Being slain by enemies no longer matters. Life as a hero has reached its highest possible peak. No more accumulation is possible save, perhaps, for a metaphysical transformation. With the impossibility of further additions, the discourse comes to a halt. For not only has he transcended mortal society so as to have become fundamentally unworried, but that in the process, he discovered that this highest freedom to move was that founded upon the separation of one's actions from their consequences. Accountability for one's own actions, though continuing to be a matter of nature, is no longer worrisome. One no longer worries; rather, one welcomes the natural response to one's prehistory.

It was this attitude that the sedentary society was to repackage under the rubric of "duty," along with its attendant replacement of heroes by prophets. That is, resting with a clear conscience became a psychic state that was possible because of an awareness that all possibly harmful outcomes that one might risk by performing according to the dictates totalized as "duty" are obviated by valuing duty as the realm whose achievement is life's highest goal. In other words, "duty" spelled out an amnesty that made thinking of consequences irrelevant. "Duty," in the sedentary setting, was therefore a formula that repositioned its performer worrilessly on the road toward the upper boundaries of life. In the process, it was discovered that such boundaries—since no heroes or witnesses were there to make them or provide infinite knowledge about them—must belong to a transcendental form of subjectivity, for which the only witness (as the Qur'an clearly spelled out) was the prophet himself. Thus, the process by which credentials are ordinarily endowed in society is reversed, whereby the requisites of witnessing are taken away from the audience and redeposited into a phenomenon called prophethood.

THE TEAR OF THE POET AND THE FEAR OF THE PROPHET: FAILURES OF BELONGING

A transformation along the lines just described requires a great deal of self-reflection, a will to metamorphosis, an agony of redefining the meaning of communal belonging. The *sira* tradition emphasizes Muhammad's early seclusion very clearly. But the process itself had clear parallels and models in existent practices and discourses. Pre-Islamic poetry provided models for identity transformation at great length, as did the tradition of tribal outcasts (*sa'alik*), who were defined by their lack of fit into existent tribal mores and who could not be easily reintegrated into the tribe once they expressed an atypical individuality. Imru' l-Qays provided an early model of such an agony, a model that was distinguished by its acceptance of the tragic nature of an irrevocable lack of belonging, even though the poet continued to act partially on the basis of the *duties* incumbent upon such a belonging. His ode opens with an alienated memory attempting to reclaim a place or, more precisely, condemned to stand in front of it and engage with it in a hopeless duel, only to withdraw in the disarray of defeat, having failed to retrieve from the jaws of its pastness that peculiar form of togetherness that it had so deceivingly promised. Here, the trace of this togetherness acts like a mirage, a deluding paradisiacal scene at the end of the horizon, which instigates a desire doomed to nonfulfillment, a desire that only reminds of what is lacking. Like the prophet who searches after traces of ancient prophethoods in the landscape of the present, the nomadic poet is cognizant that the lack of completion of an old project is an essential property of the *present*. For the prophet, this lack instigates a hope of retrieval. For the poet, it also instigates such a hope but simultaneously decrees its unfulfillability.[35]

For both poet and prophet, ruins and remembrance go hand in hand. Whereas the prophet recognizes mental ruins—such as the faith of Abraham existing in corrupted forms—the poet recognizes physical ruins, which indicate a lost condition of earlier harmony, tranquillity, and togetherness. Ruins are traces of a past state of meaningful totality, since the trace is noticed as a trace of something larger in the first place. The remembrance itself seems to emulate the nature of that which instigates it, being itself assembled in the form of fragments. Unlike the eventual prophet, however, the poet strives after no recognizable "system." His is a nomadic remembrance: One remembers at will and responds to stimuli as they come. Prophetic remembrance, on the other hand, is ultimately oriented toward a "system," understood as a purposeful kind of discourse in that it ties various discussions together for the sake of delivering a judgment or positing a context. The nomad, by contrast, remembers at will, and likewise aborts the memory at will. He returns to himself. He forgets the confrontation. There is no lingering remorse. There is no discernible impact, no sign of indelible injury brought about by this sudden awareness of nonreturning time.

Whereas the prophet moves on to revisit the stories of past prophets as a chronicle leading up to him, the poet interrupts the meditations on the past in order to tell a *unique* story of the *self*. The narrating poet begins the story of the self always after having remembered. A trace in the midst of nature, barely recognizable, introduces him as a narrator with an individualized story of a unique and namable love. That love is now entrusted to the hands of a trace upon a certain topography, which is referenced, described, cried upon, and given a name, and the journey continues. The trace, after all, is something that is itself departing. Its very feebleness confirms the reality of time, the irreversibility of its unilinearity, the finitude of all things dear to the heart, the impending demise of the observer himself. A trace of the thing is the warning that all things are moving toward a prescribed nullity, that all movement will ultimately halt. For the prophet, on the other hand, the trace is nourished and carefully cultivated until it comes back to life in his own personhood. The poet, by contrast, commences the story of the self after having realized the ends of time, his story now being told from beneath the overwhelming weight of finitude and the overbearing weight of the halt, informed by the knowledge that what had been is unrepeatable. The poet emerges, not as a total subject but as a trace of the self, "perishing of sorrow" (Imru' l-Qays, c. 5), slowly reconstituting, painfully crystallizing.

To perish of sorrow is that essential experience that allows the self to shed the skin of its past and reemerge anew in order to populate the rest of the ode. One stands facing the ruins not to ponder their wisdom, to register their difference, to linger in one region of memory, nor to measure the magnitude of time's revenge against life. The fundamental experience of the ruins transports the observer into their essence of dilapidation. He himself becomes the ruins. As the fundamental experience that instigates the discourse, the appreciation of the ruins consists not of a simple commentary on their being or logic; rather, it is lodged in an act of dissolution in front of them. To notice nomadically is to inhabit, to possess, to become of the same element. Noticing, after all, is a precondition of halting; that is, it is the promised experience that causes the nomad to momentarily abrogate his habitual wandering.

This abrogation endows acts of halting and meditation with an apparent extremism of character. The halting poet and the meditating prophet are reconstituting a prior order that had been synonymous with nature—a certain notion of the self; thus the tear of the poet, the fear of the prophet. These are the rituals of metamorphosis which, in some way, are prefigured in the original seclusion (of the prophet) and lonely interrogation of traces (of the poet). For the poet, to shed a tear is the explicit "purpose" of halting ("Halt, friends both! Let us weep, recalling a love and a lodging" [c. 1]). Likewise, Muhammad's fear, occasioning the command to recite, his escape, and his search for refuge, commence his prophethood and offer unmistakable signs of its authenticity, for him as well as for the early faithful. For the poet, the tear is offered as an authenticating stamp of the new self, understood as the fruit of dissolved or departing experiences. The intensity of the crying itself seals the rupture between the unreclaimed trace and the impending future of this self, as the poet himself acknowledges: "Yet the true and only cure of my grief is tears outpoured: / what is there left to lean on where the trace is obliterated?" (c. 6). The fear of the prophet fashions a new self, a self with a project, a mission, and a tradition. While the tear pronounces healing and freedom from prehistory—whence the new self could commence—the fear pronounces that healing is impossible until the mission is *completed;* hence, the intensification of the weight of a vast prehistory.

For this reason, unlike the poet, the prophet cannot afford the luxury (or agony) of a socially unanchored or exiled self as a foundational trope of his identity, since his discourse could engender healing in the world only through the active endorsement of an audience to which he belongs. However, Muhammad's proselytization in Mecca was a failure by any standard. Eight years after his emergence as a prophet, he had accomplished no social breakthrough and was beginning to suffer disorienting personal losses as well: the death of his wife Khadija and, perhaps more significantly, of his protective uncle Abi Talib. Abi Talib's death had a more immediate and severe outcome, for Muhammad then had to act as *nothing but a prophet,* being for the first time without his traditional protection, which had up until then allowed him to blaspheme the established order without fear of repercussion. The traditional *sira* reports the beginning of unprecedented abuse of Muhammad at that point, especially as no universally respected Hashemite figure surfaced to protect him immediately after Abi Talib. By then, most of the traditionally significant Hashemites had already joined Islam, many of them doing so out of clannish solidarity with their kin rather than out of conviction. And many of them were already living far away in Abyssinia.

For the prophet, such events constituted a severe lesson in social irrelevance, and not only because seemingly influential clan members could no longer provide the traditional protection. The death of Abi Talib brought to the fore the sad truth that the uncle could protect and perpetuate the mission of a prophet in the community only because he was a universally respected infidel, just like the infidels who were to assume Muhammad's protection afterward. Meccan Muslims then needed protection not so much because they were another sect in Mecca as because they insisted on replacing the established ontotheological order. That insistence, coupled with numerical weakness, meant that Muslims who would otherwise be prominent society members could no longer be immune from reprisals. Prominent Muslim merchants then had to forge individual protection agreements with specific infidels who were either their relatives or with whom they had commercial or other dealings.

Though the tribal/communal experiences of exclusion encountered in pre-Islamic poetry often instigate a (half-hearted) poetic effort at reconciliation, a similar experience by a prophet allows reconciliation only at the cost of the prophetic identity itself. Even when motivated by specific communal concerns, prophetic discourse transcends the bounds of the tangible community. Thus more than the poet, the prophet can *voluntarily* break away from the tangible community, an alternative already exemplified in the earlier migrations of some followers to Abyssinia. But such migrations, in turn, confirmed to the rest of the Meccan society the irrelevance of the Muslim community in its midst, thereby accentuating the harassment of the Muslims and thereby stimulating even further the prophetic temptation to universalize the mission. An early experience with the world outside of Mecca at that point materialized as a desperate venture into the agricultural community of Ta'if, where Muhammad underwent a level of mockery and humiliation he had never endured in Mecca; he was ultimately forced to leave empty-handed.[36] But that episode in itself illustrates the resilience of prophetic identity, which is based on the ability to detect signs of success and retrieval among the ruins, where the poet saw only death, an unfulfilled desire for healing, and eventual departure. The isolation in Mecca and the cataclysmic failure in Ta'if occasioned the Qur'anic revelation of the *surah* of al-Jinn, which proclaimed—in a rare reversion to the mystical realm—Muhammad's success in bringing a community of jinn into Islam, precisely as he was heading back to the increasingly inhospitable Mecca, suffering from a major failure.[37]

The disentanglement of the project of prophethood from the specificities of Mecca was sealed, however. After the dialectic of worldly debacle in Ta'if and an otherworldly triumph with the jinn, Muhammad reentered Mecca in a way that must have confirmed the degree of the prophet's dependence on temporal and tribally based (rather than otherworldly and divine) protection. Muhammad spent days awaiting a favorable response to a request for a traditional protection (*ijara*) that he submitted to notable Meccan infidels. After two rejections, an *ijara* was finally extended to him, and he could enter the city again without fear of harassment.[38] But though Muhammad continued to dwell in the city, he was essentially on his way out, as the project of prophethood had reached a standstill there. The pilgrimage season became a period of intense activity for him, as it became an opportunity to meet other Arabs who came from throughout the peninsula. From then until his migration with the *Muhajirun* to Medina, traditional Islamic history records less communication between the Muslims and the rest of Meccan society. The exclusive preoccupation with the fate of the "mother of towns" was abandoned, the Muslim creed being gradually universalized in orientation. Always attentive to angles that might lead to success in his mission, the prophet began to apply the mission to all people equally, regardless of tribal affiliation, as Mecca increasingly seemed like a lost cause. The seeds of this orientation were already there in an earlier discovery that prophethood was there to guide the rich and the poor alike, irrespective of *established* rules of social hierarchy and valuation of human worth.[39]

From the vantage point of traditional society, such an expansion of the mission is problematic mainly because it reveals a rift within the community to the world outside; thus, the community would need to account for Muhammad or, more precisely, for a prophetic phenomenon that had weakened the harmonious image that Mecca held in the peninsula. According to Ibn Hisham, the elders of Quraysh convened in order to unify their position on refuting Muhammad (or, perhaps more probably, on explaining his behavior to the pilgrims). They debated whether to describe him to the visitors as a *kahin* (a soothsayer), a madman, or a poet. They finally resolved to describe him to the Arabs as a *magician,* on one ground, namely, that his sayings were magic insofar as they alienated otherwise indivisible entities: "the one from his father, his brother, his wife, and his kinsfolk."[40] In other words, Muhammad was to be defined as a spoiler of nothing less than the self-evident nature of human bonding. His "magic" consisted of his ability to subvert such an entrenched order by using no more than *words.*

Thus, though one of the grounds that frustrated Muhammad's mission in Mecca was his failure to produce the miracles demanded as justification of his prophetic claims, he was freely advertised as having a capacity for magic (that is, the ability to subvert nature) by the same people who had once demanded the miracle that would accomplish a comparable feat. The clear difference between the magic and the miracle, at least in this case, is that the nature that the magic overturns is *human* rather than physical nature. On the other hand, the source of this magic, more than in the case of the miracle, can be isolated and dealt with more easily: *Words,* after all, furnish the modality by which magic does its work. Unlike the miracle, therefore, the treatment of the effects of magic takes place through rendering words inaudible to an unreceptive ear.

Thus, the "magic" of words is silenced by excluding the author, who had subverted nature, from the community to which he otherwise belongs irrevocably—that is, *by nature.* Tarafa Ibn l-'Abd and Imru' l-Qays, it must be recalled, were thrown out of the tribe as much for their poetic proclivities as because their musical words threatened social nature, since they stood in the way of the poet's expected assumption of normal tribal obligations. Like Muhammad, Tarafa, following his ostracism, always navigated the borderline between the new territory of the self and the old territory of the tribe, between an uncharted region of possibilities and a known region of confinements and responsibilities. Whereas Muhammad's prophetic identity had already been well formed by the time of his departure from Mecca, Tarafa's experimentations with new identities began largely after his expulsion, with his words—the source of his dilemma—being also the means to his new faces. Thus, for Tarafa, the protestation of his lonely fate is just loud enough to be audible but not so resolute as to blazon a thoroughly novel march of a notion of the self beyond its collective prehistory. Thus, his wisdom, defenses, logic, and thoughtful deliberations are always placed *after* a discourse of carefree hedonism. Unlike the early Imru' l-Qays before embarking on his tragic quest after his father's withered kingdom, who spoke of his pleasures matter-of-factly as they came, Tarafa, like Muhammad, is aware of his history, his society, and his audience. But unlike the prophet, his discourse is also attentive to the ever present accusation of dereliction of duty.

With the notion of "duty" becoming more important after the institutionalization of poetry (as already exemplified in the cases of 'Antara, Labid, Zuhair, 'Amru, and others), pre-Islamic poets became less confident of their entitlement to carefree, tribally detached self-reference, in spite of the originality of their "magic" of words. Even Imru' l-Qays, whose hedonistic pursuits were also responsible for his ostracism, found himself compelled to eventually perish in a preordained and half-hearted quest after the lost kingship of the same father who had expelled him in the first place. The ostracized poet, just like the ostracized prophet, was incapable of becoming indifferent to his own collective prehistory. Tarafa was always at work on a new synthesis of morality, asking the tribe to grant this first subject in its history, the poet, a new right for a special behavior, for an individual name, for a distinct voice to speak with. He was only slightly ahead of his times, for that right was granted at a later stage, when the power of the poetic word was appropriately recognized and when a subsequent generation came to reverse the low opinion that Maʻbad—Tarafa's eldest brother—held of Tarafa's usefulness, and also to reverse Maʻbad's opinion of poetry in general (that it could never return a herd that had wandered off or been stolen while the shepherd was transfixed on poetic meditations).

Until that point, however, words continued to be the means to discover the new possibilities of the ostracized self, a self devoid of affiliation and duty. As Tarafa challenges his relatives to leave him alone with his own habits, he immediately realizes that that could not be done unless they abandoned him (c. 79). This sudden discovery propels a desire for an otherness of being (c. 80–81), a desire complete with names and characterizations, circumscribing wealth and power. After speculating on the consequences of his hypothetical attainment of the identity of empirical dignitaries ("then I'd have been a man of much substance, visited / by all the springs of nobility, chiefs and sons of chiefs" [c. 81]), Tarafa's ode announces the completion of his transition toward a new identity of the self (c. 82–92). The new identity acquired at this stage pronounces not the finitude of separation from the tribe but, rather, the modality upon which the poet, like the migrating prophet, will be transported back to his society at the prestigious moment of his death (c. 93 and afterward). For the poet, the transition into the new identity allows a return by relieving him from having to defend himself before his kinfolk.

The new identity begins with a self-definition (c. 82): "I'm the lean, hard-bitten warrior you *know of old.*" As in the case of ʻAmru and ʻAntara, this identity is conveyed to an audience that should have *known* his qualities before the speech itself began. The recognition that the audience does not need to be told what it is actually being told, as in the case of the prophet, is a source of crisis precisely because the speaker here knows beforehand that what should have been known before the speech will continue to pass unrecognized after its delivery. But in this case, the declaration of this self-standing identity is *followed* by (rather than logically leading to) a reconciliation, whereby the desires of the poet lead not to exclusion but to a harmonious communal festival (c. 87–92). That is a significant event in the ode, since the festival is arrived at teleologically by an act of deviance; the story commences with an attempt by the poet to steal a camel and ends with neither his success in the undertaking nor with his punishment but with all parties concerned enjoying the benefits of such a grand animal. As we shall see, the reconciliation of the prophet with Mecca at the end of his mission follows similar dynamics: The final fight is avoided, the blood of the infidels is spared, and their social position is maintained and incorporated into Islam. The struggle of the ostracized voice with the source of ostracism is not a ground of total annihilation of either party by the other but itself furnishes a new dialectic of reintegration and reunion. This reunion is possible only when the community displaces its definition of the new words from magic to miracle. Unlike the divisive magic, the miracle—in Muhammad's case it was to be divine words themselves—becomes the ground for new harmony.

seven

The House of the *Umma*
and the Spider Web of the Tribe

THE TRIBE

The beginning of open proselytization by Muhammad in Mecca, after three years of reclusive confinement within the small network of the early faithful, was reportedly instigated by the Qur'anic instruction: "Admonish your nearest kinsfolk and show kindness to those of the believers who follow you."[1] This delineation of the audience spelled out an entire range of presumptions, foremost of which was that the new religion intended to speak to society according to its existing terms of social organization. It also marked the emergence of the *social* nature of religion; though the early *Sahabah* (companions)—as a cult of semi-Hanifi mystics—came from diverse family backgrounds, the open propagation of faith called for an approach outlined in terms of traditional mechanisms of exerting influence in society. Open propagation, as opposed to selective and slow-paced recruitment, brings forth a hitherto less-vexing question of grand rules of social valuation. And here, as in Bedouin society, it was the recruitment of the close *nasab* (line of descent) relatives that established a sense of social security, around which less-durable alliances with members of farther *nasab* lines could be forged. As far as grand alliances were concerned, that

179

was the only structure that tribal society, and Muhammad himself, knew. It was on the basis of its logic that the first attempt at expanding the network of faith took place. The quick failure of that attempt, which the tradition condenses in the devastating mockery of the prophet by his uncle Abi Lahab, left Muhammad with the task of inventing a path-breaking paradigm of social solidarity. In fact, the Qur'anic singling out of Abi Lahab—as a personification of this essential predicament—for eternal damnation could be seen as a hint at the frustration felt at the magnitude of such an additional and unanticipated task occasioning the aftermath of the Qur'anic command.[2]

Immediately after designating the closest of kinsmen as the first recipients of divine news, Allah instructs his messenger to be humble toward any followers. In this second element, the highly distinguished responsibility of single-handedly salvaging the world is balanced out by prohibiting the prophet from worldly eminence should he succeed.[3] Muhammad is allowed thereby to claim no personal political design, no self-interest, and no subjective accountability for his actions, as he simultaneously deflects the question regarding his particular selection to prophethood. In this case, the Qur'an sees parallels to Muhammad's role, predicament, mission, and social position in earlier prophetic traditions. Thus, the prophet Salih is none other than a simple member of the brotherhood of Thamud, distinguishable only by an arbitrary prophetic assignment. And like Muhammad, he denies receiving any gratification from the necessity of his prophetic assignment.[4] The notion of the *brotherhood* of the prophet to his community is abundantly evident elsewhere in the Qur'an. The idea possessed the unique quality of containing an implicit allusion to egalitarianism, while invoking a traditional notion of mutual obligations. Thus, though they expound deep trepidation about the fate of their societies as an exemplary form of brotherly concern,[5] ancient prophets shield themselves thereby from the social irrelevance awaiting those who perceive of a crisis of communal meaningfulness without being able to produce a consensus behind their diagnosis of it.

At some points in the early Qur'an, the attempts to incorporate the imagery of strong kin relationships seems to overpower the barrier that otherwise divides the believers from the unbelievers; among all of the in-fidels, for instance, Abraham singles out his father for a special appeal for divine clemency.[6] Thus, having accepted traditional kinship ties as the model for the ideological battle in the open community, at least for the time being, the Qur'an sought to generalize—rather than replace—such a conception of social cohesiveness. At what was evidently a later stage, the Qur'an rendered Noah's last requests to Allah before the flood as follows: "Forgive me, Lord, and forgive my parents and every true believer who seeks refuge in *my house*. Forgive all the faithful, men and women, and hasten the destruction of the wrongdoers."[7]

Thus, immediately before the deluge was to cleanse the earth, and after nearly a thousand years of fruitless preaching, Noah humbly makes his last statement, specifying who ought to be forgiven. Significantly, this is the only instance in the Holy Book in which Noah's parents are mentioned; they are neither denounced nor praised nor historicized anywhere, not even in this context. They are to be forgiven not because they belong among the believers but solely in their capacity as the prophet's parents. In the sequence of Noah's requests for salvation, they come immediately after Noah himself and, interestingly, before the believers who join Noah of their own volition. The believers themselves, to be sure, appear in the *aya* (Qur'anic verse) only after they had been united with Noah at the familial level: They are those who join him not simply in an abstract bond of coreligiosity, but *in his own house.*

Here, the Qur'an transcended the predeterminacy of familial linkages, but only by extending their domain. The idea of the family was reasserted on grounds that were supposedly more solid than blood relationships: Now all believers, men and women, were one family. The *nasab* line was losing its monopoly over the direction and content of social loyalties. Nonetheless, that was not the whole story. Side by side with the development of that concept of familial cohesiveness of the faithful, there developed a dynamic aiming at reuniting the entire divided community, faithful and not so faithful alike. The substitution of the social cohesiveness of believers for that of genealogical families divided in faith implied a threat to the established order of social bonds. As such, it pointed the way to a lurking, novel paradigm of social solidarity that could challenge the antiquated one if the community as a whole failed to listen to the harmonizing message of Allah.

The heroic poetry of pre-Islamic times, by contrast, viewed the question of tribal/communal solidarity almost exclusively on the basis of conflicts with outside threats, without which the question of solidarity could scarcely be articulated. The most representative discourse in this genre is perhaps the ode of 'Amru Ibn Kalthum, whose portrayal of tribal solidarity as a natural certitude is spelled out largely in the context of addressing its nemesis, the king of al-Hira in lower Mesopotamia. Here, the poet wants from the outset to *inform* the king of a *certitude (yaqin)* (c. 20). In a highly pitched heroic tone, this certitude flows thereafter from a collective subject "we." The poet becomes the spokesman of his tribe, and the poetic discourse becomes its collective and embodying speech. In that case, poetry had already become, much like the Qur'an after its socialization, more than a pure, socially unanchored, wide-eyed ontology inspired by being out amid the limitless horizons: It had also become a medium of political speech and an ingredient in the games of power. In 'Amru's ode, therefore, one encounters one of the longest thematic continua in ancient poetry, propelled into motion by immediate sociopolitical concerns. The speech on behalf of the tribe (much as in the ode of al-Harith, 'Amru's poetic competitor) is conditioned by what the forms of solidarity that instigate it presuppose: a minimum common denominator, a permanent meeting ground, a stable collective character, and perhaps an enemy (or at least a distinct notion of outsidedness).

A discourse obsessed with the imperatives of predetermined sociability, like the poetry just mentioned and the social Qur'an, with a persistent pedagogic posture toward the community with which it was concerned, ultimately forfeits an earlier aura of spontaneity, discontinuity, and proximity to a less-demanding realm of nature or outsidedness. In the heroic ode, the collective subject imposes itself on the scene, thereby forcing the poet to exhibit responsibility toward a *preexistent* tradition of solidarity and to profess a thematic continuity incumbent upon the threat facing such an order. These elements rapidly deplete the poetic discourse of all meditative potential and cosmological, encyclopedic effort evident elsewhere in the pre-Islamic *mu'allaqat* (odes). There are no secrets of being here, no mysteries of nature or exteriorities, no reflections on life, no codes from a house of wisdom, not even an ontological ground for the ethic of responsibility itself. In 'Amru's ode, the speech flows in one direction, to an addressee who had been named only once but who continues to be addressed throughout, as though his eternal presence has become so natural that no reminders of his identity need ever be reissued. From the dissipation of the hedonistic mist (c. 20) to the end, no couplet is sufficiently attuned to the dizzying array of ontological hints to carry it onto a new path—as is frequently the case elsewhere in pre-Islamic poetry as well as in much of the Qur'an. No verse is independent or discontinuous enough to form a curvature in the discourse, none excavates beneath the surface of the obvious confrontation. A straight line persists all the way through, exposing no more than a single unchanged scene, exposed by no more than the dim light of a normalized, socially entrenched, and serviceable poetry. As we shall see, the Qur'an also displays this awareness of threat to the community from an outside source, which is less namable nonetheless.

As a communal discourse, the heroic sequence in pre-Islamic poetry shares with the Qur'an as well as with that of other poets (for example, Labid) an orientation toward planned, purposive speech. But this mode of planning exists at a level somewhere between the Qur'an's referential tableaux and Labid's cyclical ordering. Unlike the Qur'an, 'Amru's ode does not so much seek to redefine the nature of communal bonds as to deliver an image to the outside world regarding what the community fundamentally *is*. And unlike Labid's discourse, 'Amru's method of ordering his speech is conditioned not so much by the imperatives of the work's internal logic as by the need to reinforce the presence and definition of the audience, the community, the addressee, the function of "speaking on behalf of," and the intersubjective common denominator. The plan is unilinear rather than multidirectional, digressional, or cyclical. Though, like most other odes, it is unhampered by fragmented, discontinuous, "mixed" figuratives, 'Amru's ode's claim to unity rests on the name of the tribe from which it ostensibly emanates. Its speaker is a collective subject (we), incapable of disbanding or forgetting the conditions acquired and gradually consolidated as the speech unfolded. Furthermore, such a collective subject is defined throughout the ode antithetically, by the continuing presence of an enemy, who is the addressee of the speech. Thus, whereas the cyclical ordering evident in Labid's ode possesses the luxury of forgetting and remembering from a large reservoir of figurals, feeling no pressure to come back home soon, no need to abort or extend a cycle beyond its natural exhaustibility, the unilinear ordering cannot forget the *social* condition keeping it together. Once that condition is dropped, the discourse of the collective subject does not know where to "come back" to but, instead, disbands on the spot.

Thus, in 'Amru's ode, the king of al-Hira is addressed at length, through figuratives of heroism and glory that accumulate on top of each other. It is impossible to abort the confrontation without annihilating one side, and the resulting stalemate imprisons the poet's speech in a cycle of endless sameness. The persistence of a tribal confrontation that could not be put down ultimately delivers not a triumph, as one would expect, but an outworn unity, illuminated in the tired fragment thrown in toward an unreachable end:

> Our bodies were hung with glittering mail-coats
> having visible puckers above the sword-belt
> that being unbuckled from the warrior
> reveals his skin rusted from the long wearing. (c. 70–71)

Like all forced continuities, this one, once lifted, discloses the erosion forming underneath the heroic surface.

In this case, the skin is more than simply a metaphor. It is an allusion to an entire method of organizing and conceiving of social cohesion. Its primal function is to clothe the body as an organically unified entity, thereby setting the boundaries of that unity apart from nature and apart from all that is designated as an exteriority. Thus, the valorization of this ultimate guarantor of the unity and oneness of the self can only be undertaken not under the dictates of subjecthood alone but also in the context of an understanding of being as responsibility for handling exteriorities from the point of view of an active, transformative project. In the case of heroic poetry, and especially 'Amru's, such a being is overextended, overemployed, rusted, restless. An unbreakable bond with power constitutes its collective definition of subjectivity, infused by and limited to an indispensable responsibility, whose fulfillment defines heroism and contours the tribe's collective speech in the noisy scene of a perennial battle.

In the Qur'an, by contrast, the notion of unity was condensed in Allah as its ultimate guarantor, rather than the leader, the prophet, the poet, or even the collective speech of the tribe. In the holy book, the very notion of skin as the most certain guarantor and metaphor of the uniqueness and unity of what it holds together is vociferously challenged.[8] Physical as well as natural unity comes here not from pure speech or human authority but, rather, from a unitary capacity (God's power) that, though capable of dismembering the human subject into noncommunicating fragments, could also collect such fragments and deposit them into a larger order of sociability, much as it gathers together pointlessly scattered clouds.[9]

The notion that the tangible community is a source of a concerned speech motivates Qur'anic speech as it does 'Amru's ode, though the conclusions are dissimilar. Whereas the threat to the tribe in 'Amru's ode is clearly definable and namable, that facing Mecca was more vague, though no less real. The Qur'an clearly compares the peace of Mecca to the terror reigning in the chaotic world just outside of its limits.[10] As mentioned earlier, Muhammad for many years did not regard the outside world to be a proper domain for the message of Islam, and its problems were a matter of concern only insofar as they provided useful instructional contrasts. Before the eventual expansion of the realm of Islam, the Qur'an merely observed that amid the terrors of the world, Mecca was luckily safe. It did not dispute the city's right to be distinctly peaceful but, rather, merely asked it to recognize the abstract force protecting it, lest it degenerate into the resemblance of its uninhabitable surroundings. If the *haram* (sanctuary) was the guardian—as most Meccans thought—then let that sacred institution stand under the protective tutelage of a supreme power that could maintain its repelling function beyond human doubt. Indeed, Allah considers himself to be the "Lord of this [hitherto pagan] House," in the same context in which he emphasizes his role in safeguarding the fragile, long-distance trade routes upon which the city's economic survival depended.[11] In addition, Allah reminds Meccans of more concrete episodes of supernatural protection, such as when the Abyssinian expedition against Mecca (circa A.D. 570) was forced to retreat without a fight and under mysterious circumstances.[12] As it traces to Allah a protective function against vague and abstract threats and challenges, the Qur'an disparages pagan effort to seek tribal safety in the objects of worship then populating the *haram*, enlikening the frailty of such constructs to that of a cobweb.[13] Here, again, the metaphor of the *house*, as in the case of Noah's last appeal, condenses the idea of tribal solidarity along familial and thus ostensibly unbreakable lines—unlike those woven in vain by the spider, only to be obliterated by the first strong wind.

This embeddedness is easily discernible in the early Qur'an's feeling of belonging in and special relevance to Mecca.[14] Muhammad was even reported to have at least once openly linked the theological aspect of his message—abstract monotheism—to a political design that would make the Arabs rally around Quraysh and subject others to its mandate. Significantly, such a statement was offered in the context of Muhammad defending himself against the charge by the elders of Quraysh that he had "insulted our forefathers, ridiculed our faith, and degraded our deities."[15] The open appeal to the parochial interests of one city was repeated as often as it was needed, at the expense of the universality of Islam, until the migration of Muhammad and the Muslims from Mecca some years later.

The "mother of towns," however, rejected such a logic precisely on the basis of local relevance: If Islam was meant to be an essentially local doctrine, then why was the messenger from the Banu Hashim branch and not, say, from Banu Umayyah? Why would the prophet not be a distinctly honorable and wealthy man, instead of that thoroughly ordinary Muhammad? The problem of relevance came back to haunt the message: If Allah wanted to play the game of relevance, then he should have played by the rules. And the rules of relevance included more than praising the locality, showing concern for its fate, promising it a fortune, and speaking its vernacular. Above all, they involved accepting the community's conceptions of proper social roles and hierarchies. Eventually, the Qur'an itself came to register such a discontent as it attempted—in vain—to reject the right of the community to select its prophet according to its own rules.[16]

The priority of kin spells out an inescapability of *belonging* in a predetermined fashion. This issue, however, is not so straightforward. Pre-Islamic poetry furnishes a variety of models by which the enigmas incumbent upon such a belonging are encountered. The theme of belonging as a background of an inescapably collective speech can be seen in the aforementioned ode of 'Amru. The expelled poets, likewise, had to renegotiate readmittance into the tribe through a variety of mechanisms. But in other cases, poetic speech expressed communal belonging by showing sophisticated social concern for the community, which was expressed through eloquent, wise sayings, in the way that Qur'anic speech was intended to introduce the prophet to his community. The right to sagehood of those poets who belonged—such as Labid and Zuhair—was more recognized than that of someone who delivered discursive novelties intended to distinguish sacred speech from ordinary wisdom. Thus for a long time, Muhammad and Qur'anic discourse occupied a status within the tribe that was closer to that of the expelled poets and, as such, exhibited similar symptoms of distress and lack of comprehension of the grounds of such an exclusion.

However, though the Qur'anic response to the community's refusal to recognize the essential belonging of the faith in it was flavored with gradually crystallizing anger, the odes of the expelled poets commented upon the dilemma with a distinct tone of sadness and surrender. In Tarafa's ode, for instance, the transition into the ubiquitous trope of the virtues of his camel commences with recognizing in the essence of the animal a distressful predicament of departure and the magnitude of the distance separating him from his community: "Ah, but when grief assails me, straightforward I ride it off" (c. 11). Tarafa is a lonely, expelled poet for whom distance presented itself not as a matter for abstract signification but as a decision by others that *could be* appealed. Thus, he does not sever this hope by proclaiming it as a "fact": Such an acknowledgment would only naturalize its threatening materiality. Finding himself at the wrong end of the horizon, he must act as though he had not yet perished. To convince oneself of this endurance, therefore, is to purge the notion of irremediable distance from the speech. It is because of such a peculiar strategy of survival that Tarafa's gestures toward the materiality of movement and involuntary wandering occur as though in the abstract, without namings, without locations, oblivious to geography and to all companions who could be defined by a name and a personality.

By contrast, in poets like Labid and Zuhair we can discern the genesis of the socially belonging, "responsible" poet, someone whose distinctive speech becomes an emblem of tribal celebration as opposed to tribal ostracism. Such a poet had a solid abode, a safe belonging, and a proud tribe. He was eminent, respected, and, unlike the nascent prophet or the *sa'luk* (tribal outcast) poet, never in danger of being expelled: His had become a permanent form of speech in social life. The poet was no longer an absolutely distinct subject, traveling with his shadow and experimenting with the wilderness of discourse: He was about to become a social institution. The poet had already become a "tradition," a widely disseminated one, an echo of an established form, already constituted in a prehistory after which it was molded. The poet's own voice could now assuredly float in the distance, reaching perhaps beyond that mountain range, beyond that "shimmering haze" in the infinite horizon (Labid, c. 53). But he himself shall not move: The poet is a tradition now, he belongs on the ground where his speech gathers itself.

Thus, we encounter in the poetry of poets who belong a sense of "realism" whereby distance assumes an irremediable form that cannot be repealed. Labid's homage to the lover Nawar, for instance, is succeeded by an elaboration of the meaning of distance. As opposed to (inexplicable) hope of crossing the distance, Labid proceeds here according to the strategy of naming as a method of mapping out the concrete meaning of separation (c. 17–19): Labid distances the lover by an association with remoteness and then piles upon the road toward her one location after another, a plenitude of hindrances, with each name being a full obstacle by itself.

As such, this strategy of naming subscribes to the construction of loss encountered in traditional poetic openings, where naming functioned so as to circumvent a loss, speak to it, then leave it behind. The multitudes of naming then confirmed not only the distance of the place itself but also the distance that the poet had crossed *away* from what is now to be acknowledged as a loss by the magnifying operation of naming. Here, Labid invokes the same technique in an interestingly new dimension; in the traditional opening, naming overwhelmed the poet to such an extent that he finally withdrew in awe, acknowledging the finitude of loss and its irreversibility, and wandered off elsewhere. The distance between the spatiotemporal dimensions of the here/now and the away/behind is increased to infinity. Now Labid's namings, occurring after an opening that had its share of them, usher in a different modality for acknowledging the loss: It is not as though he is being refused entrance to or being repulsed from a realm beyond the lived reality of loss. Rather, it is that, as a fundamentally belonging poet, he shall take it upon himself to leave on his own cognizance, as a man free of love ought to: "So cut off your longing for one whom you may no more attain" (c. 20). This mode of realism reconfirms a resolute power over passions, a utilitarian vision of reality, and a sense of freedom. The impediments to all such moments, rather than pursued until the poet perishes of his sorrows, are now summarily dismissed by a swift acceptance of "reality." Yet it is this expression of freedom that, paradoxically, only a firmly rooted narrator could expound.

Thus, to be free is essentially to be *entrenched* in one's own society. Labid explicitly asserts the lover's freedom to depart, to cut off, to break, to acknowledge the irremediability of distance. Furthermore, the lover's resolution to break appears ambiguous: Not only does the lover speak in the second person, he also generalizes the identity of the lover. It becomes apparent, then, that what is meant is not the simple delivery of the poet's decision regarding the lady Nawar but, rather, the delivery of a universal pedagogy. This privileged location, ostensibly possible only by an entrenched belonging, is paradoxically the fountain of a general advice regarding the subjective will over the matter of breaking bonds.

In this ancient poetry, the poet could habitually slip quietly out of feelings of defeat, isolation, nullification, disenfranchisement, and so on with as little noise as possible,[17] sometimes abruptly, signifying annoyance, impatience, knowledge of unfreedom. The belonging poets, such as Labid, make, on the other hand, a distinction between topics whereby the honorable things in life, the worthy possessions, and the great adventures are not pronounced or dispensed with the same ease as other topics (and we will see how another great belonging poet, Zuhair, had to reason *at length* for such a thing as the futility of a hopelessly stalemated tribal war). Labid makes a decision implying a rational austerity of character rather than continuing to gaze at a present state of impossibility that waits for the decision to actualize itself, by some other externality that is impervious to his pronouncement: A free poet sets the terms. A break is legitimated here by what other nomads would regard as a mediocre factuality of distance.

For most of his tenure as a prophet, Muhammad oscillated between the two models of belonging evidenced in the discourse of the pre-Islamic poets, where belonging and freedom cohabited an uneasy conceptual landscape. The impossibility of continued belonging in Mecca of a proselytizing prophet, his eventual migration and war with the city, all exhibit a consistent theme of belonging in spite of being an outsider to his city for most of his career as a prophet. According to traditional accounts, by the eighth year after he had left Mecca, Muhammad had assembled all of his loyal followers, sedentary and nomadic alike, and captured Mecca in an astonishingly bloodless assault. Unlike in previous battles of the Muslims outside the city or with other communities, there was no plundering or dividing up of spoils of war. The city that had "thrown out" its son and his followers only a few years before, the city that broke its commitment to peace in order to marshal against him the biggest armies it could muster, offered no resistance to speak of and proved to be very receptive to Islam, as if the entire conflict, from beginning to end, had been devoid of any meaning. The estrangement of Islam from pagan Mecca was rectified on the basis of a peculiar synthesis, a synthesis to which most Bedouins paid little attention. Such a synthesis, furthermore, left many *Ansar* (Backers) wondering whether they were little more than a bridge across which Muhammad was to return to his original community, almost forgetting them afterwards.[18] Once firmly in control, Muhammad proclaimed Mecca to be as peaceful as it ever was and again forbidding violence: reversing the permission for killing that he had issued only the day before when anticipating a fight to capture it. These are his words to that effect:

> People! Allah has prohibited [violence in] Mecca on the day He created heavens and earth. Thus it shall remain prohibited until the day of resurrection. No one who believes in Allah and the Last Day shall shed in it a drop of blood or cut a tree. [The violation of the prohibition] was sanctioned to none before me, and shall be sanctioned to none after me. That was allowed me only at this hour, for [Allah's] anger at its people. But now it is as prohibited as it was in the yesterday. Let the present among you inform the absent one. Whoever says to you that the messenger of Allah had fought in it, say [in response]: "Allah has allowed it to his messenger, but not to you."[19]

The transhistorical nature of Mecca in particular as a city of peace was thus affirmed by a prophet who had led a merciless war against the city—and intermittently against others. The fact that the *Muhajirun* (Meccan Muslims who had migrated to Medina) and the *Ansar* retained distinct communities spelled out the incorporation of frames of tribal belonging into communities formed by the new faith. There are some reports that indicate that the *Ansar*, even at the peak of their usefulness to Islamic campaigns, continued to be regarded by Muhammad as outsider "people" (*nas*). This vision was expounded many years before, when Muhammad first sensed his ability to defeat Mecca at Badr precisely by the power of his non-Meccan allies. At that episode, Muhammad was reported to have addressed the corpses of the Meccan notables killed in the battle shortly before their burial: "You had denied me and the *outsiders* [*nas*] believed me; you had ostracized me and the *outsiders* sheltered me; you had fought me and the *outsiders* supported me."[20]

The predicament of belonging is abundantly apparent here, where Muhammad and the *Muhajirun* decry their unfreedom and the fact that they were *driven* to rely on strangers in order to restore a natural order to their own city. Like so many of the paradoxes with which history books overflow, the *Muhajirun*'s incessant concern for safeguarding the sanctity of their city by an omnipotent power set in motion a complex chain of events that ultimately returned the *Muhajirun* to their abode at the same time that it unintentionally expanded the social boundaries of Islam. With the final conquest of Mecca, Allah had finally accomplished the simple mission of anchoring the loosely guarded livelihood of the community on more solid theological foundations, but not without having to add many unforeseen adjustments and teachings in the process. The full-bodied Islamic state that ultimately emerged from such a complex web did not only protect the Meccan socioeconomy and unite the societies of the peninsula; it also conquered the outside world to such an extent that it almost forgot Mecca itself, developing in the process a much broader, more complex, and more variably integrated sociopolitical order.

THE RUINS OF THE TRIBE

Traditional Islamic narrative, then, presents with the conquest of Mecca a picture of reconciliation that engendered a reformulation of the meaning of belonging, which integrated some tribal dimensions.[21] The prophet, much like the expelled poet but with a more social strategy and under more favorable circumstances, cannot simply lament his kinfolk's lack of understanding. After all, the tribe is not like ruins over which one could weep for a while and then go on. One must continue to belong. For the originary poet, ruins signified not so much the tribe as a loss of possibilities. Standing by them, he ponders what has not happened: his own emancipation as a subject free to belong and dwell where he loves, a subject whose promised emergence from underneath the weight of the history of predetermined sociability is continually frustrated. Here, ruins periodically remind the poet that the promised emancipation had been postponed once more, that freedom to love—which here defines subjecthood and individuality—is uncertain, that lovers will continue to depart, that separation must be accepted, against one's will and in spite of the uncontrollable passions, as the nature of things. As the dwelling of a past lover, the ruins furnish firm evidence that a promise of harmonizing individuality and sociability in a naturally expressed flow of desire—a promise of which no more than traces are left—had been frustrated.

In the prophet's case, this frustration is symbolized by the unforgiving divine pronouncement of the fate of Abi Lahab. The anger, which originally distinguishes the prophet from the poet, dissipates quickly, however. Deep, lonely, and fruitless anger is soon replaced by a compassionate humility of the color of sorrow: "If they deny this revelation, you may destroy yourself with grief, sorrowing over them," the Qur'an ponders, before proceeding with a vengeful promise: "But We will surely destroy all that is on [earth] to barren dust."[22]

Here, the rejected prophet's gaze at his society is refocused in the familiar poetic modality, whereby all but traces is lost to sight. The prophet would grieve over the remnants of his own tribe exactly as the pre-Islamic poet reminisced over the ruins of the deserted lodgings of long-departed affinities. But whereas the pagan poet blames nothing other than time's eternal cycles for the separation, the messianic messenger attempts to warn of its potential materialization in the *future*. Unlike the expelled poet, the sedentary prophet was not immediately in danger of being ostracized, and the early Qur'an itself frequently instructed the prophet to approach the infidels with patience and a good demeanor.[23] In fact, Muslim historians point out that the first time Muhammad suffered harassment in the community was when he began to directly degrade pagan objects of worship rather than when he propagated the idea of a transcendental monotheistic God.[24]

In the context of the worldly prophetic mission, the specter of eventual estrangement nullifies the value of fulfillment of individual desire, which for a hedonistic poet like Imru' l-Qays would have adequately counterbalanced the gloom of the ruins. In one instance, the Qur'an illustrates the point through the case of an (unnamed) believer who is invited to enter heaven as a reward for his responsible conduct. But instead of proclaiming his speechless delight at the offer, the lonely believer stands sadly at the gate to eternal bliss to reminisce over the sad fate of his adulterous tribe.[25] Here, one is offered not merely paradise but also individual uprootedness and eternal separation from one's society, past, and memory. The believer who had to be estranged from his community on this earth cannot forget the estrangement, because the ability to forget means an essential lack of belonging. The *social* conception of paradise allows occasional estrangement from the community on earth because of the deferred possibility of belonging. Once the deferral becomes eternal, the lonely believer must lament not so much the fate of his people as the irremediability of his own irrelevance to an essentialized form of sociability.

In pre-Islamic poetry, a comparable sense of loneliness is mitigated by the invention of companions, to whom the poetic speech is explicitly directed (for example, Imru' l-Qays's "Halt, friends both!"). There are exceptions, however. 'Ubayd Ibn l-Abras's ode is distinct in that it stubbornly resists such a temptation and chooses to exalt the experience of aloneness to its ultimate end, with no reference to a prehistory or a social being. Such a behavior was rare and, as the early Muslim biographers were to notice, nearly prophetic in character. However, most of the other ostracized poets, exemplified best by Imru' l-Qays and Tarafa, always make an effort to speak to someone, and their odes are populated with societal imagery. The odes of Tarafa and Imru' l-Qays are saturated with a desire to return to the fold, yet only on the poets' own terms. Imru' l-Qays returns eventually, being forced through a strange twist of fate to assume a position of responsibility within the tribe. He is, after all, the son of a king who was murdered while the poet was still an outcast. He is the legitimate heir to the throne, even though the kingdom itself vanished from the face of the desert before the poet's return to the tribe. The poet returns, but only to the ruins of what he must claim in the name of social responsibility.

The news of the father's death came to Imru' l-Qays, so the legend goes, one night when he was drinking and playing backgammon with his companions. He responded: "He left me to rot when I was a boy, and now I am a man he's loaded me with his blood. We'll not be sober this day, neither drunken tomorrow. Wine today, tomorrow business [al-yaumu khamr wa ghadan amr]!" There is a characteristic swiftness in this resolution of a grown man suddenly finding himself burdened with responsibility toward a sphere of belonging that had previously disowned him. Yet as he finds himself saddled with the task of avenging his father's death and reclaiming the kingdom of Kinda, his subsequent poetry continues to be extremely sparse on the matters of heroism or social duty, especially when compared to other poetry of the period. It was only the pure operation of fate, rather than his design, that had placed him in the unforeseen, and a bit unfortunate, position of being heir to a kingdom that had just been swallowed up by the sand. Imru' l-Qays barely regrets the fate of the kingdom, for women, nature, wine, and the horse continue to be his favorite companions. Yet there is the force of destiny moving him to reclaim it, and there is a sense of naturalism in such a quest, in whose impossible pursuit the poet ultimately perishes.

As discussed earlier, Imru' l-Qays was born into a royal social hierarchy that was the first of its kind under nomadism, only to witness its destruction by nomadic societies that stubbornly resisted all claims for and obligations encumbent upon such a novelty. The coming—and eventual departure—of the idea of kingship indicated no emergent social space for hedonistic or status-based luxuries. In expelling the poet, the father-king reaffirmed that the timeless nomadic ethic of austerity, which poetic indulgence was seen to threaten, had not been affected in the least by the coming into being of his "kingdom." Shortly thereafter, such a reaffirmation was furnished once more when the nomads destroyed the kingdom, which, in attempting to enforce taxation, had begun to misunderstand the nomadic limits of tolerance for authority in general and for deductions from subsistence conditions of survival in particular.

In the case of Imru' l-Qays, then, we can sense the beginning of a realization that a seemingly timeless format of belonging was becoming less meaningful. Being the heir to a throne at the precise moment when it no longer existed meant nothing but an obligation toward a form of belonging from which the one on whose shoulders the obligation was suddenly placed was expelled. Thus, the one who had demonstrably failed in fulfilling his obligations when the kingdom was still intact was nonetheless still obligated toward it when it no longer existed. That is, the threat of ostracism, which regulates the fulfillment of obligations incumbent upon belonging, could never result in an actual ostracism, even for one whose ostracism had been publicly proclaimed. The ostracized person would still be obligated not only to seek to regain membership but also to defend the order of belonging from which he had already been expelled. When belonging is deemed to be a natural gift to which subjectivity is irrelevant, a total loss of belonging is, in effect, impossible. Therefore, the conditions of belonging appear to be eternal: One's destiny is to seek a readmission, to perform, and to re-prove one's worthiness to belong. With Imru' l-Qays and the withering kingdom, we see a personification of tension between two impossibilities: the impossibility of not belonging, given the nomadic conception of natural order, and the impossibility of not indulging, which grew out of the self-definition of the kingdom as an institution above ordinary and habitual society. But after the collapse of the kingdom and the death of the poet, no traces were left except for a distinct form of speaking. Poetry survived in the ashes, since in the primal act of being thrown out of the kingdom's domain, the *phenomenon* of poetry ceased to be any longer a part of the self-definition of the kingdom or a tribally distinct form of speech. Thus, it shared neither the fate of the kingdom nor that of the poet.

For Imru' l-Qays, therefore, the naturalism of belonging entailed also a naturalism of a particular social position within the tribe that he was expected to fulfill, even though he was thrown out precisely because he was *not* expected to be able to fulfill it. The prophet, on the other hand, may or may not need to belong in some predestined fashion. For the Qur'an, the requirements of belonging became increasingly subordinate to the fact that the existent social structure failed to either realize the earnestness of the prophetic mission at hand or to allot a distinct social space for such a phenomenon. In this light, the success of the prophetic mission *within* the community required a compromise of the rules of social order and harmony, along with the traditional formats of belonging. The Qur'an characteristically begins this task by citing the stories of ancient prophets, who had challenged not only their societies but their own parents as well. However, they are portrayed as having managed to do so without being thrown out and losing social relevance thereafter. Thus, Abraham faces his own father in the same way that Muhammad faces his adulterous community: as an estranged yet passionately belonging member, who in addition bestows upon himself an unrecognized authority to change society's beliefs. Abraham confronts his idol-worshipping father as well as the entire tribe, scandalizing social customs by assuming a pedagogic role toward his elders. His expected failure results not in certain divine punishment for the tribe but, rather, in his asking Allah to forgive his unrepentant father in particular.[26]

In the Qur'an, there is a major antithesis to Abraham's failure to communicate with his father, for which the model is indirectly provided in the story of Joseph. An entire Qur'anic *surah* (chapter) is devoted to Joseph, who succeeds in being reunited with his distressed and aging father; in the story's culmination, the entire family prostrates itself before Joseph, the youngest of all. Joseph thereafter heals the divisive familial rift by accepting the allegiance of the entire crowd, including his criminally sinful brothers. Throughout the story of Joseph, the brothers, who stand for the infidel majority of the community to which the prophet belonged, are portrayed as a conspiratorial ring whose sole aim is to deprive Joseph—not by accident the youngest and thus weakest member of the family—from enjoying his rightful place in the heart of his father. The father stands for the traditional *and* just order of social relations. Far away from his dangerous family, and following decades of social disunity and injustice, Joseph resurfaces as the glorious king of Egypt. Though not totally forgetting the evilness of his outwardly repentant brothers, Joseph nonetheless seeks their forgiveness as a necessary step toward reuniting the family, at least in appearance, under God and his young messenger.[27]

The emergence of a *new* and just tutelary authority defuses the threatening potential of the brothers' treacherous natures, which the Qur'an continues to detect beneath the facade of their repentance.[28] On the other hand, the parents, standing for traditional order, share no comparable potential for treachery. By prostrating themselves before their son, they endorse the possibility of a messenger of Allah breaking through the recognized order of social hierarchy. The entire community is happily reunited ever after, without having to shed a drop of blood in the process of attaining the union, and even without having to evict any of its members, including those of suspect faith. Such a vision was indeed a welcome relief from the scenarios utilizing ancient stories of mostly futile and lonely prophets, whose communities were routinely obliterated by a frustrated divinity after the prophets' failure.

One of the elements that had made Joseph's visions significant enough to have a long Qur'anic *surah* devoted in its entirety to them was that they were presented in the form of a well-known dream that could be made to fit an interpreted reality. As a youngster, Joseph saw "eleven planets, and the sun and the moon"—symbolizing, as it turned out, brothers and parents—prostrating themselves before him. The significance of the dream was its relationship to the future: It predicts the future as no dispassionate, wakeful analysis could. In other words, the dream frees the concept and actuality of the future from the limitations of both reality and hope. The dream is superior to reality not only because its events may take place beyond the moment of dreaming or because its images are fantastic, but because it allows the prophetic dreamer to become oblivious to calculations of possibility, practicality, and instrumental means/end rationality. The dream in this sense is not a goal that can be reached with an amount of worldly effort that can be assessed on the basis of the dream; rather, it is a *substitute* for reality, for the world itself. This is why a prophet could spend a lifetime in a dream without considering himself a failure, for the real failure of such a dreamer is to fall to the temptation of accepting a stubborn reality and abandoning an unfulfillable dream. In this sense, the dream is *not* a metaphor on behalf of reality but an independent sphere habituating a self-sufficient logic. As such, the dream is not a simple hope either, for as a self-sufficient substitute for the world, the dream is predicated on the fully grounded certainty of its existence in the world in some temporal dimension. It is life in a dream world, rather than the desire for the dream to become a reality, that provides the energy to abandon necessity, practicality, and means/end rationality incumbent upon particular forms of belonging in the world.[29]

The story of Joseph, therefore, consists not of transforming a dream into reality but of transforming reality into a dream. The world is transformed only in consciousness. Consciousness, enriched by the vivid nature of the dream, becomes self-sufficient in that it no longer needs the profane logic of a mortal or passing reality. Perpetually transforming the world into a dream becomes possible because of a type of logic that is continuous and self-reflexively resourceful, a logic uncontaminated by the invasion of reminders of the logic of the world outside. Thus, the continuity of the Qur'anic text consists not in providing a compendium of disparate stories of individual prophets but in continuing the thoughts of one prophet in the mind of another, in placing one prophet in the unconscious of another, in having one prophet conclude the story of another, in the same way that Muhammad saw himself as belonging to an integral family of prophets, being the last of them, finishing their work, whereafter prophethood becomes no longer possible on earth.

FITNAH, HIJRA, WAR

In the story of Joseph, traditional order can only be interrupted or temporarily reversed by a prophet, who fortifies it with a needed moral account and then leaves the scene without further deliberation. The dream ends. The object is a social order that the prophet cannot fail to belong to, even though such an order becomes increasingly treacherous and menacing toward those who have its best interest at heart. Thus, as Mecca continued to be at least an implicit focus of the return project for the ostracized Muslims and Muhammad in Medina, it was becoming increasingly obvious that war was the only means of return to what they continued to regard as their essential community. In some important sense, the war exhibited many symptoms of a campaign being waged against an unfaithful but still much adored lover.

In his comprehensive documentation of the wars of Muhammad, al-Waqidi reports on eight organized Muslim expeditions that took place during the first two years after the *hijra* (migration), in addition to numerous smaller ambushes against the caravans of Quraysh and some of its allies, all preceding the decisive battle of Badr.[30] The *Muhajirun,* who were apparently more clearly involved in such early adventures than the *Ansar,* were also being instructed on the novel duty of fighting by the Qur'an, which also in the process noted that it might appear detestable to them.[31] Such raidings, for the *Muhajirun* at least, involved clear economic gains, which decreased the extent to which they were a burden on the *Ansar.* However, the Qur'an legitimated the war by referring to a root cause, the infidels' disruption of normative social harmony (*fitnah*), an act that appalled Allah more than did acts of killing in the war.[32]

The war developed its rules while it was in progress. The category of targeted infidels had to be narrowed down so as not to alienate other Arab societies outside of Mecca or Medina, societies that had no prior animosity toward the Muslims and that showed no interest in the whole affair. The war was to be waged exclusively against the infidels of the "Mother of Towns," where the *Muhajirun* ultimately belonged.[33] Many of the rules of war, however, conformed to prevailing traditional norms instituted by Mecca, notably abstention from fighting during the sacred months.[34] At a later stage, however, more detailed Qur'anic teachings allowed Muslims to fight during those months if they were attacked, and in the holy *haram* of Mecca only if they were assaulted while visiting it.[35] As the warlike attitudes deepened, the Qur'an temporarily abandoned the observance of the sacred months; according to classical accounts, such a radical departure was triggered by an incident during the last recorded skirmish before Badr, when an enthusiastic Muslim band raided a Qurayshan convoy, killing some, taking others prisoner, and appropriating the cattle. Mecca used the incident to denounce Muhammad's breach of such a sacred time of the year, and the bewildered Muslims were gravely disappointed at the shameful behavior of their compatriots. For a number of days, Muhammad was unable to decide on the proper handling of the crisis. Faced with the options of either apologizing to the infidels or justifying the unforeseen breach by a group of Muslims, the Qur'an chose the latter, reaffirming in the process the horror of *fitnah* as a more appalling source of evil than any other form of transgression: "They ask you about the sacred month. Say: 'To fight in this month is a grave offense; but to debar others from the path of God, to deny Him, and to expel His worshippers from the holy mosque, is far more grave in His sight. [*Fitnah*] is worse than carnage.'"[36]

The *fitnah*, consisting here of the disruption of a natural flow of communal harmony causing migration, had the status of original sin. Medina, where the *Muhajirun* and *Ansar* maintained separate communities and assumed distinct roles in the war against Quraysh, was yet to replace the "lost" harmony of Mecca. Initially, most of the *Ansar* declined to join the war, merely regarding it as a legitimate way of survival for the resourceless *Muhajirun*. But the development of a common approach to the world outside of Medina was making itself more imperative with the passing of time and events. Probably as early as the first pilgrimage season following the *hijra*, the Qur'an had to instruct the Muslims regarding the nature of their relationship to that great Meccan and peninsular tradition. In spite of the pagan ontotheology surrounding the pilgrimage, it was nonetheless the tradition that most expressed the preeminence of Mecca in the peninsula. Thus, rather than being entirely disowned, the sanctity of the pilgrimage was modified in the Qur'an so as to avoid the pagan rituals. The Muslims were told that, with the exception of visiting the idols, pilgrimage practices were now Allah's own decreed rituals (*Sha'a'er*), although Muslims were still not strictly bound to follow them.[37] The sanctity of the *haram* of Mecca was reaffirmed, and so was the pilgrimage, although the nature of the Islamic rituals to accompany it remained ambiguous until more explicit instructions on the matter were provided at a later point in time.[38]

A year and a half after the *hijra*, the raids on Meccan caravans were beginning to provide the *Muhajirun* with more than simple sustenance. They were beginning to acquire a confidence in their ability to harass, if not to eventually conquer, the city they loved. It was around that time that the

Qur'an instructed *all* Muslims to face Mecca in their prayers, rescinding the earlier specification of the direction of prayer (*qibla*) as being toward Jerusalem.[39] It is significant that in both cases, the *qibla* was oriented specifically toward a city, rather than toward some other cosmological or natural locus. The religion looked upon itself as a religion for the cities, for cities defined the world of approachable, organizable society. Locating the *qibla* ordains a vision of distinct sanctity and an idealization of the destination. In this case, it was also a deposition of hope in concretizing the idealized society through the efforts of the faithful on earth, a moment that was much less evident in the case of Jerusalem.[40] Though Jerusalem had furnished an early link to ancient prophetic and mono-theistic traditions, the crystallization of a distinct Muslim identity outside of Mecca called for symbolizing such a distinction. This was especially the case given the futility of Muhammad's efforts among the Jews in Medina, who remained indifferent to the intrusion of the Muslims. This fact was clearly registered in the Qur'an, at the same time that it noted the increasing self-confidence and self-sufficiency of Muslim doctrines, crystallizing through incrementally revealed, distinct *knowledge*.[41] Significantly, such a change was announced both in terms of ending an earlier state of uncertainty ("Many a time have We seen you [Muhammad] [shifting] your face [around in the sky]") and also in terms of acknowledging communal desire over and above theological connections ("We will [then] make you turn towards a *qibla* that will *please you*").[42]

Such reorientations were taking shape shortly before Badr, when sporadic raiding finally gave way to a full-scale battle, which the Muslims won, and at whose conclusion Muhammad, in the memorable speech mentioned earlier, reproached the corpses of slain Meccan notables for having forced him to use outsiders to defeat them. Badr marked not merely the first major military episode of the Muslims but also, and more importantly, the beginning of an irreversible expansion of clan-based and tribally based notions of communal obligations, which had heretofore weighed in different ways among different Muslims. That accomplishment, however, was not straightforward. Though Badr was the first joint assault by both *Muhajirun* and *Ansar,* there was no consensus among the *Ansar* with regards to their new role under Muhammad, even though they made up the majority of the Muslim army. Reportedly, many *Ansar* refrained from joining the fight, while others were dismayed that the capture of the wealth of the caravan, which was their sole intention, was no longer possible without a fight after Quraysh mobilized to protect it.[43] In subsequent battles, many *Ansar* either resolutely refused to join or joined only half-heartedly. Beyond the direct (and uncertain) acquisition of spoils, the wavering elements saw little point in such adventures. But as the escalating cycle of fighting called for an ever-increased number of committed soldiers, increasingly vocal opponents of the war among the *Ansar* were sharply denounced in the Qur'an as two-faced (*Munafiqun*).

The extent of denunciation of the *Munafiqun* in the Qur'an indicates the degree to which they were perceived as threats, especially as the Muslim community was becoming more warlike and thus in need of disciplined unity. In addition to an earlier defection of some Aussians to the side of Mecca, Muslim historians report more extensively on another, apparently more serious, defection by a notable Khazrajite chief by the name of 'Abdullah Ibn Ubay. He was reportedly held in deep respect by both Medinian tribes, and was on his way to being crowned as a king of Medina shortly before Muhammad and his followers came to the city. As king, Ibn Ubay would have fulfilled a political function that Muhammad himself eventually took up, which consisted of transforming Medina from a city in which each tribe lived in a castle built in anticipation of the ever-present danger of tribal wars in the town to a place where intercommunal relations were regulated by a consensual central authority.[44] The intervention of Muhammad seemingly added a supernatural ontological dimension to the trend, a dimension that, unlike a local kingship, had the added advantage of promising to relieve local authority from consistent questioning on the basis of tribal credentials.

The details of the story of Ibn Ubay show the evolutionary nature and politicization of the idea of prophethood. Ibn Ubay continued to attract some respect from the prophet, even after he repeatedly reversed decisions made by the latter. In the Qur'an, his denunciation was never as condemning as that directed at the more humble *Munafiqun*. He is further reported to have forcibly prevented Muhammad from massacring the Medinian Jewish tribe of Banu Qainaqa' after the Muslims' euphoric return from Badr, a dispute that ended with the Muslims sparing the Jews' lives but exiling them from the city and confiscating their wealth. He is also reported to have resolutely refused to aid the Muslims in Uhud, rightly considering the battle to be an unwise adventure on their part, and to have repeatedly complained about the submission of many of the *Ansar* to whatever confrontation Muhammad resolved to herd them to.[45] That as a political movement Islam now had to negotiate terms of belonging with local notables is testified to in the fact that in spite of his independent-mindedness, Ibn Ubay was never pronounced to be a complete infidel. Ultimately, however, the course of events dragged him along into the fold. Faced with the fact that his tribe had already been involved in enough acts of aggression to be practically at war with Mecca, with the consolidation of Muhammad's rule in the city, and with the increasing indulgence of the *Ansar* in the new war economy, Ibn Ubay followed the practical course of submitting to what had to be considered the will of Allah in the land.[46]

Thus, the foundation of the new transtribal community was built upon the ruins of another. After that moment of intertribal consolidation, the Qur'an rarely revisits the idea of ruins and divine destruction with the tone of sadness flowing from frustrated belonging or concerned prophetic attachment. Rather, the notion of destruction becomes more clearly associated with the idea of construction, whereby the dead mode of social life that the ruins evidence begins to be seen as a sign of natural evolution and displacement by better virtues. As a foundation for a new form of community, the idea of destruction—up to and including martyrdom in the cause of Allah—begins to be addressed in terms of the future dimensions of sociability that it opens up rather than in terms of irremediable loss of all objects of love and belonging, which the early Qur'an expressed much as did the traditional *mu'allaqat.*

THE SATANIC VERSES AND THEIR BACKGROUND

A politicized prophet is no longer simply one of the ideal types of estranged and reconstituted belonging. Rather, his discourse is more heavily flavored with the impulse toward eventual reunion. Thus, symbols of Mecca's preeminence in Arabia, such as the *haram,* are never assaulted by the Qur'an in general. To the contrary, the very ground of the *haram*'s sacredness is traced back to Allah. Such a proposal sought to strengthen the ground upon which the city's prime symbol stood beyond and above uncertain tribal voluntarism, which was appealed to by filling the space with objects of worship that various peninsular tribes could identify with separately. That system of faith broke down repeatedly, as evidenced by the many stories describing the Bedouins' indifference to the spiritual claims of sacredness that Mecca proclaimed about the *haram* among the Arabs before Islam. By placing the *haram* under Allah's tutelage, Islam's social relevance could be accentuated *without* risking Allah's monotheism, for the *haram* itself was not the object of pagan worship, unlike the idols that populated it.

The manner by which communal peace was traced to Allah followed an interesting trajectory, which at the conceptual level seems to have paralleled the trials and tribulations of the emerging Muslim community. In the very early *surah* of al-Qalam, a mild show of Allah's potential capacity for destruction leads wrongdoers to repent, after a relatively minor commission of injustice, whereafter the divided society is reunited under God:

> We have afflicted them as We afflicted the owners of the orchard who had declared that they would pluck its fruits next morning, without [saying: "If God wills."]. A visitant from your Lord came down upon it while they slept, and in the morning it was as black as midnight. . . .
>
> And off they went, whispering to one another: "No beggar shall enter the orchard today." . . .
>
> And they began to blame one another. "Woe to us!" they cried. "We have been great transgressors. We hope Our Lord will give us a better orchard in its place."[47]

Here, what the holy scripture abhors most is not the effort to seal off private property and protect one's orchard from the theft of its fruits but, rather, a condition of acrimonious social disunity. Privileged access to productive private property and the individual greed that is seen as symptomatic thereof are recognized as main sources of social schism. Interestingly, however, such a recognition does not lead to a denunciation of individual claims to distinct wealth or possession but, rather, to its regulation by empowering God over all novel notions of individual earthly distinction. The verses above hint that the ill-fortune of the orchard's owners might not have been so bleak had they appended a note regarding Allah's will to their exclusionary resolution. Even when such a recognition is withheld, divine punishment was not necessarily irrevocable. At the conclusion of the story, Allah remains silent in the face of the owners' wish that their doomed orchard be replaced by a better one, suggesting the possibility of such a generous recompense once the wrongdoers realize the socially divisive outcome of their self-consuming obliviousness to divine interest in communal harmony.

Such an early message implied that everything in the social order could stay in its place, provided that Allah's presence held emerging individual distinctions in check. Such an early conception of Allah apparently attempted to antagonize as few people as possible; even God's entitlement to issue threats or punish seem demure: The statement that retribution in the other life would be worse than losing one's orchard on earth is immeasurably weaker than the horrifyingly detailed portrayals of life in hell in the later Qur'anic *surahs*. In any case, what can be discerned here is the genesis of a response to the emerging inegalitarian disharmony of sedentary life, as well as an awareness of the threats facing such a state of affairs in the material world.

According to this view, a divided society is self-evidently in error; indeed division is a sin in itself. Thus, though Thamud is announced to be a sinful village deserving divine obliteration in many passages in the Qur'an, the only instance at which the criteria for its evilness are specified involves a brief allusion to its factionalism.[48] In a similar vein, though the parable of the confrontation between the erring pharaoh of Egypt and Moses is recounted many times over in the Qur'an, only once are we told why pharaoh's sin is so unforgivable: "Now Pharaoh made himself tyrant in the land. He divided his people into castes, one group of which he persecuted [*yastad'ef*], putting their sons to death and sparing only their daughters. Truly, he was an evil-doer."[49]

The evilness of the division assumes a more concrete meaning here, as "dividing the people" means that one faction will suffer. The source of suffering in society is detected in a comparative fashion: The austere Bedouin society could recognize no suffering as an absolute, concrete manifestation as long as the standards of well-being were gauged within that society itself. The Bedouins only realized their poverty once they compared their austere life to that of the prosperous city. Within the city itself, likewise, the idea of suffering had no comprehensible meaning until its opposite was encountered. The development of different levels of wealth within the different branches of Quraysh not only concretized the concept of suffering but also associated it with a disunity of the people.

Unjust persecution (*yastad'ef*) of one section of the divided people was therefore the potential outcome of any division of them in the first place. The result of this injustice is driven home picturesquely: It is tantamount to physically eliminating the sons of the weak caste while sparing its women, a tactic reminiscent of the Bedouin raid. Thus, the brutality of the Bedouin economy is comparable to pharaoh's terror, indicating no desire on the Qur'an's part to substitute the antiquated cohesiveness of the nomadic social unit to the vicious divisiveness of the city society. Thus, in one stroke, the Qur'an identifies major pictorial aspects of *badawah* and *hadarah* life as evil. First it points out the evils of the city society, but it then proceeds quickly to make it clear that an impossible retreat to the Bedouin past is not its intention at all.

The encroachment upon natural order of an alienating and distorted system of social relations cannot be easily rectified by a God whose powers are still uncertain, and who refuses to interfere with a world gone astray, a refusal that extends to the point of refraining from revealing the Qur'an by himself to his own messenger. He announces, thus, that no angels can or will ever be allowed to dilute the *distant* perfection of his kingdom in heaven by mixing in an unworthy earthly world, that the poisoned and mortal world should be satisfied with a plainly human messenger: "Say: 'Had the earth been safe enough for angels to dwell in, We would have sent down to them an angel from Heaven as an apostle.'"[50]

Such an idea of a "proper place," whereby a world contaminated by disharmony is set apart from a world beyond that nonetheless produces impulses toward perfection in the former, means that Muhammad—like *all other prophets*—must remain perfectly human. Other apostles, therefore, can only respond humbly and affirmatively to suspicions of their human normalcy, proclaiming their astonishment that such a point is an issue at all.[51] Subsequently, the prophet is explicitly relieved of individual responsibility for his community by being forbidden to assume the role of guardian (*wakil*), being told instead to be nothing more than simply one who warns (*nadhir*).[52]

In this case, reduced prophetic responsibility is consistent with the desire for the effacement of distinct and potentially disharmonious individualities, which God himself was protesting. The passion for communal harmony requires an exemplary altruism that borders on self-sacrifice. For instance, in his last cries of despair and compassion, the estranged Noah calls upon his people to destroy him personally if such an act would result in social good, displaying thereby a heroic trust in both Allah and the tribe.[53] Here, it is the duty of the messenger to remain socially relevant at all cost and to maintain a bridge of communication with his brethren, to the point of martyrdom. Along with his followers, he is further instructed to repair the communication damage caused by his early vocal eccentricity by strictly following a nonrepulsive course of preaching.[54]

Following that strategy, the Qur'an even sought a temporary ideological truce that was originally expressed in the *surah* of al-Kafirun, which did not call upon idolaters to do any more than leave the Muslims in peace with their newly discovered faith, in return for the latter's abandonment of their insistence on their ideological hegemony in the community.[55] Meccan society, as a whole, apparently had little desire for a total ideological war against Muhammad and his followers over spiritual hegemony, a hegemony that was inconsistent with the pluralistic ethic underpinning the function of the idols. According to al-Tabari, when the Qurayshan chiefs complained to Abi Talib about his nephew's divisive proclamations, they showed little interest in winning Muhammad back to their faith: "Let him quit insulting our Gods," they offered, "and we will leave him alone with his God."[56] According to different accounts, the aforementioned *surah* of al-Kafirun was revealed in response to even more generous offers by Qurayshans, namely, that all Meccans, Muslims and non-Muslims alike, worship the idols one year and Allah the next, or that the entire community worship everything it knew without distinction: Muhammad's Allah and the idols simultaneously.[57] In other words Allah, who had long been accepted as a divine concept, could be easily integrated into existing ontotheology by being assigned the status of a somewhat more prominent idol. The pluralistic impulse of the pagan tradition was malleable enough to absorb Allah's idea within it, even though it had no place for a hegemonic deity, much less for an arbitrarily selected messenger of God.

Thus, regardless of his wishes, the prophet found himself acting almost exclusively within the bounds of existing social structure for much of his tenure in Mecca. *Sira* sources (traditional biographies of the prophet) are unanimous in reporting that the branch of Quraysh to which he belonged, Banu Hashim, and in particular his eminent uncle Abi Talib, shielded him from abuse while other less socioeconomically fortunate Muslims bore the brunt of humiliation and mistreatment. But more significantly, not many members of Muhammad's clan became Muslims. Abi Talib himself declined the invitation to convert to Islam, citing reasons that had more to do with his social status in the community than with theology.[58] (On the other hand, clannish solidarity produced legendary recruits, such as Muhammad's cousin Hamza, who announced his conversion to Islam without having harbored any prior theological convictions while thundering his outrage at the ill-treatment of Muhammad by his infamous adversary Abi Jahl.)

Working within the bounds of existing social structure gradually overshadowed early Meccan Islam with clannish perceptions, and at the same time it cut off communicative links between Muslims and the rest of Quraysh. This ensuing closure is symbolized in a (premature) Qur'anic conclusion that whatever could be done had been done: "Can you make the deaf hear, or guide the blind or those in gross error? Whether We take you hence or let you live to see Our threats fulfilled, We shall surely take vengeance on them. Therefore hold fast that which is revealed to you: you are on a straight path."[59]

This rigidification of the frontiers roughly coincided with an initially broadly based conclusion among Quraysh that Muhammad's protective kin, Banu Hashim and Banu 'Abd l-Muttaleb, had earned themselves total social and economic exclusion. According to the lore, the rest of Quraysh resolved that marriages and commerce could no longer take place with the two clans. Instigated by Muhammad's infamous uncle Abi Lahab, who defected from his own Banu Hashim, the confederated Qurayshans affixed a declaration of ostracism to the wall of the *haram*. The ostracism, which collapsed after three years, was porous in any case, as evidenced by reports concerning sporadic communication between the clans throughout those years.[60] There was a growing realization that Muhammad's eccentricity did not warrant such harsh treatment for his clan, along with a growing suspicion that a few merchants, notably Abi Lahab and some of Banu Umayyah, had benefited economically from the boycott against the Hashemites, even at the expense of smaller clans that had agreed to participate in their exclusion.

In addition, the network of *nasab* relations that had developed between the branches during the years of sedentarization in Mecca made any such exclusion impossible to impose. The city was no longer a Bedouin society where *nasab* lines possessed (at least in imagination) transhistorical clarity and distinction. In the city, the myth of distinct *nasab* lines needed only an attempt at exclusion to make evident its meaninglessness.[61] According to the lore, when some Qurayshans with affinities to the Hashemites decided to tear down the declaration of exclusion, they went to the wall of the *haram* only to find out that moths had devoured every word in it that entailed injustice, transgression, and communal disharmony, leaving intact only the name of Allah (which was routinely used by Quraysh to open contractual statements).[62] In attributing the end of the isolation to the will of Allah, this version of the story avoids admitting the unbelievers' capacity to rectify injustice of their own volition.

On the other hand, the termination of the boycott made more pressing the point that the community was *capable of reuniting on principles other than Islam.* The entire affair began and ended in a strictly tribal manner, with little reference to the theological novelty that had ostensibly originated the friction. As the crisis was settling, there was an evident tendency to minimize the theological substance of the affair. Muhammad was facing arguments to the effect that the whole matter was not worth a social split, such as the assertion that Quraysh had always worshipped Allah through his "daughters," namely, the idols.

For Muhammad and the Muslims, the removal of the ostracism presented pressure toward a synthesis, since the rapprochement could not be rejected simply because it occurred without the triumph of Islam. The legend of the moths notwithstanding, one glaring result of the affairs was that the infidels showed themselves to be capable of recognizing their error *without* converting to Islam. The revelation of the "Satanic verses," which resulted from this tension, was introduced in the Qur'an by a conciliatory tone indicating an unmistakable desire to remove the animosity of former times. After excusing Muhammad's lack of choice in being the carrier of God's message and making further overtures by a rare permission of "minor sins,"[63] the *surah* proceeded to offer a remarkable concession, which was eventually to be rescinded by Muhammad, who traced it to demonic intervention in the transmission of God's words. The two Satanic verses were to be the only recorded departure from monotheism, as they dignified the two most important Meccan idols by ratifying their intercessionary credentials with God.[64]

According to the *sira*, the entire community, Muslims and non-Muslims alike, prostrated themselves at the conclusion of the *surah*. This remarkable show of unity could have dramatically altered the course of Islam had it been allowed to stand. However, the bases of such a unity were soon to be made clear to Muhammad, as the infidels relayed to him what they had understood from the revelation: "Now we know that Allah is the One who gives life and causes death, and that He is the One who creates and gives sustenance, but these deities of ours will intercede for us with Him. As you have made an allowance [for them], we are with you [in faith]."[65] Thus, though the Satanic verses could lead to communal unity and harmony, they did so at the cost of further expanding pagan spiritual pluralism, accomplishing thereby the opposite of what the notion of a spiritual communion safeguarded by a monotheistic God had entailed.

Thus, the theological grounds for deleting the Satanic verses are clear. Less clear, however, are the *sociological* grounds. More precisely, the question is why, given a choice between social reunion and undiluted theological purity, did the latter choice prevail? At the level of discourse, at least one fundamental reason can be detected. The pronouncement of the grounds for unity in the form of a Qur'anic recitation returned the discourse to a theological sphere, which had been largely ignored throughout the ordeals of boycott and reunion. The departure from the immediacy of the social into theological discourse revealed the temporality of social events, including the prevailing atmosphere of social reunion. This is a classic example of the societal unpredictability of ideological discourses, in which advocates of an ideology set in motion processes whose implications they do not fully comprehend. Their initial transsocial theological immersion caused early Muslims to become oblivious to questions of immediate social relevance. Struggling to be readmitted on the basis of habitual traditional connections, they lost track of the theological source of their early social estrangement. Redeploying theological discourse once they were invited to belong *with* that distinction, they discovered the full range of the *logic* their estrangement. If the social rapprochement was to result in a theological one, as Muhammad sought in an-Najm—and especially in the deleted verses—then the "rapprochement" meant no more than the declaration by Allah of his uselessness, pronouncing thereby to the Muslims the futility of their continued estrangement from society for something as trivial as a God who had always existed in the collective consciousness, a God who could easily be persuaded by the stones that the community was already serving.

In the orthodox verses replacing the Satanic ones praising pagan stones, the stones are pronounced to be no more than subjectively chosen "names" with no *essential* authority vested in them.[66] The subjectivity of man himself seems thus to consist of establishing relations to objects by "merely" naming them. Naming, then, signifies a relationship to an object that designates its existence, without an essential experience of its truth. The pagans are denounced, therefore, not for naming as such but for allowing the activity of naming to substitute for thinking of and experiencing the nature of objects in the world. This being the nature of subjectivity, it is then questioned as a valid regulator of belief: Man cannot, by his own desires, assign to himself a deity of his liking. The deity has to come from outside of society, from above it, and objectively impose itself on man, since the latter, having proven himself to be an imperfect source of harmony, could no longer be entrusted with visibly manufacturing a deity that is likely to be imperfect as well.

The facts that many Muslims were willing to endure the agony of discontent and find themselves subjected to unusual moral questioning, mockery, harassment, and isolation and that many of them were willing to leave the city and settle far away in Abyssinia indicate the level of ideological investment that the "Satanic verses" summarily annulled. On the other hand, the deletion of the verses and the loss of the temporary display of unity pronounced a realization that the conflict was irremediable. For the Muslims, that meant that ideology had to guide sociability and that ideology should never again appear to be moved by sociability. Indeed, at a later stage, the Qur'an explicitly rejected any possibility of harmony resulting from Satanic interjection, pointing out in the process what it saw as a state of extreme dissension among the infidels.[67] That move occasioned a gradual shift in the idea of harmony to a conception of harmony as being strictly within a *Muslim* community, transcending inherently schismatic tribalism, which—as epitomized by the *hijra*—was eventually pronounced to have lost its claim as the most normative embodiment of social solidarity.[68]

The classic sources chronicle an ill-advised return from Abyssinia by the Muslims either shortly before or around the same time as the lifting of the boycott against the Hashemites.[69] These two processes, which coincided with a short-lived easing of tensions, led, as outlined above, to a quick discovery of the magnitude of the actual schism. The reinvigoration of the theological discourse caused not only the highlighting of religious rather than tribal lines of demarcation. It subsequently entailed a reexamination of traditional standards of individual worth on the basis of where ideological success was registered. The Qur'an itself registered this reorientation, as it reproached the prophet for his unwarranted insistence on devoting his energies to the largely futile effort to recruit the traditionally honorable society members while almost ignoring the weak. The *surah* of 'Abasa is the clearest illustration of this reexamination, as it denounced Muhammad, the messenger of Allah, for ignoring repeated requests to recite the Qur'an by an ignoble blind man, as Muhammad was in the midst of a promising dialogue with a tribal notable. The *surah* is interesting not only for its manifestation of divine displeasure with the prophet's conduct, but also because the Qur'an here addresses not Muhammad but the community at large in drawing conclusions from this valuable lesson.[70] In some sense, such a reorientation reflected a recognition of the fact that only a few of the socially prestigious followers of Muhammad stayed with him in Mecca throughout the years of persecution, when he was left with only the most helpless and miserable among the believers.[71]

It is possible, in principle at least, to identify in the nature of this wretched crowd certain venues that could enable the group or the message to reenter normal society. In one pre-Islamic ode, Tarafa, as the tribe gathers at his graveside (beginning c. 93), addresses the crowd in a way that effects a redistribution of the network of speakers and listeners. The poet here no longer delivers his discourse to figures of authority in the tribe; rather, he speaks to its less-powerful components (the daughter of Ma'bad, for instance). As he nears the end of his wanderings and reaches his end, the expelled poet expresses a final hope that his name would be redeposited with the tribe in a way that would be free of the play of power, that his name would signify more than simply glamorous credentials, inhabiting instead more salient, gentle, and tranquil moments within an everlasting collective memory.

In a gesture that is closer than Tarafa's to Muhammad's predicament, Noah expresses the feelings of a prophet surrounded by an ignominious crowd that he had not specifically intended to be restricted to. Among the recorded criteria according to which Noah's people rejected him was the very low social position of his followers.[72] But though Noah responds by refusing to dissociate himself from the socially obscure believers, he hesitates, interestingly, to strongly defend them either. In fact, he does not defend them at all, stating merely that they would face Allah's judgment if they had committed any wrongs of which he had no knowledge.[73] In the same context, Noah asserts that the fundamental reason for his inability to drive away such believers is his status simply as one who warns, with limited responsibilities. This passive acceptance of all who would submit to the faith is transformed into an active posture of inclusion with the *surah* of 'Abasa, in which Muhammad is commanded to approach all members of his community *equally*, manifesting thereby a behavior exemplary of the order to prevail in a united and just Mecca.

In much of the early Qur'an, distinct wealth was often seen as a source of disharmony, but *only* to the extent that it was not placed under Allah's tutelage. In the Meccan *surah* of al-Kahf, a sociotheological confrontation between a rich unbeliever and a poor believer ends, characteristically, with the rich man being stripped by Allah of his continued enjoyment of the fruits of his possessions.[74] But the punishment is far from being fatal or even irreversible, as the rich man comes to regret his earlier indifference to the faith. Interestingly enough, however, the poor man asks for no share for himself in the rich man's abundant gardens. He merely asks Allah for better gardens than those of the wealthy man, which he wishes to become barren. In the meantime, he denounces in the rich man *nothing* other than his refusal to (at least verbally) recognize the source of his bounties. The rich man is never denounced for being uncharacteristically wealthy, nor for excluding the poor from his unusually rewarding private property. Neither does the poor man ask to share in such wealth, as would have been the case among the nomadic tribes. In fact, the poor man is never portrayed as being compensated at all; there is merely an allusion to a reward in the life to come in heaven. The clear message here concerns wealth and *not* poverty. The rich man is the background against which all social lessons are drawn. His very existence seems to be the whole issue. He is rich because of Allah's (unexplained) generosity to him. His indifference to such a fact, taught through the tongue of the deprived man, commences his immiseration. But again, he is never thrown mercilessly into the blazing fires of hell; at the end, he is portrayed as an almost repentant man, whereafter his story ends abruptly. In other instances, the Meccan Qur'an seemed to appeal shamelessly to the upper classes, whose very existence in the world alluded to God's activity and potential:

God makes this comparison. On the one hand there is a helpless slave, the property of his master. On the other, a man on whom We have bestowed Our bounty, so that he gives of it both in private and public. Are the two equal?

...God also makes this comparison. Take a dumb and helpless man, a burden on his master: Wherever he sends him he returns with empty hands. Is he as good as he that enjoins justice and follows a straight path?[75]

When the functions narrated in such seemingly strange comparisons are examined more closely, it appears that they contrast not rich and poor but, rather, notions of usefulness versus uselessness. The growth of inequality is significant not because of its intrinsic evilness but because it entails a possibility of reducing human usefulness and worth and magnifying the concern with the *comparative value* of human action.[76] *Distinct* wealth is thus variably explained as a "test,"[77] a divine reward awaiting acknowledgment,[78] and a source of evilness and transgression.[79] But if Allah was the source of wealth, and if wealth was the source of evil on earth, then Allah would be the original source of evil. Allah responds to the possibility of such a chain of thought by simply confirming the inevitable conclusion of that mercilessly straightforward logic: "When We resolve to destroy a city, We first [command] those of its people who live in comfort [so that they commit grave sins in it. Whence Our judgment is vindicated], and We raze that city to the ground."[80]

That astoundingly deterministic language does not, however, entail the encasement of Islam as a religion of the poor. Rather, by being framed in terms of *individual* distinction, the discourse on inequality habituates noncollective modalities of rapprochement. Thus, the people of Mecca would not inhabit hell and paradise according to clan membership but, rather, according to individually determined credentials of faith. This potential, though redressing the disharmonizing reality of growing sedentary inequality and fragmentation, nonetheless presents an uncomfortable logical consequence: The disunited society in this world will become even more so after the Day of Judgment. Society, therefore, cannot entertain a harmonious totality at any given time. This realization apparently preceded the evolution of the notion of the *umma*, coming at a moment when the prophet himself was aware that many "good" Qurayshans (for example, Abi Talib) declined to join Islam. The heartening goodness shown by many idol-worshipping Qurayshans when they lifted the boycott against the Hashemites added further complications to this image of dual accountability along lines of faith versus lack of it. Could all those infidels, whose moral character was obviously diverse, be thrown into a blazing hell of fire that almost burst with rage as it consumed them?

At some points, the Qur'an entertained the possibility that not all unbelievers were equal in guilt, as it depicted wrangling among them in hell regarding the higher responsibility of their "leaders" for bringing upon them that unbearable fate, where some of them would ask Allah to double the punishment of those who were responsible for misguiding them.[81] When Allah acknowledged that non-Muslims were not uniform in their wrongdoing, he pondered as well the possibility that not all Muslims were uniform in their submission to him either. Classical sources abound with stories of defection and repentance among Muhammad's followers. Some joined before others, and some showed more dedication and endurance than others. At one point, Allah acknowledged the fact by constructing a hierarchy among the Muslims in paradise itself, a project that was quickly abandoned, however.[82] Though the hierarchy of the otherworld pronounced a sort of acknowledgment of differential suffering, faith, and transgression, the more important mission was to actually erase such differentiations, to construct a paradise in which *all* believers "will pass from hand to hand" a plenitude of blessings.[83] As a now ideologically distinct community, the faithful were to be one united people, as bound together as an ancient Bedouin tribe, but on a larger and more sophisticated scale: They were now to be one "*umma.*"

THE BOUNDARIES OF THE *UMMA*

As a term referring to the ideal community, the concept of *umma* metamorphosed in meaning several times while it was being added to the early Islamic discourse. At various points, it was couched in terms of tribal and transtribal bonds, used in reference to the population of Mecca regardless of belief, to the followers of all prophets, and to the Muslim community at large. The standards of solidarity prevailing in such an ideally united society were frequently altered or redefined. At one point, the Qur'an revealed to Muhammad that on the Day of Judgment, humankind would be assembled according to their *umma* category, but it did not elaborate on what the concept exactly meant.[84] Elsewhere, he was assured that because of the wisdom of Allah, humanity will not become one *umma* of unbelievers.[85] And though at some points the *umma* linked Muslims to Jews and Christians as descendants of a single imagined family of brotherly prophets, it was also used to condemn the Christians for their wrangling factionalism and general failure to establish the ideal *umma* in the world.[86] Nonetheless, with its main obsession being the overthrow of pagan pluralism, the Qur'an refrained from diverting valuable energy from this central task, accepting in the process the possibility of *monotheistic pluralism* (including Christians and Jews) as long as the diversity of its texts could be traced to a single source: "Do not follow their desires, but say [instead]: 'I believe in all the scriptures that God has revealed. I am commanded to exercise justice among you. God is our Lord and your Lord. We have our own works and you have yours; let there be no argument between us. God will bring us all together, for to Him we shall return.'"[87]

This notion of *umma* is prefigured in pre-Islamic poetry, which spoke of times of unusually intense and lengthy tribal conflicts. Poets such as Zuhair and Labid are prominent in this regard, each displaying an entitlement to a transtribal moral authority expressed through distinct poetics. Though the notion of *umma* itself is hardly used in such poetry, one encounters efforts to construct a system of harmony that encompasses "foreignness." This is evident in Labid's ode, where the identification of quarreling referents is less important than the *general* resolution of disputes (for example, c. 70: "And oft in an *unfamiliar* muster of many strangers / where gifts were hoped for, and the voice of reproach was feared").[88] Here, Labid describes a location of great acrimony, "unfamiliar" (*majhulah*) in terms of population, cause, and outcome of the conflict. There is a location (or event) where (when) angry people are exchanging wild threats. Like the anonymous enemy pursued earlier in the ode, this gathering (or the battlefield) is strange, unspecifiable, unnamable, undefinable, unbounded by characterizations.[89] Unlike 'Amru's confident voice, which presents the tribal adversary clearly and described them as having committed specific, punishable deeds, the enemy here refuses to emerge.

The inconclusive confrontation gives way, unglamorously, to a scene resonating with the image of a caring community, toward which one owes a duty that encompasses more than the readiness to take up arms in its defense. Here, the poor, the weak, the wayfarer, the orphan—in short, all rejects and outcasts—are invited in (together with the "neighbor") to a feast presided over by the poet. Moving further away from scenes of potential confrontations and threats in the world outside, this scene inaugurates an inward movement, toward an enlarged sense of home. The grand feast that announces such an expanded togetherness establishes the basis for a subsequent rethinking of the sources (the whys) of the earlier disorientative, futile, directionless, unsettling, long chase after an elusive enemy. Expanded togetherness in Labid's ode acts as a shield for such a contemplative activity. The festive relief from the wilderness at the conclusion is used as an opportunity to reformulate ideas of sociability, from the vantage point of a nonalien location where such thinking could flow, free from the fear of the unknown, a fear lurking in the unfamiliarity of otherness, in the renounced expanse of emptiness outside of the home, in the undecidability of darkness, and in the pointlessness of the strangers' feud.

The expanded home becomes the model for addressing transtribal anonymities in the outside world, a model whereby the multitudes of such a world are ordered and its pluralist composition is ascertained. What is to become of the world outside is what is becoming of the expanded abode. Thus, toward the end of Labid's great ode, we reach what resembles a code of morals or justice, consisting of ethics, behaviors, and duties incumbent upon belonging to this kind of *community of strangers.* There is the image of an assembly, of a community in a state of meaningful togetherness, encompassing both the tribe and its outside. Like the *umma* that was to coalesce at a later point in Medina, Labid's assembly is a site of resolutions and a new form of just governance: Its conditions of being are still those of claims and counterclaims (very much like that conflict-ridden "unfamiliar muster of many strangers"), but here there is an arbitrator to dispense justice (c. 78–80). Unlike Zuhair's general wisdom, Labid's comes with a mechanism for effecting the code. As presumably the last of the great pre-Islamic poets, Labid offers a significantly different vision of communal organization and hints at the desire for experimenting with expanded yet still vague notions of belonging.

In Muhammad's case, the actual expansion of the domain of Islam begins most clearly with the second *bay'ah* (pact), when the *Ansar* declared their readiness to shield the prophet upon migrating to Medina. The *bay'ah* inaugurated a cautious yet ultimately successful expansion of Islam, which until then had been confined to a besieged community in Mecca and whose earlier attempts to escape such confines, such as Muhammad's distressing ordeal in Ta'if, met with even more pronounced failure. The second *bay'ah*, however, was more overshadowed by tribal than theological paradigms. According to the *sira*, Muhammad barely spoke during the deliberations, his alliance with the *Ansar* being instead negotiated by an infidel uncle. Unlike the more ethical conditions of the first pact with the *Ansar*, those of the second one spelled out little more than a declaration of war on any common enemies. Tribal alliance figured here more than the constitution of a single *umma*, signified by Muhammad's original abstention from assuming the leadership of the *Ansar*, delegating the task instead to twelve Medinian notables, while reserving for himself leadership over the Meccan Muslims (*Muhajirun*). But as far as Medina was concerned, the selection of the twelve overseers (*nuqaba'*) was tantamount to forging a pathbreaking union of the main non-Jewish Medinian tribes. Although Muhammad was soon to abandon the division of Muslim leadership between himself and the twelve overseers, its introduction nevertheless could be construed as marking a suspicion—on the part of Muhammad at least—that Islam was not as clearly meant for Medina as it was for Mecca. Once in the city, he reportedly pleaded, speaking for the *Muhajirun*, "Lord, make us love this town as much as You made us love Mecca, and even more so,"[90] clearly indicating that Mecca continued to be the point of reference.

In addition, the enshrinement of Islam in Medina before Muhammad's migration was probably made even easier by the prophet's absentee status, because he could neither be seen "eating food and walking about the marketplace" as he was in Mecca, nor could he be implicated in the long history of local tribal tensions. This aloofness from profane associations was maintained for a while; *sira* sources mention that Muhammad, upon entering Medina, turned down various clan's offers of residence, leaving the decision to his unguided she-camel, whose meandering path and choice of resting place was attributed to divine commandment.[91] Following blind destiny here establishes the foundation for transtribal solidarity, since the decision regarding prophetic residence in a multitribal minefield is taken away from human as well as prophetic subjectivities.

Gradually, the Medinian Qur'an moved away from its Meccan centricity, expressing in its place an ecstasy at discovering the possibility of transtribal union. This paralleled a gradual consolidation of the *umma* in Medina, as one of the first orders of business for Muhammad in the new town was to "fraternize" (*mu'akhah*) the believers by assigning to each of his Meccan followers a "brother in belief" from among the *Ansar*. In the same line, the separation of leadership over the two communities was abandoned as soon as the first of the twelve Medinian overseers died, with Muhammad declaring himself to be the new *naqib* (overseer) of his constituents rather than delegating the post to someone else from the deceased man's clan.

Though the fraternization indicated a higher level of commonality than "alliance," it did not mean a complete overturn of the laws of clannish bonding. As it strove to account for the nature of the new and diverse community, the Qur'an made a clear distinction between the *Muhajirun* and Muslims who chose to stay in Mecca, subordinating the relation between the two groups to that between the *Muhajirun* and *Ansar,* who were more distant from each other in terms of lineage. The nature of the new bond was first seen in terms of a synthesis between the feeling of distinction from other societies and blood lineages: "The unbelievers give aid and comfort to each other. If you fail to do likewise, there will be disorder in the land and great corruption. . . . Those that have since embraced the Faith and fought with you—they too are your brothers; although according to the Book of God those who are bound by ties of blood are nearest to one another."[92]

The *hijra* meant that Mecca *as a whole* was defined as a site of evil. This all-inclusive definition, which laid down the foundation for the war, meant that the *Muhajirun* had to dissociate themselves from their brethren in faith who had stayed in the city, but without equating them with its infidels. The synthetic formula was to reduce them to the status of tribal allies, the obligation toward whom being no higher than that toward other social units with which the Muslims had treaties. From then on, the notion of blood relations was gradually subordinated to an increasingly ideologized and organized *umma* that was becoming aware of its distinct and original nature in the land. Earlier Qur'anic instructions to approach idolaters with patience and humility sharply contrasted with emergent instructions in Medina, where at one point believers were forbidden to befriend "the enemies of Allah" or even to entertain warm feelings toward the infidels in their immediate families. At some point in that new exposition, the Qur'an found it worthwhile to assert a point that might otherwise have been missed, namely, that kin relations counted for nothing on the Day of Judgment.[93]

Along with such an overhaul of relations, the Medinian Qur'an began to reinterpret tales of earlier prophets that had emphasized their pre-ordained and inescapable communal belonging. The most significant of such reinterpretations was perhaps that concerning the story of the patri-arch Abraham, who in the Meccan Qur'an was portrayed as leaving his infidel father on good terms and even promising to intercede for him be-fore Allah.[94] In the context of Medina, however, the Qur'an now explicitly instructed the believers *not* to emulate that particular episode of the story of Abraham.[95] The context of such emergent teachings and reinterpre-tations brought about not only the rigidification of the boundaries sepa-rating Muslims and non-Muslims but also the need to consolidate the unity among the transtribal Muslim community of Aus, Khazraj, and the *Muhajirun,* now territorially confined to a city from which non-Muslim tribes were being gradually expelled. The fact that Meccan Muslims were not uniformly ready to follow Muhammad in the *hijra* and the fact that the population of Medina continued to harbor the not-so-distant memory of previous animosities among tribes now united in faith led to an ac-knowledgment that conflicts could indeed occur *within* this *umma* as well. Should this recur, however, such conflicts were now to be resolved through a standard method:

> If two parties of believers take up arms the one against the other, make peace between them. If either of them commits aggression against the other, fight against the aggressors till they submit to God's judgment. When they submit, make peace between them in equity and justice; God loves those who exercise justice.
>
> The believers are a band of brothers. Make peace among your brothers.[96]

Elsewhere, conflicts within the necessarily harmonious *umma* were seen as either illusions or as the result of unintentional mistakes.[97] Thus, a Muslim who kills another, for example, is not automatically thrown into the raging fire of hell; rather, he is allowed one of four ways to quickly erase the happening from social memory, listed in an interesting order: He may free a Muslim slave and pay "Islamic" blood-money (*diyyah*) to the family of the victim (with a divine recommendation that the family give it away in alms), or he may fast for two consecutive months in penance. If the Muslim victim was from a clan that was an enemy of the faith, the *diyyah* requirement was waived, but it was reinstituted, in addition to freeing the slave, if the victim belonged to a non-Muslim clan with which Muslims had a treaty. The novelty of this compensatory scheme consists partially in its simultaneous incorporation of the traditional *diyyah*—which generally sufficed by itself otherwise—and expanding the range of compensatory actions beyond the idea of "private" right. A freed Muslim slave supplemented the *umma* with one life that substituted for the one lost *to the umma* in an episode of inner conflict. Within the pluralist communalistic perspective sanctified by independent idols and conceived along the lines of autonomous clans, the family of a victim could not benefit from a freed slave, but it obviously could from the *diyyah*. By contrast, under the emergent *umma* conditions, the perpetrator would pay back the entire *umma* for the crime, and no longer exclusively the kinfolk of the victim.

The introduction of more elaborate modes of punishment must be understood in the context of this redefinition of the nature of sociability. Here, a just punishment is not a straightforward restitution or revenge; it must above all preclude *general* societal futility. The modality of penance allows the very acts of conflict to strengthen the *umma* within which they take place. It is in this context that the downgrading of pointless revenge as a guide to retributary behavior can be understood. But it is also in this context that one can understand why the socially impotent, self-torturing practice of fasting (*for God*) for two consecutive months was left as a *last* option, to be used only when the Muslim perpetrator was unable to fulfill more socially communicative retributary requirements.

Thus, for the *Muhajirun* and the *Ansar*, "Islam" gradually came to be a regulator of inner conflicts, as it simultaneously grew to assume the status of the milestone that marked the boundaries of exterior conflict. But such was not the case for the Muslim Bedouins, for whom allegiance to Islam meant little more than a declaration of alliance with a powerful sedentary community. The fact that such sedentary Muslims were periodically involved in raiding the caravans of Mecca was not, after all, that dissimilar from what Bedouins had traditionally understood as familiar *ghazw* (plundering), which for them hardly needed theological justification.

Furthermore, the Bedouin socioeconomy was inherently incompatible with the central control that was gradually being experimented with in Medina, an incompatibility that had imploded the Kinda kingdom before Muhammad's time and seriously threatened the nascent Islamic polity after him through Musaylimah's revolt.[98] Though the Muslim Bedouins continued to be relatively out of reach of the *umma* as it was being constituted, they were nevertheless of strategic value as military allies. During the first few years after the migration from Mecca, the Muslims could count on the allegiance of so many tribes in the western and northern coastal areas of the peninsula that they could severely undermine the security of the trade route to Syria—an irreplaceable lifeline for the Meccan economy.[99]

In spite of the geographic separation, the *umma* was beginning to be imagined along the lines of uniform practices and rituals that were expected to act as markers of faith everywhere. This expectation, which many Muslim nomads frequently failed to fulfill, arose as the geography of the *umma* became less certain because of its expansion into nomadic territory. One interesting report even seems to indicate that the prophet did not know where Bedouin Muslims lived: "The messenger of Allah, peace be upon him, never raided a people whom he had targeted until dawn; then, if he heard a call to prayer, he would hold still, and if he did not hear [it], he would attack."[100]

Muslim historians trace the "conversion" of the Bedouins back to Muhammad's later period in Mecca, where he regularly proselytized among Arabs from throughout the peninsula during the pilgrimage season. The same sources also report that when he ventured to visit the Bedouins, Muhammad was consistently met with rejection, scorn, and mockery. The stronger the core sedentary Muslim community became, and the more willing it was to raid for acquisition, the more the nomads proceeded to form alliances with it and express them through verbal allegiance to Islam. Having reneged several times on promises of aid to sedentary Muslims at times of crisis, fighting only when it suited them, nomads were sharply denounced in the Qur'an in words that avowedly suspected their motivation to join the faith.[101]

Nomadic life remained otherwise outside of the sociological concerns of the new faith. As the Qur'an and the sedentary Muslims became entangled with experiences emanating from urban and transtribal forms of union, Bedouin life stood out unexplained, unaccounted for, and unin-structed. Like all other societies that the sedentary Muslims did not know, the nomads were called upon to *migrate* to those locations where Muslims lived, so that they could be incorporated into the harmony of the seden-tary community, which until then had been the only real success story of Islam in the peninsula. Historical reports mention that, in his instructions to the Muslim army that was marshaled to Mu'tah—shortly before the conquest of Mecca—Muhammad told its commanders to call upon the infidels whom they encountered to join Islam *and* to migrate from their homes to the "home of the *Muhajirun*," so that they might be incorporat-ed into the body of the *umma* with some certitude. If they accepted Islam but chose to stay where they lived, the instructions went on, the terms of relation with them would be similar to those prevailing with the "Bedouin Muslims," with a share of the spoils of war going to them only in those in-stances in which they fought alongside the Muslims of Medina.[102] In this respect, continuing to live apart from the *tangible umma* indicated not only suspicious theological commitment but, moreover, lack of suscepti-bility to organizational control. As the sedentary community revealed it-self to be the stable core in the social life of the faith, the spontaneous sense of closeness and proximity was seen to be one of the most impor-tant virtues of the *umma*, so much so that it became difficult to imagine true believers existing without being empirically touched by a prophet who belonged to it.[103]

HUDAYBIYYAH AND THE PARADIGMS OF THE *UMMA*

The empirical definition of the *umma* was to a large extent foreshadowed by the experience of Islam in Mecca, and the early feeling that Islam showed for distinct belonging of the *umma* in a sanctuary that excluded its inhospitable, terror-ridden surroundings. The *hijra*, while creating another tangible community, inaugurated a more complicated system of relations in which figured both distant allies and distant Mecca, which continued to function as a spiritual magnet for the Arabs. One of the most interesting episodes in the story of Islam at that point concerned the dynamics by which a synthesis was forged between all such facets and communities of faith, a synthesis that did not fail to unsettle theological purists and show that the larger and less tangible the *umma*, the more polyphonous it became. Such tensions were epitomized in the *Sulh al-Hudaybiyyah,* or the Peace of Hudaybiyyah, which was signed between Muhammad and Mecca almost two years before the fall of the city, and ended a promising Muslim expedition against it without a fight.

The sources emphasize that Muhammad's army, consisting of 700 to 1,400 sedentary followers, did not intend to wage war during that episode. Rather, the force was intended as more of an army of preachers that would proselytize among the Arabs during their pilgrimage and participate with them in glorifying Mecca's *haram.* The Qurayshans went on alert, vowing not to let their enemy, with whom they had so much bloodshed already, enter the city without their explicit and humiliating approval. The standoff resulted in the *Sulh al-Hudaybiyyah,* which stipulated, among other conditions, that the war would be halted for ten years, that individuals in both camps would be free to ally themselves with whichever side they chose, and that Muhammad and his followers would postpone their visit to the *haram* to the following year and would restrict their stay to three days, during which Quraysh would stand impatiently vigilant. One important condition that incensed many Muslims was that Muslim Meccans who thereafter migrated to Medina without the consent of their guardians were to be sent back to Mecca, while Quraysh was exempted from reciprocating such treatment in the case of Muslims who defected to Mecca.

Many of the Muslims considered the agreement to be an unwarranted humiliation, with the faithful giving away much and ending the war in exchange for almost nothing. (In the *sira,* the later caliph 'Umar Ibn al-Khattab largely personified the opposition to the treaty among the Muslims.) At first glance, Muhammad's concessions at Hudaybiyyah do indeed look perplexing, even if one takes into account strategic calculations, such as that the fight against Mecca was different from a Bedouin raid, where the balance of forces is calculated more directly. When negotiating the treaty, Muhammad even agreed to replace the Islamic heading of "In the name of Allah, the Compassionate, the Merciful," with the more general Qurayshan "In Your name, our Allah," and to replace the reference to himself as "Muhammad, the messenger of Allah," with the more traditional designation of his name followed by that of his father.

The *sira* condenses the contradictory passions toward Mecca around that time in an incident that is said to have in some mystical way precipitated the agreement: Once Muhammad's army was near Mecca and unable to decide on a course of action after the march had put the Qurayshans on a determined and defensive alert, God once more offered a sign. Muhammad's she-camel suddenly lowered itself to the ground in the valley of Huday-biyyah, prompting the prophet to an immediate explanation: "She was halted by Him who had halted the elephant from Mecca,"[104] in reference to the earlier expedition of the elephant-riding Abyssinians, whose retreat without a fight was traced earlier in the Qur'an to God's intervention. Now that same Allah was to protect Mecca from his own messenger, a messenger whose motives were originally meant to be the exact opposite of those of Abraha, with his elephants bent on destroying the sacred *haram* of Mecca and Abraham. Muhammad, whose year of birth coincides in the *sira* with that expedition, could only kneel down before the symbol of Mecca's greatness and apologize for having appeared to be attacking it in the same way he had attacked the caravans in the desert, to repent and grieve for having appeared as an Abyssinian invader, from the likeness of whose might the city was to be shielded through the tutelage of the monotheist deity to begin with.

At a different level, the agreement of Hudaybiyyah emerged from the predicament that Islam, as a social force, had been experiencing since its departure from Mecca. War caused the spread of Islam in the form of verbal allegiances (which could mark the possible origin of the verbal *shahadah* [pronouncement of belief] as the first pillar of faith), which could not be ascertained and monitored without the beholders' migration to the dwellings of the only community under continuous control, namely the "home of the *Muhajirun.*" Confined within the boundaries of Medina, the Muslims could partially count on their allies, as well as on their own force, to sustain a war economy that was growing to obscure the original mission of the religion. But as a theologically committed force, not a single tribe was converted to Islam by the force of arms. The ten-year peace treaty was the outstanding testimony to that fact. To spread the faith by peaceful means, or at least to reestablish thereby peaceful contacts with the peninsular Arabs, who continued to revere Mecca, as well as with Mecca itself, was, after all, the Muslims' professed motivation for visiting the *haram*. According to traditional accounts, such a bargain paid off: The Muslim ranks multiplied several times over after the agreement, to such an extent that two years after its inception, Muhammad—using a minor breach as a pretext—could marshal ten thousand dedicated men to Mecca and finally capture the city.

But at the time of the agreement, it was not clear whether such a bargain could be expected to pay off, although some Muslims probably regarded it more as a way out of the war's failure to bring to Islam other converts than the lukewarm and unreliable Bedouins. War, however, added to the faith an important political dimension. Muhammad was no longer a lonely prophet but one with a deeply dedicated following in Medina and with allies elsewhere. The war itself, if unsuccessful in bringing in theologically committed recruits, did at least establish the Muslims as a force to be taken seriously among the Arabs. Thus, once arms were laid down, Muhammad could capitalize on the novel facts that the earlier lack of prophetic credentials that had isolated him in Mecca had by then been almost compensated for by a show of success, endurance, and following and that the societies that had always expected a prophet were therefore prepared to consider him. At the same time, though many of the concessions of the agreement appeared unnecessary, they did nonetheless defuse the tense atmosphere of war to such an extent that Islam could be considered by minds that were free from presupposed hostility.[105]

The time of Hudaybiyyah, furthermore, witnessed evident cleavages in both camps, cleavages that in themselves could have caused a rethinking of the viability of total war. Muhammad, who was painfully aware of the refusal of the Bedouin Muslims to join the expedition, was further reminded of both his belonging in Mecca and the unreliability of his own forces by a notable Qurayshan negotiator: "O Muhammad! So you have gathered the *medley of people* by whom you came back to break the might of *your own* tribe. Quraysh has come out [for you], with them are the women and the children . . . vowing that you [will] never enter [Mecca] without their approval. By Allah, I could see *those* [the Muslims] disbanding from around you tomorrow."[106] But it was not only the Muslims whose ranks were shaky. The same reports mention that the leader of the Ahabish, one of the non-Qurayshan components of Mecca, protested against preventing Muhammad and his followers from paying respect to the *haram*, reaffirming meanwhile the principle of openness and peace upon which the city was founded. The reports also mention that the Ahabish protected some of Muhammad's emissaries to Quraysh. Further cleavages appear in the treatment of negotiators, as some of the Qurayshan messengers were respected by Muhammad more than others, and like-wise, the Muslim messenger 'Uthman Ibn 'Affan could count on more honorable treatment in Mecca than another Muslim messenger, 'Umar Ibn al-Khattab.

At that juncture, 'Uthman and 'Umar represented two opposing para-digms within the Muslim community. For Quraysh, the difference be-tween the two had to do with the former's abundance of notable relations. That was not a purely accidental difference, for it affected the positions and worldviews of these two later caliphs. While 'Uthman, being firmly rooted in Mecca, represented the visions of most Meccan Muslims like himself and Muhammad, the relative outsider 'Umar spoke to most of the new converts, who were either strangers to Mecca or were held at a disad-vantage within its old socioeconomic rules: the poor, the non-Qurayshan allies, and the semi-Bedouins. Those sectors compensated for their lack of power within the social structure of the city by claiming it in the realm of a theology that held, from their perspective, the only set of ideas that could stand above the established social order that had nullified their sig-nificance. Precisely because of its position with regard to the established social order, the theology could be used to overthrow the social order rather than to further protect it, an idea condensed in the 'Uthmanist vi-sion. In that unpronounced unevenness of vision, the seeds were planted of the later conflict that was to destroy the Rashidi caliphate, although the conflict gathered other ingredients while it was maturing.

Realizing theology's power to affect the established social order re-inforced the *general* commitment to it among diverse Muslims. But when the possibility that the same theology could deal with the established order in diametrically opposed ways was exposed in Hudaybiyyah (to the satisfaction of the 'Uthmanists), the bewildered faction attempted to force its own purist vision to account for what was happening. Traditional ac-counts acknowledge a widespread disappointment among the Muslims after the treaty became known;[107] many of them echoed 'Umar's incom-prehension of the entire affair. They could not possibly comprehend the commitment of Muhammad and the 'Uthmanists to the "mother of towns" itself, nor their not-so-inaudible drive to have Allah himself protect what they thought to be a social order that lacked legitimate ontotheological foundations. Though the 'Umarist paradigm recognized the unstable foundations upon which the Meccan socioeconomic order stood, it only discerned in that realization an opportunity to demolish it completely, to replace it with one that would allocate a place for all on the basis of theological commitment rather than clannish and class affiliations. It was in Islam that adherents to such a paradigm saw the perfect ideological vehicle to accomplish that work, even when the Meccan Qur'an was saying little more than pure, abstract theology. In part, the Qur'anic daring and vocal objection to Meccan theodicy and outlook to the world must have appeared, at least to some outsiders, as a rejection of the centerpiece of the differentiated status quo. Thus, it was little noted that, in an attempt partially motivated by the desire to elicit the attention of the established social order, the message addressed some of the social concerns of the dispossessed largely when the selfsame social order ignored the warnings. But once integrated into the message, the outsiders were led to believe that the new religion meant to speak to them and, as such, entailed a radical reorganization of the order of cosmological as well as social totality.[108]

Such paradigmatic differences in Muslim ranks emerged from the fact that Islam was becoming a larger social mantle for discontent, recognizing the existence of each group it met along the way. Seeing his followers' crestfallen spirits after he had spontaneously made so many concessions in Hudaybiyyah, including some that even his own enemies had not asked for, Muhammad could offer no reason other than that Allah had dictated the terms of the treaty. When one paradigm, such as the 'Uthmanist in Hudaybiyyah, dictated terms to its own satisfaction, none of the others interpreted the matter in the self-reflexive way that would have led them to conclude that they were the "wrong" recruits to Islam, even when some of the "wrong" recruits began to be turned away or sent back to Mecca. Ibn Hisham reports at least one mutiny, in which a rebellious Muslim refused to be sent back to his masters in Mecca, escaping Medina instead to form a band consisting of other scattered Muslims, reportedly Meccans of low socioeconomic origins, who had refrained from migrating to Medina earlier. The band independently recommenced raiding Meccan caravans to such an extent that Quraysh eventually asked Muhammad to take them into his custody in Medina, relieving him of the treaty obligation of having to extradite them to Mecca.[109]

Such rebellious and purist spirits were now utilized in wars against other communities with which the peninsular Arabs had few connections. The expeditions taking place between Hudaybiyyah and the eventual conquest of Mecca were larger in scale than previous skirmishes and were characterized by an elevated spirit of adventurism.[110] Such expeditions brought back unity to Muslim ranks while allowing the negativity of the treaty to be erased from memory. Muhammad now commanded the faithful to look the other way, to the north, ignoring thereby the existence of Mecca. This strategy discharged the energies of the purist recruits at the same time that it allowed Muslims to avoid endangering their newly established good relations with the peninsular Arabs and to proselytize to sedentary communities in a less highly charged atmosphere.

Once Muslim ranks were large enough, the focus of the wars moved back to Mecca, which was taken without a fight only two years after Hudaybiyyah. The manner in which the city was overrun, however, is extremely instructive. The sources mention that shortly before entering Mecca, Muhammad announced three categories of people to be immune from reprisals, on the basis of their location: those seeking refuge in the *haram,* those seeking refuge in their own homes, and most interestingly, those seeking refuge in the house of Abi Sufian, then the most eminent chief in pagan Mecca. In other words, with the exception of the idols, all former dignitaries, whether represented by the *haram* or by traditional hierarchies, were announced to be safe enough for Islam to live with. So many things stayed in their former order that all the acrimony of the previous conflict would seem bewildering. The most important *haram* service function, *siqayah* (providing water), was reassigned by Muhammad to the same man who was already holding it, the sanctity of the *haram* and of the city were reiterated, and even some of Muhammad's most hated enemies were rehabilitated.[111] One report spells out the dialectical puzzle of a struggle whose roots remained inaccessible to the protagonists because such roots could be expressed only in the metaphors of transhuman authority; when Muhammad was about to reassign the function of *siqayah* to the Meccan notable who had just given him the key to the *haram,* Muhammad asked him: "You can surely see now that this key is in my hand, that I can assign it to whomever I want?" The notable, thinking that the key was going to land in the hands of one of those medley of Arabs who composed the bulk of Muhammad's army, commented with the grief of eternal loss: "Then, the glory and might of Quraysh is gone!" Muhammad promptly corrected him: "To the contrary, today [Quraysh's name] is entrenched and glorious!"[112]

The 'Uthmanist vision, thus, involved the irony that Quraysh was to become "entrenched and glorious" not because of its own pursuit of such merits but through the imposition of such honors from without, that is, under the banner of a religion that it had rejected and by a "medley" of people it had despised. The specific character of such an irony consists in that it was neither calculable from the onset nor intentional throughout. But such seems to be the destiny of any process that eventually comes to be called "historical": What sets it in motion runs the risk of becoming unrecognizable in the end product. As it unfolded upon various societies, Islam was no longer free from the bondage of that "medley" of people by whose efforts it had become victorious. For in order to enlist them in the struggle to safeguard Mecca from itself, they had to be addressed in a way that made Islam into their own religion.

But in some cases, such as that of the Bedouin Muslims, the Qur'an resolutely refused to speak in terms of constituents. Rather, it explicitly abhorred their overtly opportunistic attitude toward the idea of Allah, while Muhammad repeatedly complained of their unreliability. However, it was that relationship that enabled Islam, especially after the conquest of Mecca, to solve the problem of Bedouin infighting and the hopeless stagnation resulting from periodic demographic expansions in a relatively resourceless landscape, by transferring such populations outside of the peninsula through the astonishingly rapid Islamic conquests. That process furnished an unintended balance between some trends emerging out of nomadism itself toward a more centralized system of arbitration for an increasingly anarchistic society (first expressed through the Kinda experiment) and the development of that authority in a sedentary setting following different dynamics and aspirations.[113] Once Islam brought the peninsula under a central authority, it deprived the Bedouins of one of the elements of their economy that demographic expansions had disproportionately aggrandized, namely, intertribal *ghazw*. When they were sent outside of the peninsula, they were sent as warriors who could rightfully enjoy a specified share in the spoils of war, as they had done previously among themselves, in a way that the sedentary Muslims emulated in their struggle against pre-Islamic Mecca.[114] Thus, in the *surah* of al-Fath, reported to have been revealed to Muhammad shortly after the conquest of Mecca, the Qur'an accentuates the authority over the nomads by reminding them of the new power of the unified sedentary communities while ordaining to those unreliable allies their future role, *far away*:

> You [the desert Arabs] thought that the Apostle and the believers would never return *to their people;* and with that fancy your hearts were delighted. You harbored evil thoughts and thus incurred damnation. . . .
>
> Say to the desert Arabs who stayed behind: "You shall be called upon to fight a mighty nation, unless they embrace Islam. If you prove obedient, God will reward you. But if you run away, *as you have done before this,* He will inflict upon you a stern chastisement."[115]

Thus, significant distinctions were already apparent within the Muslim community even before the death of the prophet. Though early Islam accepted the preexisting distinction in social order between *hadarah* and *badawah* lifestyles (but no longer recognizing their political independence), it harbored simultaneously the seeds of unprecedented future ideological splits among the *hadaris* themselves, which first came into evidence in the landmark peace of Hudaybiyyah; the contradictions of various societies simply regrouped under the mantle of an Islamic *umma,* where they continued to galvanize, metamorphose, and develop further discursive camouflages along their way into forms of explication more multifarious than those expressed by tribal pluralism.

The success of Islam, and Muhammad, in a land that was not only expecting prophets but teeming with them stems from the fact that a multitude of modalities of reception compelled the message to synthesize all the contradictions it had thought of as such once it encountered them along its way. It was born in the relatively advanced society of Mecca, and from that vantage point it looked upon the fissions of what it judged to be less-fortunate, brute, or transitional surroundings. It passed judgment on everything it encountered, filling up the enormous ontological void that was magnified by the willful self-enclosure of its most important ideological alternatives. In other words, it became a "system," which in a dialectical fashion created and was re-created by a vast and polyphonous social order, an order that did not know whom else to ask, among other issues of life, the question of its own justification.

eight

Austerity, Power, and Worldly Exchange

The Qur'an words, amid the heat of the war against Mecca, revealed a sense of torment about the raison d'être of the war: "They have hearts they cannot comprehend with; they have eyes they cannot see with; and they have ears they cannot hear with. They are like beasts—indeed, they are more misguided."[1] Apart from the war's profane and visible association with the potential for economic remuneration, it remained more lodged in an incomprehensible resistance of the old system of belief to natural extinction.[2] But while this perception was simmering among the estranged *Muhajirun* (Meccan Muslims in Medina), the rest of infidel Quraysh went about its business as usual, with no apparent concern for the possibility that the small raids on its caravans by the former could escalate into a full-scale war. The difference in attitudes was most evident at the battle of Badr, the first major confrontation between the two sides, where a Muslim contingent of three hundred warriors defeated a Qurayshan convoy protected by three times their number. Traditional accounts lengthily portray the prebattle determination of the Muslims, sharply contrasting it with the unwillingness of many Qurayshans, who were more traders than warriors, to engage in a real fight. The hastily marshaled Qurayshan army was meant largely as a show of strength; its mission was only to camp in the area of Badr for three nights and then stage an orderly withdrawal back to Mecca rather than to actually fight according to a preset stratagem. The Muslims' swift attack caught it by complete surprise, especially because most Qurayshans continued to entertain the belief that the blood relations between them and the *Muhajirun* could not possibly be superseded to the extent of intertribal war waged in the name of a transtribal faith.[3]

But another dimension of the story here, which nonetheless should not be too exaggerated, had to do with the comparative ontology of life and death. The Muslims' battle adversaries knew of no other life than this one. For them, justice could not be postponed to another life or relegated to a weak deity that had no jurisdiction over this area of human relations. In sharp contrast to the restless, vengeful attitude of Mecca after its defeat in Badr, the remembrance of the Qur'an for the Muslims killed in Uhud was overwhelmingly compassionate, with no mention whatever of a need to avenge their deaths. Rather, they were portrayed as enjoying the richness of paradise, desiring only to be joined in it by their other comrades, and repudiating the survivors' need to mourn their glorious fate.[4] With the consolidation of such an ontotheological development, one of the ancient standards of behavior attached to the concept of honor, namely insuring the certitude of avenging unnatural death, was demurred.

DEATH, SUBJECTIVITY, AND IDENTITY

In neighboring social contexts, however, natural death was a final destination that had nullified the need for grandiose individual planning in life, especially under nomadism. An outstanding example occurs in Tarafa's ode, where death is shown to reduce all contrasting virtues—the niggardly and the indulgent wastrel—into a sameness of nonbeing:

> All you can see is a couple of heaps of dust, and on them
> slabs of granite, flat stones piled shoulder to shoulder. (c. 64)

Here, death equalizes all and erases all difference. Death is the permanent abode of the same. The awareness of this impending sameness is mobilized here to negate the purposefulness of the present quest after, or demand for, an ethical difference (which in this case is related to a difference in social status). Here, there is a clear, overpowering desert landscape that furnishes the immense background of the two similar grave markers, where an anonymity of death blurs vision and makes distinctions improbable. Past achievement, human effort, projects, designs, life itself are all so visibly ephemeral. This fundamentally nomadic conception of natural death was inherited by the pre-Islamic sedentaries, whose differentiated socioeconomy was yet to provide a more differentiated idea of natural death, an idea that would be expected to exist in tandem with the new conceptions of the virtue of status and the introduction of more-stable social hierarchies. To be sure, the Qur'an itself seems at some points to allude to an archaic image of death, articulated in terms quite distant from those postulating it as a total finitude of a normative and coherent subjectivity: "When they enter it [the hell of fire], their ears, their eyes, and their very skins will testify to their misdeeds. 'Why did you speak against us?' they will say to their skins, and their skins will reply 'God, who gives speech to all things, has made us speak. . . . You did not hide yourselves, so that your ears and eyes and skins could not be made to testify against you.'[5]

Thus, though disunited as they seek to account for sins, the organs would still address the self to which they belong as a unit. Here, though the physical unity of the body is torn asunder by divine power, an ethical stand-in is kept in place for the purpose of interrogating the *source* of sinful acts. Organs are separated and endowed with tongues of their own in order to give credence to an act of witnessing, which is to be transmitted to a divine court of justice at a later point in time. This procedure is grounded upon the need to produce a most credible witnessing, especially in the case of major sins such as fornication.[6] In fact, failure to produce witnesses in such cases could result in those making the accusation being punished almost as severely as the adulterers themselves, with all their subsequent rights to witness being suspended until they repent.[7] Eventually, they would be torn into conflicting organs, each of which would testify against the organism as a whole for the ultimate sin of speaking of unprovable scandals and thereby causing undue social discord.

Here, the entire human body begins to mirror existence itself, as nothing more than an aggregate of disjointed parts, individually controlled and collectively made into meaningful ensembles by a divine power. The integrity of physical oneness, much like questions of belief, infidelity, and repentance, is no longer the sole property of a coherent self. Coherence here is condensed not in the idea of naturally endowed and physically referenced subjectivity but in a totality of discoverable acts played in the context of a game of justice, a game whose players must be testified for and against by a reliable system of surveillance and witnessing, a system which, in turn, can be deposited in an assemblage of breakable physical oneness, unsuspectedly called the self.[8]

AUSTERITY, JUSTICE, PERISHING: MOSES AND 'UBAYD

This notion of human subjectivity, here articulated for the purposes of anchoring a process of restoring justice and argued in the context of death and an afterlife, recalls some elements of the pre-Islamic vision of self-hood. In much of that heritage, and especially from the nomadic point of view, subjective integrity is questioned on the grounds of the austere conditions of life and the recurrent nonheroic, passive exposure to the storms of fate. In the tradition surrounding the *mu'allaqat* (odes), one of the most illustrative cases of this view is the story of 'Ubayd Ibn l-Abras, the least known and reportedly most destitute of the great pre-Islamic poets. In fact, so his story goes, he was not a poet at all. He was an impoverished wanderer, accompanied in the desolate landscape by his sister and a few goats. Being a man of neither means nor power, he was prevented from watering his goats at a well by a certain figure from Banu Malik. Despondent, he departed, agonizing over his fated weakness. Exhausted, he rested next to his sister in the shadow of a tree. The same man who had kept them from the water, so the legend goes, saw the siblings sleeping next to one another. He uttered a disparaging allusion to incest, and his words found their way to the ears of the poet-to-be. Awakened, he could do no more than appeal to a God to deliver him justice, since he himself was so completely disinherited and feeble. Like all those who thus wish to vindicate their cause, he resumed sleeping. Eventually, divine help arrived in the form of an angel descending from heaven and armed with a "bundle of poetry" (*kubbaton mina l-shi'r*), which he hurled into the poet's mouth. Then, before disappearing, he commanded the poet to rise. When the poet awoke, he immediately discovered within himself a mass of poetry that stampeded out of him without control, poetic sentences forming by themselves out of the flood of words.

Here, poetry is produced by itself, and the speaking subject is no more than a medium. Such a spontaneous, subjectless production of testimony and meaning arrives from a source located outside of the speaker, with the product appended to him in such a way that the balance of power between the speaker/witness/plaintiff and his enemies is altered. Yet the appendage has to be structured so as to appear to be spontaneous, in other words, unforeseen by all parties involved—the enemy as well as the speaker, since it is the *novel and unexpected* nature of this balance of justice that makes this speech so effective. This appendage also must deny having belonged to a prepoetic nature of the speaker, whose original identity is that of a faceless nonpoet.

In the Qur'an, such an invasive assumption of command over what could otherwise be assumed to be subjective qualities is likewise connected to a need to restore justice, but in a way that disempowers individuals in the face of God rather than empowering them over earthly adversaries. The unity in nature that God symbolizes means that in spite of God's sporadic intrusions, the fundamental building blocks of subjective action and being are, after all, far from being arbitrarily deposited: "God has never put two hearts within one man's body. He does not regard the wives whom you divorce as your mothers, nor your adopted sons as your own sons. These are *mere words* that you utter with your mouths: . . . God (in contrast) declares the Truth and guides to the right path."[9]

The assertion of such a parallel uniformity of both physical constitution and transsubjective relations is evidently rooted in the suspicion that some "utterances," like 'Ubayd's, possess the potential to reorder nature by themselves, even though they originated for a different purpose, namely, to restore justice in an ad hoc, pastoral fashion. It is as if such words, to the extent that they fail to refer precisely to the known nature of things, are in themselves dangerous, perhaps even indicative of uncontrolled desires. For in this case it would be one's unanchored wishes that would be ruling, wishes that, as has been proven time and again, without proper guidance could lead to injustice: "We offered Our trust to the heavens, and to earth, and to the mountains, but they refused the burden and were afraid to receive it. Man undertook to bear it, but he has proved to be [unjust and ignorant]."[10]

Thus, the coming into being of a religion speaking of "a trust" indicates that such a trust, a novel or an unexplained proposition, was in any case no longer to be held strictly in the hands of those addressed as if they were its holders. While the ontological existence of such a trust had distinguished man from and given him priority over nature, the story of trust was necessarily a story of failure to meet the responsibility. In salvation religions, the transcendental deity always justified its actions on the basis of man's failure in that regard. Thus, the withdrawal of the trust inaugurated the social aspects of the faith, whereby not merely theology and worship but all the practical affairs of social life, exchange, and political order were regulated. It was precisely that grand reorganization of all the details of life that absolved that unjust and ignorant creature of sin, replacing it with an unshakable belief in lawful self-righteousness; it was becoming impossible to be a wrongdoer, because human action no longer emanated from avowed desire or inner sources of inspiration. When merchants sold and bought in the marketplace, they sold and bought what Allah had allowed according to prescribed rules and congratulated themselves for avoiding what he prohibited. Many of the prohibitions, though by no means all, do not seem to have had any meaning other than to serve as a measurement of commitment to the communal faith, a measurement that would allow the faithful to give other than preordained tribal credence to their social standing and citizenship. The cosmos itself was organized with built-in signals to allow for this social exchange to proceed in an orderly fashion: The new moons were to indicate dates and times of pilgrimage, the day was *made* for earning a living, and the night for resting.[11]

The Qur'anic exchange rules began by sanctifying private wealth but at the same time strictly rejecting "unnatural" wealth, that is, wealth for which no labor was visibly exerted. This connection between wealth and labor was clearly illustrated by the single stroke in which two unrelated transactions were summarily forbidden: usurping an orphan's trust fund, and enlarging charity to the feeble-minded to an extent that would amount to giving away to them wealth that Allah had entrusted to those who had labored for it.[12] In general, many of Muhammad's reforms of economic life in Medina were directly aimed at ending speculative activities and encouraging production, wage labor, land use, and trade in empirically existing items instead.[13] Legitimate exchange meant, above all, the possibility of "trusting," which was regulated along the same lines that had occasioned the procedure laid out for the general restoration of justice: The act of witnessing was of paramount importance in this type of exchange. Once the orphans came of age, their money was to be given back to them in its entirety, while witnesses were present.[14] Witnesses were also to be present at any occasion in which there was to be a transfer of wealth, such as loaning or making a will.[15] In most instances in which the Qur'an called for witnesses to oversee a transaction, it went into unusually detailed expositions, surveying all possible scenarios, displaying thereby little faith in human ability to act justly without proper guidance and surveillance. So suspicious was the Qur'an of having to leave anything to human agency that, when it contemplated the scenario of death in a remote place where no credible witnesses could be found, it first dictated that whoever purported to witness must be ritually imprisoned after prayer until they swore their trustworthiness, after which they could still be replaced by other witnesses should they arouse suspicion regarding their reliability. But realizing the lack of definition of reliability in such a system (not to mention its cumbersome nature), the Qur'an soon abandoned it and introduced uniform and elaborate schemes for dividing up the resulting inheritance.[16]

Such formulaic and elaborate strictures belong to the Medinian period and were clearly part and parcel of the practical necessities of governance and adjudication. The principle of safeguarding exchange and justice through some form of "trust," however, was already evident not only in the Meccan Qur'an but also, and perhaps even more so, in some pre-Islamic institutions in Mecca, such as the *hilf al-fudul* (pact of the virtuous ones) and, more amorphously, the sanctified atmosphere and claims surrounding the city. In fact, at some points the Meccan Qur'an seems necessarily less formulaic on this theme than pagan Mecca was willing to entertain, illustrating instead the idea of the restoration of justice through parables reminiscent of austere nomadic conditions, such as those that had instigated 'Ubayd's poetic outburst. Here, a slightly revised Biblical story offers the story of Moses as the Qur'anic counterpart to 'Ubayd's story:

> When [Moses] came to the well of Midian he found around it a multitude of men watering their flocks, and beside them two women who were keeping back their sheep. "What is it that troubles you?" he asked.
>
> They replied: "We cannot water them until the shepherds have driven away their flocks. Our father is an aged man."
>
> Moses watered for them their sheep, then retired to the shade. . . . The old man said: "I will give you one of my daughters in marriage if you stay eight years in my service." . . . "So be it between us," said Moses.[17]

Unlike in 'Ubayd's fable, justice here is restored without discursive or poetic accentuation of the conflict. Here, Moses offers a helping hand in what may seem to be a minor incident, but the very simplicity of the picture makes it exceptionally earthly and vivid. Shepherding in desert areas involves occasional conflicts of claims for the scarce water, which is one of the main sources of friction within pastoral nomadic societies. The mundane, everyday nature of this conflict calls for no more than an equally straightforward, nonmiraculous resolution by a passing prophet.

These Qur'anic passages are obviously not as powerful as others dealing with the concept of restoring justice. But the picture they provide is realistic. They depict a normal Bedouin and semisedentary economic activity, introduce one important and real source of disharmony that could conceivably accompany its practice, and offer a means by which it is resolved. Through the entirely traditional means of marriage, the weak are then attached to nothing less than a herald of invincible justice. For years thereafter, Moses becomes a humble shepherd, wandering like a Bedouin who is totally freed from any source of alienation; not only had he restored justice, but he confidently expected not to be wronged in the future. His explicit announcement of such a prediction clearly addressed not the immediate nomadic conflict over water but a more original wrong from which he himself had escaped and to whose source he was to return at a later stage as a prophet: the unjust, disunited world of the pharaoh. In this sense, the restoration of harmony in the desert is not part of the logic of the desert itself but, rather, part of a logic residing outside the desert in the sedentary setting from which the idea of God was exiled. It is significant, in this respect, that though Moses stayed behind in the desert for many years after the Midian incident, nothing more was heard from or about him until he returned to the sedentary fold. His story is interrupted, as though it could flow forth only under conditions of sedentary pain.

In contrast to Moses's small-scale, self-actualized triumph in the desert, 'Ubayd's comparable episode displays the poet as a weakling who is reinforced by an exterior source with a poem intended to empower him over conditions of injustice. The poem itself commences with an extremely pessimistic and austere opening—which is nonetheless profoundly traditional in the genre of the *mu'allaqat*. To be sure, the traditional opening of standing by the ruins itself seems to be hospitable to the generally agonized nature of 'Ubayd's discourse. Unlike many of the other *mu'allaqat*,

'Ubayd's staunchly refuses to balance the lugubrious beginning with amorous adventures and other reminiscences from a more pleasant past. His is a fundamentally lonely environment, unmitigated by the slightest human referent. Although there is an abundant succession of locations—nine in all—their former occupants are only anonymously identified as "they" (c. 3). Thus, even though geography is abundant, it stands by itself, with little human anchor or identity. (This remarkable absence of humanity can be contrasted to the lengthy portrayal of desert animals, which abound throughout the second half of the ode [c. 27–48].) What further distinguishes this opening from the rest of the tradition of the *mu'allaqat* is that the poet seems to be weeping over what has never been lost, since it is never claimed to have existed. While past attainment is not clearly established, a profound sense of loss pervades 'Ubayd's opening, which is laden with such terms as *maslub, mahrub,* and *mauruth* (dispossessed, pirated, and disinherited). Such a dispossession seems to be occurring naturally in the due course of time, with no apparent causality. Perishing (*halak*), and the aging that will accompany the simple passages of time permeate the picture (c. 6, 11, 16, and elsewhere). The only manifestation of life, interestingly enough, flows from the metaphors of weeping: Tears flow like a spring, or a river, in the shadow of the palm trees, or down the hill, or through the valley (c. 7–10). The appearance of life is not an object for joy as much as it is another transformation in a nature whose evanescence is noted with sad contentment. There is a profound, nearly prophetic inability to refuse to follow the brutality of fate to its logical conclusion.

In an important way, however, this ascetic vision anticipates some features of the early Islamic God, especially as it highlights distance from and disillusionment with both human society and the record of material nature, neither of which promises any more hope or redemption than would a possible world beyond. Thus, in spite of the pervasive despair, hope is still possible and is evidenced first by the very ability to compose a poem. In order to hope to deliver this discourse on absolute hopelessness, the poet must speak through the medium through which philosophy and wisdom became singularly receivable. This tribute to a traditional form of delivering sagacity constitutes the fundamental hope of 'Ubayd's discourse: the hope for an audience. But then, this was to be not simply an audience for the rhythms but also one that could hear the great ontological barrenness effected in 'Ubayd's ode—the shortest among the legendary ten—where nothing is left in place but the glaring severity of unmitigated nihilism.

'Ubayd delivers himself therefore without modification. He is defined not in terms of absolute powerlessness but, rather, in terms of powerlessness *knowable* by virtue of an encounter with a source of power, whereafter this knowledge becomes immutable. His dispossession is presented as an irremediable condition of existence. One cannot transform what must be presented as nature. Thus, 'Ubayd stands by the ruins and declares his alienation from that which he could never attain, whereby the dispossessed condition of being is absolutized as irreversible nature. The oppositions between potential possession and actual dispossession are not presented as belonging to the same temporal dimension; rather, one condition belongs to the past, which had defined the fallen status of the present, and the other belongs to the present, which is the impossibility of past and reclamation. Thus, the present becomes known as an absolutely dismal condition.

Thus, 'Ubayd denies hope rather emphatically (c. 14). From the abyss of this existential gloom, general wisdom flowers suddenly in the form of a monotonous, figuratively austere, despondent, pessimistic ontology, wishing death, disbelieving in struggle, and suspicious of those strictures of human togetherness known to the poet, namely, those provided in the form of tribal allegiance (c. 14–26). Allah makes an appearance, openly contrasting his resourcefulness to the unreliability of the human spirit. The ontology here speaks of the randomness of fate, nullifying all notions constructed around human effort: This is perhaps why this ontology is so remarkably nonpedagogical—in sharp contrast to those of Zuhair and Labid, whose codes are directed at specific audiences to which they belonged and could be entrusted with lecturing. 'Ubayd not only has no audience, but his discourse even negates the determinacies of audience and doubts the fruitfulness of pedagogic effort. There is no point in lecturing when all are mortals, the lecturer, the lectured, and by extension, the lecture itself. Nothing shall be preserved. The best one can do, from this word until consumed by death, is to dealienate oneself. One must shed the skin of outworn morality of attachments—particularly to a social entity as pointless as a tribe; distrust the normative closeness of kin (especially c. 24–25); forget alienation, borne out by the severance of links to society; make no effort to structure one's life, according to *any* code of manners, ethics, or labor, for the way fate operates is completely independent of human design: Fate will take its course regardless (c. 21–23) and will proceed up to and including the point of *reversing* the presently established order of human relations. Even wishing life, over and above destiny, merely prolongs the torture of the "lie" of which human life consists (c. 26).

Such ethical postures are predicated upon a vacant ontology, which calls for withdrawal and meditation, an approach exemplified by the early extended seclusions of Muhammad prior to the revelation. The ontological presupposition proceeds to remove all those ideological strictures, modes of belonging, and social ethics, substituting for them a passive wait for either death or overpowering revelation. This moment of emptying, which inhabits the same sphere as death, is also that of possible refilling, which inhabits the same sphere as hope. To detect a "lie" of human life (c. 26), after all, is to be interested in a nonlie that, since it is not already provided, is placed as a matter for search. Here, one relinquishes the received wisdom of sociability so as to return to an originary moment preceding it, a moment that—as used in the genealogy of prophets in the Qur'an—both precedes society and reconstitutes its source of legitimate knowledge and pedagogy. Here is born the desire to begin the story, life, creation itself, over again. To desire death, therefore, is to set oneself on the road toward an immense project.

This social being's mode of existence is conditioned by an awareness of an exogenous power toward which he is helpless except, as in this instance, when armed with words arranged according to a certain method. And exclusively through such words does he enter the category of the great poets, even though the conditions of his life do not establish him as a hero like 'Antara, a sycophant like an-Nabigha and to a lesser extent Tarafa, a tribal spokesman like al-Harith and 'Amru, a suitably placed moralist like Zuhair and Labid, a kingship claimant like Imru' l-Qays, or even a polyglot lover like al-A'sha. Nothing at all establishes him other than his desire to attain for himself justice through speech, even though the speech does not speak to the instance presumably instigating it. He has no prehistory to introduce his credentials, thus, other than that help from outside of himself, from outside of all society, from beyond all nature, arriving while all are asleep, withdrawing before they wake, leaving no witnesses behind—unlike in the case of prophetic constitution, when a prophet is left behind as the witness and social medium of this exogenous power. In this case, all that was left behind was a poetic discourse, which was to become known as 'Ubayd's ode, rather than as the speech of the gods. That elusive pre-Islamic Allah, who commanded little definition or regard, could on occasions interject himself briefly in order to rectify or solidify a poorly supported person or sentence, quickly dissipating thereafter, with only fragments of a record of such an interjection left behind.

'Ubayd's supreme austerity was not a unique and unrepeatable story, however, but rather a memorable archetype still in circulation by Muhammad's time. The prevailing image of perishing as the norm of nature, lurking just around the corner, contrasted sharply with the long-term contractual postures occasioning the emergence of a relatively wealthy trading community in Mecca. This wealth, as outlined before, could not dispel the specter of vulnerability to fate, especially as there was neither the ideology nor the instrumentality to account for it or to maintain it into perpetuity. The Qur'an itself began this story by unambiguously registering this adjoining coexistence in both geography and consciousness of fortune and deprivation.[18]

GOD'S CONTRACTS

Thus, in light of a system of faith motivated by an awareness that the world presented acute dangers to the city's livelihood, it was indeed an ironic twist that it was ultimately possible to bring Mecca into Islam precisely by accentuating such conditions of terror upon the city by the migrating Muslim community. Contrary to expectations implicit in the Qur'anic observation just noted, it was not a Mecca fearful of its disorderly environs that willingly followed Muhammad but, rather, that chaotic outside itself—more specifically, Medina, home to perennially warring semisedentary communities—that exhibited the most voluntary willingness to follow an instrumental (rather than simply spiritual) prophetic leadership. The ramifications of this transition included the evolution of increasingly instrumental and detailed regulations for the idea of social justice and social exchange, virtually all of which developed in Medina. This development proceeded in a piecemeal and experimental fashion and was largely based on economies of exchange and production that the faithful were familiar with. The gradual cosmology that was ostensibly the background of this legalistic formulation dictated that even economies that Muslims were less familiar with by then—for example, agriculture[19]—could still be divinely regulated by being seen, at the level of their essences, as parts of a general human effort to sustain and reproduce life.[20] In general, however, the idea of exchange itself was seen as the model of the relationship between the faithful and Allah, a relationship whose nature flowed specifically from the metaphors of commercial activities and contractual obligations: "God has *purchased* from the faithful their lives and worldly goods and *in return* has promised them the Garden. They will fight for the cause of God, slay and be slain. Such is the true promise which He has made them in the Torah, the Gospel and the Koran. And who is more true to his pledge than God? Rejoice then in the *bargain* you have made."[21]

On other occasions, details of such a (transhistorical) bargain were clarified; the bargain itself was available only to those who did not allow their economy to obscure their relation to Allah *and,* more innovatively, their obligation toward other members of the *umma.*[22] To give alms was the central new point, and Allah's command to do so was articulated in a novel way that went beyond the simple promise of heavenly reward: Alms were not being given to the poor but in effect to Allah himself, who had to assume the role of an authoritative tax collector until an Islamic state that could assume such a responsibility could come into existence.[23] This lack of instrumentality is further evidenced by the fact that the redistribution of wealth within the community through alms was not introduced as a "tax" at all but, rather, as a "loan" to God, who guaranteed repayment of the principle along with a hefty interest: "Who will grant God a generous loan? He will repay him many times over. It is God who enriches and makes poor. To Him you shall return. . . . Believers, bestow in alms a part of what We have given you before a day arrives when commerce and friendship and intercession shall be no more."[24]

The practice of setting aside a sum of wealth for charitable purposes had its roots in pre-Islamic practices and traditions.[25] The old *rifadah* tax in Mecca, which the city's inhabitants paid in order to provide pilgrims with sustenance, was inseparable from the city's self-propagated image of open sanctity toward various tribal communities. But otherwise, the practice of giving condensed in the concept of *sadaqah* (charity) was largely confined within a tribe. With the advent of the *Muhajirun* and the war economy, as outlined before, new groups of legitimate recipients of the spoils were added, groups that no longer coincided with the older social structures of charity.[26] The introduction of alms, in this context, was clearly meant to enforce charity as a religious obligation rather than leaving it to individual decision, as in the case of the *sadaqah,* or restricting it to specific times and ends, as in the case of the *rifadah.* Alms (*zakah*) were meant to transcend temporality and immediacy and act as a continuous link of attention between the transtribal faithful.

The way alms were introduced testified to the incomplete consolidation of and control over the *umma.* Allah solemnly decreed the manner in which believers were to divide the spoils of war; in contrast, he pleaded with them to give alms to Allah, promising them in every such instance a generous repayment—which in its spirit went against the Qur'anic frowning upon speculative wealth enhancement through usury. The recognition that alms created a debt owed by God to the faithful flowed from the commercial mentality that had shaped the socioeconomic horizons of Islam and that had already been experimented with in the symbiosis between commercial and charitable exchange introduced early on in Medina in the "market of the prophet."[27]

The issue of alms, generally revealed in the context of the war economy and the distribution of its spoils, was of crucial importance with regards to the idea of social justice within the community of the faithful, especially in a community that was to be typified by cross-class and cross-tribal solidarity. Thus, the Qur'an became increasingly more assertive in furthering the issue. That assertiveness gradually evolved out of both the increased instrumental and legal authority of Islamic leadership and the continued reluctance of many of the rich faithful to pay when the demand was couched in terms of seemingly voluntary loaning. There are passages, for instance, in which those who withhold alms are threatened with being replaced by others as recipients of divine bounty and mercy.[28] Resistance to this taxation is well noted in the Qur'an, up to and including mockery by those who found the idea of giving Allah a "generous loan" to be quite humorous: "God has heard the words of those who said: 'God is poor, but we are rich.' Their words We will record, and their slaying of the prophets unjustly. We shall say: 'Taste now the torment of flagration.'"[29]

Despite the extent of the insult to divinity, Allah does not, in that early

Medinian passage, decree eternal punishment *exclusively* on the basis of the blasphemous statement. Instead, he assigns to them another imaginary evil act (unjustly slaying their prophets). At that point, the refusal to pay alms, though not being regarded as infidelity, was made punishable by being seen in the context and with the appendage of the grave and unanchored but transhistorically recurrent sin of murdering God's messengers. In the late *surah* of at-Tauba, thought to be one of the last *surahs* of the Qur'an, when the Islamic *umma* had become a more abstract and widespread phenomenon, involving various societies and tribes and permeating the major cities and towns, withholding alms became *by itself* a reason for eternal punishment, from which even the intercession of the prophet himself could not save the sinner.[30]

These discursive events concerning the question of almsgiving involve more than mere differences in time and space. The variety of discourses regarding almsgiving indicate the immense importance of the issue. The gradual emergence of the transclass and transtribal *umma* made a certain form of wealth redistribution an irreplaceable mechanism for ensuring the cohesive solidarity of diverse social strata, especially because Islam became in an important sense a placeholder for this grand peace, among other things. Thus, in the final version of early, textual Islam, almsgiving grew to be one of the "five pillars" of the faith, especially as the claim that Islam was intended as the religion of the "mother of towns" was relinquished in practice, when that town itself had to be overcome by a force consisting of many more *Ansar,* nomads, and seminomads than authentic Meccan *Muhajirun,* who had become a small minority of the *umma* by then.

WAR AND THE CODE OF JUSTICE

The notion of social justice is prevalent in some of the main themes of pre-Islamic odes, being propounded mainly not by the outcast or heroic poets but, rather, by those who had recognizable social standing. In such cases, there are indications of growing social complexity, particularly when dispensing justice ceases to refer, appeal, or adhere to rules of straightforward nomadic egalitarianism (for example, Labid, c. 79; 85–86). In Labid's ode, the notion of "right" is abundantly general, and the main concern seems to be the mechanism of pronouncing justice rather than its content. The worry was about the methods of ruling, legalizing, super-structuring, and promulgating already existing morals in a society that had become more conflictual and complex. Such orientations sought not to change common ethics but to encase them by binding statute.

The interest, thus, was with the distinct *appearance* of ethical discourse rather than with its substance. The appearance of ethical discourse, in turn, became possible only when some discursive form, like poetry, had become endowed with power. In this case, the "legal superstructure" was formed not through institutions or similar describable objectivities but primarily through language and speech. Ultimately, however, it was the source of that speech that became the institution of dispensing justice. Toward the end of Labid's ode, while parties to a conflict are being advised to be content with the judgment of the arbitrator (c. 85), the poetics sud-denly discover that the poet and the arbitrator are by definition the same. The poet had belonged, had severed his ties to earlier moments of love for the sake of a tribe's communal sensibilities. He composed thereupon a code and, with that armory, he returned, fulfilling the new set of responsi-bilities to the letter. A monumental edifice of trustworthiness became the basis for institutionalizing common notions of justice.

Zuhair was the other great moralist of those ancient times, times of wandering and witnessing, with an increasingly blurred vision, the creep-ing confoundment between moments of self and society, freedom and duty, belonging and estrangement, war and peace, sobriety and hedo-nism, nomadism and sedentarism, movement and halting. Such elements were to intermingle, to be sure, in ways much more complicated than simple binary oppositions. What is interesting about Zuhair's ode is that it seems to occur at a middle point, so to speak, of this tradition, to pay homage to and witness all those transformations of social elements. The introductory moment of his *mu'allaqa* copiously reproduces the tradi-tion. The images of ruins, caravan movement, and extensive naming in situations of halting and movement—which populate the first fifteen couplets—had all been visited by the other great poets, particularly Tarafa. Yet unlike Tarafa, Zuhair afterward averts the route toward hedo-nism, when he establishes his true distinction: There is this responsibility confronting him, which is to help pacify a warring society. The two tribes of 'Abs and Dhubyan had been at war for forty years. Peace seemed to be finally at hand—when the ode was composed—mainly because of the generosity of two resourceful chiefs, who gave out of their own wealth to settle all remaining claims to *diyyah*.

After the long tribute to the tradition, Zuhair begins to record the peace. The two arbitrators are praised for patching up a breach in nature, when a state of concord within a purportedly single, albeit overarching, tribal community was shattered. A war broke out that, despite its legendary duration, continues to be recognized as an anomaly. Those who bring it to an end are praised for restoring a natural order. They have not developed new methods but, rather, have "restored," revived, and made workable again old and forgotten rules for the resolution of conflicts. The end of a tribal war means more than that there would be no more bloodshed: The freely wandering nomad would be restored to a natural order, defined by the freedom from the restriction upon movement and expansive associations, restrictions borne out by the fact of war, of having to take sides, of having to walk cautiously upon the land, of having to stand by a too broadly defined kinfolk beyond the periodicity of economic necessity. The order that is restored is that transcendental freedom from a burdensome and demanding frame of belonging that the war situation had so valorized. *The order that is being restored is that under which the social being is less definable by sociability than by being.* The promise of this fluid "order" is thus a return to conditions of unconfined wandering.

But in this case, when tribal wars gradually became unforgettable legends—in a way that the Qur'an did not fail to take note of, as it showed concern for the durability of the brittle peace of Mecca—the advent of peace introduced new and memorable dimensions into the traditional process of the restoration of justice. In Zuhair's rendition of the story, peace became possible because of the emergence of a new form of *active* leadership, replacing the passive arbitrator of times past. Because of the irreplaceability of their function, the two chiefs in question became *models* for a possibly novel method of attaining justice. The description of the restorationist effort entailed describing the restorers as well as the way they had accomplished the celebrated effect.

In the ode, those models signify a single-handed accomplishment by outsiders to the conflict. The memory of the war's enormous bloodshed and great length is wiped out by "ample giving and fair speaking" (c. 20). Though the abundance of the ample giving could be duly described (c. 22–25), "fair speaking," a less calculable but no less essential precondition for justice, induces a more complicated assessment. "Fair speaking" (*ma'rufen mina l-qawl*) is opposed in this case to hidden, inarticulable desire. Couplet 27 speaks of "whatever is in your breasts," that is, of surreptitious vindictives. According to at-Tibrizi, what was "hidden" was the proud claim by Dhubyan that they were not necessarily thirsting for peace and that they could go on with the war. The poet, however, is not any more explicit about what he means (for example, couplet 27 could also mean that he is suspicious of their agreement to peace). The nomadic context of this transmutation between war and peace is that of a lack of an instrumental central authority capable of guaranteeing either the conditions of peace or the pronouncements to that effect. In this particular case, an incident was to contribute to the great doubt about the efficacy of the whole discourse of peace: Husayn Ibn Damdam, a Dhubyanist whose father was killed in the war, almost single-handedly destroyed the entire peace project by turning his vindictiveness on an unsuspecting 'Abside. The two arbitrators intervened again at this crucial juncture, compensating for the crime with their own camels. Thus, though the lack of a normalizing instrumentality was being deliberated, this incident functioned as an empirical confirmation of such a lack.

Thus the vulnerability of "fair speaking" and of speaking of intentions in general; whence comes God—who rarely occurs in the *mu'allaqat*—as a guarantor. He guarantees by virtue of his "knowledge" of the unspoken intentions. The succeeding couplet (c. 28) is surprisingly "Islamic" in character ("Day of Reckoning"), seemingly attempting to further instrumentalize this God who, in any case, is abruptly aborted thereafter.[31] Allah is here merely an experiment in a large parade of possibilities that Zuhair sets to march in the quest after guarantees of peace and pronounced intentions. Thus, it is interesting that in the very next couplet, he announces his intention to tell the audience of another mighty externality, which (unlike Allah?) "*ma huwa bil-hadithi l-murajjami* [is not a tale told at random, a vague conjecture]": It is to be the concrete evidence of the horror of war itself.

The only external guarantee of peace turns out to be a continual attendance to the imagery of warfare. The phenomenon of war thus brings forth an intricate set of morals lodged in specifically preserved memories of carnage, thereby producing knowledge that could be expected to guarantee peace by itself. The ultimate guarantee, thus, is founded upon a permanent knowledge of an extensive experience with a phenomenon *that is about to pass away.* Such a project leads to some of the most eloquently composed lines in the ode (c. 29–33). Images of war stumble over each other (a flame, a grindstone, a mother pregnant with ill-omens, a field yielding a poisoned harvest). War is expected to be a producer. But such an expectation, which had traditionally accompanied the *ghazw* practice, is shown in light of the legendary pre-Islamic wars to be increasingly unable to function as such. Thus the metaphors of war in Zuhair's ode render a particular and vivid kind of knowledge. As the field disclaims the harvest, all producers in nature are summoned to pronounce their disdain for their productions.

Thus, in its quest after the guarantor of peace, the poetic discourse here only finds itself. By Zuhair's time, the poet had already become a significant locus of authority (many believed that poets produced their speech with the aid of the jinn). Unlike an outcast like 'Ubayd, the socially anchored poet here directs his speech to specific, namable, or describable audiences (for example, c. 26 and 34). Here, poetics serve to define the audience that is to hear the message. In other words, what is being defined is the type of audience deemed appropriate for the task of interpreting the lines. In some sense, this formula possesses a structure of delimitation similar to the primary act of standing at the ruins: One "begins" by carving out from the vast expanse a certain space (a certain geography in the case of the ruins, a certain *social* space here), defining it by features, names, references, boundaries, history. One begins by setting the limits of the receiver, which in this case is a diseased, torn society. In contrast to Tarafa's helplessly defensive discourse—which critiques the customary societal obligations that ultimately led to his ostracism—one hears in Zuhair's a credible voice of authority, stemming from a socially concerned, socially relevant poet, from within the walls of a supposed tradition of harmony and justice. This is an affirmative speech by a speaker confident of a listening crowd. Unlike the earlier poets—that primordial Imru' l-Qays, who, because there was no one to listen to him, went to the ruins and delivered to them his story—this one is capable not only of speaking from within but of remodeling the fabric of his social abode from within as well. By delivering a discourse that commences by defining the audience, this authorial voice can reasonably hope to make such a transitory *audience* into a continually present *society.*

The general characteristics of Zuhair's audience/society are remarkably simple. They are mighty, proud, secure, and naturally mobile; they do little else: They pasture their flock, quench their thirst, renew their energies, and go on (c. 36). As an outcome of their movement, they become involved in a feud. They have no explicit intention to go to war, neither is there any indication that they had a foreknowledge of the outcome of their habitual migrations, and thus they could not be blamed. It is not clear, nor apparently is it all that important to ascertain, whether they prevail or simply survive stalemates and continue wandering beyond them:

> They pastured their flock awhile, thirsting, then brought them down
> to pools gushing with weapons and gouts of blood;
> there they fulfilled dire doom together; then they led back
> their beasts to a pasture noisome and unstomachable. (c. 36–37)

Who is their enemy? An unimportant detail.[32] They clash with some other force, some obstacle along the road, some hindrance in nature, but they survive with a strength sufficient to carry them to another troublesome destiny; of this one, again, they may have no foreknowledge. Yet they have no need to worry, for they had already been introduced as being indestructible, undefeatable, safe from all danger, and, above all, they are always marching along or residing together (*hillon halal*). Such is Zuhair's audience. It is the body so constituted that is now to be advised on how to refrain from involvement in future wars.

As transtribal peace is reconstituted, war must be made to lose its heroic appeal, its moralism of duty, its claim to normative necessity, its positivity. The whole sequence finds its conclusion in couplets 44 to 46, where the ultimate outcome of the vicious cycle of war is seen to consist of an overstatement of purpose, thus of unfulfillable and unacceptably high claims by the warring factions. These three couplets, congested with specific references, are clearly meant for the ears of a specific historic audience. The names here are of tribal members who were killed long before the war but who were later added by each tribe to the list of those whose deaths the war was to avenge—and, by extension, the peace agreement was to honor by adequate compensation. Their inclusion illustrates the war's ultimate illogic. The modes of thinking produced by this war, therefore, include an inadmissible extension into spheres incongruous with it. The discourse of peace begins by disarming war of all that is not a part of its clearly discernible history. And with this proclamation (c. 46), images of war dissipate, giving way to an extended but relatively simple code of wisdom and ethics.

As opposed to customary nomadic raids, war thus required the introduction of novel, or the reinvocation of "forgotten," values to extinguish its fire. In this regard, the ideological background of the war of the Muslims with Mecca led to profoundly nontraditional attitudes with regards to its settlement, elements of which appeared in the Peace of Hudaybiyyah. In that case, the agreement was not based on a traditional code of ethics but, rather, was couched in procedural/contractual language that specified the obligations of the signatories without reference to universal moral background, as was imperative in Zuhair's code.[33] For the Muslims, the war was an element of a new economy of acquisition sanctioned by God and *not* by the antecedent nomadic tradition of *ghazw*. The novelty of the legitimating background of acquisition in itself called for novel methods of rationalizing its distribution, lest the *umma* fall pray to the whims of an emergent warrior caste. According to *sira* accounts (traditional biographies of the prophet), the earliest revelations concerning the division of the spoils of war were prompted by sharp disagreements among the victorious warriors in Badr regarding the matter, whereafter the Qur'an swiftly assigned the responsibility for the spoils to the prophet, who divided it up equally among the participants in the battle.[34] Upon arrival in the city, a more elaborate distribution scheme was introduced, taking a fifth of the spoils from the warriors and giving it to "God." God in this case represented both a general idea of social good as well as specific social categories, such as the family of the prophet, orphans, paupers, and wayfarers.[35]

FATE AND THE LEGITIMACY OF ACQUISITION

This "taxation" of the proceeds of war preceded the institution of almsgiving and was clearly intended to enhance social welfare within the *umma*. What is of interest here are the specific categories of recipients (beyond God and his messenger's family), which coincided with the forms of dispossession experienced among the believers. Orphans and paupers, whose very existence was evidence of injustice in the world, had already been addressed with compassion in the early Meccan Qur'an,[36] and the wayfarer had come to mirror and stand for the migratory experience of the *Muhajirun*.

This redistribution did not, however, entail a nostalgia toward no-madic egalitarianism. Rather, it affirmed that nonspeculative labor legitimated exceptional individual wealth. Thus, even after war proceeds were taxed, Muslim warriors could still monopolize fully four-fifths of the spoils, since in some way they were seen as deserving to enjoy the fruits of their physical labor. This understanding of fighting as remunerable labor is clearly evident in the case of Fadak, a small Jewish settlement that had agreed to peaceably give the Muslims half of its wealth, a proportion equivalent to that forcibly acquired from neighboring Khaibar. Muhammad used the fact that no army was sent to Fadak to decree that the acquisition from the town was not to be divided up among the warriors, but that he himself would have sole authority over its distribution. That manner of distributing wealth acquired without the "labor" of war was inscribed into an explicit Qur'anic instruction, which viewed such an acquisition as the property of God, his messenger, and the disinherited in the *umma*, explicitly rejecting any claim upon it by the warriors.[37]

The connection between rightful possession and "actual" labor could be discerned only within the paradigm of a trading community, where wealth could accrue through speculation and loaning as well. And it is within that paradigm that the Islamic approach to usury in the cities emerged, seeing in it an illegitimate exemption from the natural law of reward for labor. The more pressing concern in this case was the fact that in Medina it was the faithful, especially many of the *Ansar*, who were indebted to Jewish and pagan as well as Muslim lenders. Though the presence of usurers had been tolerated earlier because they fulfilled urgent needs during times of distress, the new war economy diminished their importance. A new theology with a promised paradise, furthermore, valorized enduring the hardships of life in a different way than did 'Ubayd's or Tarafa's passive wait for death, and subsequently distanced to an extent the lure of temporal alleviation, such as in taking on usury-laden loans. In that context, usury could be seen as the most scandalous example of "unnatural" methods of enrichment, namely, as accumulation without labor. The Qur'an first abhorred the act of "doubling your wealth many times over"[38] through usury and then moved on to ban the practice through unusually threatening edicts, emphasizing the divine distinction between usury and other sanctioned forms of exchange such as trade and charity.[39]

In contrast to the Islamic use of the war to fortify the boundaries of the *umma* against the outside and develop a distinct, institutionally guarded ethic of obligations within it, the context of war and its claims under the *Jahiliyyah* (pre-Islamic era) invited broader codes of morals, which were seen to be part of the nature of universal human interaction rather than results of any specific theodicy. Some of those were rendered poetically, as mentioned before in the case of Zuhair. Indeed, the treasure of ancient wisdom in Zuhair's ode (c. 47–59) begins with the realization that a war is grudgingly withdrawing its monstrous self from the scene, a fact calling for acquiescence to the message of reconciliation, an attitude endorsed in the ode's promise of praise (or at least nonvilification) for those who open their hearts to the possibility. From that point on, moralisms follow each other with breathtaking speed: the certitude of mortality, the virtue of inner tribal generosity, the importance of individual pride, the disorienting impact of individual migration on the capacity to properly judge enemies from friends, the virtue of self-respect, the necessity of self-reliance in defending one's own possessions, a conceptualization of offensive posture as a guarantee against being wronged, versatility as a necessity for survival, benevolence as a shield for the good name, unknowability of the future, and so on.

Now if we halt to look at this dizzying sequence, we can readily detect *the ideal citizen* in the addressee of this fragmentary wisdom. What we have in this sequence is a manual for proper civic behavior, a code for manners. It contains Zuhair's own point of view, needless to say. But the voice speaking here is that of an effective pedagogic authority. After all, once an audience for moral vision has been created, the poet does not find it possible to close the door and go on reflecting with his own soul. Zuhair, one of the great poets to function "within" society, could discern in the cloud of prestige following his presence an enormous task and a request for witnessing the conditions of the times, much as in the case of the more socially anchored Muhammad in Medina.

Thus, Zuhair finds it appropriate to codify a general morality in what such an audience deems a high form of discourse. Yet unlike Qur'anic instructions, which are confronted and shaped by adventures, maneuvers, and diverse constituencies, Zuhair's codification is simply structured and flows effortlessly, for it requires no logical chains and justifications for transitions across topics. And as such, each of its portions can be taken by itself and re-presented by any common person as a common wisdom. To a certain extent, Zuhair's perspicacity shares with at least some Qur'anic codes an archetypal form of law pronouncement, in which each sentence possesses a proverbial generality, a rhythmic harmony, and the possibility of easy confluence with popular wisdom. The simplicity and immediacy of Zuhair's code of manners readily delivers it not only as the outcome of a rich life experience but, even more so, as a series of dictums to be used in any selection deemed appropriate by the protagonist, but always with respect to the empowering *form* of the legal statement. The poetic form here repackages and reorganizes the discourse of everyday life in such a way as to be able to simultaneously stand above it.[40]

We know that Zuhair is producing this general wisdom after a long war. More precisely, he is speaking at its final moments, when peace is yet to be restored as the norm, when bloodletting is still fresh in people's memories, when the air is still poisoned by animosities that only time could heal. So Zuhair becomes, like the messenger of God, a witness (c. 57: "I have seen the Fates"). He first takes note of general human conditions and proclivities, where normal human action regularly leads to warfare, which could in turn be untangled by the reinvocation of traditional authorities and forms of resolution. But *witnessing* the creeping weakness of such methods, Zuhair begins a search for a guaranteeing instrumentality. This he finds in his own metaphors, which reassemble a memorable portrayal of the evil of war, tracing its course all the way to its final degeneration into a profound anomaly of illogic and irrationality.

Pessimism and uncertainty abound in the cleavages of this world outlook. Such moments, however, are as essential for the reception of this code as are continuous Qur'anic reminders of the negligibility of human impact in the face of Allah's power. By being reminded of its natural deficiencies, the audience realizes its need for further guidance. Zuhair's code thus begins (c. 49) by belittling the individual in the face of fate: Mortality is certain. After being reconfirmed, this old discovery is reintegrated into and properly placed within this experiment of general ethics. The individual being advised from this angle is one who is continually threatened not by an abstract world but by social life itself. One must structure one's behavior so as to avoid being excluded, reviled, abused, disrespected, dispossessed, trampled upon, or thoroughly obliterated. There is nothing of concrete value to *add* to this certainly perishable life, only things to *avoid.* Human action is therefore always motivated by a fear of loss, not a desire for improvement. Such a threat, in turn, could be circumvented by adhering to the provided code. Thence, a purposeful, instrumental morality is introduced that, for the time being, could regulate behavioral responses within an existential void of positive purpose, a void waiting to be reapportioned and refilled at a later stage by Muhammad's abstract God.

Zuhair's Allah, as we have seen, was quickly purged from the ode, after only a short appearance in two belated couplets (of debatable origin). Instead of an abstract God capable of intervention in this world, the source of instrumental action was located in what seemed to be a more solid foundation: The individual could be guaranteed to respect the code of manners out of an innate interest in avoiding dying from forces as destructive, but more manageable, than time. What the code promised, therefore, was for the individual to languish until claimed by the irreversible progression of the *dahr* (time as a total, self-enclosed natural phenomenon). Thus, that vision of human capabilities, potentials, and modes of fulfillment edified a loosely nomadic but essentially nonadditive posture. That posture seemed to suffice for a world weary of war and aggrandized claims and yearning for the restoration of the habitual cycle of periodic human destruction by fate alone. And as such, it sufficed until the predicament of migration, dispossession, and sedentary wars restructured and instrumentalized a different kind of code, which was distinguished by the positivity it assigned to the category of labor, over and above the passive wait for reclamation by fate.

nine

In Lieu of a Conclusion:
The Origins, the System, and the Accident

*An Arab state, framed according to Arab ideals, tailored to the new condi-
tions and yet sufficiently close to the Bedouin life that it had to incorporate, and able to take its place on an equal footing with the great empires—this was the great need of the times. The way was open for the man
of genius who could respond to it better than any other. That man was
about to be born.*

—*Rodinson, 37*

Successive events, understood in terms of continually changing micro-
contexts, may show the grand historical narrative that they collectively
construct to be simply the product of a series of accidents, whose ultimate
outcome could not have been predicted from the outset. This does not
necessarily entail the complete absence of "structure"; rather, it highlights
the ex post facto organization of a grand narrative into meaning. This
posterior meaning would then, once apprehended according to a common enough conceptual formula, make the grand phenomenon appear
natural and even necessary. Thus, though everything is perfectly accounted
for in the epigraph to this chapter, what remains as an unexplored mys-
tery is the question of whose "need" it was that the emergence of a state
fulfilled. It could be that an "Arab state," rather than being the "great need
of the times," was in effect the unintended result of many developments
based on pronouncements of less-profound needs. The emergence of a
state out of this story can be understood in terms of structural imperatives

coalescing out of unpredictable and unforeseen actions and counteractions rather than in terms of preexistent needs.[1]

The debate on whether a state was at the intentional roots of Islam is quite old.[2] The point here is not that the question of state is itself intrinsically interesting but, rather, that the concept of state offers one organizing device by which the sum total of countless affairs and accidents can be gathered in an ordered fashion. For example, Marxist authors like Husayn Muruwah, Sulayman Bashir, and E. A. Belyaev introduce, rather too confidently, the claim concerning a link between the coming into being of a centralized authority and the displacement of polytheism by monotheism. But even if one detects in the shift toward monotheism a desire for cosmically referenced social totality, one cannot be certain that that desire alone would furnish the basis for and be necessarily meditated in terms of a central state.

Other organizing devices are used by other practitioners in the field. For instance, Ibrahim argues that Islam caused a social reorganization that was ultimately advantageous to the merchants.[3] Though this may be true, the story of Islam cannot be reduced to a straightforward tale of class conflict, although to a certain extent that was a factor; nor can it be assumed that such an outcome was planned or intended from the point of view of the "origins." Overall, one sees a widespread effort to deduce a general and socially or ideologically structured meaning of this historical tale, an effort seen obviously in traditionalist schools of thought but also seen in the heritage of orientalism and in the anthrosociologism of William Watt and Ernest Gellner.[4] Throughout such works, the interest is in the religion's "persistent major themes," in its stillness, homogeneity, and continuity. To do otherwise would open one to the charge of seeming to suggest that all that has been recorded was a set of scattered responses to contingencies carried across unpredictable contours, or are fragments of no solid genealogical base. If such is the claim, then how, if at all, can one account for the apparent coherence of the text, or for its apparent ability to systematize the reflections and reference points of those who believe in it?

The urge to systematize is ubiquitous in historical research. A Marxist like Belyaev, for instance, shares many of the tropes of the grand categorical thinking one would usually associate with orientalism, finding little problem in employing descriptive terms such as "underdeveloped religion" and "distorted mixture."[5] But for the believers, and this is the heart of the matter for the historical sociology of consciousness, the body of knowledge in which they believed was logically integrated and developed in comparison to what preceded it (that is, the earlier system of knowledge that it had to dislodge) and to what existed synchronically outside it. An exotic term like "distorted mixture," apparently employed to imply an unacceptable level of logical heterogeneity, is grounded on the thesis that some pre-Islamic and "Judaeo-Christian" themes had survived throughout the Qur'an. What is not deemed significant is the early believers' own awareness of such a "foreign" penetration, let alone their own way of signifying it.

In sociological terms, a *system* is to be found outside of the text proper, since a text is supposed to *express* a system existing in some sociohistorical condition. For instance, the Islamic state was a system not simply because it was "objectively" a system but because its meaning and self-definition were referenced to the text. It cited the Qur'an and Hadith (sayings attributed to Muhammad) in any way it found fit for the purpose of administering territories, distributing wealth, legitimating various ways of governance, and judging on, or laying aside, newly encountered areas of legality. Though ironic, the eventual ascension over the Islamic state machinery by the Umayyads, once Muhammad's most resolute opponents in Mecca, was possible precisely because the Umayyads also could become an integral part of the new system.[6]

The text, however, came into being not in order to systematize the superstructure of the Islamic state but to systematize a less-institutional arrangement of the social life to which the prophet was told he was a "witness" (*shahed*). Thus, in contrast to its elaborate rules on the problems it recognized as such in its immediate historical surroundings, the Qur'an never spelled out any direct proposals on how a state was to be governed, and so these rules had to be extrapolated from various prophetic and Qur'anic judgments. This lack is evident in the succession of the first four caliphs: After each one passed away, a different method was used for selecting a successor. (Each of those methods, however, emphasized the assent [*bay'ah*] of the community of believers.) It was only after the fourth caliph, 'Ali, during whose reign it was becoming obvious that the Muslim *umma*, demographically magnified, territorially expansive, and ideologically factionalized, was not likely to assent in its entirety to any single subsequent ruler that a forcible takeover of the state machinery was undertaken by the Umayyads, whereafter a hereditary rule of succession was invoked.

Could the Islamic state have displayed different patterns had the Qur'an discoursed openly about it? Any answer must remain hypothetical. What we have at hand is a context of original composition of a holy book in which neither a state nor any of the structural foundations of an empire were thought of as being necessary consequences of an Islamic system. Such matters, therefore, were not part of divine revelations. If anything, there is a great deal of evidence to suggest that Islam was deeply embedded not only in predating ideologies such as Hanifism or the book religions but also in antecedent rules of social hierarchies and structure—even as it ultimately went beyond them in the constitution of Medina and its aftermath. But even then, one could detect the persistence of many of the old rules of social hierarchy. For instance, Ibrahim observes correctly that the transtribal fraternization of *Muhajirun* and *Ansar* in Medina maintained class positions, with individuals from the two camps fraternizing with those of comparable socioeconomic standing in the other.[7] Others stress that in spite of massive opposition, the nobility ultimately came to identify its new role with political governance in a way that Muhammad himself had to acquiesce to toward the end of his career. According to this view, the first two caliphs, Abi Bakr and 'Umar, were exceptions who failed to abrogate a normative connection to governorship that the nobility claimed for itself and that, in spite of massive opposition, was ultimately put into practice with the third caliph 'Uthman.[8]

Of course, it should be remembered that Muhammad's early insistence on emphasizing the conversion of the nobility was itself condemned in the Qur'an in the *surah* of 'Abasa. But the issue then was the contestation by the nobility of Muhammad's right to be a prophet, himself being of a relatively humble background. It was only a matter of time before the nobility could see not only the danger posed by Muhammad's power to mobilize outsiders and less-fortunate groups but also Muhammad's continued willingness to allocate a political space for class differentiation. The most remarkable episode in that regard must be the Peace of Hudaybiyyah discussed earlier, in which, by and large, the interests of poor Muslims were—at least temporarily—sacrificed in exchange for allowing more prominent Meccan factions to ally themselves freely with Muhammad when bonds within Mecca were weakening.[9] Nagel argues that Hudaybiyyah marked the beginning of incorporation of Meccan nobility into prominence within Islamic political structures in a way that antagonized those who had been their main opponents up to that point, namely, the disenfranchised *Muhajirun*. He sees the election of 'Uthman, who was both a noble Meccan and one of the *Muhajirun,* as a sign of compromise between the two social forces.[10]

Thus it would seem that believers who joined on strictly ideological grounds were continually supplemented by those who were persuaded on the basis of their own social values or because of calculations having to do with their position within the social hierarchy. Aside from eventually confirming the status of the nobility, Muhammad also found himself, as we saw previously, using a strictly city-centered appeal in Mecca at large or, when venturing to Islamicize the nomads, arguing in terms of tribal discourse of alliance, genealogy, and obligation. The peaceful Islamicization of Asad, for example, is explained in the sources in terms of a clear tribal paradigm, which emphasized the tribe's genealogical affinity with the prophet and which wedded allegiance to faith to a practical deal, allowing the tribe to water its herd outside of its territories in years of draught and to assume local control over the dispensation of the *sadaqah* (charity).[11]

Such embeddedness in and appeal to various forms of social values and ideas, while progressively expanding the range of social groups deemed fit for Islamicization and to which Islam proved to be a fruitful ideological investment, also opened the door for political opportunism from within the house of the *umma.* The *ridda* (renegade) wars immediately following Muhammad's death indicate that even when it seemed socially integrative and all-encompassing, Islam, much like pre-Islamic, vaguely Meccan-centered Arabian spiritual orders, was far from commanding a universally deep following. Rather, it was often understood, particularly among the nomads, as a revocable oath of allegiance possessing a status comparable to a loose, voluntary transtribal alliance. The Islamic use of tribal bonds and language itself testifies to its experimental nature, all the way down to the aftermath of the unification of Arabia. It was only the Islamic conquests (*futuhat*) outside of the peninsula that resolved the structural impediments to the full consolidation of Islam— whence the religion's life as an irrevocable, standard, and complete text began in earnest.

The remarkable survival of references to and associations with momentary or parochial logics into transhistorical tropes suggests that texts, rather than simply referencing sociological systems, actually create systems of their own, to which subsequent events are referenced in ways that cannot be predicted. For instance, the unusual consistency throughout the Qur'an on the question of God's transcendental monotheism can be seen as a direct result of its moment of introduction, when it had to legitimate itself against an ontotheological landscape dominated by a multiplicity of "harmless and helpless" idols. The attributes of Allah then were determined not merely on the basis of their social function but also on the basis of the multitude of functions that the then-prevailing, yet weak, ontotheology was seen as failing to fulfill.[12] Many centuries later, when paganism was no longer a threat, it did not go unnoticed that the recorded attributes of Allah—since the text speaking of them was irreplaceable—needed to be accounted for by extraneous efforts, namely, by reoriented and elaborate philosophical reformulations.[13]

A similar logic can be applied to the legal system. As we have seen, the evolving text was not proposing an abstract constitutional framework against which subsequent concrete and multifaceted scenarios could be judged; rather, it was commenting on real, experienced, isolated cases as they were encountered. That is why the highly elaborate Islamic jurisprudence, with its four major schools, had to await the coming into being of a vast empire, uniting various ethnicities for the first time, and requiring, as one element of its standardized centralism, a more coherent set of judicial standards. Each of the four major schools followed the changing realities, and though they amplified new methods of exegesis and reframed the boundaries of legitimate human reason and inference, they continued to accept the final referential status of the original text, to which further traditions of commentary were appended.

The context of the text's moment of introduction also determined its urban-commercial-contractual air. We have seen that agrarian life was barely mentioned and that Bedouin life was looked on less often as a sphere of existence demanding ontological justification and regulatory divine rules than as a foreign or only tenuously loyal form of living and behavior. We have seen, for instance, how the nomads were not regarded as true believers until they migrated to *Dar al-Muhajirun* (Medina), where they could be put under control. Otherwise, they were merely looked upon as, at best, temporary allies, even when they professed a belief in

Islam. To see how this state of affairs, born of practical strategic concerns in Arabia, then became the basis for one model for the political organization of the faithful, one only needs to examine another example, when the Muslims became a minority in Spain many centuries later in a completely different context. In Spain, they were frequently called upon to migrate to Grenada, where Muslims retained control, precisely on the basis of Muhammad's model of *hijra* (migration) and his seemingly comparable appeal to the faithful who lived away from the domain of territorial control of an Islamic political organization.[14]

What order of coherence, then, does the stage of origins speak of? Even if the foundational text of Islam was grounded in the failure of pre-Islamic culture, its visionary, futuristic outlook was not disconnected from that culture either. The cosmological vision of Allah was a direct judgment on the failure of the idols in what shortly after the time of Muhammad would seem like a modest task: to safeguard Mecca's precarious role in the world, a world in which it reverted back to an insignificant politico-economic (though not spiritual) footnote precisely after the triumph of Islam.

The other metaphysical grounds for Islam consisted in the scattering of spiritual ideas and meditative practices floating upon the land, which co-existed largely at peace with paganism, commonly known as Hanifism. This background is freely acknowledged in the Qur'an and throughout the tradition. As it coalesced, the new faith not only incorporated the content of such ideas, but it also nurtured the aura of their metaphysics, moral concerns, meditative air, and critical wisdom. But the significant point was that it was Islam, a code name for a full-fledged system, rather than Hanifism, that came to be referenced as the complete body of knowledge. The process of that becoming involved more than pure persuasion. Unlike Hanifism, Islam also became implicated in ushering in novel methods of social organization that transcended tribal solidarity and thus resulted in the formation of a new level of community life, which could not have been predicted at the outset of Muhammad's prophetic career in Mecca.

In this sense, the differences between Islam and Hanifism can be seen in formal rather than substantive terms. In the first place, if Hanifism entailed an anticipation of a prophet, then Islam entailed an empirical representation of such an expectation. That is, Islam became possible when an "anticipation" was understood strictly in its temporal significance, rather than, say, as an expression of indefinite alienated existence, as a willingness to live without a belief in what contemporaneity provided, as a state of truce with a hegemonic ideology, as a resigned foreignness, as a state of optimism expressing faith in the future without necessarily being invested in an empirically validated anticipation, or as a yearning for a mystical reunion with a lost past. The announcement of prophethood, on the other hand, deduces a temporal/practical logic out of the phenomenality of anticipation. The radicalism seen in the announcement of prophethood comes, paradoxically, from an avowed attempt to express a widespread ethic in a manifestly logical fashion rather than from a desire to contradict social norms.

The second formal difference between Islam and Hanifism flows directly from the first. The announcement of prophethood—as the mouthpiece of Hanifism—invited a social resistance that had not been a part of the experience of Hanifism. The ideas, then, were no longer communicated in their inert and undistorted significance. Indeed, one can argue that "undistorted communication" of the essence of a message (as, for instance, would be advocated in Jürgen Habermas's theory of communicative action), is possible only in self-dialogues, which the phenomenon of prophethood aborts for the sake of social communion. The divergence between the paradigms advocated by 'Umar and 'Uthman around Hudaybiyyah, as well as Muhammad's earlier communicative predicament in Mecca, are crucial episodes insofar as they demonstrate just how such distorted communication moves historical events. In the context of Muhammad's phenomenon and the antecedent ethic of anticipation, the empirical presence of a prophet contaminates the integrity of the holy idea, since with a prophet the question concerns not purely what God is saying but the entitlement to prophethood of a hitherto ordinary member of the community, whose ordinariness is well established in the first place and must be maintained to the extent that God's omnipotence is not to be eclipsed by the phenomenality of his messenger. On the one hand, the messenger is validated as such to himself by God; on the other, God's qualities of transcendence, which are to be communicated by the messenger, require that the messenger downplays his phenomenality, exceptionalism, and idiosyncrasy, which, save for miracles (none of which were to be had) were all he would be expected to draw on in order to legitimate his prophethood.

Such a crisis became the basis for the third formal difference between Islam and Hanifism, namely, the aforementioned communicative predicament that was so detrimental to Muhammad in Mecca. The failure to legitimize prophethood was, as indicated above, part of a formal logic implicit precisely in the strong Islamic idea of Allah. On the other hand, the need to announce the prophethood was premised on a formal and radical interpretation of a floating idea of anticipation. The possibility of such an interpretation, in turn, was premised on an ethical actualization of the idea of anticipation. That is, if the existence of an anticipation of prophethood indicates a social crisis, then the need to actualize such an anticipation is at least in part predicated on the conviction that the resolution of the crisis is for the good of society. The rejection of such an announcement, which in Muhammad's case was based on a lack of distinctive legitimacy, which the aloof Allah could not furnish, was nonetheless understood by Muhammad's few followers to mean only that the community could not know its own good. Such an interpreted lack of capacity to determine what was good for oneself seemed, therefore, to defy the logic of nature, so much so that war against Mecca, for which Allah had shown so much concern and love, became inevitable. Defiance of a radical formal logic could only invite war, which had the paradoxical objectives of taking revenge on and saving what one loved at the same time.

But as we have seen, Meccan society totally rejected neither Muhammad himself nor his ideology. More than anything else, the city's power structure challenged Muhammad's tribal credentials as bases of prophethood, in spite of the fact that he usually refrained from basing his prophethood on such credentials. Mecca's ontotheological crisis, as I have argued, was intensified precisely because its society had no social mechanism through which the crisis could be articulated, confronted, and resolved through a method that the entire community assented to. Thus, it was only a matter of time before the band of believers would break away from a society that was incapable of appreciating their constructive role and real concern for the fate of their brethren. We have also seen how the *Muhajirun* later adopted a vengeful attitude toward Mecca precisely because, in "rejecting" them, it showed itself to be going against its own natural product. It is in this context that one can understand why, for instance, the believers changed the direction of their prayer (*qibla*) toward Mecca at the very moment they were about to commence a bitter war against the city.

The rejection was thus due not so much to Muhammad's performance as to the communicative limits set by the prevailing social organization and its rules. The relevant question is, therefore, nothing like "What if the prophet had not been born, or had been born somewhere else, or at some other point in time, or had a different personality, or died prematurely, or abandoned the project altogether?" The question is: "Through what social dynamics was the idea of anticipation to present its bill to the world?" Needless to say, the prophet, as an empirical person, was but one component of the total pattern in which Meccan society received a transformative pedagogy. We have seen, for instance, how a different method of transformation in a roughly comparable society played itself out in the case of the *Ansar,* later to be Muhammad's most crucial followers, most of whom believed in Islam before ever having seen the prophet. Their need to believe had not been contaminated, as in Mecca, with an irreversible experience of the prophet's ordinariness. Thus, by the time Muhammad migrated to their dwellings, he had already passed what may be called "the threshold of legitimation."

In this sense, passing a threshold of legitimation entails the establishment of a trajectory for the emergence of a recognizable "system" out of an unpredictable, chaotic sequence of events. To pass a threshold of legitimation means more than acquiring the ability to persuade by pure argument. It means that the process of attaining such a legitimation itself must be both extratextual and appearing to deserve social respect. The authenticity of the text here is established against a background and through a process that legitimize the field of concerns evident in the text even as they ignore such concerns. Note, for instance, the Medinian Qur'an's radical shift of emphasis away from Mecca once the Muslim community was relocated away from the city. That is, once the need to acquire universal legitimation becomes more pressing, the text avoids restricting the dialogic experience to a single "addressee." Rather, it also resorts to an extraneous logic that, in seeming to be universal, can also claim to transcend the communicative restrictions engendered by the presence of an addressee, so that such an addressee is made aware that it does not monopolize the rules governing the scene of the dialogic experience underway.

But in abstracting and universalizing the addressee of the divine message in this fashion, the entire world moves inside the gradually opened up pages of the grand text. Unlike the text proper, however, the social transactions taking shape on its periphery never spelled out a transhistorical last word. But the recording activity of the religious text, which witnessed and directly commented on such transactions, rendered the heterogeneity of the extratextual sphere noiseless. The potentially explosive nature of the relations between the various social segments and worldviews claiming unity in the text moved inside the new ideological house, where they furnished the ground for continued social conflict and dynamism within the *umma*.[15]

This heterogeneity is prefigured in pagan pluralism, which itself illustrates the lack of a unifying referential basis, in whose absence the notion of unanimity was highlighted as a basis of collective decisions. Paradoxically, such an insistence on unanimity seems to have resulted from the breakdown of earlier conditions of nomadic egalitarianism in sedentary communities such as Mecca, where the drive toward consensus is reported to have typified the deliberations of the gathering (*al-mala'*) in *Dar an-Nadwah*. By contrast, in the less-differentiated nomadic setting, the loyalty of the individual to the tribe was underlined by an experience of normative belonging to a social unit where likelihoods of fortune and misfortune were more equitably distributed. The insistence on unanimity in the sedentary setting not only expressed the emergence of unenforceable conditions of differentiation but was also a prelude to the struggle for certainty, which in that case was eventually found in surrendering the human will to an active but unaccountable God. Unanimity, under conditions of awareness of the lack of perfection of the community as a system of unalienated reciprocities, could provide authorization for action but could not surround the authorized act with ethical or normative certainty. With such a lack, it became possible to experiment with different forms of authority, such as prophetic authority. The prophet cancels the need for unanimity, since the source of certainty is then relocated outside of society and given back to its creator.

Thus, under practical circumstances and through a convoluted process, Islam was woven out of the interaction of such concerns, conditions, limits, and expressive and communicative venues. Ancient consciousness could hardly posit a question anticipating unilinear systematicity, such as

"Whose ideology fashioned the Islamic religion?"[16] The final form and content of the religious text were not shaped through solitary meditations of a prophet; they were shaped with respect to the conditions and criteria that the societies he faced deemed worthy of divine or prophetic judgments and with respect to contours of expression prefigured by grand genres such as the encyclopedic ode. Having to contend with the most miserable of Meccans as original followers; having failed, despite a special effort, with the prosperous Meccans; having lost his tribal belonging and having migrated; having had to contend with the transitory society of Medina and with the unreliable Bedouin allies; having had to act as a situational statesman more often than as a detached and universal prophet; having had to wage war; having had to accept the allegiance of social sectors he never thought of at the beginning of his prophethood—all such happenings were independent of the subjective choice of the prophet. His most important legacy, the reason for his unparalleled immortalization, lies in the fact that by the time his prophetic credentials were beginning to be established, many unintegrated and often antagonistic social units, classes, and detached individuals were already attracted to his message. Each responded to it through the dynamics of its own life, each claimed him, along with the rest of the holy text, in their own way, but all were equally incapable of comprehending their unintended and unprecedented unification in terms that would preclude overloading the text with the meaning of their circumstantial relationship to it. We have seen an important manifestation of such an incomprehension already appearing before the death of the prophet, namely, in the sharp dichotomy between the 'Umarist and 'Uthmanist paradigms toward the Peace of Hudaybiyyah.

Thus the Book, like the prophet, is a witness *and* an instigator of this grand flux. A witness because the raw materials for it were long in supply and an instigator because it endowed the raw material with textual clothes that allowed it to speak and eventually wreak havoc upon the established order. As it took textual form, the religion was confounded with such a diversity and found itself chasing a continually evolving reality with continually evolving modes of witnessing, commentary, and acknowledgment. Thus, at its point of origin, it had no consciousness of itself that could be defined in any terms that could be restricted to a particular and unchanging way of categorizing social reality. Its terms of speaking were guided by the perception that an antecedent condition of social harmony had collapsed together with its ontological set of references, leaving society with the task of experimenting with a reconstruction. The reconstruction, which invoked the discourse of harmony, found itself amplifying such a theme as a grander-than-foreseen system came to house diverse groups. Those groups could not have been intended or even detected as legitimate addressees from the original point of view. But it was such an accomplishment that molded the foundational text of the origins as a transhistorical point of reference for a *variety* of systems. For being such a plenum, for such a lack of essentiality, Islam remains with us today, like all other incidental yet formative and imposing plenums of which the world is made.

Notes

INTRODUCTION

1. For an outline of this argument, see Gates, 11–22; Said (1983), 89–107.

2. See Crone's *Meccan Trade* and Sulayman Bashir's *Muqqadimah fi al-Tarikh al-Akher* (1984). For a critical assessment of the documents that the revisionist historians rely on, see Ibrahim (1987).

3. Crone, 203–230.

4. Such an attitude is perhaps best exemplified in the following passage by Maxime Rodinson, a rather sympathetic reader of the tradition: "Those who forged the traditions certainly had a true literary gift; they gave their fictions that vivid, easy, familiar quality that makes them so delightful to read—those animated dialogues, those details that seem as though they must have been experienced, those turns of phrase in reported speech, those moments of humour, all seem more redolent of literary talent than of historical authenticity" (xi). One could counter this argument by noting that receptiveness to the Islamic message was enhanced to the extent that the media of its transmission could transcend daily life normalcy, at both levels of discourse and manners of behavior. Though historical facts matter, as far as the study of a worldview is concerned so do what protagonists in the story wanted to believe as facts, which are subsequently surrounded with significations, animated structures, poetics, and mythologies.

5. For example, Crone's account of the story of Ibn Ubay's opposition to Muhammad in Medina, which is examined in Chapter 7 of this book, does not reveal a

contradiction in the sources as she claims. Rather, the seeming contradictions in the story of Ibn Ubay can be seen to highlight the experimental nature of the political employment of religion, as Islam oscillated between practical verdicts implicated in the immediacy of everyday life, on the one hand, and the notion of abstract and general authority already prefigured in the phenomenon of an absentee prophet, as Muhammad was for Medina before his migration, on the other. If anything, the story of Ibn Ubay indeed registers a significant social transformation in the role of a new faith, as it became increasingly implicated in the question of regulatory, instrumental authority. This type of authority was foreign to the meditative orientation of Muhammad and the earliest faithful.

6. Lukàcs, 30–34.

1. THE IDEOLOGY OF THE HORIZONS

1. The Arabs themselves associated the term "Arabia Felix" only with Yemen, unlike the Greeks and Romans, who associated it with the entire Arabian Peninsula.

2. Al-Istakhri, 24.

3. Qur'an 14:37.

4. Imru' l-Qays (circa A.D. 500–540), of the tribe of Kinda. He was a son of the last king of Kinda—a short-lived order of sovereignty in Najd in the north central Arabian Peninsula that acted to arbitrate between and pacify warring nomadic tribes. Imru' l-Qays, so the legend goes, was thrown out by his father for his indulgence in poetry. The legend presents him as an irreverent, sensual, highly versatile lover. He was nonetheless to be entrusted with reclaiming his family's withering kingship. Being deserted by all his former allies, including his own brothers, he resorted in vain to asking the help of Justinian, the emperor of Byzantium. He died on the way back from Constantinople. An illuminating biography is available in Tuetey, *Imrulkais of Kinda.* A. J. Arberry, in *The Seven Odes,* handsomely elucidates the life stories of Imru' l-Qays and six other major pre-Islamic poets.

5. Al-Alusi, vol. 1, 188, 194.

6. Al-Hamawi, vol. 2, 203.

7. See 'Aqel, 28–29.

8. Al-Hamawi, vol. 4, 1026–1034.

9. Al-Istakhri, 26.

10. Al-Mas'udi, vol. 2, 64.

11. Some authorities argue that the eastern region of Bahrain (not to be confused with the modern-day island of Bahrain) was the most densely inhabited region in the peninsula. See 'Ali, vol. 1, 192. The number of *suqs* held there seems both to partially support this and to account for its intermediary role in global trade, especially after the interruption of the land route passing through Persia in the sixth century A.D.

12. Al-Alusi, vol. 1, 264–270; al-Hamadani, 296. Other sources, such as Marzuqi, Ibn Habib, and Ya'qubi, offer slightly differing accounts. For a general assessement of this literature, see Simon, 78–91. The varying accounts also leave the impression that

not all traders moved with the cycle, with a number staying behind in Hadramaut and another contingent continuing northward to Khaibar after 'Ukaz.

13. Al-Istakhri, 27–28; al-Alusi, vol. 1, 185–186.

14. For a discussion of this theme, see 'Ali, vol. 1, 198.

15. On average, a camel can carry 600–700 pounds, which can be increased to 1,000 pounds if speed is not required or reduced to 300 pounds if fast delivery is the main concern. See Blome, 4.

16. The beast acting as a symbol on behalf of the camel here is reminiscent of Labid's ode. The beast is lonesome, cold, threatened by the hunters, and forced to fight their hounds for survival. Unlike in Labid's construction, however, there are no indications that the beast survived in the ode of an-Nabigha, whose audience was generally more sedentary and sovereign.

2. SOCIOECONOMY AND THE HORIZON OF THOUGHT

1. Ibn Khaldun, 211. For a more comprehensive survey of theories pertaining to the comparative origins of nomadism, see Khazanov, 85–118. Although it could be argued that the protection of wealth does not in and of itself require a sedentary framework of existence—since a network of mutual defense obligations within the nomadic tribe itself could be mobilized for that purpose—the investment and *regular* accumulation of such wealth is rooted in sedentary prerequisites. The sedentarizing imperatives of the various facets of wealth depend on whether the mutual defense obligations, comprising subtribal units, could supersede the threat posed by *individual* wealth to the principle of austere egalitarianism. In this case, the individual conception of wealth will seem to invite a move outside of nomadism into a protective framework of sedentarism.

2. Al-Mas'udi, vol. 2, 94. His observations indirectly suggest that nomads were continually seeking to settle, though most such attempts failed.

3. Some reports indicate that Meccans began organizing their own caravans to Yemen and Syria during the days of the Qurayshan chief Hashem Ibn 'Abd Manaf, probably during the first half of the sixth century A.D., as a way of escaping the hunger and destitution that prevailed among them; see al-Alusi, vol. 3, 386–387.

4. Qur'an 34:18–19. The passage clearly ordains and blesses traveling in "measured stages," a norm that the Shebans sought to violate. The lesson was of course directed at more contemporaneous traders. For interpretations of this passage, see Paret, 406; al-Baydawi, 568.

5. Khazanov, 157–158.

6. A series of droughts in Arabia occurred between A.D. 591 and 640. See Planhol, 443–469; Butzer, 359–371.

7. Frederick Barth offers comparable models of sedentarization on the basis of his observations of nomadism in southern Persia. The four models he lists are given the illuminating headings "drought and decline," "defeat and degradation," "failure and fall-away," and "succeed and surpass."

8. For a critical discussion of the sources, see Simon, 91–95.

9. Simmel, 510.

10. The "steps" outlined in the text should be seen as part of an ideological continuum rather than as discrete, historically recognizable moments.

11. For Max Weber, such a value determines the selection of spheres of interest in human action. See his *The Methodology of the Social Sciences* (1949), chapters 1, 2.

12. Qur'an 3:14 (translation altered). Other passages, e.g., 18:46 or 16:72, also list offspring among God's bounties in this world.

13. What must be kept in mind, however, is that such a discourse does not necessarily identify the way the faithful actually thought of values. As Islam spread, many adherents from various socioeconomies joined for different reasons. The important element here is the development of a *discourse* that, as is evident in this passage, seeks to ground the "self-evident" claim of abstract value upon an irrefutable source.

14. This attitude, which is perhaps related to the often noted "materialism" of pre-Islamic poetry, will be examined in more detail in Chapters 3 and 5.

15. For a comprehensive listing, see al-Karmali; also, al-Alusi, vol. 1, 264–266.

16. For details, see al-Maqrizi, ed. in al-Karmali, no. 25, 26–27. One of the more interesting local standards was the weight of the coin in grains of barley. This of course called for a further definition of what a "grain of barley" was; it was defined as one of average size and free of long ends. The increase in the variety of coins is also evident in the increase in the use of several denominations of the coinages of the empires in Mecca before Islam.

17. This is not to suggest a simple-minded connection between a money economy and the decline of tribal solidarity. Rather, the idea is more that the growth of a general method typified by abstract valuation indirectly and unintendedly furnishes new ways of approaching an older system of social values.

18. Ibrahim (1990), 95–96.

19. The absence of coercion did not mean, however, the absence of threats, which more often came from uncontrollable nomadic incursions upon the trade route than from the empires. It also manifested itself in Abraha's campaign, which in its own failure foreclosed future imperial adventures.

20. The prototypical example of such an attitude is Immanuel Kant's "aesthetic indifference," whereby the concern for the real existence of an object is distanced by the occurrence of its "form." For example, a painting could claim a legitimate existence on its own regardless of the existence of the object it purports to represent. See Simmel, 73–75.

21. For example, 53:23 and elsewhere.

22. The development of intertribal trade may have cushioned the flourishing *hadarah* lifestyle from the side effects of the opening of a direct maritime route between Egypt and India during the first century A.D. Although by then Mecca was scarcely visible in the trade routes, other peninsular merchants, from Yemen, Hadramaut, and Bahrain, continued to import from India and east Africa for local consumption and soon thereafter took advantage of the great increase in the Roman Empire's consumption of luxury items coming from those parts. See Rostovtzeff, 95.

23. Braudel, vol. 2, 407–408. For discussion see Bamyeh, 28–29.

24. Al-Mas'udi, vol. 2, 33.

25. Ibid., vol. 2, 188–191.

26. The same nonseasonal framework was preserved in setting the Islamic calendar.

27. Unlike in Bedouin society, where the accounts of raids mention negotiated set-tlements, there are reports that indicate more standard methods of calculating *diyyah* (blood money) in Yathrib. See, for instance, Ibn al-Athir (1965), vol. 1, 659.

28. Testifying to Mecca's obsession with the preservation of order, some reports trace the city's name to the ancient word "*bekka*," which connoted a certain and swift punishment for anyone who violated its peace; see al-Alusi, vol. 1, 227.

29. Simon, 24–31.

30. Ibid., 30.

31. See al-Alusi, vol. 1, 268–270.

32. For indications that the sacred months failed to garner much reverence among many Arabs, see Ibn Khaldun, 405; al-Mas'udi, vol. 2, 197.

33. Ibn al-Athir (1965) reports that some Arabs, known as *an-Nasa'ah* on the basis of their calendar, exchanged one of the forbidden months for the following one be-cause they needed to raid during the month designated by the Quraysh as sacred. Al-Mas'udi (vol. 2, 30–31, 188) gives a relevant report about a month (an-Nasi') that some added to the lunar calendar once every three years in order to make up the dis-crepancy between it and the solar calendar that was used by others. The result, in terms of the forbidden months, would be an increase once in three years of a month in which fighting was permitted, which did not sit well with the sedentary commercial society, as is evidenced in the Islamic verdict against such an addition to the calendar.

34. One report mentions that Safar, the month immediately following three suc-cessive forbidden months, was given that name because it indicated that houses be-came vacant, as its inhabitants went to war. See al-Masu'di, vol. 2, 188–89. Whether this philological deduction is correct is not the point here; what is important is, rather, the observation itself, which, as is often the case in ancient histories, is *then* traced to philological foundations. (Many modern historians, by contrast, proceed in the oppo-site direction, moving from philology *into* historical deduction.)

35. Al-Hamadani, 299.

36. For an extended narrative, the best source is al-Azraqi, vol. 1, 157–165.

37. Ibn al-Athir (1965), vol. 1, 503. The report concentrates on the status of the *haram* as the central point of contention. Significantly, it does not mention any acqui-sition of spoils as a result of the campaign.

38. Ibid., 442. The failure of that attempt was probably one reason behind Abraha's subsequent campaign against Mecca, a campaign whose expressed sole purpose was not "conquest," permanent occupation, or acquisition but, rather, the destruction of the Meccan *haram*.

39. Serjeant, 45.

40. For a summary of such reports, see Simon, 90.

41. The *siqayah* office had the responsibility for providing water, which involved

digging wells or transporting it from a distance on the back of camels. *Rifadah* involved the responsibility for providing the pilgrims with food. The holder of *hijabah* was responsible for the general upkeep of the *haram*. *Nadwah* and *liwa'* were positions more involved in the internal organization of the sedentary community, with the former referring to general, noncoercive leadership and coordination of meetings of heads of tribal branches and the latter referring to the holder of the tribal flag in battle, whose collapse signaled defeat.

42. For a thorough discussion, see Simon, 95, 102–103.

43. For an illustrative example, see al-Jahiz 57. The ideological point is not restricted to trade per se but also covers a spectrum of financial activities related to it, most importantly usury, the insuring of transported goods, and currency exchange and valuation services. These could become legendary preoccupations for reasons not of economy or accumulation but, rather, because of some behaviors associated with them that reveal traditional moral qualities. This is illustrated in the legendary status of the Jewish usurer al-Samau'al, whose name became a poeticized shorthand for fidelity to agreements. Reportedly, he refused to surrender the collateral of a dead debtor to the deceased man's enemies, even when they killed al-Samau'al's own son in front of him in an attempt to pressure him to do so. Testifying to usury's entrenched hold, prefigured in the legend, the Qur'an had to use an unusually threatening tone when it prohibited usury.

44. Al-Baghdadi, 280. For pertinent discussions, see Rubin, 106; Kister (1990), 144, among others.

45. Al-Bekri, 49–50; al-Hamawi, vol. 6, 13–14. These sources are contrasted in Simon, who elaborates on the differences between them, 80–82. There are various explanations given for the estrangement. Some emphasize Thaqif's growth to such a size that it ceased to need 'Amer's protection; others note 'Amer's reluctance to help Thaqif against nomadic threats, forcing the latter to spend more energy in surrounding the colony with a defensive wall. See also Ibn al-Athir (1965), vol. 1, 684–686.

46. Al-Azraqi lists about thirty pre-Islamic wells in and around Mecca; vol. 2, 214–224.

47. See Al-Sharif, 109.

48. A report indicative of the inferior value ascribed to the *haram* before such developments is given by al-Mas'udi, who mentions that it was bought by Qusay from the Khuza'ayan caretaker (Ibn Ghabshan) for no more than a goat and a jug of wine. That this story became a ground for a reported common superlative (*akhsar min safqat Ibn Ghabshan*, "worse than Ibn Ghabshan's bargain") may be based upon the recognition of the evolutionary status of the *haram*.

49. Al-Azraqi, vol. 1, 109.

50. Ibrahim (1990), 73. According to this thesis, this trajectory is personified in the lore by Abu Sufyan.

51. Muhammad was thus rejected by many noble Qurayshans on the grounds that he was not entitled to the distinct spiritual honor of prophethood, precisely because he was not wealthy. This episode is documented in Qur'an 43:31–32. Interestingly,

however, the same passage traces the evolution of a class society to God's targeted blessings.

52. The Qur'an adopts such an ethic as well, especially in its version of the story of Sodom, where the lack of hospitality toward guests was sufficient reason for God to obliterate the village.

53. See al-Azraqi, vol. 1, 195.

54. Ibid., vol. 1, 257; al-Mas'udi, vol. 2, 270–271. This embeddedness of the agreement in formal and general trade logic shows that it is not as embedded in clannish power politics as some commentators (e.g., Ibrahim [1990], 72) suggest.

55. Al-Alusi, vol. 3, 386–387.

56. For an illuminating discussion, see Ibrahim (1990), 41; Kister (1990).

57. The basic form of this argument can be found in a hitherto little known anthropological essay by E. R. Wolf (1951).

58. The confoundment of class and clan can also be seen in the original conflict over the *haram* services, which is reported to have taken place entirely within the Abateh of Quraysh, with the Zawaher maintaining neutrality.

59. The prime example being its rejection of the offer of alliance from the Aus of Yathrib. See Ibn al-Athir (1965), vol. 1, 677.

60. *Ilaf* agreements are reported to have existed with various local rulers in Syria, Yemen, east Africa, and Persia and are said to have been organized by the descendants of 'Abd Manaf, one of the most important branches of the Abateh of Quraysh. For an overarching review, see Hamidullah. The caravans could also forge a similar agreement with the nomads controlling the route by marketing the nomads' products and returning a profit to them on the way back; for a discussion, see Simon, 64–65.

61. Of the dynasties of Yemen, they knew only the last, the Himyari (115 B.C.–A.D. 525), and to their north, they did not know the Nubtean state, which did not vanish until its annexation to the Roman Empire in A.D. 106. They had no knowledge of Rome, but knew only Byzantium.

62. History records not a single foreign military expedition directed at Arabia itself. The Abyssinian campaign in the sixth century—the year of the elephant—was intended not so much to lead to a permanent occupation or annexation as much as to damage Mecca's highly advertised role as a safe haven for trade, thereby allowing the Abyssinian-occupied Yemen to compete with Mecca on that score. The Roman expedition of Gallus Aeilus, targeting Yemen circa 24 B.C., avoided western Arabia and sailed instead to the Red Sea coast north of Yemen. The expulsion of the Abyssinians from Yemen at the hands of the Persians toward the end of the sixth century A.D., and the subsequent transformation of Yemen into a Persian province, did not lead to any further Persian expansion into the rest of the peninsula. The seaborne Persian expedition, just like the Roman one preceding it, also avoided the peninsular land route.

63. For an examination of caravan routes, especially those connected to the southern trade, see Simon, 39–42.

64. Pliny counted sixty-five camel stations over a distance of 4,436,000 paces, which is equivalent to approximately one station for every twenty-two miles. The most

important station was undoubtedly the relatively large oasis of Taima', which was situated at an important crossroads in the northern frontiers. See Blome, 12; O'Leary, 53.

65. In addition to the aforementioned remunerative *ilaf* that was possible for some tribes, a standard fee was apparently paid to other tribes in exchange for protecting caravans in specified territories. The tribe offering such protection would return its fee if harm was done to the caravan in its territory. There is evidence that this system was further enshrined, especially in light of a report that statutes were enacted in Palmyra to honor caravan protectors who "acted at their own cost." See O'Leary, 185.

66. For a detailed description of the *hums* ritual, see 'Ali, vol. 5, 227; Hurgronje, 181.

67. Simon, 63–70.

68. Ibid., 186.

69. Muhammad, who was then barely beginning his prophetic career, reportedly was enthused by the news of victory, while claiming a spiritual role for himself in it. See Ibn al-Athir (1965), vol. 1, 482–491.

70. Rostovtzeff, 271, 400, 735n36.

71. The Persian army that was sent to Dhi Qar consisted to a major extent of Arab soldiers, some of whom reportedly deserted in the subsequent battle. After a few rapid shifts in policy, Mundherite rule over al-Hira was ultimately discontinued by Persia during the rise of Islam in Arabia.

72. The Abyssinians occupied Yemen twice. On the first occasion, they left after an internal rebellion, and on the second they were driven out by a joint Persian-Yemenite force, although Persia annexed Yemen thereafter. Al-Mas'udi reports a poem that is said to have been engraved at the main gate of Zufar, enumerating the several loyalties of Yemen to the Himyari dynasty as well as to the Abyssinians, the Persians, and even Quraysh. See al-Mas'udi, vol. 2, 63.

73. For instance, reports surrounding the Basus war mention that one of the parties, hoping to avoid the war, made exactly such an offer at the beginning.

74. This of course only partially accounts for the increase in the frequency and magnitude of tribal wars. After all, the aforementioned sources of arbitration and authority, even at the peak of their power, had limited influence in the peninsula proper, an influence that could be enhanced by sporadic infiltrations into the desert on their peripheries. A more important contributing factor had apparently to do with population increase, a recurrent historical phenomenon that had been responsible for previous Semitic emigrations for four millennia before Islam. Indeed, Islamic conquests can themselves be regarded as later versions of Semitic emigrations. As is well known, the armies settled the areas they occupied, and soldiers were eventually joined there by their families rather than returning to the political center in the peninsula. This theory is usually rejected on the ground that there is no evidence for major ecological changes that would drive people out for many millennia before Islam (Simon, 82). The point, however, concerns not ecological change as much as population growth *coupled* with the emergence of empires that defined their frontiers against such population movements.

75. O'Leary, 182.

76. See, for instance, al-Mas'udi, vol. 2, 96.

77. This nomadic trope was also adopted at a later stage by prominent Muslim philosphers of history, notably Ibn Khaldun, as they used it to trace the degeneration of their age to its distance from the graceful austerity of the Bedouin heritage.

78. Khazanov, 143–144.

79. For instance, at the onset of the Basus war—the stories around which seem to condense a large number of nomadic ethos of attachments—the Taghlib expelled from their ranks the sister of the killer of a fellow Taghlibite because she belonged to Bakr, the tribe of the killer. It made little difference that she also happened to be the wife of the murdered Taghlibite. In this sense, tribal loyalty is presented as a law of nature, determined objectively by blood and unalterable by reversible human bonds.

80. Cited in Meeker, 11–13.

81. For further discussions, see Salzman, 8–9.

82. Ibn Khaldun, 230–231, addresses this phenomenon in terms of the distinction between the "general" and "particular" *nasab.*

83. Khazanov, 127. For a summary of similar anthropological observations, see 132. Khazanov notes that in some instances, a *dar* (home) could consist of several households that pasture separately but eat together and are obligated to defend each other (136).

84. In this sense, intertribal separation was a free choice among equal members, rather than a decision on the basis of class or rank. The split was usually determined along the immediacy of lines of descent.

85. The Basus war, again, provides a good example of this. Within the tribal confederations of Bakr and Taghlib, many smaller units tied by lineage to each could freely decide at the beginning not to be involved (even though many of those were ultimately dragged into the war as it intensified and as they found themselves the target of raids).

86. It may be noted here that if one observes the histories of other discourses of collective identification—e.g., modern nationalism—and their relationship to war, one realizes that the nomads are far from being alone in this story. The flexibility of the mobilizing potential of their grand ethos is not fundamentally different from modern modalities of mass mobilization; in some instances, nomadic ethos show greater discursive flexibility—not to mention far less capacity to do damage.

87. That war itself was the objective—rather than, say, the restoration of justice—can be seen in its pretexts. The Basus war was triggered by a conflict arising from the killing of a camel, owned by the Bakrians, that had wandered into Taghlibite territory. The war proceeded in spite of offers of compensation. The Dahes wa l-Ghabra' war had no explicit justification other than an argument over a horse race.

88. Meeker, 11.

89. See 'Ali, vol. 3, 332.

90. See, for instance, Ibrahim (1990), 25; Simon, 42–48.

91. This point is emphasized by Hamidullah, 308.

92. Zaidan, 225, estimates Kinda at 30,000 individuals at the time of its earlier migration from Bahrain to Hadramaut.

93. See 'Aqel, 212.

94. The title al-Maqsur (the confined one) was reportedly given him because he confined the domain of governance strictly to what he had inherited from his father.

95. See Abu al-Fida', vol. 1, 92.

96. For a comprehensive survey of the accounts regarding that episode, see 'Ali, vol. 3, 333–338.

97. In a relatively short period, nearly all major tribes in the region could be accounted among the Kinda's constituents. Some of the main ones that can be found listed in the sources include the Asad, Ghatfan, Bakr, Taghlib, Handhalah, Rabab, Nimr, Qays, and branches of the Tamim, in addition to the previously subjugated tribes.

98. Olinder, 70.

99. Olinder, 122–128, lists different accounts concerning the allocation of the tribes to the sons. The important point, sociologically speaking, is the very fact of this division rather than its exact lines.

100. Kinda rule over al-Hira lasted for only three to four years, commencing around A.D. 524 or 525.

101. For an examination of such reports, see Olinder, 131–136.

102. Thus, for example, Bakr and Taghlib, which submitted at least nominally to two different sons of al-Harith, reportedly caused the brothers to lead them in fighting each other.

103. For a summary of the reports regarding this episode, see Olinder, 159-161.

104. The idea of this obligation permeates some of Imru' l-Qays's poetry, in a tone that also addresses it as an unchosen and—because it undermines hedonistic possibilities in life—a clearly distracting goal.

3. SOCIAL TIME, DEATH, AND THE IDEAL

1. The three components formed a single economy in the sense that, taken together, they maintained and reproduced Bedouin life.

2. This feature is not a "weakness" of thought but, rather, a method of rendering the world according to the same manner of systematicity by which it offers itself. On this score, it is not far removed from the correspondence between pre-Islamic sedentary sociopolitical pluralism, on the one hand, and pagan polytheism, on the other.

3. Arberry (121–122) credits him with discovering Labid.

4. The only one that does not commence with the theme, that of 'Amru Ibn Kalthum, includes it nonetheless shortly afterward. Indeed, many compilers and philologists have regarded that placement as marking the ode's "true" opening.

5. As late as a couple of centuries after the coming of Islam, poetry lacking the traditional opening continued to be held (at least officially) in less esteem. Some of the reports surrounding the flamboyant poet Abu Nuwwas, for instance, mention that he was forced by the Abbasid caliph to commence some of his poems with the narrator standing at the ruins. In the preserved poem, Abu Nuwwas explicitly bemoans having to revisit ruins that for him had little significance.

6. Hegel, 56. See also 114–118.

7. An-Nabigha's aforementioned couplet 7, which abrogates the scene of the ruins, clearly spells out how little value there is in such a site. Unlike the agonized withdrawal found among earlier poets, an-Nabigha here feels confident enough to recommend a specific and admirable mode of departure, upon which all belongings are to be taken away: "*Wan-mi l-qutuda 'ala 'ayranaten ujudi* [And gather the rafters on the back of a stiff-boned, energetic mare]" (c. 7). The health and vibrancy of the animal stands out in contrast to the ruins' dilapidated essence.

8. Al-Mas'udi, vol. 2, 96 (emphasis added).

9. Ibid., 96–97.

10. Poetry is a significant source here precisely because it was not an exercise in elite aesthetics. It was a depository of memorable forms and sayings, a widely disseminated oral tradition, and a compilation of events and heroic deeds. The poet gradually became an important tribal institution.

11. Another arena for idealization is the individual himself; the only poem among the legendary ten that does not commence with a reminiscence of the past opens instead with a valorization of pleasures, signified by excessive wine consumption.

12. The tribe as a major poetic theme appears more prominently in the odes ascribed to poets said to belong to a generation later than that of Imru' l-Qays and Tarafa. In the odes of these two individuals, the tribe is in essence a lost home, having shown itself oblivious to their talents and in fact seeing their talents as justification for their expulsion on the grounds that their innovation is incompatible with traditional tribal duties. At a later point, when the poet became a significant social institution and a useful tribal propaganda machine, tribal themes became more established as parts of the compositions.

13. For an extended examination of ritualistic structures in the tradition, see Stetkevych.

14. For a more theoretically elaborate discussion of the social embeddedness of distinctive language, see Mukarovsky, 49–56.

15. See 'Ali, vol. 6, 102–162.

16. One may want to speculate on the relation between this materialism and the necessity of revenge as an earthly redemption of a life that cannot be redeemed in any other realm of existence.

17. For an extended discussion, see 'Ali, vol. 5.

18. Ibn Hisham, cited in 'Ali, vol. 5, 125–126. The Qur'an itself documents this attitude; 45:24.

19. In al-Harith's opening, one encounters an element of sense perception that is more prevalent only in the more sedentarily informed schemes of an-Nabigha and, to a lesser extent, Labid. In the earlier odes, standing by the ruins was an exercise in memory invocation and similarly structured abstractions. In other words, one used none of the senses. But in the case of al-Harith, the ruins are paralleled by a sight in the distance, where the social life from which the poet was separated could be seen to reemerge someplace else. The whole experience is sensed: The poet is *told* of an

impending departure, then *shown* fire in the distance (i.e., the inevitable has already occurred). The impact of the ruins is retrievable by the senses, even though the reality of separation will persist. Here, we have, at last, a "social being," inseparable from a community of some sort, accustomed to feeling the presence of a society. The poet here wanders alone no more; even when thinking abstractly, he finds his reference points always outworn, and, even in their most inert state, eroded by the wind of society.

20. This term is both temporal and spatial. It denotes periodicity since it is the term for pilgrimage, and it also refers to well-trodden pathways (*mahajja*).

21. For a somewhat useful history of the calendar, see al-Mas'udi, vol. 2, 177, 188–196.

22. The "good morning" salute to the ruins begins another long poem ascribed to Imru' l-Qays (*ala 'im sabahan ayyuha t-talal l-bali*), which suggests common structures of recognition and commencement.

4. PRE-ISLAMIC ONTOTHEOLOGY AND THE METHOD OF KNOWLEDGE

1. For one example of this attitude, see Hawting, 23–47. While far from being unique in this approach, the article is a good demonstration of it.

2. Various reports seem to corroborate or hint at the weakness or even stark novelty of paganism within Arabia. One such report mentions that the Hanifa consumed their own idol, made of dates and ghee, in times of hunger (Ibn Qutaybah, 266). Another mentions that the transaction transferring ownership of Mecca's *haram* to Quraysh involved no more than a goat and a jug of wine (al-Mas'udi, vol. 2, 31).

3. For a compendium of pre-Islamic belief and ritual systems, see 'Alwan.

4. Ibn al-Kalbi, 8.

5. One possible explanation for the higher degree of respect for some idols has to do with the relative power or prominence of the tribe with which it was identified. The three most prominent idols, Lat, 'Uzzah, and Manat, belonged respectively to Thaqif of Ta'if, Quraysh of Mecca, and Aus-Khazraj of Yathrib. Hubal, probably a later addition, was also Quraysh's. See Ibn al-Kalbi, 27. This pattern seems reminiscent of Mesopotamian allocation of status and authority among different city's gods in a way that paralleled cities' relative sociopolitical centrality.

6. Ibid., 9, 29.

7. I do not mean to imply that poets were all uprooted but merely that how they began their odes was judged to a great extent on how eloquently they articulated the idea.

8. The most important of such attempts, discussed in Chapter 2 in connection with Abraha's campaign, was in Yemen. Two others are mentioned in the sources, one by Ghatfan, which was reportedly despoiled by Mecca. See Ibn al-Kalbi, 45.

9. Ibid., 22.

10. Qur'an 53:23.

11. The idea of "function" here is used merely to allude to some aspects of idol influence and role rather than to indicate straightforward instrumentality. The notion

does not presume that any such functions were *intended* to be fulfilled as such, and it certainly does not restrict the idols to the realm of functionality.

12. Meeker, 105–107.

13. See 'Alwan.

14. The earlier attempts to exclude the less-wealthy traders are judged in Qur'anic hindsight as acts that displeased God and hence as the cause of the decline of Yemen's trade. See Qur'an 34:18–19, and the discussion of this verse in Chapter 2.

15. Here, the notion of stages is not meant to be chronological. Rather, it is employed merely to indicate three different circles, or discourses, or modes, or communicative practices, cohabiting a single formal tradition as it becomes more established.

16. It must be noted that the Qur'an itself, particularly in the early revelations, shows a clear tendency to deliver wisdom through poetic structures. This aesthetic dimension was maintained even when Qur'anic language shifted to *saja'* (rhymed speech), a less commonly used form of rhythmic speech than the circulating poetry. The impact of the early rivalry with poetry lingered on and is explicitly addressed in the Qur'an at one point, 26:221–226.

17. For some listings, see Ibn Qutaybah, 27–29; al-Alusi, vol. 2, 244–286.

18. This offer is strikingly similar to the one made to Muhammad during the debacle of an-Najm revelation, to be discussed in Chapter 7. A variant on it is also documented in an early Qur'anic revelation, *surah* 109.

19. For a discussion of some of the most important compilations, see Kister (1980), 33–57.

20. Ibid., 48.

21. The use of such a statement in opening the treaty of Hudaybiyyah was, according to the sources, a reason for consternation among many Muslims, who protested Muhammad's acquiescence to the use of that Qurayshan formula instead of the Islamic "In the name of Allah, the compassionate, the merciful." See the discussion of Hudaybiyyah in Chapter 8.

22. Ritual suicide by starvation, or *i'tifad,* seems to have been specific to early Meccan settlement. It was apparently an outcome of an unanchored concept of misfortune, whereby misfortune was not connected to any particular individual or group. Thus, the experience of misfortune and the concept of justice remained delinked.

23. This opening, it may be said, finally answers the observation made by another heroic poet of the period, 'Antara, namely, that the tradition of the ruins imagery had become too congested. It is perhaps no accident that such challenges to the tradition could be spelled out only by tribal heroes.

24. This state of affairs may be contrasted to the thoroughly different example of China, where early political centralization, though clearly connected to regulatory efficiency and grand ethical systems such as Confucianism, was also correlated to the absence of any high God other than cosmic representation via the emperor.

25. This does not contradict the fact that an Islamic state did eventually emerge. In fact, many of the political contests following Muhammad's death took place in the context of a lack of clear prophetic or Qur'anic instructions regarding the rules and

methods of human governance. Such a state, thus, can be seen as one of the unintended outcomes of the Islamic venture.

26. Ibn Qutaybah, 28.

27. Al-Alusi, vol. 2, 244–246.

28. Bravmann, 288–295.

29. At least one significant poetic eulogy (*marthiyyah*), namely, that of Sa'd Ibn Ka'b al-Ghanawi, clearly expresses such an attitude. See al-Qurashi, 325. See also further discussion of related themes in Bellamy, 44–61.

30. Visions of hierarchy on the Day of Judgment were not confined to the dual categories of the condemned and the saved until the intensification of the conflict with Mecca required clear and irrevocable allegiances. Before that, however, hints at a possible, more multiplicitous hierarchy are evident in some early Qur'anic revelations, such as 56:10–14, 38–40.

31. Ibn Qutaybah, 29.

32. Al-Bukhari.

33. See Umayyah Ibn al-Salt, cited in al-Alusi, vol. 2, 254, on the authority of Ibn Qutaybah. The sources list a long list of anticipators (see 253–275). The point concerns not the credibility of this information as much as the aura of anticipation evident in its availability.

34. They were Abu Qays Ibn Abi Anas and Waraqah Ibn Nawfal, who was later a companion of the prophet. See al-Alusi, 269–275.

35. For an extended discussion of the phenomenon of the Medinian opposition to Muhammad along partially similar lines, see Gil, 65–96.

36. This reasoning was the basis of the Islamic insistence that Muhammad was the "last of the prophets."

37. See at-Tibrizi, 53–66, 159–164.

38. See al-Mawardi. 'Abd l-Muttaleb refers to the otherworld as *dar* (home).

39. Bravmann, 7–12. Other root meanings include the idea of "self-sacrifice," an attitude defying death by welcoming it. The term could also be related to the quest after the distant and the unknown (38). Bravmann's psychological explanations, however, are clearly superficial, to say the least, and must be evaluated apart from the philological evidence presented.

40. Al-Alusi, vol. 2, 275.

41. This line of thought may be seen as consistent with both Hegelian dialectics and existential philosophy. My prime intention, however, is not to "prove" one or the other but to work from the sources outward, since some of the recorded sayings do suggest their own paradigms and also abrogate or interrupt such paradigms on an ongoing basis.

42. This theme is explored at length in 'Alwan.

43. Al-Kisa'i, 294.

44. See Ghannun, 16–17.

45. Al-Tha'labi, 194. For an extended discussion of David's subsequent shortcomings, see 154–162.

46. Ibid., 194.

47. Ibid., 156. Of the other two-thirds of his days, one-third were devoted to his women and one-third to worshipping and reading about the trials and tribulations of his ancestors and earlier prophets.

48. Another possible symbol in that regard is the legendary warrior-poet 'Antara, an erstwhile slave, who came to assume tremendous prestige, even though he could not be allowed to marry the daughter of his ex-master. This complicated story may have several significations, including lack of necessary correlation between prominence in the community and entitlement to actual benefits and fulfillment of desires.

49. One of the most remarkable portrayals of a contemporary relative of this form of "political" life (and of the dynamics instructing a move into a more authoritarian and continually intervening governance), can be found in Abdelrahman Munif's epic novel *Cities of Salt.*

50. Al-Tha'labi, 195.

51. See Ghannun, 82.

52. Qur'an 31:13–15. In the same breath, however, the son is excused from the duties of parental obedience when parents' instructions tamper with the idea of Allah. But even in that context, outward animosity toward parents is still not allowed.

53. Al-Tha'labi, 194. See also a saying in Tarmadhi attributed to Muhammad, cited in Ghannun, 20.

54. See Ghannun, 70.

55. See, for instance, 31:17–19.

56. For a discussion of the sources, see Ghannun, 29, 49. Some sources insist that the story refers to a different Luqman. For our purposes, however, Luqman is not treated as an actual historical figure about whom myths and stories were told but, rather, as a placeholder for folk conceptions of wisdom and pedagogy.

57. Ibn Hisham, 165.

5. THE DISCOURSE AND THE PATH

1. See Fakhry, esp. 56–81.

2. Said (1983), 35–39.

3. Al-Zarkashi, *Burhan,* cited in Abu Zaid, 138.

4. Abu Zaid, 9.

5. Arkoun (1970), 14–36.

6. Abu Zaid, 34.

7. Qur'an 2:31. After the fall, Adam's first sign of forgiveness consists of (yet to be outlined) "words" (*kalimat*) from God; 2:37.

8. Zarkashi, cited in Abu Zaid, 189–190.

9. Examples abound in the Qur'an. Since ruined cities are cited as lessons, their tales are usually listed together or sequentially; there is little interest in discussing each as its own theme. See 9:69; 25:35–40; 29:31–40; 41:13–18; 51:32–46; 53:50–56; 69:4–8; 89:6–13, and elsewhere.

10. For a discussion of this theme, see Abu Zaid, esp. 263.

11. The "Ahmar of 'Ad" refers to a mythico-historic incident in which a holy camel was slaughtered.

12. Qur'an 4:150; 47:26.

13. Ibid., 2:106. The Qur'an freely admits that some verses could be ambiguous, since their meaning was yet to be revealed even though their text was already available (e.g., 3:78). An interesting episode of "forgetting" is a late Qur'anic reproach to Muhammad for having failed to free himself from an impossible promise he had made to one of his wives (see 66:1–2), even though the Qur'an had detailed a method by which commitments of that nature could be absolved (5:89).

14. Couplet 36, which connects two sets of images, warrants some elaboration. In Arberry's translation, it begins thus: "Is such my camel? Or shall I enliken her to . . ." In the original, this statement is contained in the brevity of two words (*afatilka, amm,* "is (she) such, or . . ."). There is no explicit reference to the camel, nor to a project of likening; nor is there a first person pronoun. The original provides a sense that there is a continuing awareness of the original object, that metaphorization is an unpronounced activity. All such eliminations allow the distance between two metaphoric cycles to be kept to a minimum.

15. Qur'an 48:29.

16. See, for instance, ibid., 63:6. The persistence of earthly conflict deflates the cosmological level of discourse, forcing it to address specific incidents on a continual basis. The specificity of context, in turn, does not reduce the grand referential nature of the corpus, as many of the early *sahabah* (companions to the prophet) were to observe. It was afterward that such specific revelations, as a rule, became grounds for general edicts. See, for example, al-Suyuti, vol. 1, esp. 39–40.

17. For example, see Qur'an 48:18, 26.

18. "How many generations [*min qarnen*], far greater in prowess, have We destroyed before them! . . . They searched the entire land: but could not find a refuge?" ibid., 50:36.

19. Ibid., 3:140.

6. PROPHETIC CONSTITUTION

1. Qur'an 48:8, 33:45.

2. Al-Tabari, vol. 2, 210–211.

3. There is one remarkable Qur'anic passage that goes one step beyond confirming that the known prophetic histories all come from the same source, asserting that the faithful must also believe indiscriminately in what had been transmitted to *all* such prophets. See Qur'an 2:136.

4. This can be seen in Qur'anic references that, even when they use earthly examples to demonstrate divine omnipotence, deny the possibility of knowing Allah through existing categories of knowledge and valuation. For a famous example, see Qur'an 2:255.

5. For example, see ibid., 14:35.

6. See Qur'an 112:1–4; 19:88–92, 107–111; 10:68; 18:4–5; 43:81–82; 6:100–101; 23:91; 3:79–80; 4:171–172; 5:17, 72–75, 116–118; 9:29–30; 2:116.

7. Ibid., 6:159; 23:53; 2:116.

8. Ibid., 45:16–18; 2:92; 5:24; and elsewhere.

9. This point emerged later in the development of the Qur'an in Medina, when ethical rules and regulations were being formulated. Since many of such rules were apparently deemed to be timeless, adherents of book religions were frequently accused of suppressing Allah's earlier directions to them. See ibid., 4:51; 3:75, 78; 5:47; 9:33; 62:50.

10. The Qur'an sought to defend Muhammad from rejection on these grounds by refraining from listing reasons for Muhammad's selection and instead invoking an incomprehensible divine will, which paid no respect to traditional habits of social rank. See Qur'an 14:11 and before; 25:20, 56–57; 6:50; 7:63, 69; 43:31–32.

11. Ibid., 108:3.

12. An interesting example concerns his approach to the Kalbians: He told them they should worship Allah because he was the ultimate cause of the glory of their "father's name."

13. See al-Tabari, 232; Ibn Hisham, 164.

14. Ibn Hisham, 568–569.

15. Qur'an 49:14. The word *aslamna* could also be rendered as "we commit ourselves to Islam" or "we commit ourselves to live in peace" rather than "we profess Islam." For stronger denunciations, see 48:11–12, 15–16; 9:97–98.

16. Compare this to the Qur'an's emphatic denunciation of the *Munafiqun* (two-faced) in Medina who, being part of a sedentary community over which the prophet could exercise more continuous control, were offered no similar option.

17. Ibn Hisham, 168. The stories of Ibn Ubay and the *Munafiqun*, which seem to contradict such a view, will be discussed in Chapters 7 and 8.

18. Al-Tabari, 248–249; Ibn Hisham, 167–168; Ibn Sa'd, 148.

19. Muhammad's final response, according to al-Tabari, Ibn Hisham, and Ibn Sa'd, was expressed invariably as follows: "I am of you, and you are of me. I will wage war on whomever you wage war on, and I will make peace with whomever you make peace with."

20. Qur'an 96:1–5.

21. Such a reclusive quest apparently did not interfere with the proselytizing mission, as many of the early and well-known recruits to Islam continued to be brought in not by Muhammad himself but, rather, by other close companions. See Ibn Hisham, 87–90. Indeed, even actual failures to bring recruits in, as in Muhammad's early trip to Ta'if, could be balanced by success in bringing in otherworldly recruits—the jinn— around the same time. See Qur'an 72:1–2; 46:29–31. Also, al-Tabari, 231; Ibn Hisham, 162–68; Ibn Sa'd, 142.

22. For example, Qur'an 73:1–7.

23. Al-Tabari, 196.

24. Ibid., 209; Ibn Saʿd, 96–97.

25. Ibn Hisham, 79–80; al-Tabari, 205–206; Ibn Saʿd, 129–130.

26. See, for example, Qurʾan 3:26. Muhammad is frequently instructed to affirm his mere humanness (e.g., 41:6, 6:50, and elsewhere).

27. During the early ʿAbbasid period, a fierce scholastic debate consumed the circles of the *Muʿtazilah* and other schools in Baghdad, whose centerpiece was the status of the Qurʾan within God's acts of creation. For a more detailed account, see Fakhry, esp. 77–80.

28. The tradition often indirectly addresses the notion of Muhammad's distance from God by showing the physical severity of the impact that each revelation had upon him. See, for examples, Ibn Saʿd, vol. 1, 131–132, Muslim, vol. 7, 82.

29. For example, 2:23; 59:21; 52:34; 10:38; 11:13; 17:88; 18:1; 13:31; 39:27–29.

30. A powerful verse in this regard is 17:88. It is significant in that it came in the context of narrating Muhammad's night journey to heaven, an episode whose truthfulness many refused to believe. The Qurʾan here cites itself as that which authenticates the story.

31. See the discussion of *Dahriyyah* in Chapter 3 and the Qurʾanic depictions of pagan mockery of the idea of resurrection in 17:49; 16:38; 37:16–17; 41:39; 6:29; 45:24–25; 23:82–83; 13:5; 50:3.

32. Ibn Hisham, 105.

33. Qurʾan 37:45–47; 56:18–19.

34. The literal translation of the second half of couplet 44, "*In kunti jahilatan bima lam taʿlami,*" is "should happen to be ignorant [of that which you do not know]" and not Arberry's "ignorant and uninformed," which, to be sure, rectifies the flagrant tautology of the original. At-Tibrizi offers a plausible rendition in prose form: The intended statement, according to him, is "Have you asked the horses of what you know not, if you should happen to be ignorant, daughter of Malik?" See at-Tibrizi, 100.

35. This hope and denial can take many forms. A variant on it is the theme of the "mad poet," who is pushed to madness by the inaccessibility of his desire. This theme is explored in Asʿad Khairallah's *Love, Madness, and Poetry.* His analysis, heavily influenced by Jungian psychology, finds in the phenomenon of the mad poet-lover-seer an attempt to visualize a distinct domain of the invisible before a *unitary* God comes to claim both domains—the Here and the Beyond.

36. Unlike in the case of his later well-planned migration to Medina, the Qurʾan never clearly gave Muhammad permission to leave for Taʾif.

37. Traditional sources illustrate Muhammad's dire need to avoid the appearance of complete loss. Upon leaving Taʾif, he reportedly pleaded with its Thaqif inhabitants not to let the Qurayshans know of the bad reception he had received there, apparently so as not to endanger a tactical project of accentuating his position in Mecca by hinting at a potential following that went beyond its boundaries. See al-Tabari, 230; Ibn Hisham, 161.

38. Al-Tabari, 231; Ibn Hisham, 178. According to both historians, the two rejections came from al-Akhnas Ibn Shariq, who based his decision on the inferiority of his

own tribal standing to that of Muhammad's clan, and Suhail Ibn 'Amru, who complained of the wide distance between his clan *nasab* (descent) and Muhammad's. Muhammad's ultimate protector was to be al-Mut'am Ibn 'Uday, who had no close kin relation to Muhammad either.

39. The instructions to Muhammad to not ignore the weak in his zeal to Islamize the rich is clearly spelled out in the *surah* of 'Abasa (Qur'an 80). The shift in emphasis to non-Meccan Arabs, however, could also be attributed to the latent desire to elicit a more favorable response in Mecca, namely, by proving the viability of Islam in other societies.

40. Ibn Hisham, 94.

7. THE HOUSE OF THE *UMMA* AND THE SPIDER WEB OF THE TRIBE

1. Qur'an 26:214–215.

2. Ibid., 111.

3. This is not to say, however, that the rest of the revelations adhered to the same spirit. Both the tone of anger and frustration and the humble positioning of the prophet were to be partially abandoned later on, when the social meaning of prophethood metamorphosed and demanded reframed orientations. In particular, the fact that the question of selection refused to subside required the invention of new strategies of approaching the community.

4. Qur'an 27:45.

5. For examples, see ibid., 26:124, 161; 29:36.

6. Ibid., 26:86.

7. Ibid., 71:28 (emphasis added).

8. Qur'an 41:20–22.

9. Ibid., 7:57; 24:43.

10. Ibid., 29:67.

11. Ibid., 106.

12. In ibid., 105, Allah attributes the failure of the expedition to birds that he sent to pelt Abraha's army with clay pellets, until they became like "withered stalks of plants which cattle have devoured." Al-Tabari hints that the collapse of the army was probably due to the outbreak of an epidemic; see 111–115.

13. Qur'an 29:41.

14. For an explicit association of the divine message and Mecca and surrounding dwellings, see Qur'an 6:92; 42:7; 43:3; 44:58; 20:113; 19:97; 16:103; 41:44; 13:37; 14:4; 54:32, 40.

15. Al-Tabari, 219–220.

16. Qur'an 43:31–32.

17. The most remarkable example is perhaps Tarafa's couplet 11.

18. See Ibn Hisham, 475.

19. Ibid., 474.

20. Ibid., 289 (emphasis added). The word "*nas*" here clearly indicates "outsiders" rather than the more generic and immediate "people."

21. It could be argued, indeed, that although the notion of transtribal *umma* was already in the making, it did not sufficiently influence political developments until the overthrow of the Umayyads by the Abbasides, partially on the strength of a multiethnic following that rejected the Umayyads' almost exclusively—and avowedly—clannish claim to legitimate rule.

22. Qur'an 18:6, 8.

23. For example, see ibid., 73:10.

24. Al-Tabari, 218; Ibn Hisham, 90–91; Ibn Sa'd, 133.

25. Qur'an 36:26.

26. Ibid., 21:51–54; 26:69–77, 81; 14:41.

27. Ibid., 12:91–93.

28. Ibid., 12:95.

29. For further discussion of similar symbols in the *mu'allaqat,* see the discussion of the odes of Zuhair, an-Nabigha, and Labid in Chapters 3 and 5.

30. Al-Waqidi, 1–19; also Ibn Hisham, 263–270.

31. Qur'an 2:216.

32. Ibid., 2:190–191, 217; 22:39–40, 58–59; 4:89–90. War began to gradually take precedence over all else. In very elaborate discourses, the Qur'an told the Muslims that even worship rituals could be compromised for its sake. The Qur'an told the faithful that they could shorten their prayers if they were on alert, that some of them could pray while others stood vigilant, how they could arrange their ranks for readiness while praying, and even what to do if it rained in that circumstance. See 4:101–103.

33. But excluded from animosity among Mecca's people were those who were members of social units with whom the Muslims had treaties and those who were neutral and unwilling to fight against either side. This group included the Muslims who stayed in Mecca. See Qur'an, 4:90.

34. Ibid., 5:2.

35. Ibid., 2:191–194.

36. Ibid., 2:217.

37. Ibid., 2:158.

38. Ibid., 22:28–37.

39. Ibid., 2:143. See also Ibn Hisham, 233–234; al-Tabari, 265.

40. Though it is true that the later *qibla* was technically directed toward the *haram* rather than Mecca itself, it must be kept in mind that it was the *haram* that epitomized Mecca's sanctity and special standing in the world.

41. "Those to whom the scriptures [Jews and Christians] were given know this [the Qur'an] to be the truth from their Lord. God is never heedless of what they do. But even if you gave them every proof they would not accept your *qibla,* nor would you accept theirs; nor would any of them accept the *qibla* of the other. If, after all the knowledge you have been given, you yield to their desires, then you will surely become an evildoer" (Qur'an 2:144–145). Hurgronje argues that Muhammad's change of the *qibla* was only due to his rejection by the Jews of Medina, which moved him to abandon symbols of affinity with the people of the book for the sake of constructing a

purely Arab religion. This argument, however, misses the continuing centrality of Mecca itself—and not Arab societies at large—in the thought of the *Muhajirun*.

42. Qur'an 2:144 (emphasis added). See also 2:149–150.

43. Ibn Hisham, 276. See also Qur'an 8:5–7.

44. For a more detailed survey of Medinian fortresses, see Lecker's "Muhammad at Medina: A Geographical Approach." Lecker argues that many further developments in Medina, such as the expulsion of the Jews, simply completed processes that had started long before Muhammad. See also Kister (1968), 145–149.

45. Ibn Hisham, 317–318; al-Waqidi, 176 and after, 219, 416. For a more extended exposition regarding other examples, see Gil, who argues that Ibn Ubay's differed from other, anti-Muslim Hanifs; 87 and after.

46. The next time Muhammad resolved to expel a Jewish tribe from Medina, Ibn Ubay reportedly showed no interest in defending them as vigorously as he had the first tribe. The consolidation of the Muslims' unity allowed them to gradually expel all the Jewish tribes from Medina, in the process confiscating their wealth. The extra income was used to relieve the *Ansar* of the economic burden of supporting the *Muhajirun*. See al-Waqidi, 368–372, 379.

47. Qur'an 68:17–33.

48. Ibid., 27:45–46.

49. Ibid., 28:4.

50. Ibid., 17:95. See also 6:8–9.

51. See ibid., 23:24–25, 47; 7:63, 69; 6:33.

52. Ibid., 17:54; 10:108; 6:107. Muhammad's role as *nadhir*, however, lasted only for as long as he was in Mecca, being referred to less and less in the later course of his career.

53. Ibid., 10:71.

54. Ibid., 50:45; 25:63; and elsewhere. In fact, the Qur'an became so defensive at that juncture that the few Muslims were for a brief period instructed to refrain from attacking the idols. See 6:108.

55. "Say: 'Unbelievers, I do not worship what you worship, nor do you worship what I worship. I shall never worship what you worship, nor will you ever worship what I worship. You have your religion, and I have mine.'" Ibid., 109.

56. Al-Tabari, 219.

57. Ibid., 225–226; Ibn Hisham, 137.

58. Muhammad, on the other hand, never pressed his uncle on the issue. According to al-Tabari, it was in connection to that encounter that Muhammad learned from God that the latter guided only whom he pleased, and not necessarily whom the prophet loved. Here, the prophet is further relieved of the responsibility to reverse traditional hierarchies and customary relations. Al-Tabari, 219. See also Ibn Hisham, 160.

59. Qur'an 43:40–43.

60. Ibn Hisham, 130–144.

61. This was evidently a gradual discovery. Though apparently no Qurayshan disputed Abi Talib's right to protect his nephew, some did question his entitlement to protect another relative from the clan of Banu Makhzum, who was not as close to him

in terms of *nasab* line. Mahmood Ibrahim (1990) argues that the failure of the boycott resulted from the fact that it was a "clan-based response to a nonclan-based social movement" (79).

62. Al-Tabari, 228–229; Ibn Sa'd, 140–141; Ibn Hisham, 142–144.

63. Qur'an 53:1–5, 11–12, 17–18, 32.

64. Al-Tabari, 226–228; Ibn Sa'd, 137. See also Ibn Manzur, vol. 10, 286-288. Ibn Sa'd introduces the report as follows: "When Muhammad saw his people abandoning their harassment of him, he sat down by himself, wishing that nothing be revealed to him which would drive them away." Al-Tabari reports two similar versions.

65. Al-Tabari, 227–228; Ibn Sa'd, 137.

66. "They are but names which you and your fathers have invented: God has vested no authority in them. The unbelievers follow vain conjectures and the whims of their own souls, although the guidance of their Lord has long since come to them" (Qur'an 53:23).

67. Ibid., 22:52–53. On the general possibility of changing verses, see 16:101.

68. Later developments, however, led to the incorporation of a certain degree of politically calculated tribalism, though it followed more theologically sophisticated deliberations.

69. *Sira* sources attribute their return to the lure of a false report of the Islamicization of Mecca following the revelation of the verses in question. Upon their arrival, however, they only saw a city bitterly divided among antagonistic camps. Those who entered it had to either immediately seek clannish protection (*ijara*) or simply hide. The rest reportedly went back to Abyssinia.

70. Qur'an 80:1–10.

71. Chief among them were the later caliphs Abi Bakr and 'Umar. The latter was reportedly more renowned and respected for his ruthless manners than for his wealth or social affinities.

72. See Qur'an 26:111; 11:27.

73. Ibid., 26:112–114; 11:29.

74. Ibid., 18:32–42.

75. Ibid., 16:75–76.

76. It is significant in this respect that when the Qur'an adopted the Biblical image comparing the passage of the rich into paradise with the passage of a camel through the eye of a needle, it replaced the rich with the more general category of those who scorn Allah's revelations. See 7:40.

77. Ibid., 6:165. A somewhat similar *aya* is 43:32.

78. Ibid., 16:71.

79. Ibid., 42:27.

80. Ibid., 17:16 (translation altered to render the original as literally as possible).

81. Ibid., 38:58–64; 40:47–48; 14:21.

82. In ibid., 56:7–40, people are amassed on the Day of Judgment in three groups rather than two. The first two constitute the believers: One band of them includes "many" of the early believers and only "a few" of the later ones, while the other con-

tains "many" of the early and likewise, "many" of the later ones. The distinction evaporates, however, when the privileges of each band in paradise are listed, for they turn out to be the same.

83. Ibid., 52:23.

84. Ibid., 45:28.

85. Ibid., 43:32–35.

86. Ibid., 23:51–53. A similar verse is 6:159, which is followed by a call to return to the common path of Abraham, the *hanif.* See also 42:14; 19:37; 11:110.

87. Ibid., 42:15. This revelation was never repealed or altered by any other. With some important exceptions, such as the issue of Jesus's divinity, the settlement of many theological sources of controversy (e.g., the sanctity of the Sabbath) was declared to be postponed until the Day of Judgment. See 16:124–125.

88. The commentator at-Tibrizi offers three interpretations regarding the nature of this "unfamiliar muster": a plan (of fate?), a war, or a meeting location (*Qubbat an-Nu'man*).

89. Interestingly, the only characterization alludes to the ghostly, trans-human world of the jinn (c. 71).

90. Ibn Hisham, 262.

91. Ibid., 196–197; al-Tabari, 256.

92. Qur'an 8:73, 75.

93. Ibid., 60:1–3, 9; 58:14, 22.

94. Ibid., 19:47.

95. Ibid., 60:4. At a later stage, and after years of bitter war, the Qur'an recalled and corrected this aspect of Abraham's story, forbidding Muhammad and the faithful from interceding on behalf of idolaters among their close relatives. See 9:112–113.

96. Ibid., 49:9–10.

97. Ibid., 4:92.

98. Both were essentially tax revolts. For a Qur'anic condemnation of the nomads' reluctance to accept any form of taxation, see 9:98.

99. At one point, the Meccans took for granted that the ancient respectability of the trade route—underwritten by the openness and peace of Mecca itself—was out of date, and they violated one of the cornerstones of the peace of their city by arresting an unsuspecting Muslim pilgrim. They released him only in exchange for some of their prisoners of war taken by the Muslims. See Ibn Hisham, 296.

100. Ibid., 444.

101. Qur'an 49:14–15, 17; 9:97–98; 48:11–12, 15–16; 22:11.

102. Al-Waqidi, 757.

103. "There has now come to you an apostle *of your own,* one who grieves at your sinfulness and cares for you; one who is benevolent and merciful to true believers" (Qur'an 9:128, emphasis added).

104. Ibn Hisham, 430; al-Tabari, 73.

105. An additional factor is that by the time of the Peace of Hudaybiyyah, the Muslims were probably not sufficiently powerful to overrun Mecca, either in number

or in resolve. Mecca itself continued to command relatively formidable resources. Slightly more than a year before, the city had organized a large army—reported to have totaled ten thousand combatants—and, with the aid of its Bedouin allies, laid a one-month siege against Medina before retreating without a fight. It is possible to argue that the march to Mecca that culminated in the Peace of Hudaybiyyah was viewed by the Muslims as a potential takeover, but the refusal of most of their own Bedouin allies to join the march without assurances of a share in the spoils of an uncertain fight quickly undermined the spirit of the expedition. According to Ibn Hisham, it was on his way back to Medina that Muhammad received from Allah the revelation of the *surah* of al-Fath (or at least portions thereof), which included extremely hostile denunciations of the treachery of the Bedouins; see 438–439. (Sociohistorical references in al-Fath, however, are ambiguous and could just as well pertain to the later takeover of Mecca.)

106. Ibn Hisham, 432 (emphasis added).

107. Al-Tabari in particular (80–81) extensively details the collapsed spirits of the Muslims after the news of the treaty.

108. The main textual landmark of this transformation is perhaps the aforementioned *surah* of 'Abasa.

109. Ibn Hisham, 440–441.

110. Two major expeditions are reported to have been organized after the treaty, one against the northern town of Khaibar, the single most important Jewish stronghold in the peninsula, and another against a massive Roman army stationed even further to the north, near Mu'tah. The expedition to Khaibar was a success; that to Mu'tah was a disaster.

111. For example, 'Abdullah Ibn Sa'd, a former Muslim who had defected to Quraysh earlier, was not only forgiven but eventually assigned provincial governorships by later caliphs. See al-Waqidi, 830–838; Ibn Hisham, 472–475.

112. Al-Waqidi, 837–838.

113. Aside from the model of Kinda, the demand for central sources of arbitration is evident in more contemporaneous reports. One such report mentions that the Christians of Najran to the south asked Muhammad to act as a regulator of their social and economic affairs, even as they declined to join Islam. See Ibn Hisham, 258.

114. The armies of conquest rarely returned to the peninsula; families eventually united with soldiers in the new frontier settlements. This massive population movement eventually had a political price; the Arabian Peninsula, soon after the conquests, reverted to a peripheral political status within the subsequent Islamic empires rather than remaining their center of gravity.

115. Qur'an 48:12, 16 (emphasis added).

8. AUSTERITY, POWER, AND WORLDLY EXCHANGE

1. Qur'an 7:179.

2. The generally more aggressive Medinian Qur'an seems to have earnestly believed in the antiquated bestiality of such heedless opponents; see, for instance, 5:33.

3. Ibn Hisham, 275, 278; al-Waqidi, 42–45. Once the war started in earnest, however, Mecca proved to be capable of fighting back. A year after Badr, the city managed to assemble a larger and more determined army, incorporating many Bedouin allies, the Ahabish, and even some expatriate Aussians from Medina, and took revenge by defeating the Muslims in Uhud near Medina. The Qur'an claimed that Allah's angels took a role in bringing about the victory at Badr. See 8:9, 17; 3:124–125.

4. Qur'an 3:157–158, 164–166, 169–174. Even those among the Muslims who retreated during that unfortunate episode were pronounced to be absolved, as the great compassion with which the dead were remembered engulfed them as well. See 3:152–155.

5. Qur'an 41:20–22.

6. For example, ibid., 24:23–24.

7. Ibid., 24:2–21.

8. A basis for this idea can perhaps be traced to the early Qur'anic affirmation of the unreliability of pathways taken by following immediate human wishes. See 6:116.

9. Qur'an 33:4 (emphasis added). "The wives whom you divorce as your mothers" refers to a pre-Islamic Arabic formula for a divorce declaration, where the husband would state to his wife: "Be [as forbidden] to me as my mother's back."

10. Ibid., 33:72.

11. Ibid., 2:189; 78:9–11. In general, passive reception of divine instructions was the model through which the Qur'an was revealed. The point is accentuated through God's periodic reproach of Muhammad, who on occasions was portrayed as either wishing to suppress some revelations or lacking firm feelings for them. See, for instance, 11:12.

12. Ibid., 4:2, 5, 10.

13. For a fuller exposition of this orientation, see Ibrahim (1990), esp. 87.

14. Qur'an 4:6.

15. Ibid., 2:282–283; 5:106–108.

16. Ibid., 5:106–108; 4:11–12, 176; 2:180.

17. Ibid., 28:23–28.

18. "Do they [the Meccans] not see how We have given them a sanctuary of safety, while all around them men are carried off by force?" (29:67).

19. Early Islam did not fare well in stable agricultural communities; Ta'if, for instance, was one of the last bastions in the peninsula to yield to Muhammad's authority, and then only by force. The animosity (or unfamiliarity of) the *Muhajirun* toward that form of economy is encapsulated in a saying attributed to Muhammad, who, upon seeing a plowshare in the house of one of the *Ansar*, reportedly commented: "This does not enter the abode of a people without lowliness following it." See Ibn Khaldun, 702. Also, al-Waqidi, 922–938.

20. See, for example, Qur'an 2:16, 268, 281; 3:117, 181; 9:120–121; 61:10; 24:37; 64:16-17; 48:29; 57:25.

21. Ibid., 9:111 (emphasis added).

22. Ibid., 24:36–38.

23. Alms may have been introduced during lulls between major military confisca-tions. As such, they redistributed income within the *umma* rather than relying on con-tinuous warfare and ultimately reduced dependence on the warriors as a major source of social income.

24. Qur'an 2:245, 254. Similar verses can be found in 2:261, 265; 64:17; 57:11.

25. For an informative though largely philological discussion, see Bravmann, 176, 229–253.

26. Ibrahim (1990) argues that Muhammad's early preoccupation with alms (*zakah*), as opposed to *sadaqah,* can be construed as an indication of abandoning tribal fellow-ship in exchange for universal individual responsibility; see 82.

27. For an example of this, see the discussion of the "market of the prophet" in Kister (1965), 272–276. See also Lecker, 53.

28. Qur'an 47:38.

29. Ibid., 3:181.

30. Ibid., 9:79–80.

31. Passages like these were used by some commentators, notably Taha Husain, to contest the historical authenticity of the *mu'allaqat.* This argument has been effective-ly challenged (for a summary of the debate, see Arberry). One point that needs to be added here, however, is that the error seems to stem from a perception that the idea of Allah is a peculiarly Islamic notion that appeared in a quantum fashion at a specific point in time rather than an *emergent* notion that underwent long mutations before it crystallized in one form.

32. My objective here—unlike the philologist's or historian's—is not to find the culprit between the lines but to ponder this ambiguity. This portion of the discourse seems to be so delicately structured as to refer simultaneously to both specific events and universal conditions incumbent upon wandering. It is impossible to *name* the party meant by Zuhair with certainty.

33. Another example of the rationalization of war was the *standard* ransom that was to be paid for the release of prisoners of war. The Qur'an specifically forbade Muslims from holding infidels as prisoners of war once such ransom was paid off. See 47:4.

34. Al-Waqidi, 131–138; Ibn Hisham, 290–291; Qur'an 8:1.

35. Qur'an 8:41. The origins of the ratio of one-fifth are not clear. It is probable that it simply represented an institutionalization of an ongoing practice; some reports indicate that before this revelation, the warriors were already, on their own volition, giving the prophet exactly one-fifth of what they gained in war (Ibn Hisham, 268).

36. Qur'an 93.

37. Qur'an 59:6–10. In this same Qur'anic sequence, the disgruntled warriors are appeased by being designated with special praise. Though they were indirectly re-minded that the *umma* could also survive through means other than permanent war-fare, no mention was made of the fact that in this instance, it was the Muslims' mili-tary might that had made other communities "voluntarily" pay the Muslim community a designated sum of their wealth.

38. Ibid., 3:130.

39. Ibid., 2:275–279.

40. In contemporary sociological theory, this theme was highlighted in the idea of ethnomethodology. With particular reference to courtroom deliberations, Harold Garfinkel argued that jurors first decide on the basis of "common sense" and then proceed to find a matching statement of law. See Garfinkel, 104–115.

9. IN LIEU OF A CONCLUSION

1. Rodinson modifies this deterministic position on 298.

2. A little-known Arab Marxist was one of the first to pose the problem, denying that the prophet had intended to construct a great empire. See al-Jawzi, 202–208.

3. See Ibrahim (1990), 8.

4. See for instance Gellner's *Muslim Society*. In Gellner there is an assumption of singular exceptionalism vis-à-vis an outside world, which may be compared to Watt's assumption of the integrative cohesion of Muslim society.

5. Belyaev, 73.

6. See for instance Rodinson, 295. In Muslim societies today, various orders of governance could use Qur'anic citations to justify various relationships toward governance. For instance, under conditions of civil strife, e.g., in Afghanistan or Algeria, the common citations tend to stress brotherhood of believers (e.g., 49:10), whereas under conditions of authoritarian rule, e.g., in Saudi Arabia, they tend to stress obedience to authorities (e.g., 4:59).

7. Ibrahim (1990), 89.

8. H. M. T. Nagel, 1982, "Some Considerations Concerning the pre-Islamic and the Islamic Foundations of the Authority of the Caliphate," in G. H. A. Juynboll, ed., *Studies on the First Century of Islamic Society*. Carbondale: Southern Illinois University Press, pp. 177–197.

9. For a discussion of this point, see Ibrahim (1990), 92–93.

10. Nagel, 188.

11. For a full discussion, see Landau-Tasseron, esp. 13.

12. This is not to suggest the primacy of "function" in interpreting the role of a deity. Rather, the idea concerns only one line of argument explicitly highlighted by Muhammad in order to show the uselessness of former deities. Other attributes of Allah, or the idols for that matter, cannot be simply confined to the functional perspective.

13. For a full discussion, see Fakhry, especially regarding the rise of scholasticism, 51–81.

14. For an interesting discussion, see Harvey, esp. 55–67. The appeal was frequently ignored or reinterpreted when conditions for the *hijra* were not appropriate. But the original experience had established a textual/referential basis for claims to its mandatory legality.

15. For a summary of one of the most obvious of such conflicts, which manifested themselves at the peak of Muhammad's power in Medina, see Gil, 65–96.

16. Bashir (1978), 77, cited in Asad, 463.

Bibliography

Abu al-Fida', Isma'il ibn 'Ali. N.d. *Al-Mukhtasar fi Akhbar al-Bashar*. Beirut.

Abu Zaid, Nasr Hamed. 1994. *Mafhum al-Nas: Dirasah fi 'Ulum al-Qur'an*. Beirut.

'Ali, Jawad. 1968. *Al-Mufassal fi Tarikh al-'Arab qabl al-Islam*. Beirut and Baghdad.

Alusi, Muhammed Shukri al-. 1954. *Bulugh al-Arab fi Ma'rifat Ahwal al-'Arab*. Ed. Muhammed S. al-Athary. Cairo.

'Alwan, Muhammed. N.d. "Mu'taqadat al-'Arab al-Bida'iyyah." Unpublished ms.

'Aqel, Nabih. 1972. *Tarikh al-'Arab al-Qadim wa 'Asr al-Rasul*. Damascus.

Arberry, A. J. 1957. *The Seven Odes*. London and New York.

Arkoun, Mohammed. 1970. "Comment lire le Coran?" In *Le Coran*, trans. Kasimirski, 14–36. Paris.

———. 1982. *Lectures du Coran*. Paris.

Asad, Talal. 1970. "Ideology, Class, and the Origin of the Islamic State." *Economy and Society* 4: 450–473.

Azraqi, al-. 1969. *Akhbar Makka*. Ed. R. S. Malhas. Beirut.

Baghdadi, al-. 1964. *Al-Munammaq fi Akhbar Quraysh*. Ed. Khurshid A. Fariq. Haydarabad.

Bashir, Sulayman. 1978. *Tawazun al-Naqa'id: Muhadarat fi al-Jahiliyyah wa Sadr al-Islam*. Jerusalem.

————. 1984. *Muqaddimah fi al-Tarikh Al-Akher.* Jerusalem.

Bamyeh, Muhammed. 1993. "Transnationalism." *Current Sociology* 3: 1–101.

Barth, Frederick. 1964. *Nomads of South Persia.* New York.

Baydawi, al-. 1939. *Tafsir.* Cairo.

Bekri, al-. 1876. *Das geographische Wörterbuch.* Ed. F. Wüstenfeld. Göttingen.

Bellamy, James A. 1990. "Some Observations on the Arabic Ritha' in the Jahiliyyah and Islam." *Jerusalem Studies in Arabic and Islam* 13: 44–61.

Belyaev, E. A. 1969. *Arabs, Islam, and the Arab Caliphate.* New York.

Blome, Walter H. 1958. *A Contribution to the History of Ancient Transportation and Trade.* Ann Arbor, Mich.

Bousquet, G.-H. 1954. "Observations sociologiques sur les origines de l'Islam." *Studia Islamica* 2: 61–87.

Braudel, Fernand. 1982. *Civilization and Capitalism.* New York.

Bravmann, M. M. 1972. *The Spiritual Background of Islam.* Leiden.

Bukhari, al-. 1862–1908. *Al-Jami' al-Sahih.* Leiden.

Butzer, Karl W. 1957. "Der Umweltfaktor in der grossen arabischen Expansion." *Saeculum* 8: 359–371.

Crone, Patricia. 1987. *Meccan Trade and the Rise of Islam.* Princeton.

Dawood, N.J. 1990. *The Koran.* New York and London.

Donner, Fred M. 1977. "Mecca's Food Supplies and Muhammad's Boycott." *Journal of the Economic and Social History of the Orient* 20: 249–266.

————. 1980. "The Bakr Ibn Wa'il Tribes and Politics in Northeastern Arabia on the Eve of Islam." *Studia Islamica* 51: 5–37.

Fakhry, Majid. 1970. *A History of Islamic Philosophy.* New York.

Garfinkel, Harold. 1967. *Studies in Ethnomethodology.* Englewood Cliffs, N.J.

Gates, Henry Louis. 1990. "Tell Me, Sir, . . . What Is 'Black' Literature?" *PMLA* 105 (January): 11–22.

Gellner, Ernest. 1981. *Muslim Society.* Cambridge, Eng.

Ghannun, A. 1969. *Luqman al-Hakim.* Cairo.

Gil, Moshe. 1987. "The Medinian Opposition to the Prophet." *Jerusalem Studies in Arabic and Islam* 10: 65–96.

Grunebaum, G. E. von. 1970. *Classical Islam.* Chicago.

Hamadani, al-. 1884–1891. *Sifat Jazirat al-'Arab.* Ed. D. H. Müller. Leiden.

Hamawi, Yuqut al-. 1965. *Mu'jam al-Buldan.* Teheran.

Hamidullah, Muhammed. 1957. "Al-ilaf, ou les rapports economico-diplomatiques de la Mecque pre-islamique." In *Mélanges Louis Massignon,* vol. 2: 293–311. Damascus.

Harvey, L. P. 1990. *Islamic Spain.* Chicago.

Hawting, Gerald R. 1982. "The Origins of the Muslim Sanctuary in Mecca." In *Studies on the First Century of Islamic Society,* ed. G. H. A. Juynboll, 23–47. Carbondale, Ill.

Hegel, G. W. F. 1977. *Texts and Commentary.* Ed. Walter Kaufmann. Notre Dame, Ind.

Hurgronje, C. Snouck. 1880. *Het Mekkaansche feest.* Leiden.

Ibn al-Athir. 1964. *Usd al-Ghaba fi Ma'rifat al-Sahaba.* Cairo.

———. 1965. *Al-Kamel fi al-Tarikh.* Beirut.

Ibn Hisham. 1961. *Al-Sira al-Nabawiyyah.* Cairo.

Ibn al-Kalbi. 1993. *Kitab al-Asnam.* Ed. Ahmad M. 'Ubed and Mohammed A. Ahmad. Cairo.

Ibn Khaldun. 1961. *Al-Muqaddimah.* Beirut.

Ibn Manzur. 1966. *Lisan al-'Arab.* Cairo.

Ibn Qutaybah. 1976. *Kitab al-Ma'aref.* Ed. M. Isma'il al-Sawi. Karachi.

Ibn Sa'd. 1905. *Kitab al-Tabaqat al-Kabir.* Ed. E. Sachau. Leiden.

Ibrahim, Mahmood. 1987. "The Petrification of Islamic Society." *Birzeit Research Review,* Winter/Spring.

———. 1990. *Merchant Capital and Islam.* Austin, Tex.

Istakhri, al-. 1961. *Al-Masalek wa al-Mamalek.* Ed. M. al-Hini and M. Ghurbil. Cairo.

Jahiz, al-. 1906. *Majmu'at Rasa'il.* Cairo.

Jawzi, Bandali S. al-. 1977. *Dirasat fi al-Lughah wa al-Tarikh al-Iqtisadi wa al-Ijtima'i 'inda al-'Arab.* Ed. Naji 'Allush. Beirut.

Karmali, Anastas M. al-. 1939. *Al-Nuqud al-'Arabiyyah wa 'Ilm al-Numayyat.* Cairo.

Khairallah, As'ad. 1980. *Love, Madness, and Poetry.* Beirut.

Khazanov, Anatoli M. 1984. *Nomads and the Outside World.* Cambridge, Eng.

Kisa'i, al-. 1978. *Tales of the Prophets.* Ed. and trans. W. M. Thackston, Jr. Boston.

Kister, M. J. 1965. "The Market of the Prophet." *Journal of Economic and Social History of the Orient* 8: 272–276.

———. 1968. "Al-Hira: Some Notes on Its Relations with Arabia." *Arabica* 15: 143–169.

———. 1980. "Labbayka, Allahumma, Labbayka: On a Monotheist Aspect of a Jahiliyya Practice." *Jerusalem Studies in Arabic and Islam* 2: 33–57.

———. 1990. "On Strangers and Allies in Mecca." *Jerusalem Studies in Arabic and Islam* 13: 113–154.

Landau-Tasseron, Ella. 1985. "Asad from Jahiliyya to Islam." *Jerusalem Studies in Arabic and Islam* 6: 1–28.

Lecker, Michael. 1985. "Muhammad at Medina: A Geographical Approach." *Jerusalem Studies in Arabic and Islam* 6: 29–62.

Lukàcs, Georg. 1974. *Conversations with Lukàcs*. Ed. Theo Pinkus. London.

Maqrizi, al-. 1939. *Kitab al-Nuqud al-Islamiyyah al-Qadimah*. Ed. al-Karmali. Cairo.

Marzuqi, al-. 1913. *Kitab al-Azmina wa al-Amkina*. Hayderabad.

Mas'udi, al-. 1965. *Muruj al-Dhahab wa Ma'aden al-Jawhar*. Ed. Yusuf Dagher. Beirut.

Mawardi, al-. 1973. *A'lam al-Nubuwwah*. Beirut.

Meeker, Michael E. 1979. *Literature and Violence in North Arabia*. New York.

Mukarovsky, Jan. 1978. *Structure, Sign, and Function*. New Haven, Conn.

Munif, Abdelrahman. 1987. *Cities of Salt*. Vol. 1. Trans. Peter Theroux. New York.

Muruwah, Husayn. 1978. *Al-Naza'at al-Maddiyyah fi al-Falsafah al-'Arabiyyah al-Islamiyyah*. Beirut.

Muslim. 1929. *Al-Jami' al-Sahih*. Cairo.

O'Leary, De Lacy. 1927. *Arabia before Muhammed*. New York.

Olinder, Gunnar. 1973. *Muluk Kinda min Bani Akel al-Murar*. Ed. and trans. Abdul Jabbar al-Muttalibi. Baghdad.

Paret, Rudi. 1971. *Der Koran: Kommentaer und Konkordanz*. Stuttgart.

Planhol, Xavier de. 1968. *Les fondaments géographiques de l'histoire de l'Islam*. Paris.

Qurashi, al-. 1986. *Jamharat Ash'ar al-'Arab*. Ed. 'Ali Fa'our. Beirut.

Rodinson, Maxime. 1971. *Mohammed*. London.

Rostovtzeff, Michael I. 1966. *Social and Economic History of the Roman Empire*. Oxford.

Rubin, Uri. 1990. "Hanifiyyah and Ka'ba: An Inquiry into the Pre-Islamic Background of Din Ibrahim." *Jerusalem Studies in Arabic and Islam* 13: 85–112.

Said, Edward. 1978. *Orientalism*. New York.

———. 1983. *The World, the Text, the Critic*. Cambridge, Mass.

Salzman, Philip, ed. 1980. *When Nomads Settle*. New York.

Serjeant, R. B. 1962. "Haram and Hawta." *Mélanges Taha Husain*. Cairo.

Sharif, Ahmad al-, I. 1965. *Makka wa al-Madinah*. Cairo.

Simmel, Georg. 1978. *The Philosophy of Money*. London.

Simon, Róbert. 1989. *Meccan Trade and Islam*. Budapest.

Stetkevych, Suzanne P. 1993. *The Mute Immortals Speak: Pre-Islamic Poetry and the Poetics of Ritual*. Ithaca, N.Y.

Suyuti, al-. 1978. *Al-Itqan fi 'Ulum al-Qur'an*. Bombay.

Tabari, al-. 1879–1901. *Tarikh al-Rusul wa al-Muluk*. Ed. M. J. de Goeje et al. Leiden.

Tha'labi, al-. 1929. *Qisas al-Anbiya'*. Cairo.

Tibrizi, at-. 1965. *Sharh al-Mu'allaqat al-Sab'*. Ed. C. J. Lyall. Ridgewood, N.J.

Tuetey, Charles. 1977. *Imrulkais of Kinda*. London.

Waqidi, al-. 1989. *Kitab al-Maghazi*. Beirut.

Watt, William M. 1961. *Islam and the Integration of Society*. London.

———. 1964. *Muhammad, Prophet and Statesman*. Oxford.

Weber, Max. 1949. *The Methodology of the Social Sciences*. New York.

———. 1963. *The Sociology of Religion*. Boston.

Wolf, E. R. 1951. "The Social Organization of Mecca and the Origins of Islam." *Southwestern Journal of Anthropology* 7: 329–356.

Ya'qubi, al-. 1892. *Kitab al-Buldan*. Ed. M. J. de Goeje. Leiden.

Zaidan, Georgy. N.d. *Tarikh al-'Arab qabl al-Islam*. Beirut.

Index

252; attitude toward Muhammad, 200–202, 216–17, 266; relation to *Muhajirun*, 218, 220, 260

'Antara Ibn Shaddad, 15, 89, 93, 125, 127–129, 133, 176, 241; knowledge in, 156–157, 163–170, 177–178

Arberry, A. J., xiii

Arkoun, Mohammed, 116

'asabiyyah. *See* solidarity

Asad, tribe of, 51, 261

A'sha, al-, xiii, 68–69, 119, 126–127, 241

Aus (of Medina), 20, 42, 154, 201, 219

Badr, battle of, 190, 198, 200–201, 231–232, 251

Bahrain, 9, 11, 21, 40, 129, 272 n. 11

Bakr, tribe of, 42, 46–47, 49, 62

Ba'laam, 101

Bashir, Sulayman, viii, 258

Basus, war of, 46, 62

Bedouins. *See* nomadism; nomads

Bekri, al-, 17

Belyaev, E. A., 258

Bilal the Abyssinian, 150

Book of Proverbs, 110

Bostra, 18, 40

Braudel, Fernand, 30

Bravmann, M. M., 96

Brockelmann, Carl, 90

Byzantium, 18, 21, 32, 40–41, 43, 50, 52

calendar, pre-Islamic, 30, 73, 275 n. 33

camel: capacity of, 12, 22, 273 n. 15; as means of transportation, 21; as

medium of exchange, 21; as a metaphor for movement, 7, 13–15; as thematic unity, 69, 135–137, 273 n. 16; value of, 24; as vehicle of escape, 187

Christianity, 79, 98; paganism and, 90, 146

Christians, 26, 119, 215

Crone, Patricia, viii, 30, 271–272 n. 5

Dabbi, al-Mufaddal al-, xiii

Dahes wa l-Ghabra', war of, 46

Dar an-Nadwah, 33, 37, 267

Daumat al-Jandal, 18

David, 101–104, 106

Dawood, N. J, xiii

Day of Judgment, 154, 213–214; hierarchies on, 284 n. 30, 292–293 n. 82; kin relation on, 219

death. *See* life

desert: demographic pressures in, 46; nature of, 3–4; in odes, 8; trade in, 29

Dhi Qar, battle of, 41, 278 n. 69, 278 n. 71

Dhubyan, tribe of, 42, 246, 248

diyyah (blood money), 12, 42, 91, 219–220, 247, 275 n. 27

Durkheim, Emile, 24

Egypt, 21, 196, 204

Empty Quarter, 3

Evans-Pritchard, Edward E., 44

exchange: hierarchy of items in, 23; in holy sites, 85; as model of relationship to God, 243; nomads and, 45; in the Qur'an, 236–237, 242; 252–253; social boundaries of, x–xi; standards of, 25, 274 n. 16. *See also* trade

Fadak, 252
feudalism, 36, 276 n. 45
forbidden months, 29, 31–32, 39, 198–199, 275 n. 33, 275 n. 34

Gabriel, archangel, 144, 161
Gadamer, Hans-Georg, ix
Gellner, Ernest, 258
geography, ancient, 9–10; notion of pilgrimage and, 32; in odes, 86
Ghassanides, 41–42, 49–50, 54
Ghatfan, Banu (tribe of), 32
Gibb, Hamilton A., 90
God: in commerce, 95, 236; contractual aspects of, 243; early meanings of, 105–106, 204, 239–240; as an experimental concept within paganism, 26, 89–91, 114, 208–209, 296 n. 31; as guarantor of peace, 203, 248; *haram* and, 185, 203; as hidden sovereign, 109; monotheistic nature of, 262; moral void and, 255; as an outcome of economic value, 29; paternal character of, 145; as recipient of charity, 243–244, 251; as sedentary construct, 6, 238; as source of economic value, 23–24; as source of human subjectivity, 233–235; as source of miracles, 67; as source of wealth, 212, 276–277 n. 51; symbolization and, 133; transcendental nature of, 78, 113, 160–161, 210, 254, 264–265, 286 n. 4; unaccountability of, 267. *See also* Qur'an

Gospel, 243
Gramsci, Antonio, 158

Habermas, Jürgen, 264
Hadramaut, 10, 11, 47
halting (in odes), 118, 123; as interruption of norm, 129; nomadic life and, 6–7, 130; realization of loss in, 13
Hanifism, 26, 34, 79, 143, 150, 260; abstraction and emergence of, 28; prophethood in, 98, 179, 263–265
haram, 11, 223; Abraham as founder of, 34, 224; compared to ruins, 85; fornication in, 81–82; as house of God, 185, 203; as house of idols, 87–88, 91, 153; as item of exchange, 34–35, 276 n. 48; migrations away from, 85; openness of, 225; in the Qur'an, 199, 202; sanctuaries competing with, 32–33, 91, 275 n. 37; as sanctuary, 31, 199, 228; service functions of, 33, 37–39, 228, 275–276 n. 41; as site of pilgrimage, 29, 32. *See also* Mecca
Harith, al-, king of Kinda, 49–50, 52
Harith, Ibn Hilliza al-, of Bakr, 94–95, 117, 119; as spokesman of tribe, 127, 182, 241
Hashemites, 148, 173, 186, 206–208, 210, 214
Hawazen, tribe of, 31, 91
hawta, 33
hedonism, 64, 70–71, 92, 138, 177, 246. *See also* odes
Hegel, G. F. W., 58
Heidegger, Martin, ix
hermeneutics, ix

Hijaz, 9, 18; agriculture in, 5, 30; isolation of, 40, 277 n. 61, 277 n. 62; marketplaces of, 29

Hijr (Akel al-Murar), king of Kinda, 47-49

Hijr Ibn al-Harith, king of Kinda, 51

Himyar, 47, 48, 50

Hira, al- (lower Mesopotamia), 49–50, 117, 162, 182, 184

history, philosophy of, viii–xii, 258

Hudaybiyyah, Peace of, 223–228, 230, 251, 260, 264, 268, 283 n. 21, 293–294 n. 105

hums, 40

Husayn Ibn Damdam, 248

Ibn al-Anbari, xiii

Ibn al-Kalbi, 82, 85

Ibn Hisham, xiii, 175, 227

Ibn Kaisan, xiii

Ibn Khaldun, 17, 19

Ibn Qutaybah, xiii

Ibn Sa'd, xiii

Ibrahim, Mahmood, 37, 258, 260

Idols. *See* paganism

Idris, prophet, 145

ilaf, 40, 48, 277 n. 60

Imru'l-Qays, 7, 57, 81, 147, 162, 272 n. 4; approach to past in, 85, 172; duty in, 193–195, 280 n. 104; as "founder" of poetry, 83–84, 249; hedonism of, 64, 177, 192–193; as kingship claimant, 51–52, 241; as outcast, 69, 74, 89, 170, 176–177; poetic structure in, 56

India, 21, 43

'Iraq, 9, 41, 67, 131

Isbahani, Abi al-Faraj al-, xiii

Islam: concept of forbidden months in, 32; in the context of paganism, 80–81, 88–89; earlier traditions in, 200, 259–260, 263–265; estrangement from Mecca of, 190, 224, 266; experimental nature of, 261; meanings of the word, 100, 151, 284 n. 39; political centralization and, 47, 52, 229, 258, 261, 263, 294 n. 113; as sedentary religion, 200, 229; social classes and, 202, 211, 213, 258; social unity in, 146, 220, 245; state and, 257–261; universalization of, 185–186, 191, 217–218, 227, 229, 266–267; as verbal allegiance, 224, 287 n. 15. *See also* Muhammad; Muslims; Qur'an; *umma*

Ismael, "father of the Arabs," 146

Istakhri, al-, 9

i'tifad. See suicide

Jehova, 145

Jerusalem, 200

Jesus, 146; disciples of, 155; miracles of, 116; Muhammad and, 98, 145

Jews, 26, 119, 215; in Medina, 20, 200–201, 252, 291 n. 46; as tribal identity, 80

jinn, 105, 119, 174

Jones, Sir William, 70

Joseph, 195–197; Muhammad and, 145

Judaism, 79–80, 98; paganism and, 90, 146

Jurham, tribe of, 36

justice: emergence of Islamic concepts of, 220, 242, 244, 262; in nomadism, 94–95, 237–238, 281 n. 16; as outcome of concept of life, 232; through poetic language, 235, 241, 246–251, 253; in poetry, 93–94; prophet and, 215; under sedentarism, 99–100, 135–136; stratification and, 68, 102–103; trade and, 91; witnessing and, 236–237

Khadija, 150, 158, 173
Khaibar, 153, 252
Khalid Ibn Sinan, 97
Khazanov, Anatoli, 19, 43–45
Khazraj (of Medina), 20, 42, 151, 154, 201, 219
Khuza'ah, tribe of, 36, 90
Kinda, kingdom of, 30, 43–44, 46–52, 106, 153, 193–194, 221, 229, 280 n. 97
Kister, M. J., 90
knowledge: believers and, 259; codification of, 119; distant, 124; divine, 158, 200, 235–236; immanence of, 94, 241; Luqman and, 101–102, 110–111; mystical, 121; in odes, 157–158, 163–170, 177–178, 240, 248–249, 253; political authority and, 107–109; prophetic, 160, 239; time and, 72, 77–78; uniqueness of, 139
Kuhn, Thomas, 86

Labid Ibn Rabi'ah, 13–14, 55, 89, 133, 157, 162, 176; approach to the past in, 57, 85; belonging in, 186–189, 215–216, 240–241; as judge, 127, 245–246; structural elements in, 134–138, 183; vision of nature in, 121–124
Lachmides, 49

Life: code of conduct in, 76–78, 253–255; as coherent subjectivity, 233–234; as ethical question, 63–65, 232; finitude in, 69–70, 96, 232; Islamic concepts of, 232; as journey back to God, 128, 130–131, 137; notion of "event" in, 73; pre-Islamic concepts of, 61–62, 67–68, 93, 234, 239; reproduction of, 243; as social chronicle, 75; stratification and the interpretation of, 68–69, 112–113, 232–233
Lineage, 43–44, 63, 65, 67; alternatives to blood, 24, 232, 291–292 n. 61, 293 n. 95; authority of, 86, 240–241; ethics and, 82, 145; in Mecca, 207–208; prophethood and, 179–181, 185–86. See also solidarity
Lukàcs, Georg, ix
Luqman the Wise, 100–104, 106, 110–114
Lyall, C. J., xiii

Malik, Banu (tribe of), 234
marketplaces, 11, 45, 272 n. 11; cultic nature of, 33, 35; cycle of, 29, 32, 87–88, 272–273 n. 12
Marx, Karl, 22, 45, 258
Mas'udi, al-, 10, 17, 30, 59
Mazdaism, 41
Mecca: attitude toward nomadism in, 54; capital formation in, 19, 37, 95; class structure in, 20, 110–111, 148; division of labor in, 33; harmony of, 198–199, 212, 214, 268–269; Hudaybiyyah and, 222–228; Islamic conquest of,

190–191, 222, 227–229; Islamic sanctification of, 200, 224; Islamicization of capital in, 25; materialist thought in, 68, 82; neutrality of, 30–31, 36, 39; peace of, 43, 185, 203, 247, 275 n. 28, 293 n. 99; political independence of, 6; propagation of paganism by, 84; as site of evil, 218; trade of, 11, 18, 30, 34, 152, 273 n. 3; vulnerability of, 34, 185, 242, 263. *See also haram;* Quraysh; trade

Medina, 9; economic reforms in, 236, 242; Islamicization of, 201; and model of migration, 262–263; Muhammad's migration to, 151, 154–155, 161, 175, 222, 268; opposition to Muhammad in, 139, 201–202, 271–272 n. 5, 291 n. 46; pacts of, 152–154, 216–217; persistence of nomadic outlook in, 20, 30, 152; political control in, 221, 225, 242, 260; tribal relations in, 54, 154, 216, 219. *See also Ansar*

Meeker, Michael, 87

Mesopotamia, 43

Mikhael, archangel, 144

monotheism, 6, 262; as ancient tradition, 146; central state and, 258; in paganism, 90, 125; pluralistic, 215, 290–291 n. 41, 293 n. 87; politics of, 185–186, 224; Qur'anic departure from, 208

Moses, 146, 204; justice of, 237–238; miracles of, 116; Muhammad and, 98, 145

mu'allaqat. See odes

Mufaddaliyyat, 74

Muhajirun, 155, 175, 190, 200, 222, 224, 245; attitude toward Mecca, 191, 198–199, 218, 261, 265–266; lineage and, 232; Muhammad and, 217; relation to *Ansar,* 220, 260; war economy of, 244; as wayfarers, 252

Muhammad, 41; *Ansar* and, 190, 216–218; approach to social classes, 211, 260–261, 268, 289 n. 39; attitude toward idols, 82, 91, 192, 291 n. 54; attitude toward the Qur'an, 121, 292 n. 64; attitude toward tribalism, 25, 180, 189–192, 195, 200, 208–211, 217–218, 291 n. 58; Biblical prophets and, 98, 144–146; compared to poets, 163, 187, 191–193, 195, 241–242, 253–254; economic reforms of, 236–237; God and, 158, 160–161, 168–169; Hanifism and, 95, 98; as human messenger of God, 26, 205, 264; Luqman and, 101, 114; migration to Medina, 151, 154–155, 216–218, 222; relation to nomads, 150, 221–222, 225, 229–230, 261–263, 268, 287 n. 12; sayings of, 118–119, 259; signs of prophethood of, 66, 165, 170; status in Mecca, 161–162, 173–175, 178, 186, 206, 261, 263–265, 276–277 n. 51; wars of, 198–202, 222–232, 251–253, 268, 294 n. 110. *See also* prophethood; prophets (pre-Islamic)

Munafiqun, 201

Mundherites, 41, 49–50, 54

Muruwah, Husayn, 258

Mus'ab Ibn 'Umair, 152

Musaylimah, 143, 150–151

Muslims: allies of, 198, 222, 224; crystallization of identity among, 200–202; defections among, 201, 214, 225; as fighting force, 223, 225, 242; links to Jews and Christians, 215; in Mecca, 206, 209–210; proselytization by, 228; as separate communities, 199, 218, 220–222, 227, 230, 260; social status of, 211–212; as transtribal community, 217–219. *See also Ansar; Muhajirun; umma*

Mu'tah, battle of, 222

Mutalammes Ibn Umayyah, al-, 90

Nabigha, an-, xiii, 14–15, 241; style of sedentary poetics in, 54–57; 103–110

Nagel, T., 260–261

Najd, 9, 35, 41, 43, 48, 153; agriculture in, 5, 30

Najran, 26

nasab. See lineage

Nippur, 88

Noah, 181, 185, 205–206, 211–212

nomadism: abstract valuation in, 20–22; adaptive strategies in, 44; authority in, 45, 47–52, 194, 247–248; concepts of justice in, 237–238; economy of, 17–18, 45–46, 53, 194, 205, 221; ethics of, 43, 45, 53, 59–63, 91–92, 94–95, 111, 246, 255, 279 n. 77; as isolated lifestyle, 46; as lifestyle surrounding Mecca, 5, 39; lineage in, 207–208; logical structure in, 128, 130–131, 171–172, 280 n. 2; mate-rialist thought in, 6, 28, 59, 66, 69, 71, 84, 96, 113, 232–233, 281 n. 16; in Mecca's governance, 37, 267; notion of death in, 232, 234; origins of, 12; protection of wealth under, 19, 273 n. 1; state development in, 19, 106–107, 229, 257; warfare in, 20, 42, 46, 49, 52, 107, 220, 229, 246–251, 278 n. 74, 279 n. 85, 279 n. 87. *See also* Kinda, kingdom of; nomads; odes; solidarity

nomads: attitude toward the forbidden months, 31–32; attitude toward Islam among, 52, 139, 220–221, 225, 229–230, 261–263; attitude toward state, 6, 105, 108, 112, 150, 194; egalitarianism among, 45, 49, 68, 71, 84, 148, 204, 212, 232–233, 245, 252, 267, 273 n. 1; image of God among, 87, 95, 229; imperial powers and, 41, 49; in the Qur'an, 151, 205, 221, 293–294 n. 105; spirituality among, 203; trade and, 19, 30–31, 40, 43, 59, 61, 278 n. 65. *See also* nomadism

Nufud wilderness, 3

Nu'man, an-, king, 103–104

odes, 70; belonging in, 187–189, 193–195, 281 n. 12, 285 n. 48; compared to the book, 120; compared to poetry after Islam, 65, 109, 280 n. 5; concept of time in, 63, 66, 124; as documentation of loss, 85, 93–94, 122–123, 188, 239–240; duty in, 216, 250, 280 n. 104; dynastic politics in,

103–110; hedonism in, 64, 76, 138, 177, 246, 281 n. 11; individualism in, 69–71, 89, 157, 194, 281 n. 11; model of nature in, 121–124, 239–240; moral themes in, 76, 89, 127, 246–251, 253–255; naming in, 85–87, 94, 187–188, 246; nomadic economy and structure of, 57, 109; notion of value in, 24; openings of, 8, 52, 55–57, 64, 82–84, 123, 126, 238–240, 281–282 n. 19; rationale in, 55–54; realism in, 188; solidarity in, 181–185, 215–216; space in, 10; structural elements in, 13, 118, 127–129, 133–139, 162–163, 183, 286 n. 14; symbolization in, 104, 122–124, 131–133, 138; tribal politics in, 58–59, 74–75, 117, 127; as unifying visions, 65–67, 157, 268; wandering in, 56, 69, 120, 127–129, 133, 187. *See also* poetry (pre-Islamic); poets

Olinder, Gunnar, 50

ontotheology, vii, , 80, 262, 265

orientalism, 79, 90

pact of the virtuous ones, 38, 91, 277 n. 54

paganism: accommodation to tribalism, 85, 87–88, 90, 202–203, 282 n. 5; end of, 228, 262; ethics of, 81–82; monotheistic elements of, 90–91; among nomads, 84–85; origins of, 85; pluralist nature of, 26–27, 32, 34, 206, 215, 267; Qur'anic overtures toward, 206, 208–210; rituals of, 91, 199; status of idols in, 28, 282–283 n. 11;

weakness of, 79–80, 88, 91, 263, 282 n. 2

Palestine, 41, 49

Palmyra, 6

past: in odes, 58, 146–147, 171; ethics and, 82; idealization of, 62–65; prophethood and, 171; ruins as, 63, 240. *See also* ruins (in odes); time

Persia, 21, 32, 41–43; Kinda and, 49–50. *See also* Sassanid Empire

Petra, 6, 18

philology, viii, 116, 119

pilgrimage (pre-Islamic): chants, 29, 32, 90; as measure of time, 73, 236; Muslims and, 199, 223; proselytizing during, 118, 175, 221; trade cycle and, 11, 29, 33

poetry (pre-Islamic), 119–120; audience in, 118; 146–147, 167–170, 176–177, 183, 239–240, 249–250, 253–254, 273 n. 16; as element of justice, 235, 241; as historical evidence, xii–xiii; as mystical production, 234–235, 241–242, 249; as tradition, 82–83, 126, 195; as tribal institution, 75, 89, 176, 187, 281 n. 10; truth and, 117. *See also* odes; poets

poets: as arbitrators, 246–249; as outcasts, 170, 186–187, 245, 249, 281 n. 12; as tribal spokesmen, 74, 89, 182. *See also* odes; poetry (pre-Islamic)

prophethood: anticipation of, 98, 160, 168, 230, 263–266; audience and, 148–153, 155, 165, 173–174; belonging and, 191–193, 195–198, 222; calling and, 156–157,

revenge: as ethical duty, 51, 91, 281 n. 16; in the Qur'an, 232
Rodinson, Maxime, 271 n. 4
Roman Empire, 6, 41
ruins (in odes), 7, 10, 56–57, 68, 82, 238–240, 246; abandonment of, 14, 281 n. 7; compared to *haram,* 85; inevitability of, 94; structural role of,126, 159–160, 171, 249; time and, 72, 74, 172; as tribe, 191–192; value of, 24, 28
ruins (in the Qur'an), 124–125, 137, 192, 202, 285 n. 9

Said, Edward, vii
Salih, prophet, 180
Sassanids Empire, 6, 18, 41. *See also* Persia
Satanic verses, 208–210
scholasticism, 115
sedentarization: concept of duty in, 170; dynamics of, 17–20, 273 n. 1, 273 n. 7; ethical uncertainty after, 267; impediments to, 43; Islam and, 200; justice under, 99, 135–136, 238; logical structure in, 128, 131; money economy and, x; poetics and, 54–58; in the Qur'an, 205; stratification in, 96–97, 204, 213; tragic vision under, 84, 96, 233; visions of nature after, 105–106, 109–110. *See also* Mecca; Quraysh
semiology, 85
Semitic migrations, 4
Serjeant, R. B., 33
Simmel, Georg, 22, 27
Simon, Róbert, 31
sinful wars, 31, 91

solidarity, vii, 25, 44, 274 n. 17; among early Muslims, 207; Muhammad and, 25, 173–174, 179–181, 190; in odes, 181–185, 215–216, 240, 247; in the Qur'an, 203–204, 210; rise of theological, 226–227, 263, 268, 293 n. 95; transtribal, 214, 216–218, 232, 244–245, 290 n. 21; tribal, 62, 65, 279 n. 79, 279 n. 83, 279 n. 84, 279 n. 86. *See also umma*
Solomon, 104–108
Spain (Islamic), 263
state: Islamic, 25, 257–262, 283–284 n. 25; nomads and, 19, 106–108. *See also* Kinda, kingdom of
suicide (i'tifad): commercial failure and, 39, 88, 95, 140, 283 n. 22
suq. See marketplaces
Syria, 12, 43, 67, 81, 85

Tabari, al-, xiii, 144, 206
Taghlib, tribe of, 42, 46, 62, 93
Ta'if, 9, 30; concept of labor in, 34–36; Mecca's food supply and, 5; Muhammad in, 174, 217
Taima', 18
Tarafa Ibn l-'Abd, 13, 24, 162, 241, 246; attitude toward status differences, 68, 211, 232; fatalism in, 69–71, 129, 252; knowledge in, 72; as outcast, 74–75, 89, 176–177, 187, 193; poetic tradition in, 83–84; thematic unity in, 136
taxation: *haram* service functions and, 38, 243; Islamic, 243–245, 251–252, 296 n. 23, 296 n. 26; under nomadism, 48, 50–51, 243–244

Thamud, 180, 204
Thaqif, tribe of, 35–36
Tibrizi, at-, xiii, 248
time: ancient notions of, 66–68, 71, 73, 100; destruction by, 255; knowledge and, 72, 77–78; language preservation and, 71–72, 74–75, 89; logic of history and, x, 147; opposition to space, 92–93, 108; remembrance and, 8, 172; separation and, 192. *See also* past; resurrection; ruins (in odes)
Torah, 243
totemism, 87
trade: commodities of, 21; community formation through, 24; concept of labor in, 252; contractual rationality and, 242, 262; ethical status of, 34; as an expansive enterprise, 27; financial aspects of, 276 n. 43; growth of commercial rationality through, 40; intermediary, 30, 43; Mecca and world, 5, 273 n. 3; nomads and, 18, 30, 278 n. 65; routes of, 31, 46, 221, 272 n. 11, 274 n. 22, 277–278 n. 64; sedentarization and, 18–19; size of, 30; spiritual dimension of, 32, 37–40, 81, 84, 91, 95; threats to, 231, 274 n. 19. *See also* marketplaces; Mecca
Tuhama, 9, 32

'Ubayd Ibn l-Abras, xiii, 99, 140, 234–235, 237–242, 249, 252
Uhud, battle of, 201, 232
'Ukaz, marketplace of, 11, 29, 55, 82, 95
'Uman, 5, 11

'Umar Ibn al-Khattab, 223, 226, 260, 264, 268
Umayyads, 186, 207, 259–260
umma, 213–215; compared to tribal alliances, 217; conflicts within, 219–220, 230, 261, 267; consolidation of, 218–219, 244–245, 261; contrasted to tribal solidarity, 54; as sanctuary, 222; selection of caliph within, 259–260, 290 n. 21; status of warriors in, 251–252, 296 n. 37; as tangible community, 221–222, 224, 262; taxation within, 243–245, 251–252. *See also* solidarity
'Urud, 9
usury, 244, 252–253, 276 n. 43
'Uthman Ibn 'Affan, 150, 223, 226–227, 229, 260–261, 264, 268

wandering: as desert lifestyle, 4–7, 250; freedom and, 15, 247; logic of, 128; as a noble lifestyle, 43, 63; in odes, 10, 69, 127–129, 187. *See also* odes; nomadism; nomads
Waqidi, al-, xiii, 198
Waraqah Ibn Nawfal, 98, 150
warfare: economy of, 244, 252–253, 296 n. 35, 296 n. 37; Islamic compared to nomadic, 25, 251, 253; against Mecca, 222–232; 242, 265–266, 295 n. 3; Muhammad and, 198–202; in odes, 246–251, 254
Watt, William M., 258

Yamama, 9, 21
Yaqut al-Hamawi, 9, 17
Yathrib. *See* Medina

year of the elephant, 41

Yemen, 6, 9, 11, 18, 73; agricultural economy of, 5; decline of, 31, 33, 42–43, 278 n. 72; extent of, 9–10; Kinda and, 47–50, 153; trade commodities of, 21

Zaid Ibn 'Amru, 97–98

Zaid Ibn Haritha, 150

Zamzam, 36

Zarqa' l-Yamama, 104, 108

Zauzani, al-, xiii

Zoroastrianism, 41

Zufar, 21

Zuhair Ibn Abi Sulma, 89, 99, 127, 162, 176; attitude toward status differences, 68; belonging in, 186–187, 215, 240–241; code of conduct in, 76–78, 114, 119, 158–159, 251, 253–255; poetic tradition in, 84; as sage, 72–73, 74, 77, 216; symbolization in, 131–132, 138; war in, 163, 189, 246–251

MOHAMMED A. BAMYEH is assistant professor at New York University. He teaches comparative civilizations and social theory at the Gallatin School and is an affiliate of the sociology department. He has been awarded a Social Science Research Council–MacArthur Fellowship and has published articles and a monograph on the history and theory of intercultural exchange. Currently he edits the journal *Passages: Journal of Transnational and Transcultural Studies* and the book series World Heritage Studies in Transnationalism and Multiculturalism.